Java Projects
Second Edition

Learn the fundamentals of Java 11 programming by building industry grade practical projects

Peter Verhas

BIRMINGHAM - MUMBAI

Java Projects
Second Edition

Commissioning Editor: Richa Tripathi
Acquisition Editor: Denim Pinto
Content Development Editor: Nikhil Borkar
Technical Editor: Mehul Singh
Copy Editor: Safis Editing
Project Coordinator: Ulhas Kambali
Proofreader: Safis Editing
Indexer: Rekha Nair
Graphics: Tom Scaria
Production Coordinator: Nilesh Mohite

First published: April 2017
Second edition: August 2018

Production reference: 1300818

Published by Packt Publishing Ltd.
Livery Place
35 Livery Street
Birmingham
B3 2PB, UK.

ISBN 978-1-78913-189-5

`www.packtpub.com`

mapt.io

Mapt is an online digital library that gives you full access to over 5,000 books and videos, as well as industry leading tools to help you plan your personal development and advance your career. For more information, please visit our website.

Why subscribe?

- Spend less time learning and more time coding with practical eBooks and videos from over 4,000 industry professionals
- Improve your learning with Skill Plans built especially for you
- Get a free eBook or video every month
- Mapt is fully searchable
- Copy and paste, print, and bookmark content

PacktPub.com

Did you know that Packt offers eBook versions of every book published, with PDF and ePub files available? You can upgrade to the eBook version at www.PacktPub.com and as a print book customer, you are entitled to a discount on the eBook copy. Get in touch with us at service@packtpub.com for more details.

At www.PacktPub.com, you can also read a collection of free technical articles, sign up for a range of free newsletters, and receive exclusive discounts and offers on Packt books and eBooks.

Contributors

About the author

Peter Verhas is a senior software engineer and software architect with an electrical engineering and economics background from TU Budapest (MsC) and PTE Hungary (MBA), and he also studied at TU Delft and TU Vienna. He created his first programs in 1979, and since then he has authored several open source programs. He has worked in several positions in the telecommunications and finance industries.

Peter works for EPAM Systems in Switzerland, participating in software development projects at various customer sites, and he supports talent acquisition by interviewing candidates, running training programs for developers, and internal mentoring programs. He regularly talks at various international conferences.

About the reviewer

Aristides Villarreal Bravo is a Java developer, a member of the NetBeans Dream Team, and a Java User Groups leader. He lives in Panama. He has organized and participated in various conferences and seminars related to Java, JavaEE, NetBeans, the NetBeans platform, free software, and mobile devices. He is the author of *jmoordb* and tutorials and blogs about Java, NetBeans, and web development. Aristides has participated in several interviews on sites about topics such as NetBeans, NetBeans DZone, and JavaHispano. He is a developer of plugins for NetBeans.

I would like to thank my mother, father, and all my family and friends.

Packt is searching for authors like you

If you're interested in becoming an author for Packt, please visit `authors.packtpub.com` and apply today. We have worked with thousands of developers and tech professionals, just like you, to help them share their insight with the global tech community. You can make a general application, apply for a specific hot topic that we are recruiting an author for, or submit your own idea.

Acknowledgments

Acknowledgment is the section of a book that everybody ignores by turning the pages. This time, this section is a bit different. I will mention a few people and their roles in the making of this book but, at the same time, I will explain why and how it is important to rely on people, being a software developer.

Doing professional work is not possible without having a life. It is quite obvious if you take that literally, but it is just as true figuratively. If you do not find the balance between your personal and professional life, you will burn out and will not operate professionally. This is the place to mention my family, my parents whom I am lucky to still have around, my brother who introduced me Java itself the first place, my wife, and my already adult kids who never stopped believing in me being able to do this work, who know more than well what a hypocrite I am, advocating personal-professional life balance, and who continually pushed me closer to this equilibrium point in life so that I could keep performing professionally.

For professional work, coworkers are almost as important as family support. It is important that you support your colleagues as much as you ask them for their support. You learn a lot from books and from experience, but you learn the most from other people. Pay attention to senior developers. You can, however, learn just as much from juniors. No matter how ace you are, from time to time, a rookie may shed light on a topic. During the years, I learned a lot from juniors who brought a fresh view to the table, asking shocking questions that were absolutely valid. I cannot name each and every junior who aided my work with fresh out-of-the-box thinking.

I can, and should, however, name some peer professionals who actively participated in the creation of this book with their advice, discussions, and suggestions.

I should certainly mention Károly Oláh who was very enthusiastic about my project, and he represented, supported, and encouraged the idea inside EPAM systems. He actively discussed with the upper management that the support for writing a book well fits the innovation line and development of the company and the people who work together. Without the official support from the company providing extra time for the task, I would not have been able to create this book.

A good company attracts good people who are clever and also good to work with. I had many discussions about the book, topics, and how to explain certain aspects with my fellow EPAMers: Krisztián Sallai, Peter Fodor, Sándor Szilágyi, Mantas Aleknavicius, Gábor Lénard, and many others.

I will separately mention István Attila Kovács from our Budapest office with whom I discussed Chapter 5 in detail, and who gave me very valuable feedback about the topic. If he does not know something about Java parallel computing, then that something does not exist.

As a summary and takeaway for the patient reader who read this section till the end, technology, knowledge, skills, and experience are extremely important for being a professional Java developer, but it is the people who really matter.

Table of Contents

Preface

Java drastically changed with the introduction of Java 8, and this change has been elevated to a whole new level with the new version, Java 9 and then further with Java 10 and 11. Java has a well-established past, being more than 20 years old, but at the same time, it is new, functional, reactive, and sexy. This is a language that developers love, and at the same time, it is the number one choice of developer language for many enterprise projects.

It is probably more lucrative to learn Java now than ever before, starting with Java 11. We encourage you to start your professional developer career by learning Java, and we have done our best in this book to help you along this road. We assembled the topics of the book so that it is easy to start, and you can feel the things working and moving very quickly. At the same time, we have tried to reach very far, signaling the road ahead for a professional developer.

The sands of time kept moving, and I discovered functional programming.

I could very well see why writing side-effect-free code worked! I was hooked and started playing with Scala, Clojure, and Erlang. Immutability was the norm here. However, I wondered how traditional algorithms would look in a functional setting and started learning about it.

A data structure is never mutated in place. Instead, a new version of the data structure is created. The strategy of copy and write with maximized sharing was an intriguing one! All that careful synchronization is simply not needed! The languages come equipped with garbage collection. So, if a version is not needed anymore, the runtime would take care of reclaiming the memory. All in good time, though! Reading this book will help you see that we need not sacrifice algorithmic performance while avoiding in-place mutation!

Who this book is for

This book is for anyone who wants to learn the Java programming language. No programming experience is required. If you have prior experience, it will help you get through the book more easily.

What this book covers

`Chapter 1`, *Getting Started with Java 11*, gives you a jump start in Java, helping you install it on your computer and run your first interactive programs using the new Jshell.

`Chapter 2`, *The First Real Java Program - Sorting Names*, teaches you how to create a development project. We will create program files and compile the code.

`Chapter 3`, *Optimizing the Sort - Making Code Professional*, it develops the code further so that the code is reusable and not only a toy.

`Chapter 4`, *Mastermind - Creating a Game*, is when the fun starts. We develop a game application that is interesting and not as trivial as it first seems, but we will do it.

`Chapter 5`, *Extending the Game - Run Parallel, Run Faster*, shows you how to utilize the multi-processor capabilities of modern architecture. This is a very important chapter that details technologies that only a few developers truly understand.

`Chapter 6`, *Making Our Game Professional - Do it as a Web App*, transforms the user interface from command-line to web browser-based, delivering a better user experience.

`Chapter 7`, *Building a Commercial Web Application Using REST*, takes you through the development of an application that has the characteristics of many commercial applications. We will use the standard REST protocol, which has gained ground in enterprise computing.

`Chapter 8`, *Extending Our E-Commerce Application*, helps you develop the application further, utilizing modern language features such as scripting and lambda expressions.

`Chapter 9`, *Building an Accounting Application Using Reactive Programming*, teaches you how to approach some problems using reactive programming.

`Chapter 10`, *Finalizing Java Knowledge to a Professional Level*, gives a bird's-eye view of developer topics that play an important role in the life of a Java developer, and that will guide you further in working as a professional developer.

To get the most out of this book

To immerse yourself into the content of this book and to soak up the skills and knowledge, we assume that you already have some experience of programming. We do not assume too much but hope that you already know what a variable is, that computers have memory, disk, network interfaces, and what they generally are.
In addition to these basic skills, there are some technical requirements you need to try out the code and the examples in the book. You need a computer—something that is available today and can run Windows, Linux, or OS X. You need an operating system and, probably, that is all you need to pay for. All other tools and services that you will need are available as open source and free of charge. Some of them are also available as commercial products with an extended feature set, but for the scope of this book, starting to learn Java 9 programming, those features are not needed. Java, a development environment, build tools, and all other software components we use are open source.

Download the example code files

You can download the example code files for this book from your account at `www.packtpub.com`. If you purchased this book elsewhere, you can visit `www.packtpub.com/support` and register to have the files emailed directly to you.

You can download the code files by following these steps:

1. Log in or register at `www.packtpub.com`.
2. Select the **SUPPORT** tab.
3. Click on **Code Downloads & Errata**.
4. Enter the name of the book in the **Search** box and follow the onscreen instructions.

Once the file is downloaded, please make sure that you unzip or extract the folder using the latest version of:

- WinRAR/7-Zip for Windows
- Zipeg/iZip/UnRarX for Mac
- 7-Zip/PeaZip for Linux

The code bundle for the book is also hosted on GitHub at `https://github.com/PacktPublishing/Java-Projects`. In case there's an update to the code, it will be updated on the existing GitHub repository.

We also have other code bundles from our rich catalog of books and videos available at `https://github.com/PacktPublishing/`. Check them out!

Download the color images

We also provide a PDF file that has color images of the screenshots/diagrams used in this book. You can download it here: `https://www.packtpub.com/sites/default/files/downloads/JavaProjects_ColorImages.pdf`.

Conventions used

There are a number of text conventions used throughout this book.

`CodeInText`: Indicates code words in the text, database table names, folder names, filenames, file extensions, pathnames, dummy URLs, user input, and Twitter handles. Here is an example: "The simplest way to do that is to initiate `new Thread()` and then call the `start()` method on the thread."

A block of code is set as follows:

```
private boolean isNotUnique(Color[] guess) {
        final var alreadyPresent = new HashSet<Color>();
        for (final var color : guess) {
            if (alreadyPresent.contains(color)) {
                return true;
            }
            alreadyPresent.add(color);
        }
        return false;
    }
```

When we wish to draw your attention to a particular part of a code block, the relevant lines or items are set in bold:

```
@Override
public boolean equals(Object o) {
    if (this == o) return true;
    if (o == null || getClass() != o.getClass()) return false;
    MyObjectJava7 that = (MyObjectJava7) o;
    return Objects.equals(field1, that.field1) &&
            Objects.equals(field2, that.field2) &&
            Objects.equals(field3, that.field3);
}
```

Any command-line input or output is written as follows:

```
Benchmark       (nrThreads)  (queueSize)  Score    Error
playParallel              1           -1 15,636  ± 1,905
playParallel              1            1 15,316  ± 1,237
playParallel              1           10 15,425  ± 1,673
playParallel              1          100 16,580  ± 1,133
playParallel              1      1000000 15,035  ± 1,148
playParallel              4           -1 25,945  ± 0,939
```

Bold: Indicates a new term, an important word, or words that you see onscreen. For example, words in menus or dialog boxes appear in the text like this. Here is an example: "If you start up **VisualVM**, you can select the **Threads** tab of any JVM process and see the actual threads that are in the JVM."

Warnings or important notes appear like this.

Tips and tricks appear like this.

Get in touch

Feedback from our readers is always welcome.

General feedback: Email `feedback@packtpub.com` and mention the book title in the subject of your message. If you have questions about any aspect of this book, please email us at `questions@packtpub.com`.

Errata: Although we have taken every care to ensure the accuracy of our content, mistakes do happen. If you have found a mistake in this book, we would be grateful if you would report this to us. Please visit `www.packtpub.com/submit-errata`, selecting your book, clicking on the Errata Submission Form link, and entering the details.

Piracy: If you come across any illegal copies of our works in any form on the Internet, we would be grateful if you would provide us with the location address or website name. Please contact us at `copyright@packtpub.com` with a link to the material.

If you are interested in becoming an author: If there is a topic that you have expertise in and you are interested in either writing or contributing to a book, please visit `authors.packtpub.com`.

Reviews

Please leave a review. Once you have read and used this book, why not leave a review on the site that you purchased it from? Potential readers can then see and use your unbiased opinion to make purchase decisions, we at Packt can understand what you think about our products, and our authors can see your feedback on their book. Thank you!

For more information about Packt, please visit `packtpub.com`.

1
Getting Started with Java 11

You want to learn Java and you have a good reason for it. Java is a modern and well-established application programming language, which is widely used in many industries, such as telecommunication, finance, and much more. Java developer positions are the most numerous and, probably, the best paid. This, among other things, makes the language lucrative for young professionals to learn.

On the other hand, this is not without reason. The Java language, the tools, and the whole infrastructure around it is complex and sophisticated. Becoming a Java professional does not happen in a day or a week; it is a work of many years. To be a Java expert, you need to know not only about the programming language but also about object-oriented programming principles, open source libraries, application servers, network, databases, and many other things. Nevertheless, learning the language is an absolute minimum. All other practices build on it. Throughout this book, you will learn Java version 18.9, also known as Java 11, and other things. You will learn not only the language but also the most important tools like maven, gradle, spring, Guice, SoapUI; protocols like http/2, SOAP, REST; how to work in an agile professional team; and what tools the team should use to cooperate. In the last chapter, you will even learn how you can plan your career that you intend to start as a Java developer.

In this chapter, you will be introduced to the Java environment, and you will be given step-by-step instructions on how to install it, edit the sample code, compile, and run Java. You will get acquainted with the basic tools that help in development, whether a part of Java or provided by other vendors. We will cover the following topics in this chapter:

- Introduction to Java
- Installing on Windows, Linux, and macOS
- Executing `jshell`
- Using other Java tools
- Using an integrated development environment

Getting started with Java

It is like going through a path in a forest. You can focus on the gravel of the road, but it is pointless. Instead, you can enjoy the view, the trees, the birds, and the environment around you, which is more enjoyable. This book is similar, as I won't be focusing only on the language. From time to time, I will cover topics that are close to the road and will give you some overview and directions on where you can go after you finish this book. I will not only teach you the language but also talk a bit about algorithms, object-oriented programming principles, tools that surround Java development, and how professionals work. This will be mixed with the coding examples that we will follow. Lastly, the final chapter will be fully devoted to the topic, what to learn next, and how to go further to become a professional Java developer.

By the time this book gets into print, Java will have completed 22 years (`http://www.oracle.com/technetwork/java/javase/overview/javahistory-index-198355.html`). The language has changed a lot during this period and got better. The real question to ask is not how long it has been here, but how long will it stay? Is it still worth learning this language? There are numerous new languages that have been developed since Java was born (`http://blog.takipi.com/java-vs-net-vs-python-vs-ruby-vs-node-js-who-reigns-the-job-market/`). These languages are more modern and have functional programming features, which, by the way, Java has also had since version 8. Many say that Java is the past—the future is Scala, Swift, Go, Kotlin, JavaScript, and so on. You can add many other languages to this list, and for each, you can find a blog article that celebrates the burial of Java. There are two answers to this concern: one is a pragmatic business approach, and the other is more regarding engineering:

- Considering that COBOL is still actively used in the finance industry and COBOL developers are perhaps better paid than Java developers, it is not too risky to say that, as a Java developer, you will find positions in the next 40 years. Personally, I would bet more than 100 years, but considering my age, it will not be fair predicting more than 20 to 40 years ahead.
- Java is not only a language, it is also a technology that you will learn a bit about from this book. The technology includes the **Java Virtual Machine** (**JVM**), which is usually referred to as JVM, and gives the runtime environment for many languages; Kotlin and Scala, for example, cannot run without JVM. Even if Java will be adumbrated, JVM will still be a number one player in the enterprise scene.

To understand and learn the basic operation of JVM is almost as important as the language itself. Java is a compiled and interpreted language. It is a special beast that forges the best of both worlds. Before Java, there were interpreted and compiled languages.

Interpreted languages are read from the source code by the interpreter, and then the interpreter executes the code. In each of these languages, there is some preliminary lexical and syntax analysis steps; however, after that, the interpreter, which, as a program itself, is executed by the processor, and the interpreter continuously interprets the program code to know what to do. Compiled languages are different. In such a case, the source code is compiled to binary (`.exe` file on Windows platforms), which the operating system loads and the processor directly executes. Compiled programs usually run faster, but there is usually a slower compilation phase that may make the development slower, and the execution environment is not so flexible. Java combined the two approaches.

To execute a Java program, the Java source code has to be compiled to the JVM bytecode (`.class` file), which is loaded by JVM and is interpreted or compiled. Hmm...is it interpreted or compiled? The thing that came with Java is the **Just in Time (JIT)** compiler. This makes the phase of the compilation that is calculation-intensive and the compilation for compiled languages relatively slow. JVM first starts to interpret the Java bytecode and, while doing that, it keeps track of execution statistics. When it gathers enough statistics about code executions, it compiles to native code (for example, x86 code on an Intel/AMD platform) for direct execution of the parts of the code that are executed frequently and keeps interpreting the code fragments that are rarely used. After all, why waste expensive CPU time to compile some code that is hardly ever used? (For example, code that reads configuration during startup and does not execute again unless the application server is restarted.) Compilation to the bytecode is fast, and code generation is done only for the segments that pay off.

It is also interesting that JIT uses the statistics of the code execution to optimize the code. If, for example, it can see that some conditional branch is executed in 99% of the cases and the other branch is executed only in 1%, it will generate native code that runs fast, thus favoring the frequent branch. If the behavior of that part of the program changes by time and the statistic shows that the ratios changed, the JIT automatically recompiles the bytecode from time to time. This is all automatic and behind the scenes.

In addition to the automatic compilation, there is also an extremely important feature of JVM—it manages the memory for the Java program. The execution environment of modern languages does that, and Java was the first mainstream language that had an automatic garbage collection (GC). Before Java, I was programming in C for 20 years, and it was a great pain to keep track of all memory allocation and not to forget to release the memory when the program no longer needed it. Forget memory allocation at a single point in the code, and the long-running program eats up all memory slowly. Such problems practically ceased to exist in Java. There is a price that we have to pay for it—GC needs processor capacity and some extra memory, but that is something we are not short of in most of the enterprise applications. Some special programs, like real-time embedded systems that control the brakes of a heavy-duty lorry, may not have that luxury.

Those are still programmed in assembly or C. For the rest of us, we have Java, and though it may seem strange for many professionals, even *almost-real-time* programs, such as high-frequency trading applications, are written in Java.

These applications connect through the network to the stock exchange, and they sell and buy stock responding to market changes in milliseconds. Java is capable of doing that. The runtime environment of Java that you will need to execute a compiled Java code, which also includes the JVM itself, contains code that lets Java programs access the network, files on disks, and other resources. To do this, the runtime contains high-level classes that the code can instantiate, execute, and which do the low-level jobs. You will also do this. It means that the actual Java code does not need to handle IP packets, TCP connections, or even HTTP handling when it wants to use or provide a REST service in some microservices architecture. It is already implemented in the runtime libraries, and all the application programmer has to do is include the classes in the code and use the APIs they provide on an abstraction level that matches the program. When you program in Java, you can focus on the actual problem you want to solve, which is the *business* code and not the low-level system code. If it is not in the standard library, you will find it in some product in some external library, and it is also very probable that you will find an open source solution for the problem.

This is also a strong point of Java. There are a vast number of open source libraries available for all the different purposes. If you cannot find a library fitting your problem and you start to code some low-level code, then you are probably doing something wrong. There are topics in this book that are important, such as class loaders or reflection, not because you have to use them every day but because they are used by frameworks, and knowing them helps you understand how these frameworks work. If you cannot solve your problem without using reflection or writing your own class loader or program multithread directly, then you probably chose the wrong framework. There is almost certainly a good one; Apache project, Google, and many other important players in the software industry publish their Java libraries as open source.

This is also true for multithread programming. Java is a multithread programming environment from the very beginning. The JVM and the runtime support programs that execute the code. The execution runs parallel on multiple threads. There are runtime language constructs that support the parallel execution of programs. Some of these constructs are very low level, and others are at a high abstraction level. Multithread code utilizes the multicore processors, which are more effective. These processors are more and more common. 20 years ago, only high-end servers had multiple processors and only Digital Alpha processors had 64-bit architecture and CPU clock above 100 MHz. 10 years ago, a multiprocessor structure was common on the server side, and about 5 years ago, multicore processors were on some desktops and on notebooks; today, even mobile phones have them. When Java was started in 1995, the geniuses who created it had seen this future.

They envisioned Java to be a *write once, run anywhere* language. At that time, the first target for the language was applet running in the browser. Today, many think (and I also share this opinion) that applets were a wrong target, or at least things were not done in the right way. As of now, you will meet applets on the internet less frequently than Flash applications or dinosaurs. What's more, the applet interface was deprecated already in Java 9, creating the opinion that applets are not good officially.

However, at the same time, the Java interpreter was also executing server and client applications without any browser. Furthermore, as the language and the executing environment developed, these application areas became more and more relevant. Today, the main use of Java is enterprise computing and mobile applications mainly for the Android platform. For the future, the use of the environment is growing in embedded systems as the **Internet of things** (**IoT**) comes more and more into the picture.

Version numbers

Java versioning is constantly changing. It does not only mean that the version numbers are changing from one release to the other. That is kind of obvious; that is what version numbers are for, after all. In the case of Java, however, the structure of the version numbers is also changing. Java started with version 1.0 (surprise!) and then version 1.1 shortly followed. The next release was 1.2, and it was so much different from the previous versions that people started calling it Java 2. Then, we had Java 1.3 till Java 1.8. This was a stable period as far as we consider the structure of the version number. However, the next Java version was named Java 9 instead of 1.9 last year, in 2017. It makes sense, because after 22 years of development and nine releases, the `1.` part of the version number did not really make much sense. Nobody was expecting a "real" Java 2.0 that is so much different from any other releases that it deserved the `2.` version prefix. In reality, the Java versions were really 1, 2, 3 and so on; they were just named as 1.1, 1.2, 1.3, and so on.

You could expect that after this huge change in the release number format, the next release of Java would be Java 10. Not at all. Oracle decided to use date-based release numbers. The first part of the release number before the dot will be the two digit year, like `18` for versions released in 2018. The part after the dot is the number of the month, usually `3` for March and `9` for September. Thus, when you look at Java version number 18.3, you immediately know that this version was released March 2018, which is actually Java 10 when following the old nomenclature.

Installing Java

To develop, compile, and execute Java programs, you will need the Java execution environment. As the operating systems that we usually use for software development do not contain the language preinstalled, you will have to download it. Although there are multiple implementations of the language, I recommend that you download the official version of the software from Oracle. The official site for Java is `http://java.com`, and this is the site from where the latest release of the language can be downloaded. At the time of writing this book, the 11th version of Java has not yet been released. An early pre-release version is accessible via `http://jdk.java.net/11/` to download. Later, the release versions will also be available from here:

jdk.java.net

GA Releases
JDK 10

Early-Access Releases
JDK 12
JDK 11
JDK 8
OpenJFX
Valhalla
JMC

Reference Implementations
Java SE 10
Java SE 9
Java SE 8
Java SE 7

Feedback
Report a bug

Archive

JDK 11 Early-Access Builds

Schedule, status, & features (OpenJDK)

Documentation

- Release notes
- Test results
- API Javadoc

Latest build: 25 (2018/8/2)

- Changes in this build
- Issues addressed in this build

OpenJDK builds

These early-access, open-source builds are provided under the GNU General Public License, version 2, with the Classpath Exception.

Linux/x64	tar.gz (sha256)	187599632 bytes
macOS/x64	tar.gz (sha256)	182050291
Windows/x64	zip (sha256)	187368712
Alpine Linux/x64	tar.gz (sha256)	186738581

Oracle JDK builds

Thank you for accepting the Early Adopter Development License Agreement. You may now download this software.

Linux/x64	tar.gz (sha256)	180869456 bytes
macOS/x64	dmg (sha256)	174786244
Solaris/SPARC	tar.gz (sha256)	196935830
Windows/x64	exe (sha256)	159419752
API Javadoc	zip (sha256)	53179697

What you can download from here is a so-called early access version of the code that is available only to experiment with it, and no professionals should use it for commercial purposes.

On the page, you have to click on the radio button to accept, but the license. After that, you can click on the link that directly starts the download of the installation kit. The license is a special early access license version that you, as a professional, should carefully read, understand, and accept only if you are agreeable to the terms.

There is a separate installation kit for Windows 32 and 64 bit systems, macOS, Linux 32, and 64-bit versions, Linux for ARM processor, Solaris for SPARC processor systems, and Solaris x86 versions. As it is not likely that you will use Solaris, I will detail the installation procedure only for Windows, Linux, and macOS. In the later chapters, the samples will always be macOS, but since Java is a *write once, run anywhere* language, there is no difference after the installation. The directory separator may be slanted differently, the classpath separator character is a semicolon on Windows instead of a colon, and the look and feel of the Terminal or command application is also different. However, where it is important, I will try not to forget to mention it.

To confuse you, the Java download for each of these operating system versions lists a link for the JRE and one for the JDK. **JRE** stands for **Java Runtime Environment**, and it contains all the tools and executables that are needed to run Java programs. **JDK** is the **Java Development Kit** that contains all the tools and executables needed to develop Java programs, including the execution of the Java program. In other words, JDK contains its own JRE. For now, all you need to do is download the JDK.

There is one important point of the installation that is the same on each of the three operating systems, which you have to be prepared for before the installation—to install Java, you should have administrative privileges.

Installation on Windows

The installation process on Windows starts by double-clicking on the downloaded file. It will start the installer and will present you with a welcome screen. Windows 10 may ask you the admin permission to install Java:

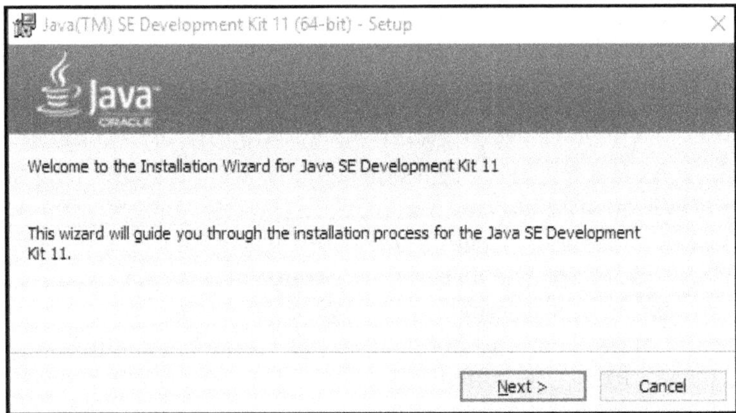

Pressing the **Next** button gets a window where you can select the parts you want to install, and also, we can change the location where Java will be installed:

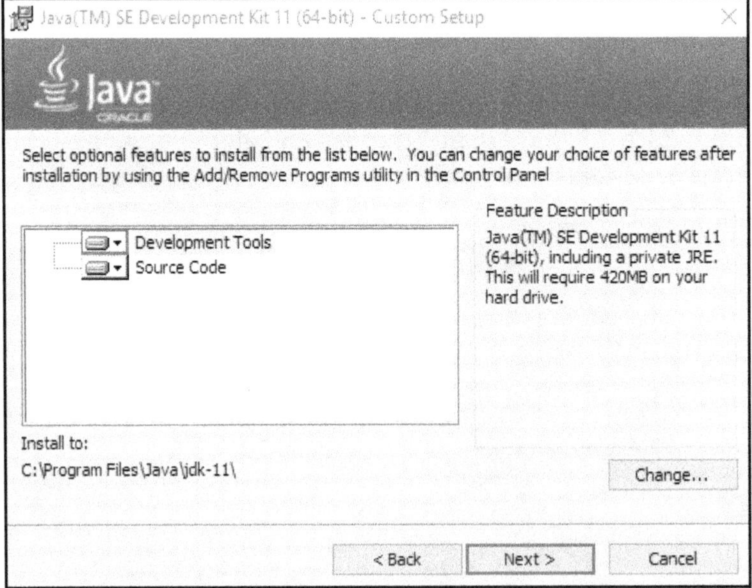

Let's leave the default settings here, which means that we install all the downloaded parts of Java and press **Next**:

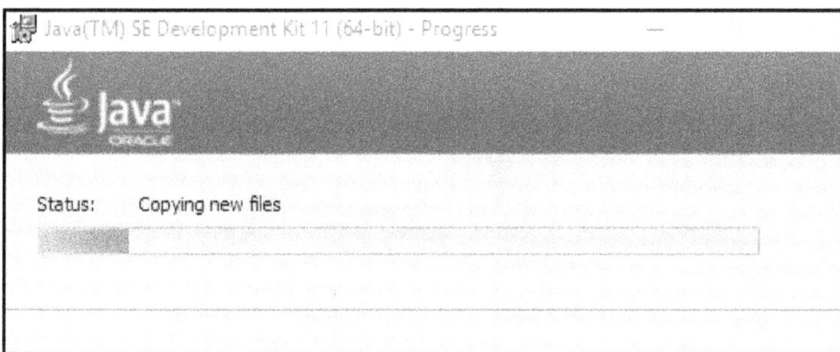

We get to a progress screen while Java is installing. This is a fairly fast process, no more than a 10-second process. After Java has been installed, we get a confirmation screen:

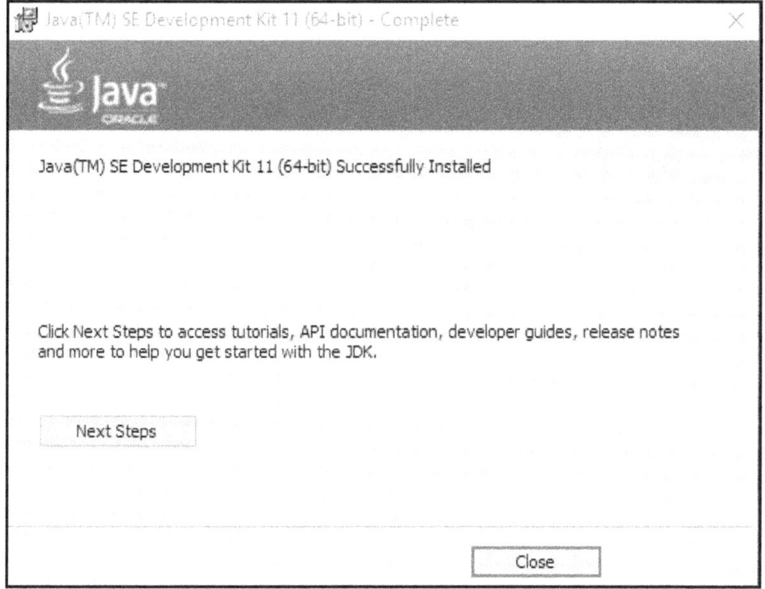

We can press **Close**. It is possible to press the **Next Steps** button, that opens the browser and brings us to a page that describes the next steps we can do with Java. Using the prerelease version results in an HTTP 404 error. This will hopefully be fixed when you read this book.

The last step is to set the environment variable `JAVA_HOME`. To do that, in Windows, we have to open the control center and select the **Edit environment variables for your account** menu:

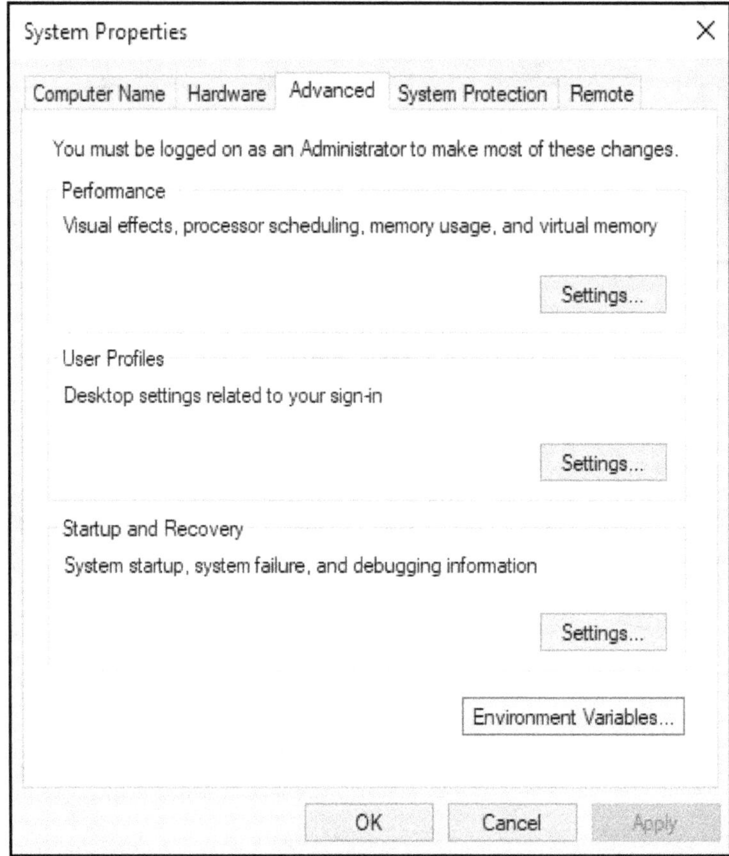

This will open a new window that we should use to create a new environment variable for the current user:

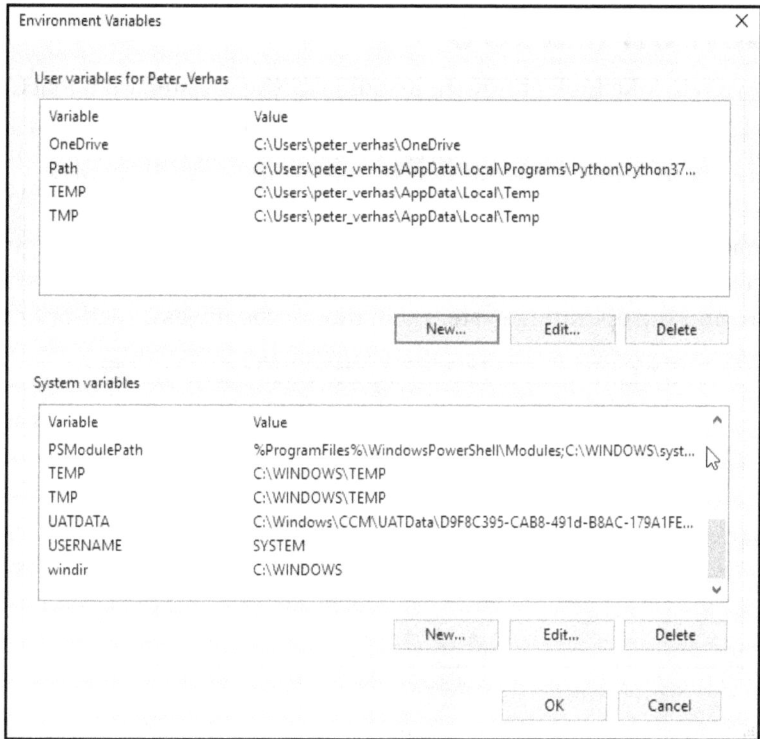

The name of the new variable has to be `JAVA_HOME`, and the value should point to the installation directory of the JDK:

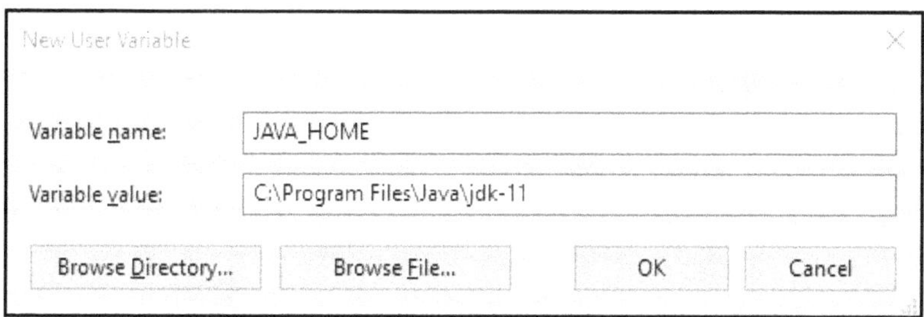

This value on most systems is `C:\Program Files\Java\jdk-11`. This is used by many Java programs and tools to locate the Java runtime.

Installation on macOS

In this section, we will take look at how to install Java step by step on a macOS platform. I will describe the installation process for the released version available at the time of writing this book. As of now, the Java 18.9 early access version is a bit tricky to install. It is probable that the release version of Java 18.9 will have similar or the same installation steps as Java 9.

The macOS version of Java comes in the form of a `.dmg` file. This is a packaging format of macOS. To open it, simply double-click on the file in the `Download` folder where the browser saves it, and the operating system will mount the file as a read-only disk image:

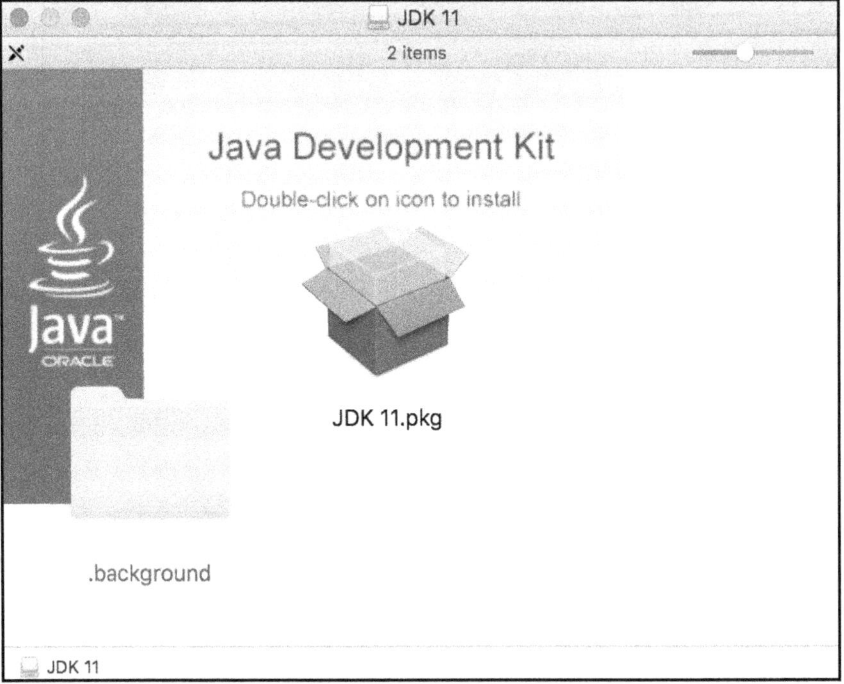

There is only one file on this disk—the installation image. Double-click on the filename or icon in the Finder application and the installation process will start:

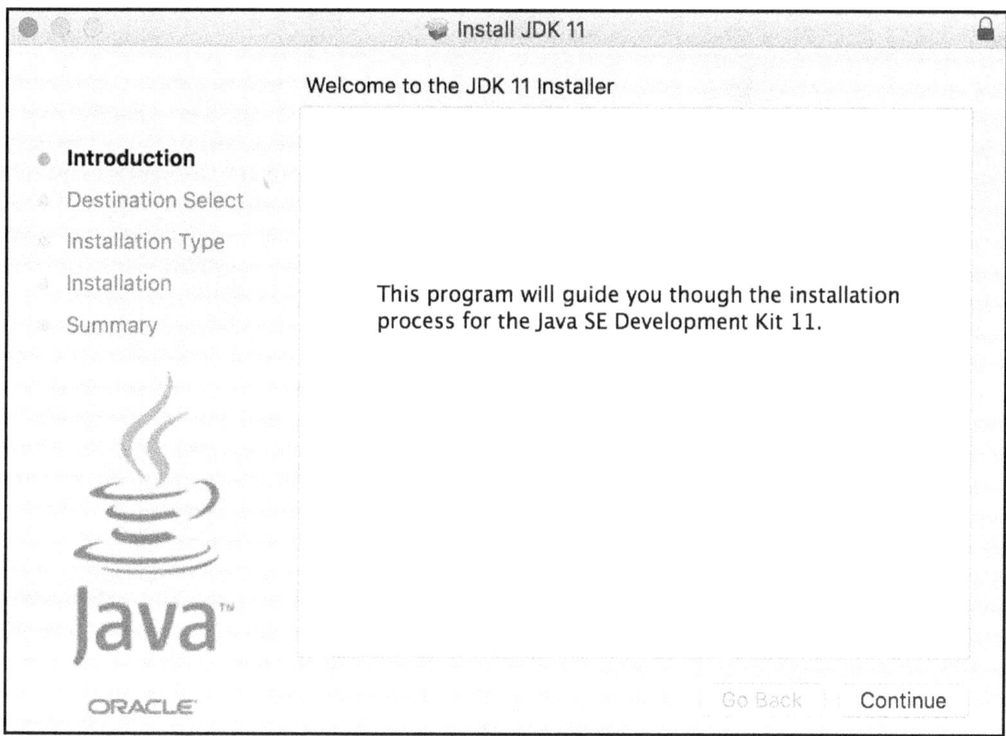

The first screen is a welcome screen. Click on **Continue**, and you will see the **Summary** page that displays what will be installed.

It is not a surprise that you will see a standard Java installation. This time, the button is called **Install**. Click on it and you will see the following:

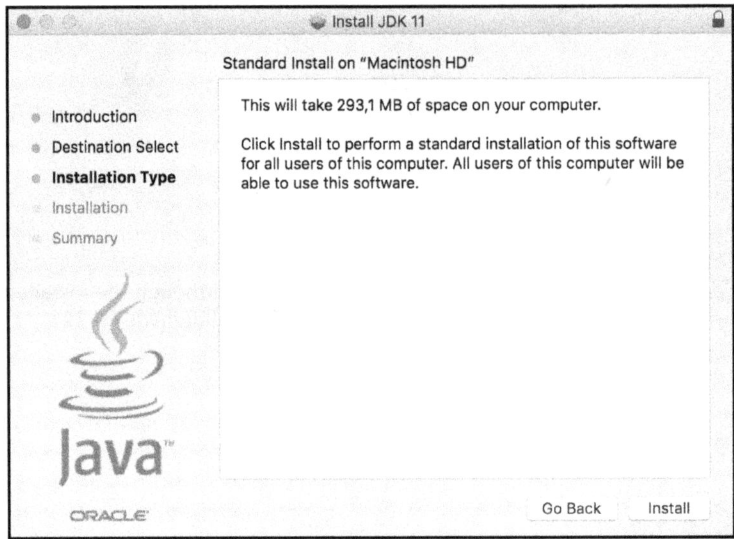

This is the time when you have to provide the login parameters for the administrative user—a username and password:

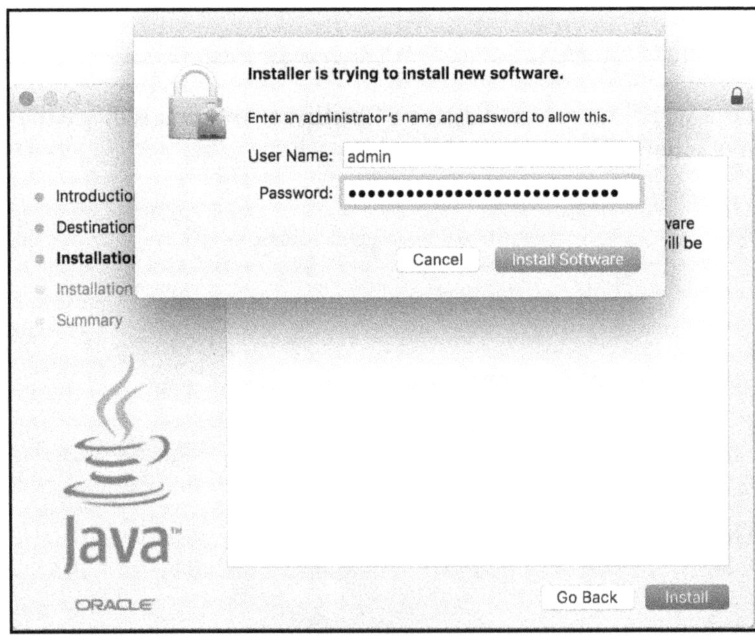

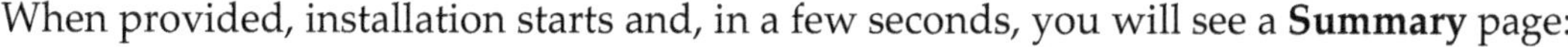

When provided, installation starts and, in a few seconds, you will see a **Summary** page:

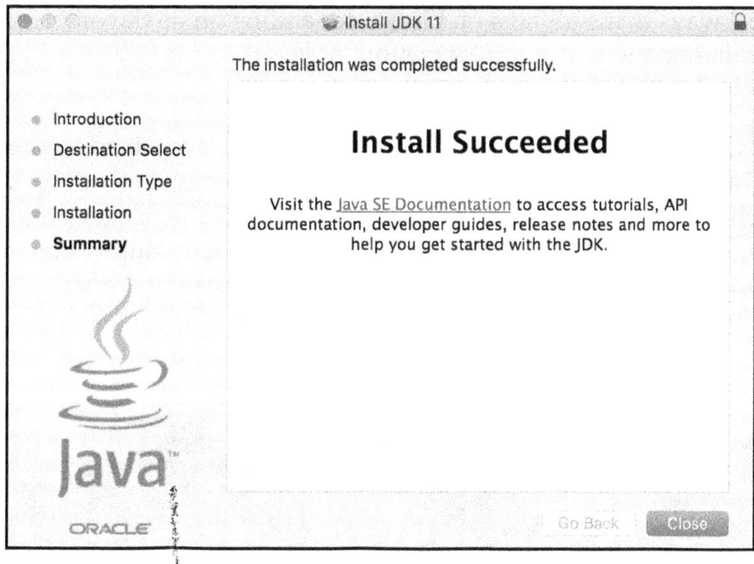

Click on **Close** and you are ready. You have Java installed on your Mac. Optionally, you can dismount the installation disk and, sometime later, you can also delete the `.dmg` file. You will not need that, and in case you do, you can download it any time from Oracle.

The last thing is to check whether the installation was okay. The proof of the pudding is in eating it. Start a Terminal window and type `java -version` at the prompt; Java will tell you the version that's been installed.

In the following screenshot, you can see the output on my workstation and also the macOS commands that are handy to switch between the different versions of Java:

```
verhasp — -bash — 68×24
~$ java -version
java version "11-ea" 2018-09-25
Java(TM) SE Runtime Environment 18.9 (build 11-ea+25)
Java HotSpot(TM) 64-Bit Server VM 18.9 (build 11-ea+25, mixed mode)
~$
```

In the preceding screenshot, you can see that I have installed the Java 11 version and, at the same time, I also have a Java 18.9 early release installation, which I will use to test the new features of Java for this book.

Installation on Linux

There are several ways to install Java on Linux, depending on its flavor. Here, I will describe an installation method that works more or less the same way on all flavors. The one I used is Debian.

The first step is the same as in any other operating system—download the installation kit. In the case of Linux, you should select a package that has a `tar.gz` ending. This is a compressed archive format. You should also carefully select the package that matches the processor in your machine and the 32/64 bit version of the operating system. After the package is downloaded, you have to switch to root mode, issuing the `su` command. This is the first command you can see in the following screenshot, that shows the installation commands:

```
root@test-Veriton-M200-H110: /home/test/Downloads
test@test-Veriton-M200-H110:~$ su root
Password:
root@test-Veriton-M200-H110:/home/test# cd Downloads
root@test-Veriton-M200-H110:/home/test/Downloads# tar xfz jdk-11-ea+25_linux-x64
_bin.tar.gz
root@test-Veriton-M200-H110:/home/test/Downloads# mv jdk-11 /opt/jdk
root@test-Veriton-M200-H110:/home/test/Downloads# update-alternatives --install
/usr/bin/java java /opt/jdk/bin/java 10045
root@test-Veriton-M200-H110:/home/test/Downloads# update-alternatives --install
/usr/bin/javac javac /opt/jdk/bin/javac 10045
root@test-Veriton-M200-H110:/home/test/Downloads#
```

The `tar` command uncompressed the archive into a subfolder. In Debian, this subfolder has to be moved to `/opt/jdk`, and the `mv` command is used for this purpose. The two `update-alternatives` commands are Debian-specific. These tell the operating system to use this newly installed Java in case there is already an older Java installed. The Debian I was using to test and demonstrate the installation process on a virtual machine came with a 7-year-old version of Java.

The final step of the installation is the same as any other operating system—checking whether the installation was successful in issuing the `java -version` command. In the case of Linux, this is even more important. The installation process does not check that the downloaded version matches the operating system and the processor architecture.

Setting JAVA_HOME

The JAVA_HOME environment variable plays a special role in Java. Even though the JVM executable, java.exe or java, is on the PATH (thus, you can execute it by typing the name java without specifying the directory in the Command Prompt) (Terminal), it is recommended that you use the correct Java installation to set this environment variable. The value of the variable should point to the installed JDK. There are many Java-related programs, Tomcat or Maven for example, that use this variable to locate the installed and currently used Java version. In macOS, setting this variable is unavoidable.

In macOS, the program that starts to execute when you type java, is a wrapper that first looks at JAVA_HOME to decide which Java version to start. If this variable is not set, macOS will decide on its own, selecting from the available installed JDK versions. To see the available versions, you can issue the following command:

```
~$ /usr/libexec/java_home -V
Matching Java Virtual Machines (13):
    11, x86_64: "Java SE 11-ea"
/Library/Java/JavaVirtualMachines/jdk-11.jdk/Contents/Home
    10, x86_64: "Java SE 10"
/Library/Java/JavaVirtualMachines/jdk-10.jdk/Contents/Home
    9.0.1, x86_64:      "Java SE 9.0.1"
/Library/Java/JavaVirtualMachines/jdk-9.0.1.jdk/Contents/Home
    9, x86_64:  "Java SE 9-ea"
/Library/Java/JavaVirtualMachines/jdk-9.jdk/Contents/Home
    1.8.0_92, x86_64:   "Java SE 8"
/Library/Java/JavaVirtualMachines/jdk1.8.0_92.jdk/Contents/Home
    1.8.0_20, x86_64:   "Java SE 8"
/Library/Java/JavaVirtualMachines/jdk1.8.0_20.jdk/Contents/Home
    1.8.0_05, x86_64:   "Java SE 8"
/Library/Java/JavaVirtualMachines/jdk1.8.0_05.jdk/Contents/Home
    1.8.0, x86_64:      "Java SE 8"
/Library/Java/JavaVirtualMachines/jdk1.8.0.jdk/Contents/Home
    1.7.0_60, x86_64:   "Java SE 7"
/Library/Java/JavaVirtualMachines/jdk1.7.0_60.jdk/Contents/Home
    1.7.0_40, x86_64:   "Java SE 7"
/Library/Java/JavaVirtualMachines/jdk1.7.0_40.jdk/Contents/Home
    1.7.0_21, x86_64:   "Java SE 7"
/Library/Java/JavaVirtualMachines/jdk1.7.0_21.jdk/Contents/Home
    1.7.0_07, x86_64:   "Java SE 7"
/Library/Java/JavaVirtualMachines/jdk1.7.0_07.jdk/Contents/Home
    1.7.0_04, x86_64:   "Java SE 7"
/Library/Java/JavaVirtualMachines/1.7.0.jdk/Contents/Home

/Library/Java/JavaVirtualMachines/jdk-11.jdk/Contents/Home
```

You will then get the list of installed JDKs. Note that the command is lowercase, but the option is capitalized. If you do not provide any options and argument to the program, it will simply return the JDK it thinks is the newest and most appropriate for the purpose. As I copied the output of the command from my Terminal window, you can see that I have quite a few versions of Java installed on my machine.

The last line of the program response is the home directory of JDK, which is the default. You can use this to set your `JAVA_HOME` variable using some bash programming:

```
export JAVA_HOME=$(/usr/libexec/java_home)
```

You can place this file in your `.bashrc` file, which is executed each time you start a Terminal application, and thus `JAVA_HOME` will always be set. If you want to use a different version, you can use `-v`, with the lowercase option this time, to the same utility, as follows:

```
export JAVA_HOME=$(/usr/libexec/java_home -v 1.8)
```

The argument is the version of Java you want to use. Note that this versioning becomes the following:

```
export JAVA_HOME=$(/usr/libexec/java_home -v 11)
```

If you want to use the Java JDK Early Access version and not 1.11, there is not an explanation for the same—fact of life.

Note that there is another environment variable that is important for Java—`CLASSPATH`. We will talk about it later.

Executing jshell

Now that we have spent a lot of time installing Java, it's time to get your fingers burnt a bit. As we are using Java 18.9, there is a new tool that helps developers play around with the language. This is a **Read-Eval-Print-Loop** (**REPL**) tool that many language toolsets contain and there were also implementations from Java, but version 9 is the first that contains this feature off the shelf.

REPL is a tool that has interactive prompt and language commands that can be directly entered without editing some standalone file. The entered commands are executed directly and then the loop starts again, waiting for the user to type in the next command.

This is a very effective tool to try out some language constructs without the delay of editing, compiling, and loading. The steps are automatically and transparently done by the REPL tool.

The REPL tool in Java 18.9 is called jshell. To start it, just type its name. If it is not on the `PATH`, then type the full path to jshell that comes installed with Java 18.9, as shown in the following example:

```
$ jshell | Welcome to JShell -- Version 11-ea | For an introduction type:
/help intro jshell>
```

The jshell starts up in an interactive way and the prompt it displays is `jshell>` to help you recognize that jshell is running. What you type is read by the program and not the operating system shell. As this is the first time you will start jshell, it tells you to type `/help intro`. Let's do it. It will print out a short text about what jshell is, as shown in the following code:

```
jshell> /help intro
|
|                                    intro
|                                    =====
|
|  The jshell tool allows you to execute Java code, getting immediate
results.
|  You can enter a Java definition (variable, method, class, etc), like:
int x = 8
|  or a Java expression, like:  x + x
|  or a Java statement or import.
|  These little chunks of Java code are called 'snippets'.
|
|  There are also the jshell tool commands that allow you to understand and
|  control what you are doing, like:  /list
|
|  For a list of commands: /help
```

Okay, so we can type Java snippets and `/list`, but that is only one example of the available commands. We can hope for more information by typing `/help`, as demonstrated in the following code:

```
jshell> /help
|  Type a Java language expression, statement, or declaration.
|  Or type one of the following commands:
|  /list [<name or id>|-all|-start]
|       list the source you have typed
|  /edit <name or id>
|       edit a source entry
```

```
|  /drop <name or id>
|       delete a source entry
|  /save [-all|-history|-start] <file>
|       Save snippet source to a file
...
```

What you get is a long list of commands. Most of it is not presented here to save paper and your attention. We will use many of these commands on our journey through the next few pages. Let's start with a small Java snippet, that is, the ageless *Hello World* example:

```
jshell> System.out.println("Hello, World!")
Hello World!
```

This is the shortest ever Hello World program in Java. Till Java 9, if you wanted to do nothing more than print out `Hello World!`, you had to create a program file. It had to contain the source code of a class, including the `public static main` method, which contained the one line we had to type in with Java 9 jshell. It was cumbersome just for a simple printout of sample code. Now it is much easier, and jshell is also lenient. It forgives us the regarding missing semicolon at the end of the line.

The next thing we should try is declaring a variable, as follows:

```
jshell> var a = 13
a ==> 13
```

We declared a variable, named `a`, and assigned the value to it—`13`. The type of the variable is `int`, which is an abbreviation for integer types in Java. Now, we have this variable already in our snippet, so we can print it out if we want to, as shown here:

```
jshell> System.out.println(a)
13
```

It's time to write something more complex into jshell than a one-liner:

```
jshell> void main(String[] args){
   ...> System.out.println("Hello, World")
   ...> }
|  Error:
|  ';' expected
|  System.out.println("Hello, World")
|                                    ^
```

The jshell recognizes that this is not a one-liner and that it cannot process what we typed so far when we press *Enter* at the end of the first line, and it signals that it expects more characters from us, so it displays `...>` as a continuation prompt. We type in the commands that make up the whole hello world `main` method.

However, this time, jshell does not let us miss the semicolon; that is allowed only in the case of one-line snippets. As jshell is interactive, it is easy to correct the mistake—press the up arrow key a few times to get back the previous lines and, this time, add the semicolon at the end of the second line:

```
jshell> void main(String[] args){
   ...> System.out.println("Hello, World");
   ...> }
|  created method main(String[])
```

This method was created for us as a snippet, and now we can call it:

```
jshell> main(null)
Hello, World
```

It works. You can list all the snippets that were created, as follows:

```
jshell> /list

   1 : System.out.println("Hello World!")
   2 : var a = 13;
   3 : System.out.println(a)
   4 : void main(String[] args){
       System.out.println("Hello, World");
       }
   5 : main(null)
```

Also, as we want to go on writing a full Java version of *hello world*, we can save our work from jshell to a file, as follows:

```
jshell> /save HelloWorld.java
```

Finally, we exit from jshell by typing `/exit`. As you get back to the system prompt, type `cat HelloWorld.java` (or `type HelloWorld.java` on Windows) to see the content of the file. It is as follows:

```
$ cat HelloWorld.java
System.out.println("Hello, World!")
var a = 13;
System.out.println(a)
void main(String[] args){
System.out.println("Hello, World");
}
main(null)
```

The file contains all the snippets that we typed in, one after the other. If you think that you have messed up the shell with lots of variables and code snippets that you do not need anymore, you can issue the `/reset` command:

```
jshell> /reset
|  Resetting state.
```

After this command, the jshell is as clean as when it was started earlier:

```
jshell> /list

jshell>
```

Listing just does not produce anything, as we deleted it all. Fortunately, we saved the state of jshell to a file, and we can also loaded the content of the file by issuing the `/open` command:

```
jshell> /open HelloWorld.java
Hello, World!
13
Hello, World
```

It loads the line from the file and executes it, just as the characters were typed into the Command Prompt.

You may recall that the `/list` command printed a number in front of each snippet. We can use it to edit the snippets individually. To do so, issue the `/edit` command, followed by the number of the snippet:

```
jshell> /edit 1
```

You may recall that the first command we entered was the `System.out.println` system call that prints out the argument to the console. When you press *Enter* after the `/edit 1` command, you do not get the prompt back. Instead, jshell opens a separate graphical editor that contains the snippet to edit, as shown:

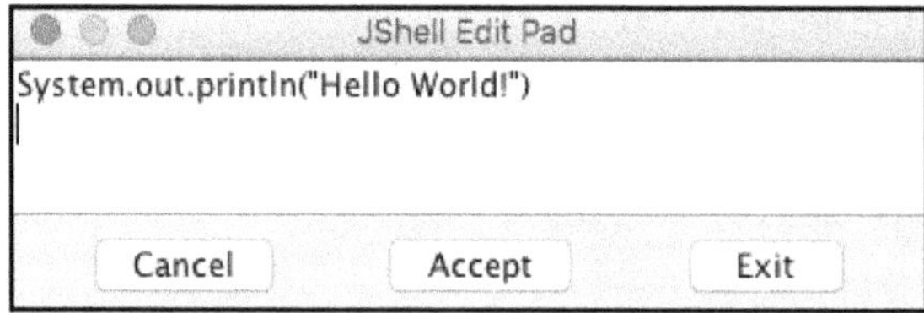

Edit the text in the box so that it will look like this:

```
void printf(String format, Object... args) { System.out.printf(format,
args); }
printf("Hello World!")
```

Click on **Accept** and then **Exit**. When you click on **Accept**, the Terminal will execute the snippet and display the following result:

```
| created method printf(String,Object...) Hello World!
```

The method that we used, `printf`, stands for formatted printing. This may be well-known from many other languages. It was first introduced by the C language and though cryptic, the name survived. This is also part of the standard Java class, `PrintStream`, just like `println`. In case of `println`, we had to write `System.out` in front of the method name. To avoid that, we defined the snipped in the editor, and it got executed and defined the `printf` method for us.

Jshell also defines a few snippets that are automatically loaded when jshell starts or resets. You can see these if you issue the `/list` command with the `-start` option, as follows:

```
jshell> /list -start

  s1 : import java.io.*;
  s2 : import java.math.*;
  s3 : import java.net.*;
  s4 : import java.nio.file.*;
  s5 : import java.util.*;
  s6 : import java.util.concurrent.*;
  s7 : import java.util.function.*;
  s8 : import java.util.prefs.*;
  s9 : import java.util.regex.*;
 s10 : import java.util.stream.*;
```

These predefined snippets help in the use of jshell. Most users will import these classes.

If you want to list all the snippets you entered as well as the predefined snippets, and also those that contained some error and thus were not executed, you can use the `-all` option on the `/list` command, as follows:

```
jshell> /list -all
  s1 : import java.io.*;
  s2 : import java.math.*;
  s3 : import java.net.*;
  s4 : import java.nio.file.*;
  s5 : import java.util.*;
  s6 : import java.util.concurrent.*;
```

```
   s7 : import java.util.function.*;
   s8 : import java.util.prefs.*;
   s9 : import java.util.regex.*;
  s10 : import java.util.stream.*;
    1 : System.out.println("Hello, World!")
    2 : var a = 13;
    3 : System.out.println(a)
    4 : void main(String[] args){
        System.out.println("Hello, World");
        }
    5 : main(null)
    6 : void printf(String format, Object... args) {
System.out.printf(format, args); }
    7 : System.out.println("Hello, World!");
```

The lines that are preloaded are numbered with the `s` prefix. The snippets that contain an error have a number prefixed with `e`. (We have none in this printout.)

If you want to execute some of the snippets again, you only have to type `/n`, where `n` is the number of the snippet, as follows:

```
jshell> /1
System.out.println("Hello, World!")
Hello, World!
```

You cannot re-execute the preloaded snippets or snippets that contained errors. There is no need for any of those anyway. Preloaded snippets declare some imports; erroneous snippets do not execute because they are, well...erroneous.

You need not rely on the number of jshell when you want to re-execute a snippet. When you already have a lot of snippets in your jshell session, listing them all would be too cumbersome; there is a shortcut to re-execute the last n-th snippet. You have to write `/-n`. Here, n is the number of the snippet counting from the last one. So, if you want to execute the very last snippet, you have to write `/-1`. If you want to execute the one before the last one, you have to write `/-2`. Note that if you already typed `/-1`, the last one is the re-execution of the last snippet, and snippet number -2 will become number `-3`.

Listing all the snippets can also be avoided in other ways. When you are interested only in certain types of snippets, you can have special commands.

If we want to see only the variables that we defined in the snippets, we can issue the `/vars` command, as follows:

```
jshell> /vars
|    int a = 13
```

If we want to see only the classes, the `/types` command will do that:

```
jshell> class s {}
|  created class s

jshell> /types
|    class s
```

Here, we just created an empty class and then we listed it.

To list the methods that were defined in the snippets, the `/methods` command can be issued:

```
jshell> /methods
|    void main(String[])
|    void printf(String,Object...)
```

You can see in the output that there are only two methods, which are as follows:

- `main`: Which is the main class of the program
- `printf`: This, we defined when using the editor

If you want to see everything you typed, you have to issue the `/history` command for all the snippets and commands that you typed. (I will not copy the output here; I do not want to shame myself showing all of my typos and failures. You should try yourself and see your own history!)

Recall that we can delete all the snippets by issuing the `/reset` command. You can also delete snippets individually. To do so, you should issue the `/drop n` command, where `n` is the snipped number:

```
jshell> /drop 1

jshell> /list

   2 : var a = 13;
   3 : System.out.println(a)
   4 : void main(String[] args){
       System.out.println("Hello, World");
       }
   5 : main(null)
   6 : void printf(String format, Object... args) {
System.out.printf(format, args); }
   7 : System.out.println("Hello, World!");
   8 : System.out.println("Hello, World!")
```

We can see that we dropped the first snippet:

```
jshell> /drop 2
|  dropped variable a

jshell> /drop 4
|  dropped method main(String[])
```

The jshell error message asks us to see the output of the `/types`, `/methods`, `/vars`, or `/list` commands. The problem with this is that `/types`, `/methods`, and `/vars` do not display the number of the snippet. This is most probably a small bug in the jshell prerelease version and may be fixed by the time the JDK is released.

When we were editing the snippets, jshell opened a separate graphical editor. It may happen that you are running jshell using ssh on a remote server and where it is not possible to open a separate window. You can set the editor using the `/set` command. This command can set quite a few configuration options of the jshell. To set the editor to use the ubiquitous vi, issue the following command:

```
jshell> /set editor "vi"
|  Editor set to: vi
```

After this, jshell will open the snipped-in `vi` in the same Terminal window where you issue the `/edit` command.

It is not only the editor that you can set. You can set the startup file, and also the way jshell prints the feedback to the console after a command was executed.

If you set the startup file, the commands listed in the startup file will be executed instead of the built-in commands of jshell after the `/reset` command. This also means that you will not be able to use the classes that are imported by default directly, and you will not have the `printf` method snippet, unless your own startup file contains the imports and the definition of the snippet.

Create the `sample.startup` file with the following content:

```
void println(String message) { System.out.println(message); }
```

Starting up a new jshell, execute it as follows:

```
jshell> /set start sample.startup

jshell> /reset
|  Resetting state.
```

```
jshell> println("wuff")
wuff

jshell> printf("This won't work...")
|  Error:
|  cannot find symbol
|    symbol:   method printf(java.lang.String)
|  printf("This won't work...")
|  ^----^
```

The `println` method is defined, but the `printf` method, which we defined earlier, is not.

The feedback defines the prompt jshell prints and then waits for the input, the prompt for the continuation lines, and the message details after each command. There are predefined modes, which are as follows:

- Normal
- Silent
- Concise
- Verbose

Normal is selected by default. If you issue `/set feedback silent`, prompt becomes `->`, and jshell will not print details about the commands. The `/set feedback concise` code prints a bit more information, and `/set feedback verbose` prints verbose information about the commands executed:

```
jshell> /set feedback verbose
|  Feedback mode: verbose

jshell> int z = 13
z ==> 13
|  created variable z : int

jshell> int z = 13
z ==> 13
|  modified variable z : int
|    update overwrote variable z : int
```

You can also define your own modes, giving a name to the new mode using the `/set mode xyz` command, where `xyz` is the name of the new mode. After this, you can set prompt, truncation, and format for the mode. When the format is defined, you can use it in the same way as the built-in modes.

Last but not least, the most important command of jshell is `/exit`. This will just terminate the program, and you will return to the operating system shell prompt.

Now, let's edit the `HelloWorld.java` file to create our first Java program. To do so, you can use vi, notepad, Emacs, or whatever is available on your machine and fits you. Later on, we will use some integrated development environment (IDE), NetBeans, Eclipse, or IntelliJ; however, for now, a simple text editor is enough.

Edit the file so that the content will be as follows:

```
public class HelloWorld {
  public static void main(String[] args){
        System.out.println("Hello World");
       }
  }
```

To compile the source code to bytecode, which is executable by JVM, we have to use the Java compiler named `javac`:

```
javac HelloWorld.java
```

This generates the `java.class` file in the current directory. This is a compiled code that can be executed as follows:

```
$ java HelloWorld
Hello World
```

With this one, you have created and executed your first full Java program. You may still wonder what we were doing; everything will be clear later. Here and now, I wanted you to get a feeling that it works.

The file we edited contained only the snippet, and we deleted most of the lines, except for the declaration of the `main` method, and inserted the declaration of the class around it.

In Java, you cannot have standalone methods or functions, like in many other languages. Every method belongs to some class, and every class should be declared in a separate file (well, almost, but for now, let's skip the exceptions). The name of the file has to be the same as the name of the class. The compiler requires this for `public` classes. Even for non-public classes, we usually follow this convention. If you renamed the file from `HelloWorld.java` to `Hello.java`, the compiler will display an error when you try to compile the file with the new name:

```
$ mv HelloWorld.java Hello.java
~/Dropbox/java_9-by_Example$ javac Hello.java
Hello.java:2: error: class HelloWorld is public, should be declared in a
file named HelloWorld.java
public class HelloWorld {
       ^
1 error
```

So, let's move it back to the original name, that is, `mv Hello.java HelloWorld.java`.

The declaration of the class starts with the `class` keyword, then the name of the class, an opening curly brace, and lasts until the matching closing brace. Everything in-between belongs to the class.

For now, let's skip why I wrote `public` in front of the class and focus on the main method in it. The method does not return any value; therefore, its return value is `void`. The argument, named `args`, is a string array. When JVM starts the `main` method, it passes the command-line arguments to the program in this array. However, this time, we do not use it. The `main` method contains the line that prints out `Hello World`. Now, let's examine this line a little more.

In other languages, printing something to the console requires only a `print` statement, or a very similar command. I remember that some BASIC interpreters even allowed us to type `?` instead of `print`, because printing to the screen was so common. This has changed a lot during the last 40 years. We use graphical screens, internet, and many other input and output channels. These days, it is not very common to write to the console.

Usually, in professional large-scale enterprise applications, there is not even a single line that does that. Instead, we will direct the text to log files, send messages to message queues, and send requests and reply with responses over TCP/IP protocol. As this is so infrequently used, there is no reason to create a shortcut for the purpose in the language. After the first few programs, when you get acquainted with the debugger and logging possibilities, you will not print anything directly to the console yourself.

Still, Java has features that let you send text directly to the standard output of a process the good old way, as it was invented originally for UNIX. This is implemented in a Java way, where everything has to be an object or class. To get access to the system output, there is a class named `System`, and it, among other things, has the following three variables:

- `in`: This is the standard input stream
- `out`: This is the standard output stream
- `err`: This is the standard error stream

To refer to the output stream variable, because it is not in our class but in `System`, we will have to specify the class name, so we will refer to it as `System.out` in our program. The type of this variable is `PrintStream`, which is also a class. Class and type are synonyms in Java. Every object that is of the `PrintStream` type has a method named `println` that accepts a `String`. If the actual print stream is the standard output, and we are executing our Java code from the command line, the string is sent to the console.

The method is named `main`, and this is a special name in Java programs. When we start a Java program from the command line, JVM invokes the method named `main` from the class that we specify on the command line. It can do that because we declared this method `public` so that anyone can see and invoke it. If it was `private`, it would be seen and callable only from within the same class, or classes that are defined in the same source file.

The method is also declared as `static`, which means it can be invoked without an actual instance of the class that contains the methods. Using static methods is usually not seen as a good practice these days, unless they are implementing functions that cannot really ever be related to an instance, or have different implementations such as the functions in the `java.lang.Math` class. However, somewhere, the code execution has to start, and the Java runtime will not usually create instances of classes for us automatically.

To start the code, the command line should be as follows:

```
java -cp . HelloWorld
```

The `-cp` option stands for classpath. The classpath is a fairly complex idea for Java, but, for now, let's make it simple and say that it is a list of directories and JAR files that contain our classes. The list separator for the classpath is `:` (colon) on UNIX-like systems and `;` (semicolon) on Windows. In our case, the classpath is the actual directory, as that is the place where the Java compiler created `HelloWorld.class`. If we do not specify classpath on the command line, Java will use the current directory as a default. That is the reason our program was working without the `-cp` option in the first place.

Both `java` and `javac` handle many options. To get a list of the options, type `javac -help` or `java -help`. We use the IDE to edit the code and, many times, to compile, build, and run it during development. The environment, in this case, sets the reasonable parameters. For production, we use build tools that also support the configuration of the environment. Due to this, we rarely meet these command-line options. Nevertheless, professionals have to understand their meanings at least and know where to learn their actual use, in case it is needed.

Looking at the bytecode

The class file is a binary file. The main role of this format is to be executed by the JVM and to provide symbolic information for the Java compiler when a code uses some of the classes from a library. When we compile our program that contains `System.out.println`, the compiler looks at the compiled `.class` files and not at the source code. It has to find the `System` class, the `out` field, and the `println` method.

When we debug a piece of code or try to find out why a program does not find a class or method, we will need a way to look into the binary of the `.class` files. This is not an everyday task, and it takes some advanced knowledge.

To do so, there is a *decompiler* that can display the content of a `.class` file in a more or less readable format. This command is called `javap`. To execute it, you can issue the following command:

```
$ javap HelloWorld.class
Compiled from "HelloWorld.java"
public class HelloWorld {
  public HelloWorld();
  public static void main(java.lang.String[]);
}
```

The output of the program shows that the class file contains a Java class that has something called `HelloWorld();` it seems to be a method having the same name as the class, and it also contains the method we have written.

The *method* that has the same name as the class is the constructor of the class. As every class in Java can be instantiated, there is a need for a constructor. If we do not give one, the Java compiler will create one for us. This is the default constructor. The default constructor does nothing special, but returns a new instance of the class. If we provide a constructor on our own, the Java compiler will not have bothered creating one.

The `javap` decompiler does not show what is inside the methods or what Java code it contains unless we provide the `-c` option:

```
$ javap -c HelloWorld.class
Compiled from "HelloWorld.java"
public class HelloWorld {
  public HelloWorld();
    Code:
       0: aload_0
       1: invokespecial #1                  // Method
java/lang/Object."<init>":()V
       4: return
  public static void main(java.lang.String[]);
    Code:
       0: getstatic     #2                  // Field
java/lang/System.out:Ljava/io/PrintStream;
       3: ldc           #3                  // String hali
       5: invokevirtual #4                  // Method
java/io/PrintStream.println:(Ljava/lang/String;)V
       8: return
}
```

It is very cryptic and is not for ordinary humans. Only a few experts who deal with the Java code generation can fluently read that. However, taking a look at it helps you get a glimpse of what bytecode means. It is something like a good old assembly. Although this is binary code, there is nothing secret in it: Java is open source, and the class file format is well documented and debuggable for the experts.

Packaging classes into a JAR file

When you deliver a Java application, usually the code is packaged into JAR, WAR, EAR, or some other packaged format. We learn something again that seems to be obscure at first sight, but in reality, this is not that complex. They are all ZIP files. You can open any of these files using WinZip or some other ZIP manager that you have a license for. The extra requirement is that, for example, in the case of a JAR file, the archive should contain a directory named `META-INF` and inside it a file named `MANIFEST.MF`. This file is a text file and contains meta information in the format, which is as follows:

```
Manifest-Version: 1.0
Created-By: 11-ea (Oracle Corporation)
```

There can be a lot of other information in the file, but this is the minimum that the Java provided tool `jar` puts there if we package our class file into a JAR, issuing the following command:

```
jar -cf hello.jar HelloWorld.class
```

The `-c` option tells the JAR archiver to create a new JAR file and the `f` option is used to specify the name of the new archive. The one we specified here is `hello.jar`, and the file added to it is the class file.

The packaged JAR file can also be used to start the Java application. Java can read directly from JAR archives and load classes from there. The only requirement is that they are on the classpath.

You cannot put individual classes on the classpath, only directories. As JAR files are archives with an internal directory structure in them, they behave like a directory.

Check that the JAR file was created using `ls hello.jar`, and remove the `rm HelloWorld.class` class file just to ensure that when we issue the command line, the code is executed from the JAR file and not the class:

```
$ java -cp hello.jar HelloWorld
Hello World
```

To see the content of the JAR file, however, it is recommended that you use the JAR tool and not WinZip, even though that may be cozier. Real professionals use the Java tools to handle Java files:

```
$ jar -tf hello.jar META-INF/ META-INF/MANIFEST.MF HelloWorld.class
```

Managing the running Java application

The Java toolset that comes with the JDK supports the execution and management of running Java applications as well. To have some program that we can manage while executing, we will need a code that runs not only for a few milliseconds but, while it runs, it also prints something to the console. Let's create a new program called `HelloWorldLoop.java`, with the following content:

```
public class HelloWorldLoop {
  public static void main(String[] args){
       for( ;; ){
         System.out.println("Hello World");
         }
       }
  }
```

The program contains a `for` loop. Loops allow repeated execution of a code block, and we will discuss them in `Chapter 2`, *The First Real Java Program - Sorting Names*. The loop we created here is a special one that never terminates but repeats the printing method call, printing `Hello World` until we kill the program by pressing *Ctrl* + C or issuing a `kill` command on Linux or on macOS X, or terminate the program in the task manager under Windows.

Compile and start it in one window and open another Terminal window to manage the application.

The first command that we should get familiar with is `jps`. To get more familiar with `jps`, you can read some content here—`http://docs.oracle.com/javase/7/docs/technotes/tools/share/jps.html`, It lists the Java processes that run on the machine, which are as follows:

```
$ jps
21873 sun.tools.jps.Jps
21871 HelloWorldLoop
```

You can see that there are two processes: one is the program we execute and the other is the `jps` program itself. Not surprisingly, the `jps` tool is also written in Java. You can also pass options to `jps`, which are documented on the web.

There are many other tools, and we will examine one of them, which is a very powerful and easy-to-use tool—Java VisualVM:

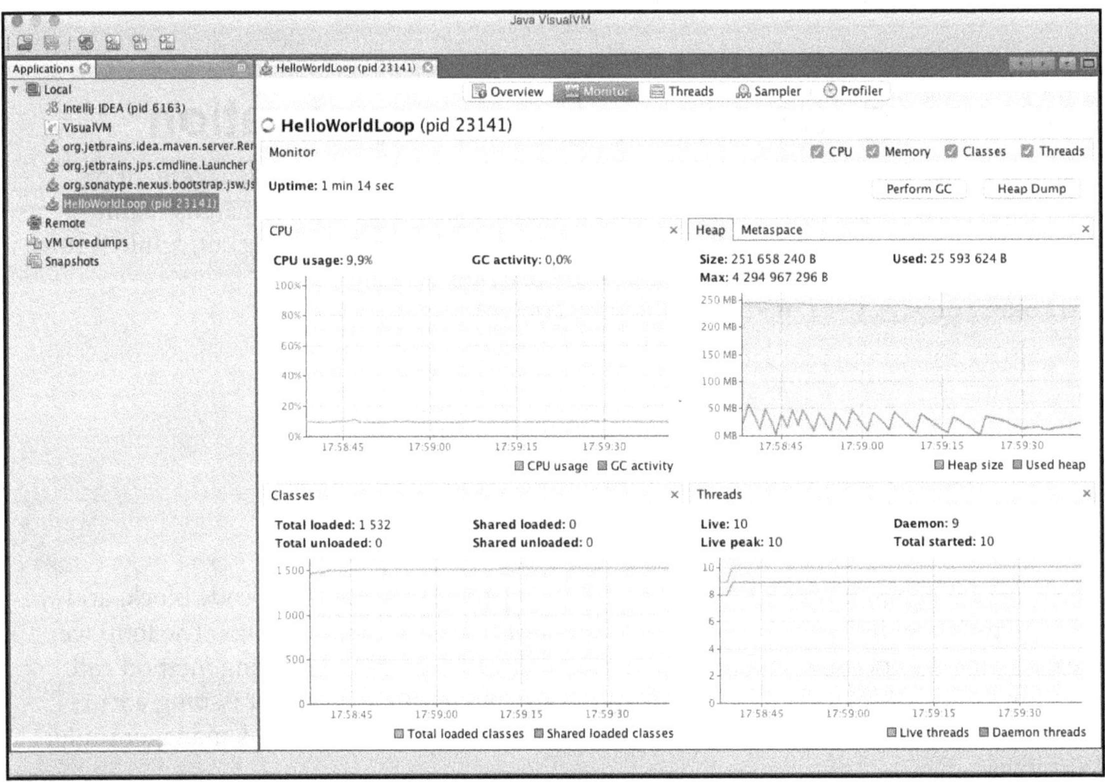

VisualVM is a command-line graphical tool that connects to the running Java process and displays the different performance parameters. To start the VisualVM tool, you will issue the `jvisualvm` command without any parameters. Soon, a window will appear with an exploring tree on the left-hand side and a welcome pane on the right. The left shows all the running Java processes under the branch named **Local**. If you double-click on `HelloWorldLoop`, it will open the details of the process on the right pane. On the header tabs, you can select **Overview**, **Monitor**, **Threads**, **Sampler**, and **Profiler**. The first three tabs are the most important and give you a good view of what is happening in JVM regarding the number of threads, CPU usage, memory consumption, and so on.

Using an IDE

Integrated development environments are outstanding tools that help the development by offloading the mechanical tasks from the developer's shoulders. They recognize many of the programming errors as we type the code, help us find the needed library methods, display the documentation of the libraries, and provide extra tools for style checking, debugging, and such.

In this section, we will look at some IDEs and how to leverage the functions they provide.

To get an IDE, you will have to download and install it. It does not come with the Java development tools, because they are not part of the language environment. However, don't worry, they can be downloaded free of charge and are easy to install. They may be more complex to start up than a notepad editor, but even after a few hours of work, they will pay back the time you devote to learning them. After all, it is not without reason that no developer is coding Java in notepad or vi.

The three topmost IDEs are *NetBeans*, *Eclipse*, and *IntelliJ*. All are available in community versions, which means you need not pay for them. IntelliJ has a *full* version that you can also buy. The community edition will be used for learning the language. In case you do not like IntelliJ, you can use Eclipse or NetBeans. These are all free of charge. Personally, I use the IntelliJ community edition for most of my projects, and the screen samples that show an IDE in this book will feature this IDE. However, it does not necessarily mean that you have to stick to this IDE.

In the developer community, there are topics that can be heavily debated. These topics are about opinions. Were they about facts, the debate would easily be soon over. One such topic is "Which is the best IDE?". It is a matter of taste. There is no definite answer. If you learn how to use one, you will like that, and you will be reluctant to learn another one unless you see that the other one is so much better. That is the reason developers love the IDE they use (or just hate, depending on their personality), but they keep using the same IDE, usually for a long time. There is no best IDE.

To download the IDE of your choice, you can visit either one of the following websites:

- `https://netbeans.org/` for NetBeans
- `http://www.eclipse.org/` for Eclipse
- `https://www.jetbrains.com/idea/` for IntelliJ

NetBeans

NetBeans is supported by Oracle and is continuously developed. It contains components, such as the NetBeans profiler, that became part of the Oracle Java distribution. You may note that when you start Visual VM and start the profiling, the Java process started has `netbeans` in its name.

Generally, NetBeans is a framework to develop rich client applications, and the IDE is only one application of the many that are built on top of the framework. It supports many languages, not only Java. You can develop PHP, C, or JavaScript code using NetBeans and have similar services for Java. For the support of different languages, you can download plugins or a special version of NetBeans. These special versions are available from the download page of the IDE, and they are nothing more than the basic IDE with some preconfigured plugins. In the C package, the developers configure the plugins that are needed when you want to develop C; in the PHP version, the developers configure for PHP.

Eclipse

Eclipse is supported by IBM. Similar to NetBeans, it is also a platform for rich-client application, and it is built around the *OSGi* container architecture, which itself is a topic that can fill a book like this. Most of the developers use Eclipse and, almost exclusively, it is the choice when developers create code for the *IBM WebSphere* application server. The Eclipse special version contains a developer version of WebSphere.

Eclipse also has plugins to support different programming languages and also has different variations that are similar to NetBeans. The variations are plugins prepackaged with the basic IDE.

IntelliJ

The last one in the preceding enumeration is IntelliJ. This IDE is the only one that does not want to be a framework. IntelliJ is an IDE. It also has plugins, but most of the plugins that you will need to download to use in NetBeans or Eclipse are preconfigured. When you want to use some more advanced plugins, it may, however, be something you have to pay for, which should not be a problem when you are doing professional, paid work, should it? These things are not that expensive. To learn the subjects in this book, you won't need any plugin that is not in the community edition. As in this book, I will develop the samples using IntelliJ, and I recommend that you follow me during your learning experience.

I want to emphasize that the examples in this book are independent of the actual IDE to be used. You can follow the book using NetBeans, Eclipse, or even Emacs, notepad, or vi.

IDE services

Integrated development environments provide us with services. The most basic service is that you can edit files with them, but they also help build the code, find bugs, run the code, deploy to the application server in development mode, debug, and so on. In the following sections, we will look at these features. I will not give an exact and precise introduction on how to use one or the other IDE. A book like this is not a good medium for such a tutorial.

IDEs differ on menu placement, keyboard shortcuts, and they may even change as newer versions are released. It is best to look at the actual IDE tutorial video or online help. Their features, on the other hand, are very similar. IntelliJ has the video documentation at `https://www.jetbrains.com/idea/documentation/`.

IDE screen structure

The different IDEs look similar, and they have the same screen structure more or less. In the following screenshot, you can see an IntelliJ IDE:

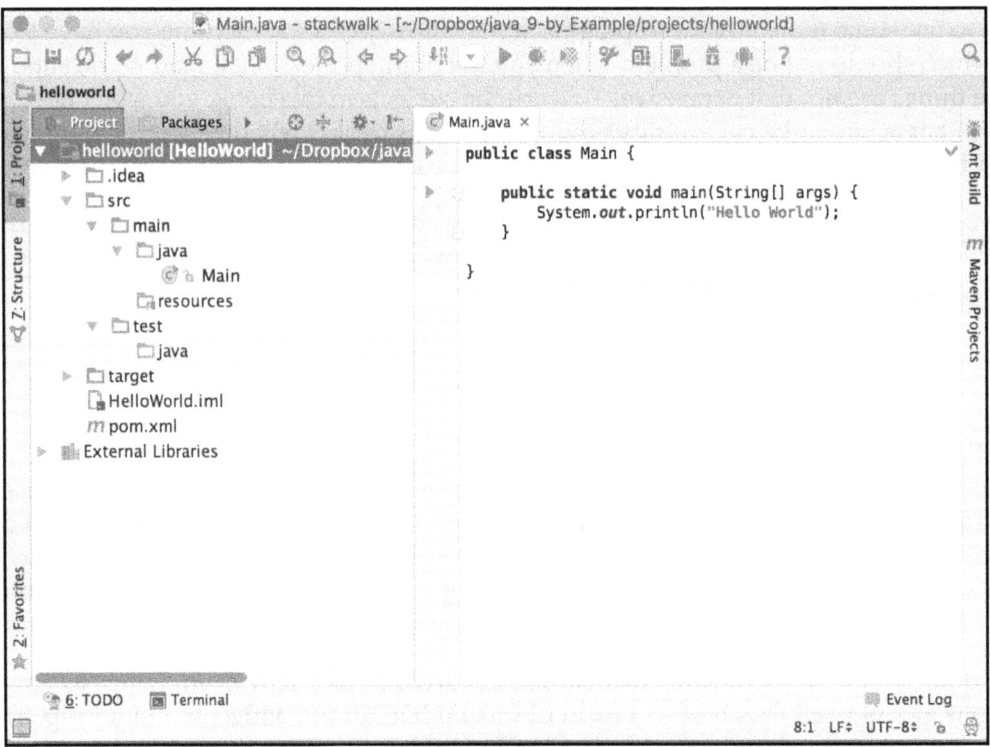

On the left, you can see the file structure of a Java project. A Java project typically contains many files in different directories, which we will discuss in the next chapter. The simple *HelloWorld* application contains a `pom.xml` project description file. This file is needed for the Maven build tool, which is also a topic for the next chapter. For now, you should only know that it is a file that describes the project structure for maven. The IDE also keeps track of some administrative data for itself. It is stored in `HelloWorld.iml`. The main program file is stored in the `src/main/java` directory and named `HelloWorld.java`.

On the right, you can see the files. In the preceding screenshot, we have only one file opened. In case there is more than one file opened, there are tabs, one for each file. Now, the active file is `HelloWorld.java`, which can be edited in the source code editor.

Editing files

When editing, you can type in characters or delete characters, words, and lines, but this is something that all editors can do. IDEs offer extra—they analyze the source code and format it, which, in turn, automatically indents the lines. It also continuously compiles the code in the background while you edit it, and if there is some syntax error, it underlines that with a red waiving line. When you fix the error, the red underlining disappears:

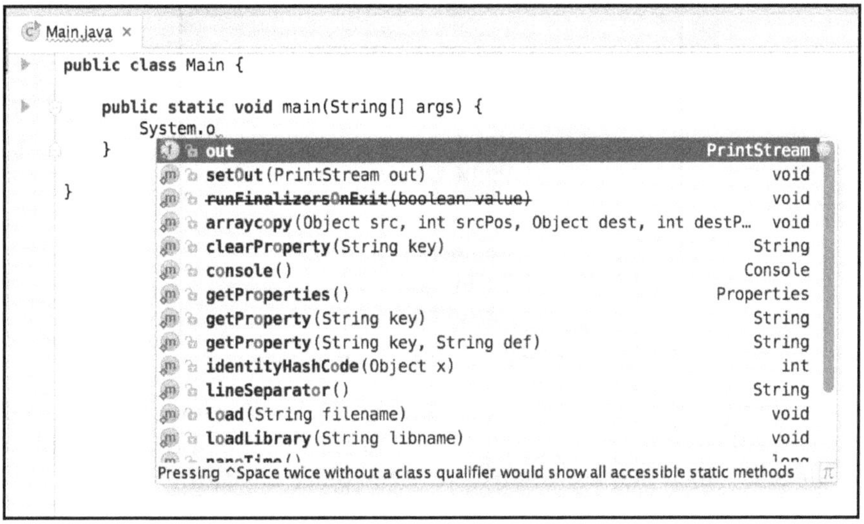

```
Main.java ×
public class Main {

    public static void main(String[] args) {
        System.o
    }             out                                              PrintStream
                  setOut(PrintStream out)                          void
}                 runFinalizersOnExit(boolean value)               void
                  arraycopy(Object src, int srcPos, Object dest, int destP...  void
                  clearProperty(String key)                        String
                  console()                                        Console
                  getProperties()                                  Properties
                  getProperty(String key)                          String
                  getProperty(String key, String def)              String
                  identityHashCode(Object x)                       int
                  lineSeparator()                                  String
                  load(String filename)                            void
                  loadLibrary(String libname)                      void
                  nanoTime()                                       long
                  Pressing ^Space twice without a class qualifier would show all accessible static methods
```

The editor also automatically gives suggestions for further characters as you type. You can ignore the window that pops up and continue typing. However, many times, it is easier to stop after a character and use the up and down arrows to select the word that needs finishing before pressing *Enter*; the word will be inserted into the source code automatically.

In the preceding screenshot, you can see that I wrote `System.o`, and the editor immediately suggested that I wanted to write `out`. The other alternatives are the other static fields and methods that are in the `System` class and which contain the letter `o`.

The IDE editor gives you hints, not only when it can type for you, but also when it cannot type instead of you. In the following screenshot, the IDE tells you to type some expression as an argument to the `println()` method that is `boolean`, `char`, `int`, and so on. The IDE has absolutely no idea what to type there. You have to construct the expression. Still, it can tell you that it needs to be of a certain type:

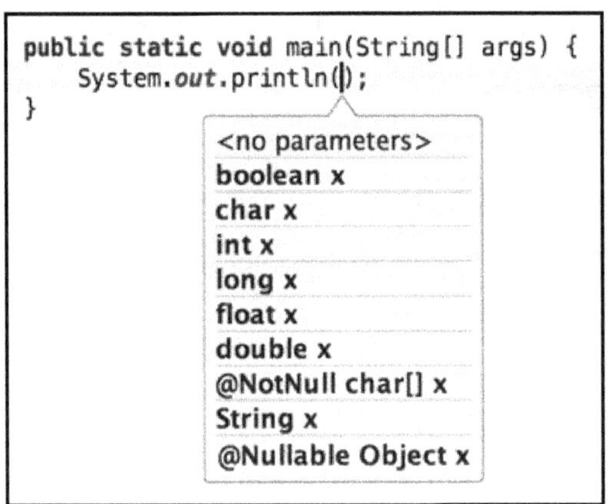

It is not only the built-in types that the editor knows. The editor integrated with the JDK continuously scans the source files and knows what classes, methods, and fields are there in the source code and which of those are usable at the place of editing.

This knowledge is also heavily used when you want to rename a method or variable. The old method was to rename the field or method in the source file and then do an exhaustive search for all references to the variable. Using the IDE, the mechanical work is done by it. It knows all the uses of a field or method and automatically replaces the old identifier with the new one. It also recognizes whether a local variable happens to have the same name as the one that we rename, and the IDE only renames those occurrences that are really referring to the one we are renaming.

You can usually do more than just renaming. There are more or less mechanical tasks that programmers call **refactoring**. These are supported by the IDEs using some keyboard shortcut and context-sensitive menu in the editor—right-click on the mouse and click on **Menu:**

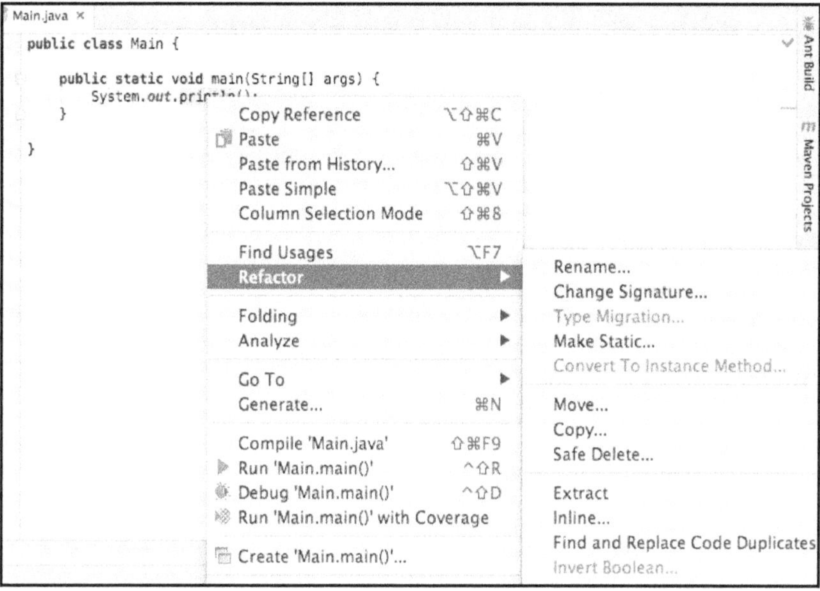

The IDE also helps you read the documentation of the libraries and source code, as shown here:

```
   class AllDefaultPossibilitiesBuilder extends RunnerBuilder {
private final boolean fCanUseSuiteMethod;
                                          [< 1.8 >] java.lang
public AllDefaultPossibilitiesBuilder(boole public class Throwable extends Object
                                          implements Serializable
@Override
public Runner runnerForClass(Class<?> testClass) throws Throwable {
    List<RunnerBuilder> builders = Arrays.asList(
            ignoredBuilder(),
            annotatedBuilder(),
```

Libraries provide *Javadoc* documentation for the `public` methods, and you should also write Javadoc for your own method. Javadoc documentation is extracted from special comments in the source code, and we will learn how to create those in `Chapter 4`, *Mastermind - Creating a Game*. These are located in comments in front of the actual method head. As creating compiled documentation is part of the compilation flow, the IDE also knows the documentation, and it displays as a hovering box over the method names, class names, or whatever element you want to use in the source file when you position the cursor on the element.

Managing projects

To the left of the IDE window, you can see the directory structure of the project. The IDE knows the different types of files and shows them in a way that is meaningful from the programming point of view. For example, it does not display `Main.java` as a filename. Instead, it displays `Main` and an icon that signals that `Main` is a class. It can also be an interface still in a file named `Main.java`, but, in that case, the icon will show that this is an interface. This is again done by the IDE continuously scanning and compiling the code.

The files are structured into subdirectories when we develop a Java code. These subdirectories follow the packaging structure of the code. Many times, in Java, we use compound and long package names, and displaying it as a deep and nested directory structure will not be so easy to handle.

Packages are used to group the source files. The source files for classes that are related in some way should go into one package. We will discuss the notion of packages and how to use them in the next chapter.

The IDE is capable of showing the package structure instead of the nested directories for those directories of the project that contain source files:

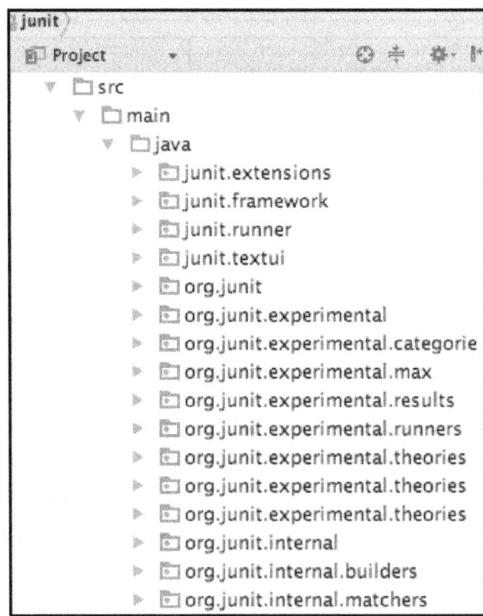

When you move a class or an interface from one package to another, it happens in a similar to how renaming or any other refactoring action takes place. All references to the class or interface in the source files get renamed to the new package. If a file contains an `import` statement referring to the class, the name of the class in the statement is corrected. To move a class, you can open the package and use the good old drag and drop technique.

Package hierarchy is not the only hierarchy displayed in the IDE. The classes are in packages but, at the same time, there is an inheritance hierarchy. Classes may implement interfaces and can extend other classes. The Java IDEs help us by showing type hierarchies where you can navigate across a graphical interface along the inheritance relations.

There is another hierarchy that IDEs can show to help us with development—method call hierarchy. After analyzing the code, the IDE can show us the graph displaying the relations between the methods: which method calls which other methods. Sometimes, this call graph is also important in showing the dependencies of methods on each other.

Building the code and running it

The IDEs usually compile the code for analysis to help us spot syntax errors or undefined classes and methods on the fly. This compilation is usually partial, covering a part of the code, and as it runs all the time, the source code changes and is never actually complete. To create the deployable file, that is, the final deliverable code of the project, a separate build process has to be started. Most of the IDEs have some built-in tool for that, but it's not recommended to use these, except for the smallest projects. Professional development projects use Ant, Maven, or Gradle instead.

Here's an example of Maven:

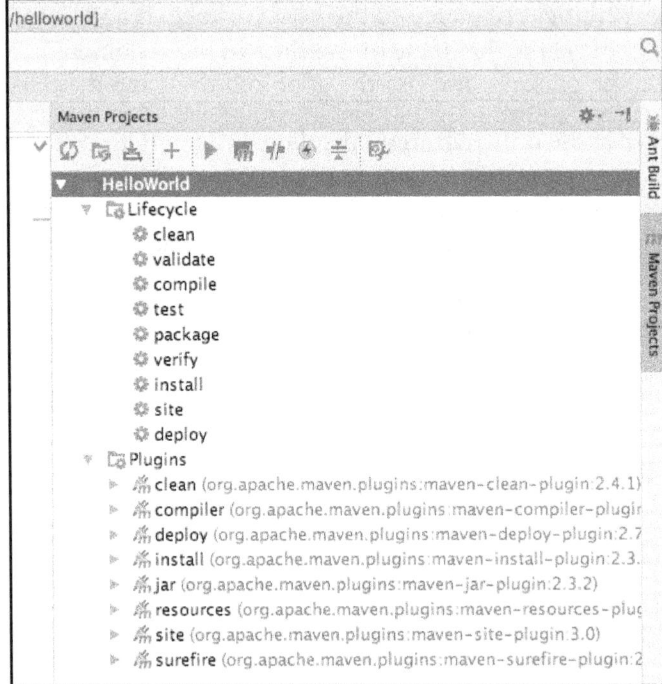

The IDEs are prepared to use such an external tool, and they can help us start them. This way, the build process can run on the developer machine without starting a new shell window. IDEs can also import the settings from the configuration file of these external build tools to recognize the project structure, where source files are, and what to compile to support error checking while editing.

The building process usually contains the execution of certain checks on the code. A bunch of the Java source file may compile nice and smooth. Still, the code may contain a lot of bugs and may be written in a terrible style. Those things make the project unmaintainable in the long run. To avoid these problems, we will use unit tests and static code analysis tools. These do not guarantee error-free code, but the chances are much slimmer.

IDEs have plugins to run the static code analysis tools as well as unit tests. Being integrated into the IDE has a huge advantage. When there is any problem identified by the analysis tool, or by some unit tests, the IDE provides an error message that also functions like a link on a web page. If you click on the message, which is usually blue and underlined, exactly like on a web page, the editor opens the problematic file and places the cursor where the issue is.

Debugging Java

Developing code needs debugging. Java has very good facilities to debug code during development. JVM supports debuggers via the Java Platform Debugger Architecture. This lets you execute code in debug mode, and JVM will accept external debugger tools to attach to it via a network, or it will try to attach to a debugger depending on command-line options. JDK contains a client, the `jdb` tool, which contains a debugger; however, it is so cumbersome to use when compared to the graphical client built into the IDEs that I have never heard of anyone using it for real work.

To start a Java program in debug mode so that JVM will accept a debugger client to attach the options to it, execute the following command:

```
-Xagentlib:jdwp=transport=dt_socket,server=y,suspend=y,address=7896
```

The `Xagentlib` option instructs the Java runtime to load the `jdwp` agent. The part of the option that follows `-Xagentlib:jdwp=` is interpreted by the debugger agent. These options are as follows:

- `transport`: This should specify which transport to use. It can be a shared memory (`dt_shmem`) socket or a TCP/IP socket transport but, in practice, you will always use the latter. This is specified in the preceding `dt_socket` sample.
- `server`: This specifies if the debugged JVM starts in server mode or client mode. When you start the JVM in server mode, it starts to listen on a socket and accepts the debugger to connect to it. If it is started in client mode, it tries to connect a debugger that is supposed to be started in server mode, listening on a port. The value of the option is `y`, meaning server mode, or `n`, meaning nonserver, which is client mode.
- `suspend`: This can also be `y` or `n`. If JVM is started in suspend mode, it will not start the Java code until a debugger is attached to it. If it is started with `suspend=n`, the JVM starts and when a debugger attaches, it stops as soon as a break point is reached. If you start a standalone Java application, you will usually start the debugging with `suspend=y`, which is the default. If you want to debug an application in an application server or servlet-container environment, it is better to start with `suspend=n`; otherwise, the server does not start until the debugger attaches to it. Starting the Java process in the `suspend=y` mode in case servlet application is only useful when you want to debug the servlet static initializer code, which is executed when the server is starting up. Without the suspend mode, you will be required to attach the debugger very fast. It is better that JVM just waits for you in that situation.

- `address`: This should specify the address that JVM communicates with. If the JVM started in client mode, it will start to connect to this address. If the JVM runs in server mode, it will accept connections from the debugger on that address. The address may specify only the port. In this case, the IP address is that of the local machine.

The other options the debugger agent may handle are for special cases. For the topics covered in this book, the preceding options are enough.

The following screenshot shows a typical debugging session where we debug the simplest program in IntelliJ IDE:

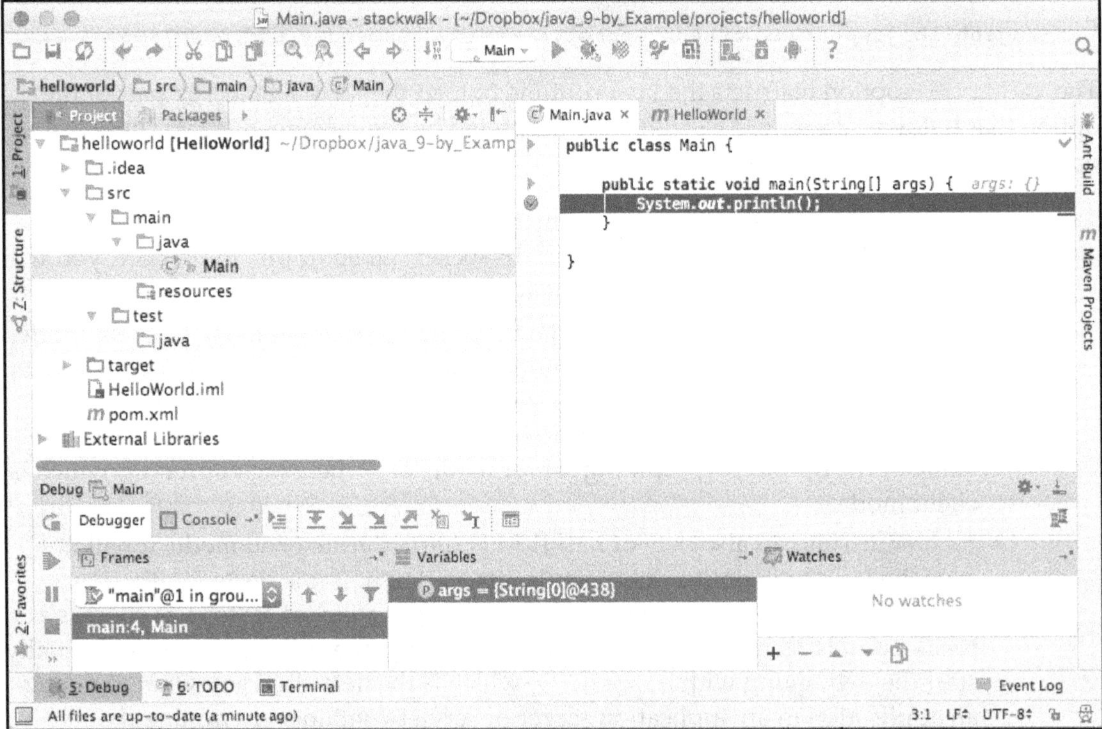

When you start a program from the IDE in debug mode, all of these options are automatically set for you. You can set a break point just by clicking on the source code in the editor. You can have a separate form to add, remove, and edit break points. Break points can be attached to specific lines or specific events, like when an exception is thrown. Break points attached to a specific line can also have conditions that tell the debugger to stop the execution of the code, but only when the condition is true; for example, if a variable has some predefined value.

Summary

In this chapter, we were introduced to each other with Java. We do not know too much about each other but we got acquainted. We installed the Java environment: Java, JDK, and integrated development environment. We wrote a small program and took a brief look at what can be done using the development tools. This is far from mastery, but even the longest journey starts with a first step, which is sometimes the hardest to take. We have done it in our Java journey. We started rolling and, for the enthusiasts that we are, nothing can stop us walking all the way along.

2
The First Real Java Program - Sorting Names

In the previous chapter, we got acquainted with Java, and especially with using the REPL tool and interactively executing some simple code. That is a good start, but we need more. In this chapter, we will develop a simple program. Using this code as an example, we will look at different build tools, which are frequently used for Java projects, and learn the basic features of the Java language.

This chapter will cover the following topics:

- The sorting problem
- The project structure and build tools
- The Make, Ant, Maven, and Gradle build tools
- Java language features related to the code example

Getting started with sorting

The sorting problem is one of the oldest programming tasks that an engineer deals with. We have a set of records and we know that we want to find a specific one sometime soon. To find it, we sort the records in a specific order that helps us find the record we want quickly.

As an example, we have the names of students with their marks on some cards. When students come to the dean's cabin asking for their results, we look through all of the cards one after the other to find the name of the inquiring student. However, it is better if we sort the cards by the names of the students alphabetically. When a student makes an inquiry, we can search the mark attached to the name much faster.

We can look at the middle card; if it shows the name of the student, then we are happy to have found the name and the mark. If the card precedes the name of the student alphabetically, then we will continue searching in the second half; otherwise, we will check the first half.

By following this approach, we can find the name of the student in a few steps. The number of steps cannot be more than the number as many times the pack of cards can be halved. If we have two cards, then it is two steps at most. If it is four, then we will need three steps at most. If there are eight cards, then we may need four steps, but not more. If there are 1,000 cards, then we may need at most 11 steps, while the original, nonsorted set will need 1,000 steps, as a worst case. That is, approximately, it speeds up the search by 100 times, so this is worth sorting the cards unless the sorting itself takes too much time. The algorithm finding an element in the already sorted set we just described is called **binary search** (`https://en.wikipedia.org/wiki/Binary_search_algorithm`).

In many cases, it is worth sorting the dataset, and there are many sorting algorithms to do that. There are simpler and more complex algorithms, and, as in many cases, more complex algorithms are the ones that run faster.

As we are focusing on the Java programming part and not the algorithm forging, in this chapter, we will develop a Java code that implements a simple and not-that-fast algorithm.

Bubble sort

The algorithm that we will implement in this chapter is well-known as **bubble sort**. The approach is very simple. Begin at the start of the cards and compare the first and the second card. If the first card is later in lexicographic order than the second one, then swap the two cards. Then, repeat this for the card that is in the second place now, then the third, and so on. There is a card that is lexicographically the latest, says Wilson. When we get this card and start to compare it with the next one, we will always swap them; this way, Wilson's card will travel to the last place where it has to be after the sort. All we have to do is repeat this traveling from the start and do the occasional swapping of cards again, but this time only to the last but one element. This time, the second latest element will get to its place—say, Wilkinson will be right before Wilson. If we have n cards, and we repeat this $n-1$ times, all the cards will get to their place.

In the upcoming sections, we will create a Java project that implements this algorithm.

Getting started with project structure and build tools

When a project is more complex than a single class, and it usually is, then it is wise to define a project structure. We will have to decide where we store the source files, where the resource files (the ones that contain some resource for the program but are not Java source) are, where the `.class` files should be written by the compiler, and so on. Generally, the structure is mainly the directory setup and the configuration of the tools that perform the build.

The compilation of complex programs cannot be feasibly done using the command line issuing `javac` commands. If we have 100 Java source files, the compilation will require that many `javac` commands to be issued. It can be shortened using wildcards, such as `javac *.java`, or we can write a simple bash script or a BAT command file which does that. First, it will be just 100 lines, each compiling one source Java file to the class file. Then, we will realize that it is the only time that CPU and power are being consumed to compile the files that have not changed since the last compilations, so we can add some bash programming that checks the time stamp on the source and generated files. In the end, we will end up with a tool that is essentially a build tool. Build tools are available ready-made; it is not worth reinventing the wheel.

Instead of creating one, we will use a build tool that is ready. There are few of them that can be found at `https://en.wikipedia.org/wiki/List_of_build_automation_software`. In this chapter, we will use one called Maven; however, before jumping into the details of this tool, we will look at some other tools that you are likely to meet as a Java professional in enterprise projects.

In the upcoming sections, we will discuss a bit about the following four build tools:

- Make
- Ant
- Maven
- Gradle

We will mention Make briefly because it is not used in Java environments these days. However, Make was the first build tool, and many ideas that modern Java build tools are based on are coming from the *good old* `make`. You, as a professional Java developer, should also be familiar with Make so that you do not freak out if you happen to see the use of it in a project for some purpose, and can know what it is and where its detailed documentation can be found.

Ant was the first build tool widely used for Java many years ago, and it is still used in many projects.

Maven is newer than Ant, and it uses a different approach. We will look at it in detail. Maven is also the official build tool of the Apache software foundation for the Java project. We will also use Maven as a build tool in this chapter.

Gradle is even newer, and it has started to catch up to Maven these days. We will use this tool in the later chapters of this book in more detail.

Make

The `make` program was originally created in April 1976, so this is not a new tool. It is included in the Unix system, so this tool is available without any extra installation on Linux, macOS X, or any other Unix-based system. Additionally, there are numerous ports of this tool on Windows and some version is/was included in the Visual Studio compiler toolset.

Make is not tied to Java. It was created when the major programming language was C, but it is not tied to C or any other language. The `make` is a dependency description language that has a very simple syntax. The `make`, just like any other build tool, is controlled by a project description file. In the case of make, this file contains a rule set. The description file is usually named `Makefile`, but in case the name of the description file is different, it can be specified as a command-line option to the `make` command.

Rules in `Makefile` follow each other and consist of one or more lines. The first line starts at the first position (there is no tab or space at the start of the line) and the following lines start with a tab character. Thus, `Makefile` might look something like the following code:

```
run : hello.jar
    java -cp hello.jar HelloWorld

hello.jar : HelloWorld.class
    jar -cf hello.jar HelloWorld.class

HelloWorld.class : HelloWorld.java
    javac HelloWorld.java
```

This file defines the three so-called targets: `run`, `hello.jar`, and `HelloWorld.class`. To create `HelloWorld.class`, type the following line at Command Prompt:

```
make HelloWorld.class
```

Make will look at the rule and see that it depends on `HelloWorld.java`. If the `HelloWorld.class` file does not exist, or `HelloWorld.java` is newer than the Java class file, `make` will execute the command that is written on the next line and it will compile the Java source file. If the class file was created following the last modification of `HelloWorld.java`, then `make` knows that there is no need to run the command.

In the case of creating `HelloWorld.class`, the `make` program has an easy task. The source file was already there. If you issue the `make hello.jar` command, the procedure is more complex. The `make` command sees that in order to create `hello.jar`, it needs `HelloWorld.class`, which itself is also a target on another rule. Thus, we might have to create it.

First, it starts the problem the same way as before. If `HelloWorld.class` is present and is older than `hello.jar`, there is nothing we need to do. If it is not present or is newer than `hello.jar`, then the `jar -cf hello.jar HelloWorld.class` command needs to be executed, although not necessarily at the moment when it realizes that it has to be performed. The `make` program remembers that this command has to be executed sometime in the future when all the commands that are needed to create `HelloWorld.class` are already executed successfully. Thus, it continues to create the class file in exactly the same way as I described earlier.

In general, a rule can have the following format:

```
target : dependencies
    command
```

The `make` command can create any target using the `make target` command by first calculating which commands to execute and then executing them one by one. The commands are shell commands executing in a different process and may pose problems under Windows, which may render the `Makefile` files' operating system to be dependent.

Note that the `run` target is not an actual file that `make` creates. A target can be a file name or just a name for the target. In the latter case, `make` will never consider the target to be readily available.

As we do not use `make` for a Java project, there is no reason to get into more details. Additionally, I cheated a bit by making the description of a rule simpler than it should be. The `make` tool has many powerful features out of the scope of this book. There are also several implementations that differ a little from each other. You will most probably meet the one made by the Free Software Foundation—the GNU make. And, of course, just in case of any Unix command-line tool, `man` is your friend. The `man make` command will display the documentation of the tool on the screen.

The following are the important points that you should remember about `make`:

- It defines the dependencies of the individual artifacts (targets) in a declarative way
- It defines the actions to create the missing artifacts in an imperative way

This structure was invented decades ago and has survived up until now for most of the build tools, as you will see in the next few chapters.

Ant

The `ant` build tool was built especially for Java projects around the year 2000. The aim of Java to be a write-once-run-anywhere language needed a tool that can also be used in different environments. Although `make` is available on Unix machines, and Windows as well, `Makefiles` were not always compatible. There was a small problem with the use of the tab character that some editors replaced with space, rendering `Makefile` unusable, but this was not the major reason. The main problem with `make` that ignited the development of Ant is that the commands are shell commands. Even if the implementation of the `make` program was made to be compatible, running on different operating systems, the used commands were many times incompatible, and that was something make itself could not change. Because `make` issues external commands to build the targets, developers are free to use any external tool that is available for them on the development machine. Another machine using the same operating system just may not have the same set of tools invoked by `make`. This undermines the portability of the `make` built projects.

At the same time, Ant is following the major principles of `make`. There are targets that may depend on each other and there are commands that need to be executed in an appropriate sequence to create the targets one after the other, following the dependency order. The description of the dependencies and the commands is XML (tab issue is solved) and the commands are implemented in Java (system dependency is solved, well... more or less).

As Ant is neither part of the operating system nor the JDK, you will have to download and install it separately if you want to use it.

Installing Ant

Ant can be downloaded from its official website (`http://ant.apache.org`). You can download the source or the precompiled version. The easiest way is to download the binary in a `tar.gz` format.

Whenever you download software from the Internet, it is highly recommended that you check the integrity of the downloaded file. The HTTP protocol does not contain error checking, and it may happen that a network error remains hidden or a malevolent internal proxy modifies the downloaded file. Download sites usually provide checksums for the downloadable files. These are usually MD5, SHA1, SHA512, or some other checksums.

When I downloaded the Apache Ant 1.9.7 version in `tar.gz` format, I also opened the page that led to the MD5 checksum. The checksum value is `bc1d9e5fe73eee5c50b26ed411fb0119`:

- `.zip` archive: apache-ant-1.9.7-bin.zip [PGP] [SHA1] [SHA512] [MD5]
- `.tar.gz` archive: apache-ant-1.9.7-bin.tar.gz [PGP] [SHA1] [SHA512] [MD5]
- `.tar.bz2` archive: apache-ant-1.9.7-bin.tar.bz2 [PGP] [SHA1] [SHA512] [MD5]

The downloaded file can be checked using the following command line: `$ md5 apache-ant-1.9.7-bin.tar.gz MD5 (apache-ant-1.9.7-bin.tar.gz) = bc1d9e5fe73eee5c50b26ed411fb0119` The calculated MD5 checksum is the same as the one on the website, which says that the file integrity is not harmed. On the Windows operating system, there is no tool to calculate MD5 digest. There is a tool that Microsoft provides, called **File Integrity Checksum Verifier Utility**, which is available at `https://support.microsoft.com/en-us/help/841290/availability-and-description-of-the-file-checksum-integrity-verifier-utility`. If you use Linux, it may happen that the `md5` or `md5sum` utility is not installed. In that case, you can install it using the `apt-get` command or whatever installation tool your Linux distribution supports.

After the file is downloaded, you can explode it into a subdirectory using the following command:

```
tar xfz apache-ant-1.9.7-bin.tar.gz
```

The created subdirectory is the usable binary distribution of Ant. Usually, I move it under `~/bin`, making it available only for my users on OS X. After that, you should set the environment variable as `ANT_HOME` to point to this directory and also add the `bin` directory of the installation to `PATH`. To do that, you should edit the `~/.bashrc` file and add the following lines to it:

```
export ANT_HOME=~/bin/apache-ant-1.9.7/
export PATH=${ANT_HOME}bin:$PATH
```

Then, restart the terminal application, or just type `. ~/.bashrc` and test the installation of Ant by typing the following command:

```
$ ant
Buildfile: build.xml does not exist!
Build failed
```

If the installation was correct, you should see the preceding error message.

Using Ant

When you see a project to be built by Ant, you will see a `build.xml` file. This is the project build file, the one that Ant was missing when you checked that the installation was correct. It can have any other name, and you can specify the name of the file as a command-line option for Ant, but this is the default filename, as `Makefile` was for `make`. A `build.xml` sample looks like the following:

```
<project name="HelloWorld" default="jar" basedir=".">
<description>
    This is a sample HelloWorld project build file.
</description>
    <property name="buildDir" value="build"/>
    <property name="srcDir" value="src"/>
    <property name="classesDir" value="${buildDir}/classes"/>
    <property name="jarDir" value="${buildDir}/jar"/>

    <target name="dirs">
        <mkdir dir="${classesDir}"/>
        <mkdir dir="${jarDir}"/>
    </target>

    <target name="compile" depends="dirs">
        <javac srcdir="${srcDir}" destdir="${classesDir}"/>
    </target>

    <target name="jar" depends="dirs,compile">
        <jar destfile="${jarDir}/HelloWorld.jar" basedir="${classesDir}"/>
    </target>
</project>
```

The top-level XML tag is `project`. Each build file describes one project, hence the name. There are three possible attributes to the tag, which are as follows:

- `name`: This defines the name of the project and is used by some IDEs to display it in the left panel identifying the project
- `default`: This names the target to use when no target is defined on the command line starting Ant
- `basedir`: This defines the initial directory used for any other directory name calculation in the build file

The build file can contain a description of the project, as well as properties in property tags. These properties can be used as variables in the attributes of the tasks between the `${` and `}` characters, and play an important role in the build process.

The targets are defined in target XML tags. Each tag should have a name that uniquely identifies the target in the build file and may have a `depends` tag that specifies one or more other targets that this target depends on. In case there is more than one target, the targets are comma separated in the attribute. The tasks belonging to the targets are executed in the same order as the targets dependency chain requires, in a very similar way as we saw in the case of `make`.

You can also add a `description` attribute to a target that is printed by Ant when the `-projecthelp` command-line option is used. This helps the users of the build file to know what targets are there and which does what. Build files tend to grow large with many targets, and when you have 10 or more targets, it is hard to remember each and every target.

The sample project with `HelloWorld.java` is now arranged in the following directories:

- `build.xml`: This is present in the `root` folder of the project
- `HelloWorld.java`: This is present in the `src` folder of the project
- `build/`: This folder does not exist; it will be created during the build process
- `build/classes` and `build/jar`: These also do not exist yet and will be created during the build process

When you start the build for the `HelloWorld` project the first time, you will see the following output:

```
$ ant
Buildfile: ~/java_11-fundamentalssources/ch02/build.xml

dirs:
```

```
    [mkdir] Created dir:
~/java_11-fundamentalssources/ch02/build/classes
    [mkdir] Created dir:
~/java_11-fundamentalssources/ch02/build/jar

compile:
...
    [javac] Compiling 1 source file to
~/java_11-fundamentalssources/ch02/build/classes

jar:
      [jar] Building jar:
~/java_11-fundamentalssources/ch02/build/jar/HelloWorld.jar

BUILD SUCCESSFUL
Total time: 0 seconds
```

Some unimportant lines are deleted from the actual output.

Ant realizes that, first, it has to create the directories, then it has to compile the source code, and finally, it can pack the `.class` files into a `.jar` file. Now, it is up to you to remember the command to execute the `HelloWorld` application. It was listed already in the first chapter. Note that this time, the JAR file is named `HelloWorld.jar`, and it is not in the current directory. You can also try to read the online documentation of Ant and create a target `run` that executes the compiled and packed program.

Ant has a built-in task named `java` that executes a Java class in almost the same way as you typed the `java` command in the terminal.

Maven

As Ant was created to overcome the shortages of `make`, Maven was created with a similar intention—to overcome the shortages of Ant. You may recall that `make` could not guarantee build portability because the commands `make` executes are arbitrary shell commands that may be system specific. An Ant build, if all the tasks are available on the classpath, is portable as long as Java runs the same way on the different platforms.

The problem with Ant is a bit different. When you download the source code of a project and you want to build, what will the command be? You should ask Ant to list all the targets and select the one that seems to be the most suitable. The name of the task depends on the engineer who crafted the `build.xml` file. There are some conventions, but they are not strict rules.

Where will you find the Java source files? Are they in the `src` directory or not? Will there also be some Groovy or other programming language files in case the project is polyglot? That depends. Again, there may be some conventions that some groups or company cultures suggest, but there is no general best industry practice.

When you start a new project with Ant, you will have to create the targets for compilation, test execution, and packaging. It is something that you would have already done for other projects. After the second or third project, you will just copy and paste your previous `build.xml` into your new project. Is that a problem? Yes, it is. It is copy/paste programming, even if it is only some build files.

Developers realized that a significant effort of the projects utilizing Ant is devoted to project build tool configuration, including repetitive tasks. When a newcomer comes to the team, they will first have to learn how the build is configured. If a new project is started, the build configuration has to be created. If it is a repetitive task, then better let the computers do it. That is generally what programming is all about, isn't it?

Maven approaches the build issue a bit differently. We want to build Java projects. Sometimes, some Groovy *or* Jython things, but they are also JVM languages; thus, saying that we want to build Java projects is not really a huge restriction. Java projects contain Java files, sometimes some other programming language's source files, resource files, and generally, that is it. Ant can do anything, but we do not want to do just anything with a build tool. We want to build projects.

Okay, after we restricted ourselves and accepted that we do not need a build tool that can be used for anything, we can go on. We can require that the source files be under the `src` directory. There are files that are needed for the operational code and there are files that contain some test code and data. Therefore, we will have two directories, `src/test` and `src/main`. Java files are in `src/main/java` as well as `src/test/java`. Resource files are under `src/main/resources` and `src/test/resources`.

If you want to put your source files somewhere else, then don't. I mean it. It is possible, but I will not even tell you how. Nobody does it. I do not even have any idea why Maven makes it possible. Whenever you see a project that is using Maven as a build tool, the sources are organized like that. There is no need to understand the directory structure envisioned by the project's build engineer. It is always the same.

How about the targets and the tasks? They are also the same for all Maven-based projects. What else would you like to do with a Java project other than compile, test, package, or deploy it? Maven defines these project life cycles for us. When you want to compile a project using Maven as a build tool, you will have to type `$ mvn compile` to compile the project. You can do that even before understanding what the project actually is.

As we have the same directory structure and the same goals, the actual tasks leading to the goals are also all the same. When we create a Maven project, we do not have to describe what the build process has to do and how it has to do it. We will have to describe the project and only the parts that are project-specific.

The build configuration of a Maven project is given in an XML file. The name of this file is usually `pom.xml`, and it should be in the `root` directory of the project, which should be the current working directory when firing up Maven. The word **POM** stands for **Project Object Model**, and it describes the projects in a hierarchical way. The source directories, the packaging, and other things are defined in a so-called super POM. This POM is part of the Maven program. Anything that the POM defines, overrides the defaults defined in the super POM. When there is a project with multiple modules, the POMs are arranged into a hierarchy, and they inherit the configuration values from the parent down to the modules. As we will use Maven to develop our sorting code, we will see some more details later.

Installing Maven

Maven is neither a part of the operating system nor the JDK. It has to be downloaded and installed in a very similar way to Ant. You can download Maven from its official website (`https://maven.apache.org/`) under the download section. Currently, the latest stable version is 3.5.4. When you download it, the actual release may be different; instead, use the latest stable version. You can download the source or the precompiled version. The easiest way is to download the binary in `tar.gz` format.

I cannot skip drawing your attention to the importance of checking the download integrity using checksums. I have detailed the way to do it in the section *Installing Ant*.

After the file is downloaded, you can explode it into a subdirectory using the following command:

```
tar xfz apache-maven-3.5.4-bin.tar.gz
```

The created subdirectory is the usable binary distribution of Maven. Usually, I move it under `~/bin`, making it available only for my users on OS X. After that, you should add the `bin` directory of the installation to the `PATH`. To do that, you should edit the `~/.bashrc` file and add the following lines to it:

```
export M2_HOME=~/bin/apache-maven-3.5.4/
export PATH=${M2_HOME}bin:$PATH
```

Then, restart the terminal application, or just type `. ~/.bashrc` and test the installation of Maven typing, as follows:

```
$ mvn -v
Apache Maven 3.5.4 (1edded0938998edf8bf061f1ceb3cfdeccf443fe;
2018-06-17T20:33:14+02:00)
Maven home: /Users/verhasp/bin/apache-maven-3.5.4
Java version: 11-ea, vendor: Oracle Corporation, runtime:
/Library/Java/JavaVirtualMachines/jdk-11.jdk/Contents/Home
Default locale: en_HU, platform encoding: UTF-8
OS name: "mac os x", version: "10.13.6", arch: "x86_64", family: "mac"
```

You should see a similar message on the screen that displays the installed Maven version and other information.

Using Maven

Unlike Ant, Maven helps you create the skeleton of a new project. To do that, you will have to type the following command:

```
$ mvn archetype:generate
```

Maven will first download the actually available project types from the network and prompt you to select the one you want to use. This approach seemed to be a good idea while Maven was new. When I first started Maven, the number of listed projects was somewhere between 10 and 20. Today, as I write this book, it lists 1,635 different archetypes. This number seems more like a historical date (the constitution of the French Academy of Science) than a usable size list of different archetypes. However, do not freak out. Maven offers a default value when it asks for your choice. The default is good for the `HelloWorld`, and we go for.

```
Choose a number: 817:
```

The actual number may be different on installation. Whatever it is, accept the suggestion and press *Enter*. After that, Maven will ask you for the version of the project:

```
Choose version:
1: 1.0-alpha-1
2: 1.0-alpha-2
3: 1.0-alpha-3
4: 1.0-alpha-4
5: 1.0
6: 1.1
Choose a number: 6: 5
```

Select the `1.0` version that is listed as number `5`. The next thing Maven asks for is the group ID and the artifact ID of the project. The dependency management that we will discuss later uses these. I selected a group ID based on the book and the publisher. The artifact of the project is `SortTutorial` as we will start our chapter example in this project.

```
Define value for property 'groupId': : packt.java11.example
Define value for property 'artifactId': : SortTutorial
```

The next question is the current version of the project. We have already selected `1.0` and Maven offers `1.0-SNAPSHOT`. Here, I selected `1.0.0-SNAPSHOT` because I prefer semantic versioning.

```
Define value for property 'version':  1.0-SNAPSHOT: : 1.0.0-SNAPSHOT
```

Semantic versioning, defined at `http://semver.org/`, is a versioning scheme that suggests three-digit version numbers as M.m.p. for Major, minor, *and* patch version numbers. This is very useful for libraries. You will increment the last version number if there has only been a bug fix since the previous release. You will increment the minor number when the new release also contains new features, but the library is compatible with the previous version; in other words, any program that is using the older version can still use the newer version. The major release number is increased when the new version is significantly different from the previous one. In the case of application programs, there is no code that uses the application API; thus, the minor version number is not that important. It does not hurt, though, and it often proves to be useful to signal smaller changes in the application. We will discuss how to version software in the last chapter.

Maven handles the versions that have the `-SNAPSHOT` postfix as non-release versions. While we develop the code, we will have many versions of our code, all having the same snapshot version number. On the other hand, non-snapshot version numbers can be used only for a single version:

```
Define value for property 'package':  packt.java11.example: :
```

The last question from the program skeleton generation is the name of the Java package. The default is the value we gave for `groupId`, and we will use this. It is a rare exception to use something else.

When we have specified all the parameters that are needed, the final request is to confirm the setting:

```
Confirm properties configuration:
groupId: packt.java11.example
artifactId: SortTutorial
version: 1.0.0-SNAPSHOT
package: packt.java11.example
 Y: : Y
```

After entering `Y`, Maven will generate the files that are needed for the project and display the report about this:

```
[INFO] ------------------------------------------------------------
[INFO] Using following parameters for creating project from Old (1.x)
Archetype: maven-archetype-quickstart:1.0
[INFO] ------------------------------------------------------------
[INFO] Parameter: basedir, Value: .../mavenHelloWorld
[INFO] Parameter: package, Value: packt.java11.example
[INFO] Parameter: groupId, Value: packt.java11.example
[INFO] Parameter: artifactId, Value: SortTutorial
[INFO] Parameter: packageName, Value: packt.java11.example
[INFO] Parameter: version, Value: 1.0.0-SNAPSHOT
[INFO] *** End of debug info from resources from generated POM ***
[INFO] project created from Old (1.x) Archetype in dir:
.../mavenHelloWorld/SortTutorial
[INFO] ------------------------------------------------------------
[INFO] BUILD SUCCESS
[INFO] ------------------------------------------------------------
[INFO] Total time: 01:27 min
[INFO] Finished at: 2016-07-24T14:22:36+02:00
[INFO] Final Memory: 11M/153M
[INFO] ------------------------------------------------------------
```

You can take look at the following generated directory structure:

```
C:\Users\peter_verhas\Dropbox\packt\Fundamentals-of-java-18.9\sources\ch02\mavenHelloWorld>tree
Folder PATH listing for volume
Volume serial number is EE2E-A381
C:.
└───SortTutorial
    └───src
        ├───main
        │   └───java
        │       └───packt
        │           └───java11
        │               └───example
        │                   └───stringsort
        └───test
            └───java
                └───packt
                    └───java11
                        └───by
                            └───example

C:\Users\peter_verhas\Dropbox\packt\Fundamentals-of-java-18.9\sources\ch02\mavenHelloWorld>
```

You can also see that it generated the following three files:

- `SortTutorial/pom.xml`: This contains the **Project Object Model**
- `SortTutorial/src/main/java/packt/java11/example/App.java`: This contains a `HelloWorld` sample application
- `SortTutorial/src/test/java/packt/java11/example/AppTest.java`: This contains a unit test skeleton utilizing the `junit4` library

We will discuss unit tests in the next chapter. For now, we will focus on the sorting application. As Maven was so kind and generated a sample class for the app, we can compile and run it without actual coding, just to see how we can build the project using Maven. Change the default directory to `SortTutorial` by issuing `cd SortTutorial`, and issue the following command:

```
$ mvn package
```

We will get the following output:

```
$ mvn package
[INFO] Scanning for projects...
[WARNING]
[WARNING] Some problems were encountered while building the effective model for packt.java9.by.example:SortTutorial:jar:1.0.0-SNAPSHOT
[WARNING] 'build.plugins.plugin.version' for org.apache.maven.plugins:maven-compiler-plugin is missing. @ line 10, column 15
[WARNING]
[WARNING] It is highly recommended to fix these problems because they threaten the stability of your build.
[WARNING]
[WARNING] For this reason, future Maven versions might no longer support building such malformed projects.
[WARNING]
[INFO]
[INFO] ----------------< packt.java9.by.example:SortTutorial >-----------------
[INFO] Building SortTutorial 1.0.0-SNAPSHOT
[INFO] --------------------------------[ jar ]---------------------------------
[INFO]
[INFO] --- maven-resources-plugin:2.6:resources (default-resources) @ SortTutorial ---
[WARNING] Using platform encoding (UTF-8 actually) to copy filtered resources, i.e. build is platform dependent!
[INFO] skip non existing resourceDirectory /Users/verhasp/Dropbox/packt/Fundamentals-of-java-18.9/sources/ch02/mavenHelloWorld/SortTutorial/src/main/resources
[INFO]
[INFO] --- maven-compiler-plugin:3.1:compile (default-compile) @ SortTutorial ---
[INFO] Nothing to compile - all classes are up to date
[INFO]
[INFO] --- maven-resources-plugin:2.6:testResources (default-testResources) @ SortTutorial ---
[WARNING] Using platform encoding (UTF-8 actually) to copy filtered resources, i.e. build is platform dependent!
[INFO] skip non existing resourceDirectory /Users/verhasp/Dropbox/packt/Fundamentals-of-java-18.9/sources/ch02/mavenHelloWorld/SortTutorial/src/test/resources
[INFO]
[INFO] --- maven-compiler-plugin:3.1:testCompile (default-testCompile) @ SortTutorial ---
[INFO] Changes detected - recompiling the module!
[WARNING] File encoding has not been set, using platform encoding UTF-8, i.e. build is platform dependent!
[INFO] Compiling 1 source file to /Users/verhasp/Dropbox/packt/Fundamentals-of-java-18.9/sources/ch02/mavenHelloWorld/SortTutorial/target/test-classes
[INFO]
[INFO] --- maven-surefire-plugin:2.12.4:test (default-test) @ SortTutorial ---
[INFO] Surefire report directory: /Users/verhasp/Dropbox/packt/Fundamentals-of-java-18.9/sources/ch02/mavenHelloWorld/SortTutorial/target/surefire-reports

-------------------------------------------------------
 T E S T S
-------------------------------------------------------
Running packt.java11.by.example.AppTest
Tests run: 0, Failures: 0, Errors: 0, Skipped: 0, Time elapsed: 0 sec

Results :

Tests run: 0, Failures: 0, Errors: 0, Skipped: 0

[INFO]
[INFO] --- maven-jar-plugin:2.4:jar (default-jar) @ SortTutorial ---
[INFO] ------------------------------------------------------------------------
[INFO] BUILD SUCCESS
[INFO] ------------------------------------------------------------------------
[INFO] Total time: 2.014 s
[INFO] Finished at: 2018-08-27T20:29:43+02:00
[INFO] ------------------------------------------------------------------------
$
```

Maven fires up, compiles, and packages the project automatically. If not, please read the next infobox.

When you first start Maven, it downloads a lot of dependencies from the central repository. These downloads take time and the time values are reported on the screen and these values may be different for different runs. The actual output may be different from what you saw in the preceding code. Maven compiles the code with the default settings for Java version 1.5. It means that the generated class file is compatible with Java version 1.5, and also that the compiler only accepts language constructs that were available already in Java 1.5. Later Maven compiler plugin versions changed this behavior to use 1.6 as the default version. If we want to use newer language features, and in this book, we use a lot of them, the `pom.xml` file should be edited to contain the following lines:

```
<build>
    <plugins>
      <plugin>
        <groupId>org.apache.maven.plugins</groupId>
        <artifactId>maven-compiler-plugin</artifactId>
        <version>3.8.0</version>
        <configuration>
            <source>1.11</source>
            <target>1.11</target>
            <release>11</release>
        </configuration>
      </plugin>
    </plugins>
  </build>
```

When using Java 11's default settings for Maven, it becomes even more complex, because Java 9 and later does not generate class format, nor does it restrict source compatibility earlier than Java 1.6. This is why the compiler plugin changed its default behavior.

Now, you can start the code using the following command:

```
$ java -cp target/SortTutorial-1.0.0-SNAPSHOT.jar packt.java11.example.App
```

You can see the result of a sample run in the following screenshot:

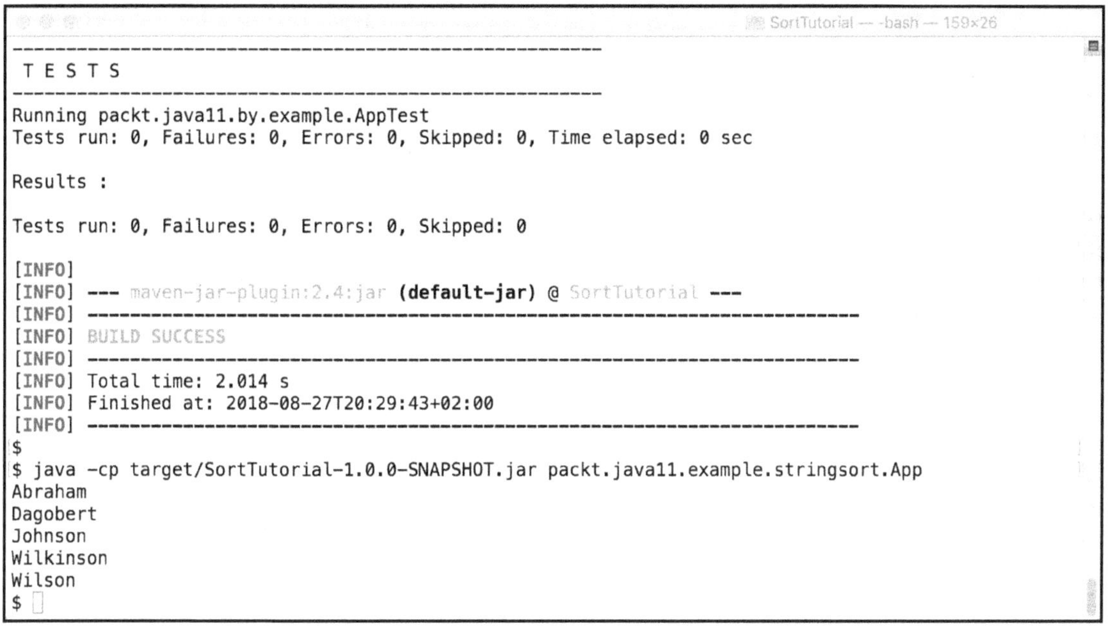

```
-------------------------------------------------------
 T E S T S
-------------------------------------------------------
Running packt.java11.by.example.AppTest
Tests run: 0, Failures: 0, Errors: 0, Skipped: 0, Time elapsed: 0 sec

Results :

Tests run: 0, Failures: 0, Errors: 0, Skipped: 0

[INFO]
[INFO] --- maven-jar-plugin:2.4:jar (default-jar) @ SortTutorial ---
[INFO] ------------------------------------------------------------------------
[INFO] BUILD SUCCESS
[INFO] ------------------------------------------------------------------------
[INFO] Total time: 2.014 s
[INFO] Finished at: 2018-08-27T20:29:43+02:00
[INFO] ------------------------------------------------------------------------
$
$ java -cp target/SortTutorial-1.0.0-SNAPSHOT.jar packt.java11.example.stringsort.App
Abraham
Dagobert
Johnson
Wilkinson
Wilson
$
```

Gradle

Ant and Maven are two worlds, and using one or the other may lead to heated debates on Internet forums. Ant gives freedom to developers to create a build process that fits their taste. Maven restricts the team to use a build process that is more standard. Some special processes that do not match any standard build, but which are sometimes needed in some environments, are hard to implement using Maven. In Ant, you can script almost anything using the built-in tasks, almost the same way as you can program bash. Utilizing Maven is not that simple, and, it often requires writing a plugin. Even though writing a plugin is not rocket science, developers usually like to have the possibility of making things in a simpler way—scripting. We have two approaches, two mindsets and styles, and not a single tool to fulfill all the needs. It's no surprise that by the time the Java technologies were developed, a new build tool was emerging.

Gradle tries to use the best of both worlds, utilizing techniques that were not available by the time Maven and Ant were first developed.

Gradle has built-in targets and a life cycle, but at the same time, you can also write your own targets. You can configure a project, just like using Maven, without scripting the tasks to do so, but at the same time, you can also script your own target just like in Ant. What is more, Gradle integrated Ant, so any task implemented for Ant is available for Gradle as well.

Maven and Ant use XML files to describe the build. Today, XML is a technology of the past. We still use it, and a developer should be fluent in handling, reading, and writing XML files, but a modern tool does not use XML for configuration. New, fancy formats such as JSON are more popular. Gradle is no exception. The configuration file of Gradle uses a **domain-specific language** (**DSL**) based on Groovy. This language is more readable for programmers and gives more freedom to program build processes. This is also the danger of Gradle.

Having the powerful JVM language Groovy in the hands of developers to create build tools gives a freedom and temptation to create complex build processes which seem to be a good idea at the start, but later may prove to be just too complex and hard, and, therefore, expensive to maintain. This is exactly why Maven was implemented in the first place.

I have to stop before getting into another area that is the ground for heated and pointless debates. Gradle is an extremely powerful build tool. You should use it carefully, just like you would use a weapon—don't shoot your legs.

Installing Gradle

To install Gradle, you will have to download the compiled binaries from the `https://gradle.org/gradle-download/` website.

Again, I'd like to emphasize the importance of checking the download integrity using checksums. I have given a detailed way to do it in the section about Ant installation. Unfortunately, the Gradle website does not provide the checksum values for the downloadable files.

Gradle is downloadable in the ZIP format. To unpack the file, you will have to use the unzip command:

```
$ unzip gradle-4.9-bin.zip
```

The created subdirectory is the usable binary distribution of Gradle. Usually, I move it under `~/bin`, making it available only for my users on OS X. After that, you should add the `bin` directory of the installation to the `PATH`.

To do that, you should edit the `~/.bashrc` file and add the following lines:

```
export GRADLE_HOME=~/bin/gradle-4.9/
export PATH=${GRADLE_HOME}bin:$PATH
```

Then, restart the terminal application, or just type `. ~/.bashrc` and test the installation of Gradle, by typing the following:

```
$ gradle -version
```

We will get the following output:

```
~$ gradle -version
WARNING: An illegal reflective access operation has occurred
WARNING: Illegal reflective access by org.codehaus.groovy.reflection.CachedClass
 (file:/Users/verhasp/bin/gradle-4.7/lib/groovy-all-2.4.12.jar) to method java.l
ang.Object.finalize()
WARNING: Please consider reporting this to the maintainers of org.codehaus.groov
y.reflection.CachedClass
WARNING: Use --illegal-access=warn to enable warnings of further illegal reflect
ive access operations
WARNING: All illegal access operations will be denied in a future release

------------------------------------------------------------
Gradle 4.7
------------------------------------------------------------

Build time:   2018-04-18 09:09:12 UTC
Revision:     b9a962bf70638332300e7f810689cb2febbd4a6c

Groovy:       2.4.12
Ant:          Apache Ant(TM) version 1.9.9 compiled on February 2 2017
JVM:          11-ea (Oracle Corporation 11-ea+25)
OS:           Mac OS X 10.13.6 x86_64

~$
```

Setting up the project with Maven

To start the project, we will use the directory structure and `pom.xml`, that was created by Maven itself when we started with the following command line:

```
$ mvn archetype:generate
```

It created the directories, the `pom.xml` file, and an `App.java` file. Now, we will extend this project by creating new files. We will code the sorting algorithm first in the `packt.java11.example.stringsort` package:

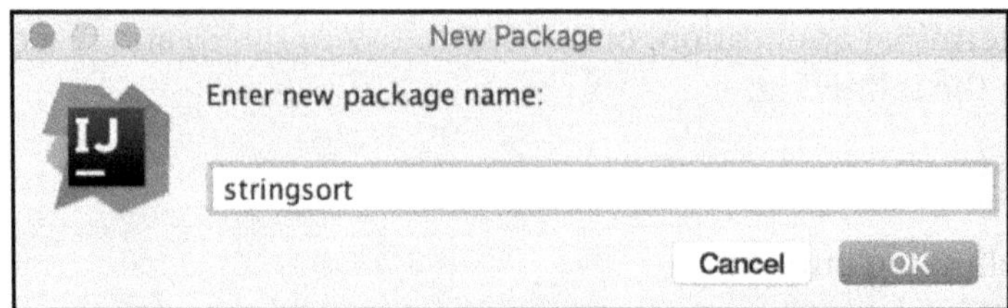

When we create the new package in the IDE, the editor will automatically create the `stringsort` subdirectory under the already existing `src/main/java/packt/java11/example` directory:

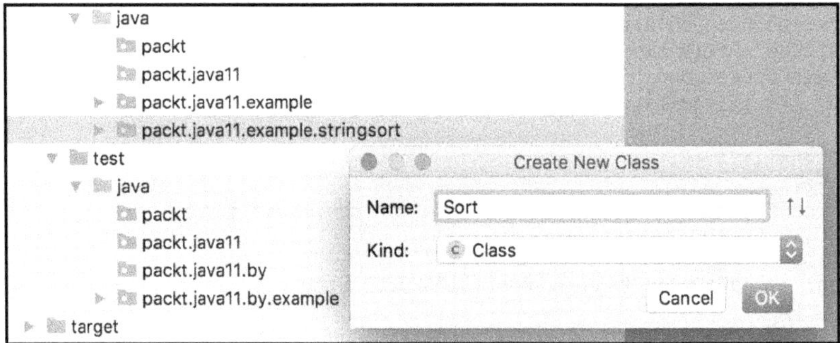

Creating the new `Sort` class using the IDE will also automatically create a new file named `Sort.java` in this directory, and it will fill in the skeleton of the class:

```
package packt.java11.example.stringsort;

public class Sort {
}
```

We will now have `App.java` containing the following code:

```
package packt.java11.example;

public class App {
    public static void main(String[] args) {
        System.out.println("Hello, World!");
    }
}
```

Maven created it as a starting version. We will edit this file to provide a sample list that the sorting algorithm can sort. I recommend that you use the IDE to edit the file and also to compile and run the code. The IDE provides a shortcut menu to start the code and this is a bit easier than typing the command in the Terminal. Generally, it is recommended that you get acquainted with the IDE features to save time and avoid repetitive tasks, such as typing terminal commands. Professional developers use the command line almost exclusively to test command-line features and use the IDE whenever it is possible:

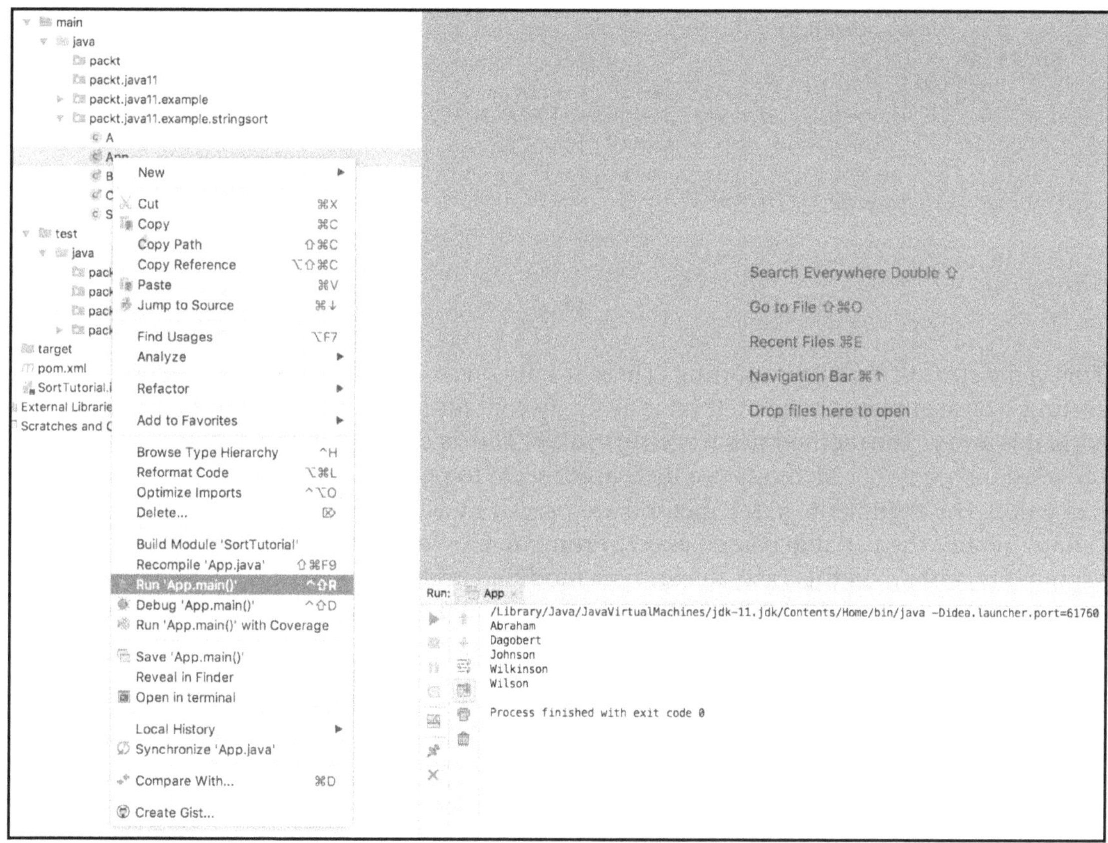

Coding the sort

Maven and the IDE created the files for the sort program. They form the skeleton for our code, and now it is time to grow some muscles on them to let it move. We spent quite some time setting up the project by visiting the different build tools, only to learn how to compile the code.

I hope that this did not distract you much, but anyhow, we deserve to see some real code.

First, we will create the code for the sorting code, and after that, the code that invokes the sorting. The code that invokes the sorting is a kind of testing code. For simplicity, we will now simply use a `public static void main()` method to start the code. We will use the test framework in later chapters.

As for now, the code for the sorting will look like this:

```
var n = names.length;
while (n > 1) {
    for (var j = 0; j < n - 1; j++) {
        if (names[j].compareTo(names[j + 1]) > 0) {
            final var tmp = names[j + 1];
            names[j + 1] = names[j];
            names[j] = tmp;
        }
    }
    n--;
}
```

This is the class that does the sorting. There is only one method in this class that does the sorting. The argument to the method is an array containing the strings, and the method sorts this array. The method has no return value. This is denoted in the declaration using the pseudotype `void`. Methods use their arguments to perform some tasks and may return one value. The arguments to the method are passed by value, which means that the method cannot modify the variable passed as an argument. However, it can modify the objects the arguments contain. In this case, the array is modified and we will sort it. On the other hand, the `actualNames` variable will point to the same array and the `sort()` method cannot do anything to make this variable point to a different array.

There is no `main()` method in this class, which means that it cannot be started from the command line on its own. This class can only be used from some other class, as every Java program should have a class that has a `public static void main()` method that we created separately.

I could also put a `main()` method into the class to make it executable, but that is not a good practice. Real programs are composed of many classes, and one class should not do many things. Rather, it's the opposite. The *single responsibility principle* says that a single class should be responsible for one single thing; therefore, `class sort` does the sorting. Executing the application is a different task, and thus it has to be implemented in a different class.

Often, we do not implement the class containing the `main()` method; a framework provides it. For example, writing a servlet that runs in a servlet container requires containing a class that implements the `javax.servlet.Servlet` interface. In this case, the program seemingly does not have a `main()` method. The actual implementation of the servlet container does. The Java command line starts the container and the container loads the servlets when they are needed.

In the following example code, we implemented the `App` class containing the `main()` method:

```
package packt.java11.example.stringsort;

public class App {
    public static void main(String[] args) {
        var actualNames = new String[]{
                "Johnson", "Wilson",
                "Wilkinson", "Abraham", "Dagobert"};
        Sort.sort(actualNames);
        for (final String name : actualNames) {
            System.out.println(name);
        }
    }
}
```

This code contains a string array initialized to contain constant values, creates a new instance of the `Sort` class, invokes the `sort()` method, and then prints out the code to the standard output.

In real programs, we almost never have such constants in program codes; we put them into resource files and have some code to read the actual values. This separates the code from data and eases maintenance, eliminating the risk of accidental modification of code structure when only the data is to be changed. Similarly, we will almost never write anything to standard output using `System.out`. Usually, we will use logging possibilities that are available from different sources. There are different libraries that provide logging functionalities, and logging is also available from the JDK itself.

As for now, we will focus on simple solutions not to distract your focus from Java by the plethora of different libraries and tools. In the upcoming section, we will look at the Java language constructs that we used while coding the algorithm. First, we will look at them generally, and then, in a bit more detail. These language features are not independent of each other—one builds on the other, and therefore, the explanation will first be general, and we will go into details in the following subsections.

Understanding the algorithm and language constructs

The algorithm was explained at the start of the chapter. The implementation is in the `Sort` class inside the `sort()` method, and it consists only of a few lines:

```
var n = names.length;
while (n > 1) {
    for (var j = 0; j < n - 1; j++) {
        if (names[j].compareTo(names[j + 1]) > 0) {
            final var tmp = names[j + 1];
            names[j + 1] = names[j];
            names[j] = tmp;
        }
    }
    n--;
}
```

The `n` variable holds the length of the array at the start of the sorting. Arrays in Java always have a property that gives the length, and it is called `length`. When we start the sorting, we will go from the start of the array to the end of it and, as you may recall, the last element, Wilson, will walk up to the last position during this first iteration. Subsequent iterations will be shorter and, therefore, the variable `n` will be decreased.

Blocks

The code in Java is created in code blocks. Anything that is between the `{` and `}` characters is a block. In the preceding example, the code of the method is a block. It contains commands, and some of them, such as the `while` loop, also contains a block. Inside that block, there are two commands. One of them is a `for` loop, again with a block. Although we can have single expressions to form the body of a loop, we usually use blocks. We will discuss loops in detail in just a few pages.

As we could see in the preceding example, the loops can be nested, and thus the `{` and `}` characters form pairs. A block can be inside another block, but two blocks cannot overlap. When the code contains a `}` character, it is closing the block that was opened last.

Variables

In Java, just like in almost any programming language, we use variables. The variables in Java are typed. This means that a variable can hold a value of a single type. It is not possible for a variable to hold an `int` type at some point in the program and later a `String` type. When variables are declared, their type is written in front of the variable name. When a local variable gets the initial value on the line where it is declared, it is possible to use a special reserved type named `var`. It means the type that is exactly the same as the type of the expression on the right-hand side of the assignment operator.

This is how the code looks like:

```
var n = names.length;
```

It can also be written as follows:

```
int n = names.length;
```

This is because the expression `names.length` has an `int` type. This feature is called local variable type inference as the type is inferred from the right-hand side. This cannot be used in case the variable is not local to a method.

When we declare a field (a variable that is on the class level outside of the body of the methods of the class and not inside an initializer block or constructor) we have to specify the exact type we want the variable to be.

Variables also have visibility scope. Local variables in methods can only be used inside the block in which they are defined. A variable can be used inside methods or they can belong to a class or an object. To differentiate the two, we usually call these variable fields.

Types

Each variable has one type. In Java, there are two major groups of types—primitive and reference types. The primitive types are predefined, and you cannot define or create a new primitive type. There are eight primitive types—`byte`, `short`, `int`, `long`, `float`, `double`, `boolean`, and `char`.

The first four types, `byte`, `short`, `int`, and `long` are signed numeric integer types, capable of storing positive and negative numbers on 8, 16, 32, and 64 bits.

The `float` and `double` types store floating point numbers on 32 and 64 bits in the IEEE 754 floating-point format.

The `boolean` type is a primitive type that can only be `true` or `false`.

The `char` type is a character data type that stores a single 16-bit Unicode character.

For each primitive type, there is a corresponding class. An instance of the class can store the same type of value. When a primitive type has to be converted to the matching class type, it is done automatically. It is called auto-boxing. These types are `Byte`, `Short`, `Integer`, `Long`, `Float`, `Double`, `Boolean`, and `Character`. Take, for example, the following variable declaration:

```
Integer a = 113;
```

This converts the value `113`, which is an `int` number, to an `Integer` object.

These types are part of the runtime and also part of the language.

There is a special class, named `String`. An object of this type contains characters. `String` has no primitive counterpart but we use it many times like it were a primitive type, which it is not. It is ubiquitous in Java programs and there are some language constructs such as concatenating strings that work directly with this type.

The major differences between primitive types and objects are that primitive types cannot be used to invoke methods on them. They are just values. They cannot be used as a lock when we create a concurrent program. On the other hand, they consume less memory. This difference between the memory consumption and its consequences for speed is important, especially when we have an array of values.

Arrays

Variables can be a primitive type according to their declaration, or they may hold a reference to an object. A special object type is an array. When a variable holds a reference to an array, it can be indexed with the `[` and `]` characters, along with an integral value consisting of 0 or a positive value ranging to one less than the array's length, to access a certain element of the array. Multi-dimensional arrays are also supported by Java when an array has elements that are also arrays. Arrays are indexed from zero in Java. Under- or over-indexing is checked at runtime, and the result is an exception.

An exception is a special condition that interrupts the normal execution flow and stops the execution of the code or jumps to the closest enclosing `catch` statement. We will discuss exceptions and how to handle them in the next chapter.

When a code has an array of a primitive type, the array contains memory slots, each holding the value of the type. When the array has a reference type, in other words, when it is an array of objects, then the array elements are references to objects, each referring to an instance of the type. In the case of `int`, for example, each element of the array is 32-bit, which is 4 bytes. If the array is a type of `Integer`, then the elements are references to objects, pointers, so to say, which is usually 64-bit using 64-bit JVM and 32-bit on 32-bit JVM. In addition to that, there is an `Integer` object somewhere in memory that contains the 4-byte value and also an object header that may be as much as 24 bytes.

The actual size of the extra information needed to administer each object is not defined in the standard. It may be different on different implementations of the JVM. The actual coding, or even the optimization of the code in an environment, should not depend on the actual size. However, the developers should be aware that this overhead exists and is in the range of around 20 or so bytes for every object. Objects are expensive in terms of memory consumption.

Memory consumption is one issue, but there is something else. When the program works with a large amount of data and the work needs the consecutive elements of the array, then the CPU loads a chunk of memory into the processor cache. It means that the CPU can access elements of the array that are consecutively faster. If the array is of a primitive type, it is fast. If the array is of some class type, then the CPU may need to access memory to get the actual value of an element of the array through the reference held in the array. This may be as much as 50 times slower.

Expressions

Expressions in Java are very much like in other programming languages. You can use the operators that may be similar to languages such as C or C++. They are as follows:

- Unary prefix and postfix increment operators (`--` and `++` before and after a variable)
- Unary sign (`+` and `-`) operators
- Logical (`!`) and bitwise (`~`) negation
- Multiplication (`*`), division (`/`), and modulo (`%`)
- Addition and subtraction (`+` and `-` again, but this time as binary operators)

- Shift operators move the values bitwise, and there is left shift (<<), right (>>) shift, and unsigned right shift (>>>)
- The comparing operators are <, >, <=, >=, ==, !=, and `instanceof` that result in the `boolean` value
- There are bitwise or (|), and (&), exclusive or (^) operators, and similarly logical or (||), and (&&) operators

When logical operators are evaluated, they are shortcut evaluated. This means that the right-hand operand is evaluated only if the result cannot be identified from the result of the left operand.

The ternary operator is also similar to the one, like it is on C, selecting from one of the expressions based on some condition—`condition ? expression 1 : expression 2`. Usually, there is no problem with the ternary operator, but sometimes you have to be careful as there is a complex rule controlling the type conversions in case the two expressions are not of the same type. It's always better to have two expressions of the same type.

Finally, there is an assignment operator (=) that assigns the value of an expression to a variable. For each binary operator, there is an assignment version that combines = with a binary operator to perform an operation involving the right operand and assigns the result to the left operand, which must be a variable. These are +=, -=, *=, /=, %=, &=, ^=, |=, <<=, >>=, and >>>=.

The operators have precedence and can be overridden by parentheses, as usual.

An important part of expressions is invoking methods. Static methods can be invoked by the name of the class and the name of the method dot separated. For example, to calculate the sine of 1.22, we can write the following line of code:

```
double z = Math.sin(1.22);
```

Here, `Math` is the class from the package `java.lang`. The `sin` method is invoked without using an instance of `Math`. This method is `static` and it is not likely that we will ever need any other implementation of it than the one provided in the class `Math`.

Nonstatic methods can be invoked using an instance and the name of the method with a dot separating the two. For example, consider the following code:

```
System.out.println("Hello World");
```

The code uses an instance of the `PrintStream` class readily available through a static field in the `System` class. This variable is called `out`, and when we write our code, we have to reference it as `System.out`. The `println` method is defined in the `PrintStream` class and we invoke it on the object referenced by the `out` variable. This example also shows that static fields can also be referenced through the name of the class and the field separated by a dot. Similarly, when we need to reference a nonstatic field, we can do it through an instance of the class.

Static methods defined in the same class from where it is invoked or *inherited* can be invoked without the class name. Invoking a nonstatic method defined in the same class or being inherited can be invoked without an explicit instance notation. In this case, the instance is the current object the execution is in. This object is also available through the `this` keyword. Similarly, when we use a field of the same class where our code is, we simply use the name. In case of a static field, the class we are in is the default. In the case of a nonstatic field, the instance is the object referenced by the `this` keyword.

You can also import a static method into your code using the `import static` language feature, in which case you can invoke the method without the name of the class.

The arguments of the method calls are separated using commas. Methods and method argument passing is an important topic that we will cover later.

Loops

Let's once again have a look at the code of the string sort. The `for` loop inside the `while` loop will go through all the elements from the first element (indexed with zero in Java) up to the last (indexed with `n-1`). Generally, this `for` loop has the same syntax as in C:

```
for( initial expression ; condition ; increment expression )
  block
```

First, the initial expression is evaluated. It may contain a variable declaration, as in our example. The `j` variable in the preceding example is visible only inside the block of the loop. After this, the condition is evaluated, and after each execution of the block, the increment expression is executed. The loop repeats so long as the condition is true. If the condition is false right after the execution of the initial expression, the loop does not execute at all. The block is a list of commands separated by semicolons and enclosed between the `{` and `}` characters.

Instead of `{` and `}`, enclosed block Java lets you use a single command following the head of the `for` loop. The same is true in the case of the `while` loop, and also for the `if...else` constructs. Practice shows that this is not something a professional should use. Professional code always uses curly braces, even when there is only a single command where the block is in place. This prevents the dangling `else` problem and generally makes the code more readable. This is similar to many C-like languages. Most of them allow a single command at these places, and professional programmers avoid using a single command in these languages for readability purposes. It is ironic that the only language that strictly requires the use of the `{` and `}` braces at these places is Perl — the one language infamous for unreadable code.

The loop in the `for (var j = 0; j < n - 1; j++) {` sample starts from zero and goes to `n-2`. Writing `j < n-1` is the same, in this case, as `j <= n-2`. We will limit `j` to stop in the loop before the end of the array, because we reach beyond the index `j` by one comparing and conditionally swapping the elements indexed by `j` and `j+1`. If we went one element further, we would try to access an element of the array that does not exist, and it would cause a runtime exception. Try and modify the loop condition to `j < n` or `j <= n-1` and you will get the following error message:

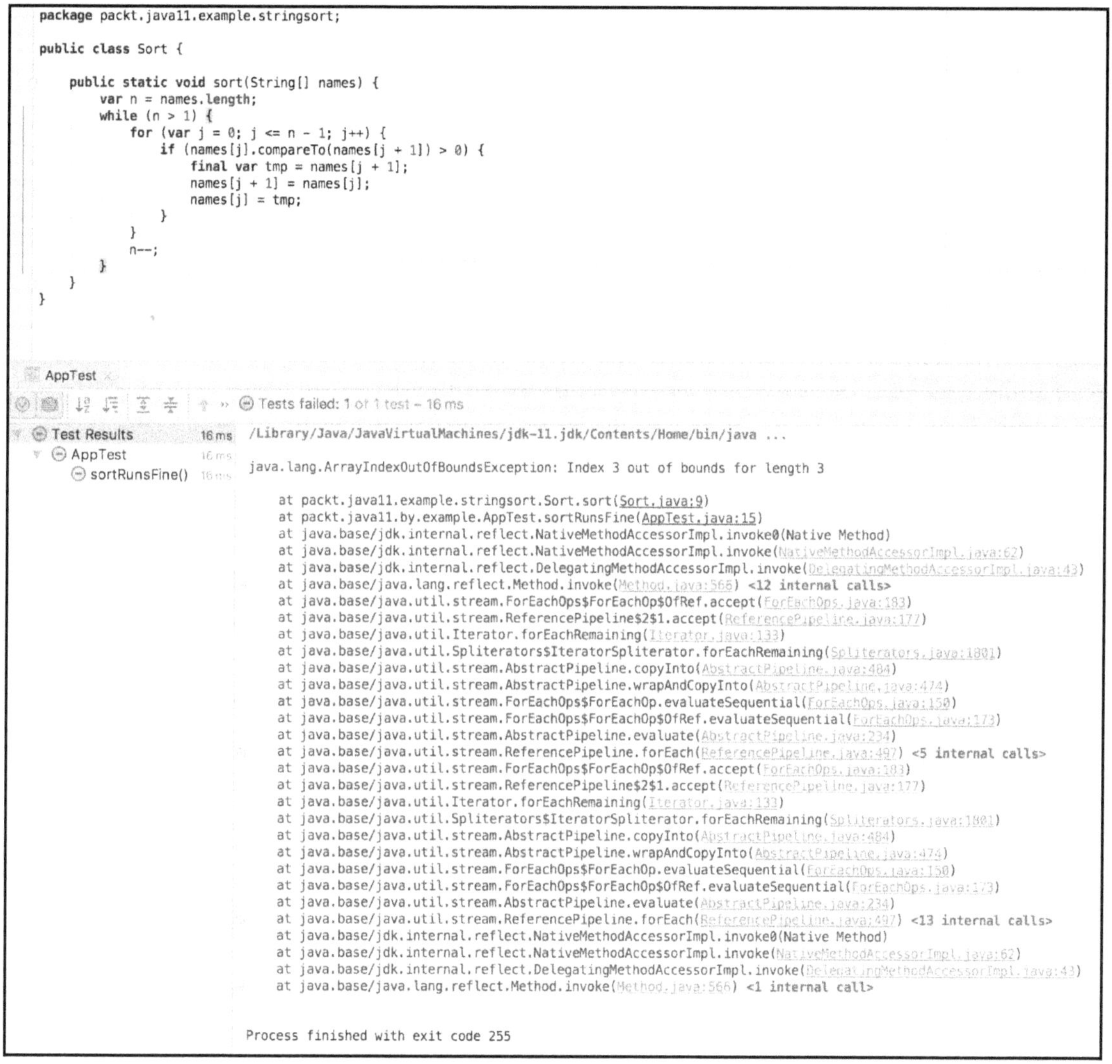

```
package packt.java11.example.stringsort;

public class Sort {

    public static void sort(String[] names) {
        var n = names.length;
        while (n > 1) {
            for (var j = 0; j <= n - 1; j++) {
                if (names[j].compareTo(names[j + 1]) > 0) {
                    final var tmp = names[j + 1];
                    names[j + 1] = names[j];
                    names[j] = tmp;
                }
            }
            n--;
        }
    }
}
```

```
AppTest
Tests failed: 1 of 1 test – 16 ms
Test Results        16 ms   /Library/Java/JavaVirtualMachines/jdk-11.jdk/Contents/Home/bin/java ...
  AppTest           16 ms
    sortRunsFine()  16 ms   java.lang.ArrayIndexOutOfBoundsException: Index 3 out of bounds for length 3

    at packt.java11.example.stringsort.Sort.sort(Sort.java:9)
    at packt.java11.by.example.AppTest.sortRunsFine(AppTest.java:15)
    at java.base/jdk.internal.reflect.NativeMethodAccessorImpl.invoke0(Native Method)
    at java.base/jdk.internal.reflect.NativeMethodAccessorImpl.invoke(NativeMethodAccessorImpl.java:62)
    at java.base/jdk.internal.reflect.DelegatingMethodAccessorImpl.invoke(DelegatingMethodAccessorImpl.java:43)
    at java.base/java.lang.reflect.Method.invoke(Method.java:566) <12 internal calls>
    at java.base/java.util.stream.ForEachOps$ForEachOp$OfRef.accept(ForEachOps.java:183)
    at java.base/java.util.stream.ReferencePipeline$2$1.accept(ReferencePipeline.java:177)
    at java.base/java.util.Iterator.forEachRemaining(Iterator.java:133)
    at java.base/java.util.Spliterators$IteratorSpliterator.forEachRemaining(Spliterators.java:1801)
    at java.base/java.util.stream.AbstractPipeline.copyInto(AbstractPipeline.java:484)
    at java.base/java.util.stream.AbstractPipeline.wrapAndCopyInto(AbstractPipeline.java:474)
    at java.base/java.util.stream.ForEachOps$ForEachOp.evaluateSequential(ForEachOps.java:150)
    at java.base/java.util.stream.ForEachOps$ForEachOp$OfRef.evaluateSequential(ForEachOps.java:173)
    at java.base/java.util.stream.AbstractPipeline.evaluate(AbstractPipeline.java:234)
    at java.base/java.util.stream.ReferencePipeline.forEach(ReferencePipeline.java:497) <5 internal calls>
    at java.base/java.util.stream.ForEachOps$ForEachOp$OfRef.accept(ForEachOps.java:183)
    at java.base/java.util.stream.ReferencePipeline$2$1.accept(ReferencePipeline.java:177)
    at java.base/java.util.Iterator.forEachRemaining(Iterator.java:133)
    at java.base/java.util.Spliterators$IteratorSpliterator.forEachRemaining(Spliterators.java:1801)
    at java.base/java.util.stream.AbstractPipeline.copyInto(AbstractPipeline.java:484)
    at java.base/java.util.stream.AbstractPipeline.wrapAndCopyInto(AbstractPipeline.java:474)
    at java.base/java.util.stream.ForEachOps$ForEachOp.evaluateSequential(ForEachOps.java:150)
    at java.base/java.util.stream.ForEachOps$ForEachOp$OfRef.evaluateSequential(ForEachOps.java:173)
    at java.base/java.util.stream.AbstractPipeline.evaluate(AbstractPipeline.java:234)
    at java.base/java.util.stream.ReferencePipeline.forEach(ReferencePipeline.java:497) <13 internal calls>
    at java.base/jdk.internal.reflect.NativeMethodAccessorImpl.invoke0(Native Method)
    at java.base/jdk.internal.reflect.NativeMethodAccessorImpl.invoke(NativeMethodAccessorImpl.java:62)
    at java.base/jdk.internal.reflect.DelegatingMethodAccessorImpl.invoke(DelegatingMethodAccessorImpl.java:43)
    at java.base/java.lang.reflect.Method.invoke(Method.java:566) <1 internal call>

Process finished with exit code 255
```

It is an important feature of Java that the runtime checks memory access and throws an exception in the case of bad array indexing. In the good old days, while coding in C, often, we faced unexplainable errors that stopped our code much later and at totally different code locations from where the real error was. The array index in C silently corrupted the memory. Java stops you as soon as you make a mistake. It follows the fail-fast approach that you should also use in your code. If something is wrong, the program should fail. No code should try to live with or overcome an error that comes from a coding error. Coding errors should be fixed before they cause even more damage.

There are also two more loop constructs in Java—the `while` loop and the `do` loop. The following example contains a `while` loop. It is the outer loop that runs so long as there are at least two elements that may need swapping in the array:

```
while (n > 1) {
```

The general syntax and semantics of the `while` loop is very simple, as shown in the following code:

```
while ( condition ) block
```

Repeat the execution of the block so long as the condition is `true`. If the condition is not true at the very start of the loop, then do not execute the block at all. The `do` loop is also similar, but it checks the condition after each execution of the block:

```
do block while( condition );
```

For some reason, programmers rarely use `do` loops.

Conditional execution

The heart of the sort is the condition and the value swapping inside the loop.

```
if (names[j].compareTo(names[j + 1]) > 0) {
                    final String tmp = names[j + 1];
                    names[j + 1] = names[j];
                    names[j] = tmp;
                }
```

There is only one conditional command in Java, the `if` command. It has the following format:

```
if( condition ) block else block
```

The meaning of the code structure is quite straightforward. If the condition is `true`, then the first block is executed, otherwise, the second block is executed. The `else` keyword, along with the second block, is optional. Creating `else` and a block after it is optional. If there is nothing to be executed when the condition is `false`, then we just do not create the `else` part. If the array element indexed with `j` is later in the sort order than the element `j+1`, then we swap them; however, if they are already in order, there is nothing to do with them.

To swap the two array elements, we use a temporary variable named `tmp`. The type of this variable is `String`, and this variable is declared to be `final`. The `final` keyword has different meanings depending on where it is used in Java. This may be confusing for beginners unless you are warned about it, just like now. A `final` class or method is a totally different thing than a `final` field, which is again different from a `final` local variable.

Note that this time we used the explicit type `String` for declaring the variable. We could use `var` and also `final var` instead and the same type would have been inferred. The only reason for using explicit typing here is for demonstration purposes.

Final variables

In our case, `tmp` is a `final` local variable. The scope of this variable is limited to the block following the `if` statement, and inside this block, this variable gets a value only once. The block is executed many times during the code execution, and each time the variable gets into scope, it gets a value. However, this value cannot be changed inside the block, and it does not exist outside the block. This may be a bit confusing. You can think about it as having a new `tmp` each time the block executes. The variable gets declared; first it is undefined, and then it gets a value once.

Final local variables do not need to get the value where they are declared. You can assign a value to a `final` variable sometime later. It is important that there should not be a code execution that assigns a value to a `final` variable that was already assigned a value before. The compiler checks it and does not compile the code if there is a possibility of the reassignment of a `final` variable. The compiler also checks that the value of a local variable (not only `final` variables) should not be used while the variable is undefined.

To declare a variable to be `final` is generally to ease readability of the code. When you see a variable in code declared to be `final`, you can assume that the value of the variable will not change and the meaning of the variable will always be the same wherever it was used in the method. It will also help you avoid some bugs when you try to modify some `final` variables and the IDE will immediately complain about it. In such situations, it is likely to be a programming mistake that is discovered extremely early.

In principle, it is possible to write a program where all variables are `final`. It is generally a good practice to declare all `final` variables that can be declared to be `final` and, in case some variable may not be declared `final`, then try to find some way of coding the method a bit differently.

If you need to introduce a new variable to do that, it probably means you were using one variable to store two different things. These things are of the same type and stored in the same variable at different times but, logically, still they are different things. Do not try to optimize the use of variables. Never use a variable because you already have a variable of the same type in your code that is available. If it is logically a different thing, then declare a new variable. While coding, always prefers source code clarity and readability. In Java, especially, the Just In Time compiler will optimize all of this for you.

Although we do not explicitly tend to use the `final` keyword on the argument list of a method, it is good practice to make sure that your methods compile and work if the arguments are declared `final`. Some experts, including me, believe that the method parameters should have been made final by default in the language. This is something that will not happen in any version of Java, so long as Java follows the backwards compatibility philosophy.

Classes

Now that we have looked at the actual code lines and have understood how the algorithm works, let's look at the more global structures of the code that brings it together—classes and packages enclosing the methods.

Every file in a Java program defines a class. Any code in a Java program is inside a class. There is nothing like global variables or global functions as in C, Python, Go, or other languages. Java is totally object-oriented.

There can be more than one class in a single file, but usually, one file is one class. Later, we will see that there are inner classes when a class is inside another class, but, for now, we will put one class into one file.

There are some features in the Java language that we do not use. When the language was created, these features seemed to be a good idea. CPU, memory, and other resources, including mediocre developers, were also more limited than today. Some of the features, perhaps, made more sense because of these environmental constraints. Sometimes, I will mention these. In the case of classes, you can put more than one class into a single file so long as only one is `public`. That is bad practice, and we will never do that. Java never obsoletes these features. It was a philosophy of Java to remain compatible with all previous versions until recently and this philosophy changes slow. This is good for the already written, huge amount of legacy code. Java code written and tested with an old version will work in a newer environment. At the same time, these features lure beginners to a wrong style. For this reason, sometimes, I will not even mention these features. For example, here, I could say—*There is one class in a file.* This would not be absolutely correct. At the same time, it is more or less pointless to explain in great detail a feature that I recommend not to be used. Later, I may simply skip them. There are not too many of these features.

A class is defined using the `class` keyword, and each class has to have a name. The name should be unique within the package (see the next section) and has to be the same as the name of the file. A class can implement an interface or extend another class, for which we will see an example later. A class can also be `abstract`, `final`, and `public`. These are defined with the appropriate keywords, as you will see in the following examples.

Our program has two classes. Both of them are `public`. The `public` classes are accessible from anywhere. Classes that are not `public` are visible only inside the package. Inner and nested classes can also be `private` visible only inside the top-level class defined on the file level.

Classes that contain a `main()` method to be invoked by the Java environment should be `public`. That is because they are invoked by the JVM.

The class starts at the beginning of the file right after the package declaration and everything between the `{` and `}` characters belong to the class. The methods, fields, inner or nested classes, and so on are part of the class. Generally, curly braces denote some block in Java. This was invented in the C language, and many languages follow this notation. The class declaration is a block, methods are defined using a block, loops, and conditional commands all use blocks.

When we use the classes, we will have to create instances of classes. These instances are objects. In other words, objects are created by instantiating a class. To do that, the `new` keyword is used in Java. When the line `final Sort sorter = new Sort();` is executed in the `App` class, it creates a new object instantiating the `Sort` class. We will also say that we created a new `Sort` object or that the type of the object is `Sort`. When a new object is created, a constructor of the object is invoked. A bit sloppy, I may say, that the constructor is a special method in the class that has the same name as the class itself and has no return value. This is because it returns the created object. To be precise, constructors are not methods. They are initializers and they do not return the new object. They work on the not-ready-yet object. When a constructor executing the object is not fully initialized, some of the final fields may not be initialized and the overall initialization can still fail if the constructor throws an exception. In our example, we do not have any constructor in the code. In such a case, Java creates a default constructor that accepts no argument and does not modify the already allocated but uninitialized object. If the Java code defines an initializer, then the Java compiler does not create a default one.

A class can have many constructors, each having a different parameter list.

In addition to constructors, Java classes can contain initializer blocks. They are blocks on the class level, the same level as the constructor and methods. The code in these blocks is compiled into the constructors and is executed when the constructor is executing.

It is also possible to initialize static fields in static initializer blocks. These are the blocks on the top level inside the class with the `static` keyword in front of them. They are executed only once, that is, when the class is loaded.

We named the classes in our example `App` and `Sort`. This is a convention in Java example `App` and `Sort`. This is a convention in Java where you must name almost everything in CamelCase.

CamelCase is when the words are written without spaces between them. The first word may start with lowercase or uppercase, and, to denote the start of the second and subsequent word(s), they start with uppercase. `ForExampleThisIsALongCamelCase` name.

Class names start with an uppercase letter. This is not a requirement of the language formally, but this is a convention that every programmer should follow. These coding conventions help you create code that is easier to understand by other programmers and lead to easier maintenance. Static code analyzer tools, such as Checkstyle (`http://checkstyle.sourceforge.net/`), also check that the programmers follow the conventions.

Inner, nested, local, and anonymous classes

I have already mentioned inner and nested classes in the previous section. Now, we will look at them in a bit more detail.

The details of inner and nested classes at this point may be difficult. Don't feel ashamed if you do not understand this section fully. If it is too difficult, skip to the next section and read about packages and return here later. Nested, inner, and local classes are rarely used, though they have their roles and use in Java. Anonymous classes were very popular in GUI programming with the Swing user interface that allowed developers to create Java GUI applications. With Java 8 and the lambda feature, anonymous classes are not so important these days, and with the emerging JavaScript and browser technology, the Java GUI became less popular.

When a class is defined in a file on its own, it is called a top-level class. Classes that are inside another class are, obviously, not top-level classes. If they are defined inside a class on the same level as fields (variables that are not local to some method or another block), they are inner or nested classes. There are two differences between them. One is that nested classes have the `static` keyword before the `class` keyword at their definition, and inner classes don't.

The other difference is that instances of nested classes can exist without an instance of the surrounding class. Inner class instances always have a reference to an instance of the surrounding class.

Because inner class instances cannot exist without an instance of the surrounding class, their instance can only be created by providing an instance of the outer class. We will see no difference if the surrounding class instance is the actual `this` variable, but if we want to create an instance of an inner class from outside the surrounding class, then we have to provide an instance variable before the `new` keyword separated by a dot, just like if new were a method. For example, we could have a class named `TopLevel` that has a class named `InnerClass`, as shown in the following code snippet:

```
public class TopLevel {

    class InnerClass { }
}
```

Then, we can create an instance of `InnerClass` from outside with only a `TopLevel` object, as shown in the following code snippet:

```
TopLevel tl = new TopLevel();
InnerClass ic = tl.new InnerClass();
```

As non-static inner classes have an implicit reference to an instance of the enclosing class, the code inside the inner class can access the fields and the methods of the enclosing class.

Nested classes do not have an implicit reference to an instance of the enclosing class, and they may be instantiated with the `new` keyword without any reference to any instance of any other class. Because of that, they cannot access the fields of the enclosing class unless they are static fields.

Local classes are classes that are defined inside a method, constructor, or an initializer block. We will soon talk about initializer blocks and constructors. Local classes can be used inside the block where they are defined.

Anonymous classes are defined and instantiated in a single command. They are a short form of a nested, inner, or local class, and the instantiation of the class. Anonymous classes always implement an interface or extend a named class. The new keyword is followed by the name of the interface or the class with the argument list to the constructor between parentheses. The block that defines the body of the anonymous class stands immediately after the constructor call. In the case of extending an interface, the constructor can be the only one without an argument. The anonymous class with no name cannot have its own constructors. In modern Java, we usually use lambda instead of anonymous classes.

Last but not least—well, actually, least I should mention that nested and inner classes can also be nested in deeper structures. Inner classes cannot contain nested classes, but nested classes can contain inner classes. Why? I have never met anyone who could reliably tell me the real reason. There is no architectural reason. It could be like that. Java does not permit that. However, it is not really interesting. If you happen to write code that has more than one level of class nesting, then just stop doing it. Most probably you are doing something wrong.

Packages

Classes are organized into packages, and the first code line in a file should specify the package that the class is in:

```
package packt.java11.example.stringsort;
```

If you do not specify the package, then the class will be in the default package. This should not be used, except in the simplest case when you want to try some code. With Java 11, you can use `jshell` for this purpose. So, as opposed to previous versions of Java, now the suggestion becomes very simple—never put any class in the default package.

The name of the packages is hierarchical. The parts of the names are separated by dots. Using package names helps you avoid name collisions. Names of the classes are usually kept short, and putting them into packages helps the organization of the program. The full name of a class includes the name of the package the class is in. Usually, we will put these classes into a package that are in some way related, and add something to a similar aspect of a program. For example, controllers in an MVC pattern program are kept in a single package. Packages also help you avoid name collision of classes. However, this only pushes the problem from class name collision to package name collision. We have to make sure that the name of the package is unique and does not cause any problems when our code is used together with any other library. When an application is developed, we just cannot know what other libraries will be used in the later versions. To be prepared for the unexpected, the convention is to name the packages according to some Internet domain names. When a development company has the domain name `acmecompany.com`, their software is usually under the `com.acmecompany...` packages. It is not a strict language requirement. It is only a convention to write the domain name from right to left, and use it as the package name, but this proves to be fairly good in practice. Sometimes, like I do in this book, one can deviate from this practice, so you can see that this rule is not carved in stone.

When the rubber hits the road, and the code is compiled into bytecode, the package becomes the name of the class. Thus, the full name of the `Sort` class is `packt.java11.example.stringsort.Sort`. When you use a class from another package, you can use this full name or import the class into your class. Again, this is on the language level. Using the fully qualified name or importing makes no difference when Java becomes bytecode.

Methods

We have already discussed methods, but not in detail, and there are still some aspects that we should meet before we go on.

There are two methods in the sample classes. There can be many methods in a class. Method names are also camel cased by convention, and the name starts with a lowercase letter, as opposed to classes.

Methods may return a value. If a method returns a value, the method has to declare the type of the value it returns and, in that case, any execution of the code has to finish with a `return` statement. The `return` statement has an expression after the keyword, which is evaluated when the method is executed and is returned by the method. It is a good practice to have only one single return from a method but, in some simple cases, breaking that coding convention may be forgiven. The compiler checks the possible method execution paths, and it is a compile-time error if some of the paths do not return a value.

When a method does not return any value, it has to be declared as `void`. This is a special type that means no value. Methods that are `void`, such as the `public static void main()` method, may simply miss the return statement and just end. If there is a `return` statement, there is no place for any expression defining a return value after the `return` keyword. Again, this is a coding convention to not use the `return` statement in case of a method that does not return any value, but in some coding patterns, this may not be followed.

Methods can be `private`, `protected`, `public`, and `static`, and we will discuss their meaning later.

We have seen that the `main()` method that was invoked when the program started is a `static` method. Such a method belongs to the class and can be invoked without having an instance of the class. Static methods are declared with the `static` modifier, and they cannot access any field or method that is not static.

In our example, the `sort()` method is not static, but as it does not access any field and does not call any non-static method (as a matter of fact, it does not call any method at all); it could just as well be `static`. If we change the declaration of the method to `public static void sort(String[] names) {` (note the word `static`), the program still works, but the IDE will give a warning while editing, as shown in the following example:

```
Static member
'packt.java11.example.stringsort.Sort.sort(java.lang.String[])' accessed
via instance reference
```

That is because you can access the method without an instance directly through the name of the `Sort.sort(actualNames);` class without the need for the `sorter` variable. Calling a static method via an instance variable is possible in Java (again, something that seemed to be a good idea at the genesis of Java, but is probably not), but it may mislead the reader of the code into thinking that the method is an instance method.

Making the `sort()` method `static`, the `main()` method can be as follows:

```
public static void main(String[] args) {
    String[] actualNames = new String[]{
            "Johnson", "Wilson",
            "Wilkinson", "Abraham", "Dagobert"
    };
    Sort.sort(actualNames);
    for (final String name : actualNames) {
        System.out.println(name);
    }
}
```

It seems to be much simpler (it is), and, in case the method does not use any field, you may think that there is no reason to make a method non-static. During the first 10 years of Java, static methods were in heavy use. There is even a term, utility class, which means a class that has only static methods and should not be instantiated. With the advent of **Inversion of Control** containers, we tend to use less static methods. When static methods are used, it is harder to use **dependency injection**, and it is also more difficult to create tests. We will discuss these advanced topics in the next few chapters. For now, you are informed as to what static methods are and that they can be used; however, usually, unless there is a very special need for them, we will avoid them.

Later, we will look at how classes are implemented in the hierarchy, and how classes may implement interfaces and extend other classes. When these features are looked at, we will see that there are so-called abstract classes that may contain abstract methods. These methods have the `abstract` modifier, and they are not defined—only the name, argument types (and names), and return type are specified. A concrete (non-abstract) class extending the abstract class should define them.

The opposite of the abstract method is the final method declared with the `final` modifier. A `final` method cannot be overridden in subclasses.

Interfaces

Methods are also declared in interfaces. A method declared in an interface does not define the actual behavior of the method; they do not contain the code. They have only the head of the method; in other words, they are abstract implicitly. Although nobody does, you may even use the `abstract` keyword in an interface when you define a method.

Interfaces look very similar to classes, but instead of using the `class` keyword, we use the `interface` keyword. Because interfaces are mainly used to define methods, the methods are `public` if no modifier is used.

Interfaces can also define fields, but since interfaces cannot have instances (only implementing classes can have instances), these fields are all `static` and they also have to be `final`. This is the default for fields in interfaces, thus we do not need to write these if we defined fields in interfaces.

It was a common practice to define only constants in some interfaces and then use these in classes. To do that, the easiest way was to implement the interface. Since these interfaces do not define any method, the implementation is nothing more than writing the implements keyword and the name of the interface into the header of the class declaration. This is bad practice because this way the interface becomes part of the public declaration of the class, although these constants are needed inside the class. If you need to define constants that are not local to a class but are used in many classes, then define them in a class and import the fields using `import static` or just use the name of the class and the field.

Interfaces can also have nested classes, but they cannot have inner classes. The obvious reason for that is that inner class instances have a reference to an instance of the enclosing class. In the case of an interface, there are no instances, so an inner class could not have a reference to an instance of an enclosing interface because that just does not exist. The joyful part of it is that we do not need to use the `static` keyword in the case of nested classes because that is the default, just as in the case of fields.

With the advent of Java 8, you can also have `default` methods in interfaces that provide the default implementation of the method for the classes that implement the interface. There can also be `static` and `private` methods in interfaces since Java 9.

Methods are identified by their name and the argument list. You can reuse a name for a method and have different argument types; Java will identify which method to use based on the types of the actual arguments. This is called **method overloading**. Usually, it is easy to tell which method you call, but when there are types that extend each other, the situation becomes more complex. The standard defines very precise rules for the actual selection of the method that the compiler follows, so there is no ambiguity. However, fellow programmers who read the code may misinterpret overloaded methods or, at least, will have a hard time identifying which method is actually called. Method overloading may also hinder backwards compatibility when you want to extend your class. The general advice is to think twice before creating overloaded methods. They are lucrative, but may sometimes be costly.

Argument passing

In Java, arguments are passed by value. When the method modifies an argument variable, then only the copy of the original value is modified. Any primitive value is copied during the method call. When an object is passed as an argument, then the copy of the reference to the object is passed.

That way, the object is available to be modified for the method. In the case of classes that have their primitive counterpart, and also in the case of `String` and some other class types, the objects simply do not provide methods or fields to modify the state. This is important for the integrity of the language, and to not get into trouble when objects and primitive values automatically get converted.

In other cases, when the object is modifiable, the method can effectively work on the very object it was passed to. This is also the way the `sort()` method in our example works on the array. The same array, which is also an object itself, is modified.

This argument passing is much simpler than it is in other languages. Other languages let the developer mix the pass by reference and the **pass by value** argument passing. In Java, when you use a variable by itself as an expression to pass a parameter to a method, you can be sure that the variable itself is never modified. The object refers to this, however, if it is mutable, may be modified.

An object is mutable if it can be modified, altering the value of some of its field directly or via some method call. When a class is designed in a way that there is no normal way to modify the state of the object after the creation of the object, the object is immutable. The classes `Byte`, `Short`, `Integer`, `Long`, `Float`, `Double`, `Boolean`, `Character`, as well as `String`, are designed in the JDK so that the objects are immutable. It is possible to overcome the limitation of immutability implementation of certain classes using reflection, but doing that is hacking and not professional coding. Doing that can be done for one single purpose—getting a better knowledge and understanding of the inner workings of some Java classes, but nothing else.

Fields

Fields are variables on the class level. They represent the state of an object. They are variables with defined a type and a possible initial value. Fields can be `static`, `final`, `transient`, and `volatile`, and the access may be modified with the `public`, `protected`, and `private` keywords.

Static fields belong to the class. It means that there is one of them shared by all the instances of the class. Normal, nonstatic fields belong to the objects. If you have a field named `f`, then each instance of the class has its own `f`. If `f` is declared `static`, then the instances will share the very same `f` field.

The `final` fields cannot be modified after they are initialized. Initialization can be done on the line where they are declared, in an initializer block or in the constructor code. The strict requirement is that the initialization has to happen before the constructor returns. This way, the meaning of the `final` keyword is very different, in this case, from what it means in the case of a class or a method. A `final` class cannot be extended and a `final` method cannot be overridden in an extending class, as we will see in the next chapter. The `final` fields are either uninitialized or get a value during instance creation. The compiler also checks that the code does initialize all `final` fields during the object-instance creation or during the class loading, in case the `final` field is `static`, and that the code is not accessing/reading any `final` field that was not yet initialized.

It is a common misconception that the `final` fields have to be initialized at the declaration. It can be done in an initializer code or in a constructor. The restriction is that no matter which constructor is called in case there are more, the `final` fields have to be initialized exactly once.

The `transient` fields are not part of the serialized state of the object. Serialization is an act of converting the actual value of an object to physical bytes. Deserialization is the opposite when the object is created from the bytes. It is used to save the state in some frameworks. The code that does the serialization, `java.lang.io.ObjectOutputStream`, works only with classes that implement the `Serializable` interface and uses only the fields from those objects that are not `transient`. Very obviously, `transient` fields are also not restored from the bytes that represent the serialized form of the object because their value is not there.

Serialization is usually used in distributed programs. A good example is the session object of a servlet. When the servlet container runs on a clustered node, some fields of objects stored into the session object may magically disappear between HTTP hits. That is because serialization saves and reloads the session to move the session between the nodes. Serialization, in such a situation, may also be a performance issue if a developer does not know the side effects of the stored large objects in the session.

The `volatile` keyword is a keyword that tells the compiler that the field may be used by different threads. When a `volatile` field is accessed by any code, the JIT compiler generates code, which ensures that the value of the field accessed is up to date.

When a field is not volatile, the compiler-generated code may store the value of the field in a processor cache or registry for faster access when it sees that the value will be needed soon by some subsequent code fragment. In the case of `volatile` fields, this optimization cannot be done. Additionally, note that saving the value to memory and loading from there all the time maybe 50 or more times slower than accessing a value from a registry or cache.

Modifiers

Methods, constructors, fields, interfaces, and classes can have access modifiers. The general rule is that in case there is no modifier, the scope of the method, constructor, and so on, is the package. Any code in the same package can access it.

When the `private` modifier is used, the scope is restricted to the so-called compilation unit. This means the class that is in one file. What is inside one file can see and use anything declared to be `private`. This way, inner and nested classes can have access to each other's `private` variables, which may not really be a good programming style, but Java permits that.

The `private` members are accessible from code that is in the same top-level class. If there are inner classes inside a top-level class, then the compiler generates separate class files from these files. The JVM does not know what an inner class is. For the JVM, a class is just a class. `private` members still have to be accessible from a class that is the top-level class or is inside the same top-level class where the `private` member (method or field) is. All the same time, other classes should not be able to access the `private` fields. To solve this ambiguity, Java generated the so-called synthetic proxy methods that are visible from the outside, and thus are accessible. When you want to call a `private` method from the same top-level class but in a different inner class, then the compiler generates a proxy class. This is the reason that many times IDEs warn that `private` methods may not be optimal from a performance point of view.

This has changed with Java 11, which introduced the notion of nest. The top-level class is a nest host and every class can tell which are in their nest and who is their nest host. That way the JVM knows if an access to a `private` member (read or write to a field or calling a method) is permissible. At the same time, Java 11 does not generate synthetic proxy methods anymore.

The opposite of `private` is `public`. It extends the visibility to the whole Java program, or at least to the whole module if the project is a Java module.

There is a middle way: `protected`. Anything with this modifier is accessible inside the package and also in classes that extend the class (regardless of the package) that the protected method, field, and so on, is in.

Object initializers and constructors

When an object is instantiated, the appropriate constructor is called. The constructor declaration looks like a method with the following deviation—the constructor does not have a return value. That is because the constructors work on the not-fully-ready instance when the `new` command operator is invoked and does not return anything. Constructors, having the same name as the class, cannot be distinguished from each other. If there is a need for more than one constructor, they have to be overloaded. Constructors, thus, can call each other, almost as if they were `void` methods with different arguments. However, there is a restriction—when a constructor calls another, it has to be the very first instruction in the constructor. You use `this()` syntax with an appropriate argument list, which may be empty, to invoke a constructor from another constructor.

The initialization of the object instance also executes initializer blocks. These are blocks containing executable code inside the `{` and `}` characters outside the methods and constructors. They are executed before the constructor in the order they appear in the code, together with the initialization of the fields in case their declarations contain value initialization.

If you see the `static` keyword in front of an initializer block, the block belongs to the class and is executed when the class is loaded, along with the static field initializers.

Compiling and running the program

Finally, we will compile and execute our program from the command line. There is nothing new in this one; we will only apply what we have learned in this chapter using the following two commands:

```
$ mvn package
```

This compiles the program, packages the result into a JAR file, and finally executes the following command:

```
$ java -cp target/SortTutorial-1.0.0-SNAPSHOT.jar packt.java11.example.App
```

This will print the following result on the command line:

```
SortTutorial — -bash — 86×7
$ java -cp target/SortTutorial-1.0.0-SNAPSHOT.jar packt.java11.example.stringsort.App
Abraham
Dagobert
Johnson
Wilkinson
Wilson
$
```

Summary

In this chapter, we have developed a very basic sort algorithm. It was made purposefully simple so that we could reiterate the basic and most important Java language elements, classes, packages, variables, methods, and so on. We also looked at build tools, so we are not empty-handed in the next chapters when projects will contain more than just two files. We will use Maven and Gradle in the upcoming chapters.

In the very next chapter, we will make the sort program more complex, implementing more efficient algorithms and also making our code flexible, giving us the opportunity to learn more advanced Java language features.

3
Optimizing the Sort - Making Code Professional

In this chapter, we will develop the sorting code and make it more general. We want to sort something that is more general and not only an array of strings. Essentially, we will write a program that can sort anything that is sortable. That way, we will bring the coding to its full extent toward one of the major strengths of Java—*abstraction*.

Abstraction, however, does not come without a price tag. When you have a class that sorts strings and you accidentally mix an integer or something else that is not a string into the sortable data, then the compiler will complain about it. Java does not allow you to put an `int` into an `String` array. When the code is more abstract, such programming errors may slip in. We will look at how to handle such exceptional cases by catching and throwing exceptions. Later, we will also look at generics, a feature of Java that can help to catch such programming mistakes at compile time.

To identify bugs, we will use unit testing, applying the industry standard JUnit version 4. As JUnit heavily uses annotations, and because annotations are important, we will also learn about annotations a bit.

After that, we will modify the code to use the generics feature of Java that was introduced into the language in version 5. Using that, we will catch coding errors during compilation time. This is much better than handling exceptions during runtime. The earlier a bug is identified, the cheaper it is to fix.

For the build, we will still use Maven, but this time, we will split the code into small modules. Thus, we will have a multi-module project. We will have separate modules for the definition of a sorting module and for the different implementations. That way, we will look at how classes can extend each other and implement interfaces, and generally, we will really start to program in an object-oriented way.

We will also discuss **Test-Driven Development** (**TDD**), and at the end of the section, we will start using the brand new feature Java introduced in version 9—module support.

In this chapter, we will cover the following topics:

- Object-oriented programming principles
- Unit testing practices
- Algorithmic complexity and quicksort
- Exception handling
- Recursive methods
- Module support

The general sorting program

In the previous chapter, we implemented a simple sorting algorithm. The code can sort elements of a `String` array. We did this to learn. For practical use, there is a ready-cooked sort solution in the JDK that can sort members of `Collection` objects that are comparable.

The JDK contains a utility class called `Collections`, which itself contains a static method, `Collections.sort`. This method can sort any `List` that has members that are `Comparable` (more precisely, members that are instances of a class that implements the `Comparable` interface). `List` and `Comparable` are interfaces defined in the JDK. Thus, if we want to sort a list of `Strings`, the simplest solution is as follows:

```
public class SimplestStringListSortTest {
    @Test
    public void canSortStrings() {
        var actualNames = new ArrayList(Arrays.asList(
                "Johnson", "Wilson",
                "Wilkinson", "Abraham", "Dagobert"
        ));
        Collections.sort(actualNames);
        Assert.assertEquals(new ArrayList<>(Arrays.asList(
                "Abraham", "Dagobert",
                "Johnson", "Wilkinson", "Wilson")),
                actualNames);
    }
}
```

This code fragment is from a sample JUnit test, which is the reason we have the `@Test` annotation in front of the method. We will discuss that in detail later. To execute that test, we can issue the following command:

```
$ mvn -Dtest=SimplestStringListSortTest test
```

This sort implementation, however, does not meet our needs. The main reason is that we want to learn something new. Using the JDK's `sort()` method does not teach you anything new, except, perhaps the `@Test` annotation that stands in front of the method.

If there is something that you cannot follow in the previous code, then you can turn some pages back in this book and consult the Oracle online documentation of the JDK (`https://docs.oracle.com/javase/9/docs/api/`), but that is all. You already know these things.

You may wonder why I wrote the URL for the Java version 9 API to the link. Well, then this is the moment of honesty and truth—when I wrote this book, the Java 11 JDK was not available in its final form. As a matter of fact, even the Java 10 JDK was only pre-release. I created most of the examples on my MacBook using Java 8 in the first edition and I only tested the features that are Java 9, 10, or 11-specific later. When you read this book, Java 11 will be available, so you can try and change that one single digit from 9 to 11 in the URL and get the documentation for version 11. At the moment, I get **HTTP ERROR 404**. Sometimes, you may need the documentation of older versions. You can use 3, 4, 5, 6, 7, 8, or 9 instead of 11 in the URL. Documentation for 3 and 4 is not available to read online, but it can be downloaded. Hopefully, you will never need that. Version 5, perhaps. Version 6 was still widely used at large corporations when the first edition of this book was published and it has not changed too much since then.

Although you can learn a lot from reading code that was written by other programmers, I do not recommend trying to learn from the JDK source code at this early stage of your studies. These blocks of code are heavily optimized, not meant to be tutorial code, and they are old. They do not rust, but they were not refactored to follow the newer coding styles of Java as it matured. In some places, you can find some really ugly code in the JDK.

Okay, saying that we need to develop a new `sort()` because we can learn from it is a bit contrived. The real reason why we need a sort implementation is that we want something that can sort not only `List` data types and a `List` of something that implements the `Comparable` interface; we want to sort a bunch of objects. All we require is that the *bunch* containing the objects provides simple methods that are just enough to sort them and have a sorted *bunch*.

Originally I wanted to use the word *collection* instead of *bunch*, but there is a `Collection` interface in Java and I wanted to emphasize that we are not talking about a `java.util.Collection` of objects.

We also do not want the objects to implement the `Comparable` interface. If we require the object to implement the `Comparable` interface, it may violate the **Single Responsibility Principle** (**SRP**).

When we design a class, it should model some object class in the real world. We will model the problem space with classes. The class should implement features that represent the behavior of the objects it models. If we look at the example of students from the second chapter, then a `Student` class should represent the features that all students share and are *important from the modeling point of view*. A `Student` object should be able to tell the name of the student, the age, the average scores over the last year, and so on. We should, however, focus on the features that are relevant for our programming needs. For example, all students have feet, and certainly, each of those feet has a size, so we may think that a `Student` class should also implement a method that returns the size of the student's feet. To make it extremely ridiculous just to highlight the absurdity, we could implement the data structure and the API to register a size for the left foot and a different size for the right foot. We do not because the size of feet is irrelevant from the model point of view.

However, if we want to sort a list containing `Student` objects, the `Student` class has to implement the `Comparable` interface. But wait! How do you compare two students? By names, by age, or by their average scores?

Comparing one student to another is not an essential feature of the `Student` class. Every class, or for that matter, package, library, or programming unit, should have one responsibility and it should implement only that and nothing else. It is not exact. This is not mathematics. Sometimes, it is hard to tell whether a feature fits that responsibility or not. Comparability can be an inherent feature of some data types, such as `Integer` or `Double`. Other classes do not have such an inherent comparison feature.

There are simple techniques to be sure whether a feature should or should not be part of a class. For example, in the case of a student, you can ask the real person about their name and age, and they can probably also tell you their average score. If you ask one of them to `compareTo` (another student), as the `Comparable` interface requires this method, they will probably ask back *by what attribute* or *how?* If they are not the polite type, they may reply by simply saying *what?* (Not to mention the abbreviation WTF, which stands for the last three working days of the week and is popular in situations like this.) In such a case, you may suspect that implementing the feature is probably not in the area of that class and its concerns; the comparison should be segregated from the implementation of the original class. This is also called **segregation of concerns**, which is closely related to the SRP.

JDK developers are aware of this. `Collections.sort`, which sorts a `List` of `Comparable` elements, is not the only sorting method in this class. There is another that just sorts any `List` if you pass a second argument, which should be an object that implements the `Comparator` interface and is capable of comparing two elements of the `List`. This is a clean pattern to separate concerns. In some cases, separating the comparison is not needed. In other cases, it is desirable. The `Comparator` interface declares one single method that the implementing classes have to provide—`compare`. If the two arguments are equal, the method returns `0`. If they are different, it should return a negative or a positive `int`, depending on which argument precedes the other.

There are also `sort` methods in the JDK class, `java.util.Arrays`. They sort arrays or only a slice of an array. The method is a good example of method overloading. There are methods with the same name, but with different arguments, to sort a whole array for each primitive type, for a slice of each, and also two for object arrays implementing the `Comparable` interface, and also for object arrays to be sorted using `Comparator`. As you see, there is a whole range of sort implementations available in the JDK, and in 99% of cases, you will not need to implement a sort yourself. Sorts use the same algorithm, a stable merge sort with some optimization.

What we will implement is a general approach that can be used to sort lists, arrays, or just *anything* that has elements we can compare with the help of a comparator, and where it is possible to swap any two elements. We will implement different sorting algorithms that can be used with these interfaces.

A brief overview of various sorting algorithms

There are many different sorting algorithms. As I said, there are simpler and more complex algorithms and, in many cases, the more complex algorithms are the ones that run faster. (After all, what would be the benefit of higher complexity algorithm if it runs even slower?) In this chapter, we will implement a bubble sort and a quicksort. We have already implemented a bubble sort for strings in the previous chapter, so in this case, the implementation will mainly focus on the coding for general sortable object sorting. Implementing a quicksort will involve a bit of algorithmic interest.

Be warned that this section is here to give you only a taste of algorithmic complexity. It is far from precise and I am in the vain hope that no mathematician reads this and puts a curse on me. Some of the explanations are vague. If you want to learn computer science in depth, then after reading this book, find some other books or visit online courses.

When we talk about the general sorting problem, we think about some general ordered collection of objects where any two can be compared and swapped while we sort. We also assume that this is an in-place sort. This means that we do not create another list or array to collect the original objects in sorted order. When we talk about the speed of an algorithm, we are talking about some abstract thing and not milliseconds. When we want to talk about milliseconds, actual real-world duration, we should already have an implementation in some programming language running on a real computer.

Algorithms, in their abstract form without implementation, don't do that. Still, it is worth talking about the time and memory needs of an algorithm. When we do that, we usually investigate how the algorithm behaves for a large set of data. For a small set of data, most algorithms are just fast. Sorting two numbers is usually not an issue, is it?

In the case of sorting, we usually examine how many comparisons are needed to sort a collection of n elements. Bubble sort needs approximately n^2 (n times n) comparisons. We cannot say that this is exactly n^2 because, in the case of $n=2$, the result is 1, for $n=3$ it is 3, for $n=4$ it is 6, and so on. However, as n starts to get larger, the actual number of comparisons needed and n^2 will asymptotically be of the same value. We say that the algorithmic complexity of the bubble sort is $O(n^2)$. This is also called big-O notation. If you have an algorithm that is $O(n^2)$ and it works just fine for 1,000 elements, finishing in a second, then you should expect the same algorithm to finish 1 million elements in around ten days to a month. If the algorithm is linear, say $O(n)$, then finishing 1,000 elements in one second should lead you to expect 1 million to be finished in 1,000 seconds. That is a bit longer than a coffee break, but too short for lunch.

This makes it feasible that if we want some serious business sorting objects, we will need something better than bubble sort. The many unnecessary comparisons are not only wasting our time, but also wasting CPU power, consuming energy, and polluting the environment.

The question, however, is how fast can a sort be? Is there a provable minimum that we cannot reduce?

The answer is yes, there is a provable minimum. The basis for that is very interesting and, in my humble opinion, every IT engineer should know not only the actual answer but also the reasoning behind it. After all, the *proof* of the necessary minimum is about nothing but pure information. The following, again, is not a mathematical proof, just a kind of vague explanation.

When we implement any sorting algorithm, the implementation will execute comparisons and element swaps. That is the only way to sort a collection of objects, or at least all other possible ways can be reduced to these steps. The outcome of a comparison can have two values. Say these values are *0* or *1*. This is one bit of information. If the result of the comparison is *1*, then we swap; if the result is *0*, then we do not swap.

We can have the objects in different orders before we start the comparison and the number of different orders is *n!* (*n* factorial), that is, the numbers multiplied from 1 to *n*, in other words, $n!=1*2*3*...*(n-1)*n$.

Let's assume that we stored the result of the individual comparisons in a number as a series of bits for each possible input of the sort. Now, if we reverse the execution of the sort and run the algorithm starting from the sorted collection, and control the swapping using the bits that described the results of the comparison and we use the bits the other way around doing the last swap first and the one that was done first during the sorting first, we should get back the original order of the objects. This way, each original order is uniquely tied to a number expressed as an array of bits.

Now, we can express the original question this way—how many bits are needed to describe *n* factorial different numbers? That is exactly the number of comparisons we will need to sort *n* elements.

The number of bits to distinguish *n!* numbers is $log_2(n!)$. Using some mathematics, we will know that $log_2(n!)$ is the same as $log_2(1)+ log_2(2)+...+ log_2(n)$. If we look at this expression's asymptotic value, then we can say that this is the same as __*O(n*log n)*__. We should not expect any general sorting algorithm to be faster.

For special cases, there are faster algorithms. For example, if we want to sort 1 million numbers that are each between one and 10, then we only need to count the different numbers and then create a collection that contains that many ones, twos, and so on. This is an *O(n)* algorithm, but this is not generally applicable.

Again, this was not a formal mathematical proof.

Quicksort

Sir Charles Antony Richard Hoare developed the quicksort algorithm in 1959. It is a typical divide-and-conquer algorithm. Here is how it goes.

To sort a long array, pick an element from the array that will be the so-called pivot element. Then, partition the array so that the left side will contain all the elements that are smaller than the pivot and the right side will contain all the elements that are larger than or equal to the pivot. When we start partitioning, we do not know how long the left side will be and where the right side will start. The precise way we work this out will be explained very shortly. For now, it is important that we will have an array divided so that the elements from the start of the array to a certain index are all smaller than the pivot, and the elements from there till the end of the array are all larger than the pivot. This also has the simple consequence that the elements on the left are all smaller than any element on the right. This is already a partial ordering. Because the pivot was selected from the array, it is guaranteed that neither side can contain the whole original array, leaving the other side to be an empty array.

When this is done, the left and right sides of the array can be sorted by calling the sort recursively. In these calls, the length of the sub-arrays is always smaller than the whole array of the previous level. We stop the recursion when there is one single element in the array segment of the actual level we want to sort. In this case, we can just return from the recursive call without comparisons or reordering; one element is evidently always sorted.

We talk about a recursive algorithm when the algorithm is defined partially using itself. The most famous recursive definition is the Fibonacci series, 0 and 1 for the first two elements, and for all following elements, the nth element is the sum of the $(n-1)^{th}$ and the $(n-2)^{th}$ element. Recursive algorithms are often implemented in modern programming languages, implementing a method that does some calculation but sometimes calls itself. When designing recursive algorithms, it is of utmost importance to have something that stops the recursive calls; otherwise, the recursive implementation will allocate all memory available for the program stack and on running out of memory, it will stop the program with an error.

The partitioning part of the algorithm goes the following way—we will start to read the array using two indices from the start and end. We will first start with an index that is small and increase the index until it is smaller than the large index, or until we find an element that is greater than or equal to the pivot. After this, we will start to decrease the larger index so long as it is greater than the small index, and the element indexed is greater than or equal to the pivot. When we stop, we swap the two elements pointed to by the two indices. If the indices are not the same, we start increasing and decreasing the small and large indices, respectively. If the indices are the same, then we are finished with the partitioning. The left side of the array is from the start to the index where the indices met minus one; the right side starts with the index finishes at the end of the to-be-sorted array.

This quicksort algorithm usually consumes $O(n \log n)$ time, but in some cases, it can degrade to $O(n^2)$, depending on how the pivot is chosen. For example, if we choose the first element of the segment of the array as a pivot and the array is already sorted, then this quicksort algorithm degrades to a simple bubble sort. To amend that, there are different approaches to the selection of the pivot. In this book, we will use the simplest—we will select the first element of the sortable collection as a pivot.

Project structure and build tools

The project this time will contain many modules. We will still use Maven in this chapter. We will set up a so-called multi-module project in Maven. In such a project, the directory contains the directories of the modules and `pom.xml`. There is no source code in this top-level directory. The `pom.xml` file in this directory serves the following two purposes:

- It references the modules and can be used to compile, install, and deploy all the modules together
- It defines parameters for the modules that are the same for all of them

Every `pom.xml` has a parent and this `pom.xml` is the parent of the `pom.xml` files in the module directories. To define the modules, the `pom.xml` file contains the following lines:

```
<modules>
    <module>SortSupportClasses</module>
    <module>SortInterface</module>
    <module>bubble</module>
    <module>quick</module>
    <module>Main</module>
</modules>
```

These are the names of the modules. These names are used as directory names and also as `artifactId` in the `pom.xml` module. The directories in this setup look as follows:

```
$ tree
   |-SortInterface
   |---src/main/java/packt/java189fundamentals/ch03
   |-bubble
   |---src
   |-----main/java/packt/java189fundamentals/ch03/bubble
   |-----test/java/packt/java189fundamentals/ch03/bubble
   |-quick/src/
   |-----main/java
   |-----test/java
```

Maven dependency management

Dependencies also play an important role in the POM file. The previous project did not have any dependencies. This time we will use JUnit, so we depend on JUnit. Dependencies are defined in the `pom.xml` file using the `dependencies` tag. For example, the bubble sort module contains the following piece of code:

```
<dependencies>
    <dependency>
        <groupId>packt.java189fundamentals</groupId>
        <artifactId>SortInterface</artifactId>
    </dependency>
    <dependency>
        <groupId>junit</groupId>
        <artifactId>junit</artifactId>
    </dependency>
</dependencies>
```

The actual `pom.xml` in the code set you can download will contain more code than this. In print, we often present a version or only a fraction that helps with understanding the topic that we are discussing at that point.

It tells Maven that the module code uses classes, interfaces, and `enum` types that are defined in the modules or libraries that are available from a repository.

When you use Maven to compile the code, the libraries used by your code are available from repositories. When Ant was developed, the notion of repositories had not been invented. At that time, developers copied versions of libraries into a folder in the source code structure. Usually, the `lib` directory was used for this purpose.

There were two problems with this approach. One is the size of the source code repository. If, for example, 100 different projects used JUnit, then the JAR file of the JUnit library was copied there 100 times. The other problem was gathering all the libraries. When a library used another library, the developers had to read the documentation of the library that described what other libraries were needed to use this library. This was often outdated and not precise. Those libraries had to be downloaded and installed the same way. This was time-consuming and error-prone. When a library was missing and the developers just did not notice it, the error manifested during compile time. If the dependency was only runtime detectable, then the JVM was not able to load the class.

To solve this issue, Maven comes with a built-in repository manager client. A repository is a storage that contains libraries. As there can be other types of files in a repository, not only libraries, Maven terminology is *artifact*. The `groupId`, the `artifactId`, and the `version` numbers identify an artifact. There is a very strict requirement that an artifact can only be put into a repository once. Even if there is an error during the release process that is identified after the erroneous release was uploaded, the artifact cannot be overwritten. For the same `groupId`, `artifactId`, and `version`, there can only be one single file that will never change. If there was an error, then a new artifact is created with a new version number and the erroneous artifact may be deleted but never replaced.

If the version number ends with `-SNAPSHOT`, then this uniqueness is not guaranteed or required. Snapshots are usually stored in a separate repository and are not published to the world.

Repositories contain artifacts in directories that are organized in a defined way. When Maven runs, it can access different repositories using the `https` protocol.

Formerly, the `http` protocol was also used. For non-paying customers, such as FOSS developers, the central repository was available via `http` only. However, it was discovered that modules downloaded from the repository could be targeted by man-in-the-middle security attacks, so Sonatype (`http://www.sonatype.com`) changed the policy to use the `https` protocol only. Never configure or use a repository with the `https` protocol and never trust a file that you downloaded via HTTP.

There is a local repository on the developer's machine, usually in the `~/.m2/repository` directory. On Windows, the user's home directory is usually `C:\Users\your_username`. On Unix operating systems, the shell, which is something like the Windows Command Prompt application, uses the ~ character to refer to this directory. When you issue the `mvn install` command, Maven stores the created artifact here. Maven also stores an artifact here when it is downloaded from a repository via **HTTPS**. This way, subsequent compilations do not need to go out to the network for artifacts.

Companies usually set up their own repository manager. These applications can be configured to communicate with several other repositories and collect artifacts from there on demand, essentially implementing proxy functionality. Artifacts travel to the build, from the far end repositories to the closer ones, in a hierarchical structure, to the local repo, and essentially to the final artifact if the packaging type of the project is `war`, `ear`, or some other format that encloses the dependent artifacts. This is essentially file caching without revalidation and cache eviction. This can be done because an artifact is never replaced.

If the `bubble` project were a standalone project and not part of a multi-module one, then the dependencies would look like this:

```
<dependencies>
    <dependency>
        <groupId>packt.java189fundamentals</groupId>
        <artifactId>SortInterface</artifactId>
        <version>1.0.0-SNAPSHOT</version>
    </dependency>
    <dependency>
        <groupId>junit</groupId>
        <artifactId>junit</artifactId>
        <version>4.12</version>
    </dependency>
</dependencies>
```

If `version` is not defined for a dependency, Maven will not be able to identify the artifact to use. In the case of a multi-module project, `version` can be defined in the parent and the modules inherit the version. Because the parent does not depend on the actual artifact, it should only define the version attached to the `groupId` and `artifactId`. For this reason, the XML tag is not `dependencies` but `ddependencyManagement/dependencies` in the top-level `project` tag, as in the following example:

```
<dependencyManagement>
    <dependencies>
        <dependency>
            <groupId>packt.java189fundamentals</groupId>
            <artifactId>SortSupportClasses</artifactId>
            <version>${project.version}</version>
        </dependency>
        <dependency>
            <groupId>packt.java189fundamentals</groupId>
            <artifactId>SortInterface</artifactId>
            <version>${project.version}</version>
        </dependency>
        <dependency>
            <groupId>packt.java189fundamentals</groupId>
            <artifactId>quick</artifactId>
```

```
                <version>${project.version}</version>
            </dependency>
            <dependency>
                <groupId>junit</groupId>
                <artifactId>junit</artifactId>
                <version>4.12</version>
                <scope>test</scope>
            </dependency>
        </dependencies>
    </dependencyManagement>
```

When the modules want to use `junit`, they do not need to specify the version. They will get it from the parent project defined as 4.12, which is the latest from *JUnit 4*. If there were to ever be a new version, 4.12.1, with some serious bugs fixed, then the only place to modify the version number is the parent POM, and the modules will use the new version when Maven executes next.

When the project developers decide to use the new *JUnit 5* version, however, all the modules will be modified because *JUnit 5* is not just a new version. *JUnit 5* is significantly different from the old version 4, and it is split into several modules. This way, `groupId` and `artifactId` also change.

It is also worth noting that the modules that implement the interfaces from the `SortInterface` module eventually depend on the module. In this case, the version is defined as follows:

```
<version>${project.version}</version>
```

That seems to be a bit tautological (it actually is). The `${project.version}` property is the version of the project and the `SortInterface` module inherits this value. This is the version of the artifact that the other modules depend on. In other words, the modules always depend on the version that we are currently developing.

Coding the sort

To implement the sorting, first, we will define the interfaces that the library should implement. Defining the interface before actually coding is a good practice. When there are many implementations, it is sometimes recommended to first create a simple one and start using it so that the interface may evolve during this development phase, and when the more complex implementations are due, then the interface is already fixed. In reality, nothing is fixed ever because there is no Archimedean point in programming.

Creating the interfaces

The interface in our case is very simple:

```
public interface Sort {
    void sort(Sortable collection);
}
```

The interface should do only one thing, sort something that is sortable. As such, we define an interface and any class that implements this interface will be `Sortable`:

```
public interface Sortable {
}
```

Creating BubbleSort

Now, we can start creating the bubble sort that implements the `Sort` interface:

```
 ...
import java.util.Comparator;

public class BubbleSort implements Sort, SortSupport {
    @Override
    public void sort(Sortable collection) {
        var n = collection.size();
        while (n > 1) {
            for (int j = 0; j < n - 1; j++) {
                if (comparator.compare(collection.get(j),
                        collection.get(j + 1)) > 0) {
                    swapper.swap(j, j + 1);
                }
            }
            n--;
        }
    }
 ...
```

Normally, the algorithm needs two operations. We implemented those specific to a `String` array—comparing two elements and swapping two elements. This time, however, the sort implementation itself does not know what type it should sort. It also does not know how the elements are stored. It can be an array, a list or something else. All it knows that it can compare elements, and also it can swap two elements. If these are provided, then the sorting works.

In Java terms, it needs a `comparator` object capable of comparing two elements and it needs a `swapper` object that is capable of swapping two elements in the collection.

The sorting object should have access to those objects. Having two fields that reference such objects is the perfect solution for that. The only question is how the fields get the reference to the comparing and swapping objects. The solution that we follow now is that we provide setters that can be used to inject these dependencies into the sorting object.

These setters are not specific to the bubble sort algorithm. These are rather general; therefore, it makes sense to define an interface that the bubble sort can implement:

```
public interface SortSupport {
    void setSwapper(Swapper swap);

    void setComparator(Comparator compare);
}
```

And the implementation in the `BubbleSort` class is simply the following code:

```
    private Comparator comparator = null;

    @Override
    public void setComparator(Comparator comparator) {
        this.comparator = comparator;
    }

    private Swapper swapper = null;

    @Override
    public void setSwapper(Swapper swapper) {
        this.swapper = swapper;
    }
```

The `@Override` annotation signals to the Java compiler that the method is overriding a method of the parent class or, as in this case, of the interface. A method can override a parent method without this annotation; however, if we use the annotation, the compilation fails if the method does not override. This helps you discover during compile time that something was changed in the parent class or in the interface and we did not follow that change in the implementation, or that we just made some mistake thinking that we will override a method when we actually do not. As annotations are heavily used in unit tests, we will talk about annotations in a bit more detail later.

This also means that we will need two new interfaces—`Swapper` and `Comparator`. We are lucky that the Java runtime already defines a `Comparator` interface that just fits the purpose. You may have guessed that from the following import statement:

```
import java.util.Comparator;
```

When you need something very basic, such as a `Comparator` interface, it is most probably defined in the runtime. It is advisable to consult the runtime before writing your own version. The `Swapper` interface, however, we will have to create:

```
public interface Swapper {
    void swap(int i, int j);
}
```

As it is used to swap two elements specified by the indices in `Sortable`, there is a method, quite obviously named `swap`, for the purpose. But we are not ready yet. If you try to compile the preceding code, the compiler will complain about the `get` and `get` methods. They are needed by the algorithm to implement the sort, but they are not inherently part of the sorting itself. This is a functionality that should not be implemented in the sort. As we do not know what type of collections we will sort, it is not only inadvisable but also impossible to implement these methods inside the sort. It seems that we just cannot sort anything. There are some restrictions we will have to set. The sorting algorithm must know the size of the collection we sort and should also have access to an element by index so that it can pass it on to the comparator. These seem to be quite reasonable constraints that we can usually live with.

The restrictions are expressed in the `Sortable` interface that we just left empty, not knowing before the first sort implementation what is required to be there:

```
public interface Sortable {
    Object get(int i);
    int size();
}
```

Now, we are ready with the interfaces and the implementation and we can go on testing the code. But, before that, we will briefly reiterate what we did and also why we did that.

Architectural considerations

We created an interface and a simple implementation of it. During the implementation, we discovered that the interface needs other interfaces and methods that are needed to support the algorithm. This usually happens during the architectural design of the code, before implementation. For didactic reasons, I followed the build-up of the interfaces while we developed the code. In real life, when I created the interfaces, I created them all in one step as I have enough experience. I wrote my first quicksort code around 1983 in FORTRAN. However, it does not mean that I hit the bulls-eye with just any problem and come out with the final solution. It just happens that sort is a too well-known problem. If you need to modify the interfaces or other aspects of your design during development, do not feel embarrassed. It is a natural consequence and a proof that you understand things better and better as time goes by. If the architecture needs change, it is better to be done than not, and the sooner the better. In real life enterprise environments, we will design interfaces just to learn during development that there were some aspects we forgot. They are a bit more complex operations than sorting a collection.

In the case of the sorting problem, we abstracted the *something* we want to sort to the most possible extreme. The Java built-in sort can sort arrays or lists. If you want to sort something that is not a list or an array, you have to create a class that implements the `java.util.List` interface with more than 24 methods it requires to wrap your sortable object to make it sortable by the JDK sort. 24 methods seem to be a lot just to make our *something* sortable. To be honest, that is not really too many, and in a real-world project, I would consider that as an option.

We do not know, and cannot know, what methods of the interface the built-in sort uses. Those should be functionally implemented which are used and those can contain a simple `return` statement that is not used because they are just never invoked. A developer can consult the source code of the JDK and see what methods are actually used, but that is not the contract of the search implementation. It is not guaranteed that a new version will still use *only* those methods. If a new version starts to use a method that we implemented with a single `return` statement, the sort will magically, and miserably fail.

It is also an interesting performance question how the swapping of two elements is implemented by the search using only the `List` interface. There is no `put(int, Object)` method in the `List` interface. There is `add(int, Object)`, but that inserts a new element and it may be extremely costly (burning CPU, disk, energy) to push all elements of the list up if the objects are stored, for example, on disk. Furthermore, the next step may be removing the element after the one we just inserted, doing the costly process of moving the tail of the list again. That is the trivial implementation of `put(int, Object)`. The sort may or may not follow it. Again, this is something that should not be assumed.

When you use libraries, classes, and methods from the JDK, open source, or commercial libraries, you may consult the source code but you should not rely on the implementation. You should rely only on the contract and the definition of the API that the library comes with. When you implement an interface from some external library, and you do not need to implement some part of it, and create some dummy methods, feel the danger in the air. It is an ambush. It is likely that either the library is poor quality or you did not understand how to use it. I do not know which is the worse.

In our case, we separated the swapping and the comparison from the sort. The collection should implement these operations and provide them for the sort. The contract is the interface, and to use the sort, you have to implement all methods of the interfaces we defined.

The interface of `SortSupport` defines setters that set `Swapper` and `Comparator`. Having dependencies set that way may lead to a code that creates a new instance of a class implementing the `Sort` and `SortSupport` interfaces, but does not set `Swapper` and `Comparator` before invoking `Sort`. This will lead to `NullPointerException` the first time the `Comparator` is invoked (or when the `Swapper` is invoked in case the implementation invokes that first, which is not likely, but possible). The calling method should inject the dependencies before using the class. When it is done through setters, it is called **setter injection**. This terminology is heavily used when we use frameworks such as Spring, Guice, or some other container. Creating these service classes and injecting the instance into our classes is fairly similar all the time.

Container implementations contain the functionality in a general way and provide configuration options to configure what instances are to be injected into what other objects. Usually, this leads to shorter, more flexible, and more readable code. However, dependency injection is not exclusive to containers. When we write the testing code in the next section and invoke the setters, we actually do dependency injection manually.

There is another way of dependency injection that avoids the problem of dependencies not being set. This is called **constructor injection**. The dependencies, in this case, are usually `final private` fields with no values. Remember that these fields should get their final values by the time the object is fully created. Constructor injection passes the injected values to the constructor as arguments and the constructor sets the fields. This way, the fields are guaranteed to be set by the time the object was constructed. This injection, however, cannot be defined in an interface, which may or may not be a problem in certain applications.

Now, we already have the code, and we know the considerations of how the interfaces were created. This is the time to do some testing.

Creating unit tests

When we write code, we should test it. No code has ever gone into production before at least doing some test runs. (Recognize the sarcasm!) There are different levels of tests that have different aims, technologies, industry practices, and names.

Unit tests, as the name suggests, test a unit of code. Integration tests test how the units integrate together. Smoke tests test a limited set of the features just to see that the code is not totally broken. There are other tests, until the final test, which is the proof of the work—the user acceptance test. The proof of the pudding is in the eating. A code is good if the user accepts it.

Many times, I tell juniors that the name user acceptance test is a bit misleading because it is not the user who accepts the result of a project, but the customer. By definition, the customer is the person who pays the bill. Professional development is paid; otherwise, it is not professional. The terminology is, however, user acceptance test. It just happens that customers accept the project only if the users can use the program.

When we develop in Java, a unit test tests standalone classes. In other words, in Java development, a unit is a class when we talk about unit tests. To furnish unit tests, we usually use the JUnit library. There are other libraries, such as TestNG, but JUnit is the most widely used, so we will use *JUnit*. To use it as a library, first, we will have to add it to the Maven POM as a dependency.

Adding JUnit as a dependency

Recall that we have a multi-module project, and the dependency versions are maintained in the parent POM in the `dependencyManagement` tag:

```
<dependencyManagement>
    <dependencies>
        ...
        <dependency>
            <groupId>junit</groupId>
            <artifactId>junit</artifactId>
            <version>4.12</version>
            <scope>test</scope>
        </dependency>
    </dependencies>
</dependencyManagement>
```

The scope of the dependency is `test`, which means that this library is needed only to compile the test code and during the execution of the test. The JUnit library will not make its way to the final released product; there is no need for it. If you find the JUnit library in some deployed production **Web Archive** (**WAR**) or **Enterprise Archive** (**EAR**) files, suspect that somebody was not properly managing the scopes of the libraries.

Maven supports the compilation and the execution of JUnit tests in the life cycle of the project. If we want to execute only the tests, we should issue the `mvn test` command. The IDEs also supports the execution of the unit tests. Usually, the same menu item that can be used to execute a class that has a `public static main()` method can be used. If the class is a unit test utilizing JUnit, the IDE will recognize it and execute the tests, and usually, give a graphical feedback on which tests were executing fine and which ones failed, and how.

Writing the BubbleSortTest class

The test classes are separated from the production classes. They go into the `src/test/java` directory. When we have a class named, for example, `BubbleSort`, then the test will be named `BubbleSortTest`. This convention helps the executing environment to separate the tests from those classes that do not contain tests but are needed to execute the tests. To test the sort implementation we have just created, we can furnish a class that contains, for now, a single `canSortStrings` method.

Unit test method names are used to document the functionality being tested. As the JUnit framework invokes each and every method that has the `@Test` annotation, the name of the test is not referenced anywhere in our code. We can bravely use arbitrary long method names; it will not hinder readability at the place where the method is invoked:

```
package packt.java189fundamentals.ch03.main.bubble.simple;

// import statements are deleted from the print for brevity


public class BubbleSortTest {
    @Test
    public void canSortStrings() {
        var actualNames = new ArrayList(Arrays.asList(
            "Johnson", "Wilson",
            "Wilkinson", "Abraham", "Dagobert"
        ));
```

The method contains an `ArrayList` with the actual names that we have already gotten familiar with. As we have a sort implementation and interface that needs `Sortable`, we will create one backed up by `ArrayList`:

```
var names = new Sortable() {
    @Override
    public Object get(int i) {
        return actualNames.get(i);
    }
    @Override
    public int size() {
        return actualNames.size();
    }
};
```

We declared a new object that has the `Sortable` type, which is an interface. To instantiate something that implements `Sortable`, we will need a class. We cannot instantiate an interface. In this case, define the class in the place of the instantiation. This is called an anonymous class in Java. The name comes from the fact that the name of the new class is not defined in the source code. The Java compiler will automatically create a name for the new class, but that is not interesting for the programmers. We will simply write `new Sortable()` and provide the needed implementation immediately, following between `{` and `}`. It is very convenient to define this anonymous class inside the method as, this way, it can access `ArrayList` without passing a reference to `ArrayList` in the class.

As a matter of fact, the reference is needed, but the Java compiler automatically does this. The Java compiler, in this case, also takes care that automatic reference passing this way can only be done using variables that were initialized and will not change during the execution of the code after the instantiation of the anonymous class. The `actualNames` variable was set and it should not be changed in the method later. As a matter of fact, we can even define `actualNames` to be `final`, and this would have been a requirement if we used Java 1.7 or earlier. Starting with 1.8, the requirement is that the variable is effectively final, and we can skip the `final` declaration.

The next thing that we need is a `Swapper` implementation for the `ArrayList`. In this case, we will define a whole class inside the method. It could also be an anonymous class, but this time I decided to use a named class to demonstrate that a class can be defined inside a method. Usually, we do not do that in production projects:

```
class SwapActualNamesArrayElements implements Swapper {
    @Override
    public void swap(int i, int j) {
        final Object tmp = actualNames.get(i);
        actualNames.set(i, actualNames.get(j));
```

```
            actualNames.set(j, tmp);
        }
    }
    ;
```

Last, but not least, we will need a comparator before we can invoke the sort. As we have `String`s to compare, this is easy and straightforward:

```
Comparator stringCompare = new Comparator() {
    @Override
    public int compare(Object first, Object second) {
        final String f = (String) first;
        final String s = (String) second;
        return f.compareTo(s);
    }
};
```

Having everything prepared for the sorting, we will finally need an instance of the `Sort` implementation. We have to set the `Sort` and the `Sort`, and finally, we invoke the sort:

```
var sort = new BubbleSort();
sort.setComparator(stringCompare);
sort.setSwapper(new SwapActualNamesArrayElements());
sort.sort(names);
```

The last but most important part of the test is to assert that the result is the one that we expect. JUnit helps us do that with the aid of the `Assert` class:

```
Assert.assertEquals(List.of(
    "Abraham", "Dagobert",
    "Johnson", "Wilkinson", "Wilson"
), actualNames);
```

The call to `assertEquals` checks that the first argument, the expected result, equals the second argument, the sorted `actualNames`. If they differ, then an `AssertionError` is thrown; otherwise, the test just finishes fine.

Good unit tests

Is this a good unit test? If you read it in a tutorial book like this, it has to be. Actually, it is not. It is a good code to demonstrate some of the tools that JUnit provides and some Java language features, but I would not use it in a professional project.

What makes a unit test good? To answer this question, we have to define what unit tests are used for. Unit tests serve two purposes. The purpose of the unit test is to validate the proper functioning of the unit and to document it.

Unit tests are not used to find bugs. Developers eventually use unit tests during debugging sessions but, many times, the testing code created for the debugging is a temporary one. When the bug is fixed, the code used to find it will not get into the source code repository. For every new bug, there should be a new test created that covers the functionality not properly working, but it is hardly the test code that is used to find the bug. This is because unit tests are mainly for documentation. You can document a class using *JavaDoc*, but experience shows that the documentation often becomes outdated. The developers modify the code, but they do not modify the documentation. The documentation becomes obsolete and misleading. Unit tests, however, are executed by the build system, and if **Continuous Integration** (**CI**) is in use (and it should be, in a professional environment), then the build will be broken if a test fails. All developers will get a mail notification about it, and it will drive the developer breaking the build to fix the code or the test. This way, the tests verify during continuous integration that the code is not broken, at least, not something that can be discovered using unit tests.

A good unit test is readable

Our test is far from being readable. A test case is readable if you look at it and in 15 seconds you can tell what it does. It assumes, of course, some experience in Java on behalf of the reader, but you get the point. Our test is cluttered with support classes that are not core to the test.

Our test also hardly validates that the code is working properly. It actually does not. There are some bugs in it that I put there deliberately, which we will locate and zap in the following sections. One single test that sorts a single `String` array is far from validating a sort implementation. If I were to extend this test to a real-world test, we would need methods that would have the name `canSortEmptyCollection`, `canSortOneElementCollection`, `canSortTwoElements`, `canSortReverseOrder`, or `canSortAlreadySorted`. If you look at the names, you will see what tests we need. Coming from the nature of the sort problem, an implementation may be reasonably sensitive to errors in these special cases.

What are the good points in our unit test, in addition to it being an acceptable demonstration tool?

Unit tests are fast

Our unit test runs fast. As we execute unit tests each time, the CI fires up a build and the execution of the tests should not last long. You should not create a unit test sorting billions of elements. That is a kind of stability test or load test. They should run in separate test periods and not every time the build is running. Our unit test sorts five elements, and that is reasonable.

Unit tests are deterministic

Our unit test is deterministic. Non-deterministic unit tests are the nightmare of developers. If you are in a group where some builds break on the CI server, and when a build breaks, your fellow developer says that you just have to try it again; no way! If a unit test runs, it should run at all times. If it fails, it should fail no matter how many times you start it. A non-deterministic unit test, in our case, would be to render random numbers and have them sorted. It would end up with different arrays in each test run and, in case there is some bug in the code that manifests for some array, we will not be able to reproduce it. Not to mention that the assertion to ensure the code was running fine is also difficult to produce.

If we sorted a random array in a unit test (something we do not), we could, hypothetically, assert that the array is sorted, comparing the elements one after the other checking that they are in ascending order. It would also be a totally wrong practice.

Assertions should be as simple as possible

If the assertion is complex, the risk of introducing bugs in the assertion is higher. The more complex the assertion, the higher the risk. We write the unit tests to ease our lives and not to have more code to debug.

Additionally, one test should assert only one thing. This one assertion may be coded with multiple `Assert` class methods, one after the other. Still, the aim of these is to assert the correctness of one single feature of the unit.

Remember the SRP—one test, one feature. A good test is like a good sniper—one shot, one kill.

Unit tests are isolated

When we test a unit *A*, any change in another unit *B* or a bug in a different unit should not affect our unit test that is for the unit *A*. In our case, it was easy because we have only one unit. Later, when we develop the test for the quicksort, we will see that this separation is not that simple.

If the unit tests are properly separated, a failing unit test clearly points out the location of the problem. It is in the unit where the unit test failed. If tests do not separate the units, then a failure in one test may be caused by a bug in a different unit than we expect. In this case, these tests are not really unit tests.

In practice, you should make a balance. If the isolation of the units will be too costly, you can decide to create integration tests; and, if they still run fast, have them executed by the *CI system*. At the same time, you should also try to find out why the isolation is hard. If you cannot easily isolate the units in the tests, it means that the units are too strongly coupled, which may not be a good design.

Unit tests cover the code

Unit tests should test all usual and also all special cases of the functionality. If there is a special case of code that is not covered by the unit test, the code is in danger. In case of a sort implementation, the general case is sorting, say, five elements. The special cases are much more numerous usually. How does our code behave if there is only one element or if there are no elements? What if there are two? What if the elements are in reverse order? What if they are already sorted?

Usually, the special cases are not defined in the specification. The programmer has to think about it before coding, and some special cases are discovered during coding. The hard thing is that you just cannot tell if you covered all special cases and the functionality of the code.

What you can tell is whether all the lines of code were executed during the testing or not. If 90% of the code lines are executed during the tests, then the code coverage is 90%, which is fairly good in real life, but you should never be content with anything less than 100%.

Code coverage is not the same as functional coverage, but there is a correlation. If the code coverage is less than 100%, then at least one of the following two statements is true:

- The functional coverage is not 100%.
- There is an unused code in the tested unit, which can just be deleted.

The code coverage can be measured, but the functional coverage reasonably cannot. The tools and IDEs support code coverage measurement. These measurements are integrated into the editor so you will not only get the percentage of the coverage, but the editor will show you exactly which lines are not covered by the coverage coloring the lines (in Eclipse, for example) or the gutter on the left side of the editor window (IntelliJ). The following screenshot shows that in IntelliJ, the tests cover the lines indicated by a green color on the gutter (in the print version, this is just a grey rectangle):

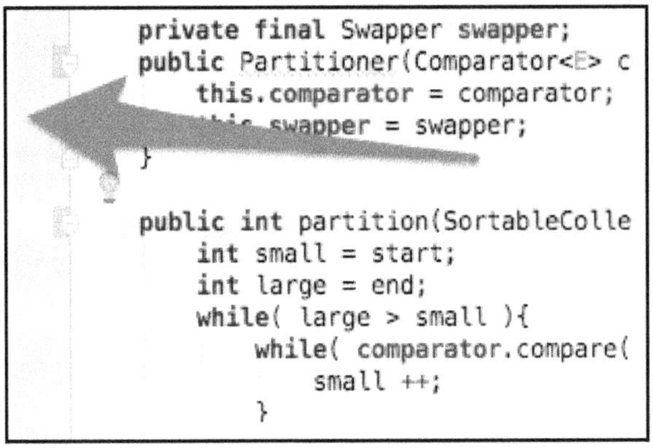

```
private final Swapper swapper;
public Partitioner(Comparator<E> c
    this.comparator = comparator;
    this.swapper = swapper;
}

public int partition(SortableColle
    int small = start;
    int large = end;
    while( large > small ){
        while( comparator.compare(
            small ++;
        }
```

Refactoring the test

Now that we have discussed what a good unit test is, let's improve our test. The first thing is to move the supporting classes to separate files. We will create `ArrayListSortable`:

```
package packt.java189fundamentals.ch03.main.bubble.simple;

import packt.java189fundamentals.ch03.Sortable;

import java.util.ArrayList;

public class ArrayListSortable implements Sortable {
    final private ArrayList actualNames;

    ArrayListSortable(ArrayList actualNames) {
        this.actualNames = actualNames;
    }

    @Override
    public Object get(int i) {
        return actualNames.get(i);
    }
```

```
        @Override
        public int size() {
            return actualNames.size();
        }
    }
```

This class encapsulates `ArrayList` and then implements the `gets` and `size` methods to `ArrayList` access. `ArrayList` itself is declared as `final`. Recall that a `final` field has to be defined by the time the constructor finishes. This guarantees that the field is there when we start to use the object and that it does not change during the object lifetime. Note, however, that the content of the object, in this case, the elements of the `ArrayList`, may change. If it were not the case, we would not be able to sort it.

The next class is `StringComparator`. This is so simple that I will not list it here; I will leave it to you to implement the `java.util.Comparator` interface that can compare two `Strings`. It should not be difficult, especially as this class was already a part of the previous version of the `BubbleSortTest` class (hint—it was an anonymous class that we stored in the variable named `stringCompare`).

We also have to implement `ArrayListSwapper`, which also should not be a big surprise:

```
package packt.java189fundamentals.ch03.main.bubble.simple;

import packt.java189fundamentals.ch03.Swapper;

import java.util.ArrayList;

public class ArrayListSwapper implements Swapper {
    final private ArrayList actualNames;

    ArrayListSwapper(ArrayList actualNames) {
        this.actualNames = actualNames;
    }

    @Override
    public void swap(int i, int j) {
        Object tmp = actualNames.get(i);
        actualNames.set(i, actualNames.get(j));
        actualNames.set(j, tmp);
    }
}
```

Finally, our test will look this:

```
@Test
public void canSortStrings2() {
```

```
        var actualNames = new ArrayList(List.of(
            "Johnson", "Wilson",
            "Wilkinson", "Abraham", "Dagobert"
        ));
        var expectedResult = List.of(
            "Abraham", "Dagobert",
            "Johnson", "Wilkinson", "Wilson"
        );
        var names = new ArrayListSortable(actualNames);
        var sort = new BubbleSort();
        sort.setComparator(new StringComparator());
        sort.setSwapper(new ArrayListSwapper(actualNames));
        sort.sort(names);
        Assert.assertEquals(expectedResult, actualNames);
    }
```

Now, this is already a test that can be understood in 15 seconds. It documents well how to use a sort of implementation that we defined. It still runs and does not reveal any bugs so far.

Collections with wrong elements

A bug is not trivial, and as usual, this is not in the implementation of the algorithm, but rather in the definition, or the lack of it. What should the program do if there are not only strings in the collection that we sort?

If I create a new test that starts with the following lines, it will throw `ClassCastException`:

```
    @Test(expected = ClassCastException.class)
    public void canNotSortMixedElements() {
        var actualNames = new ArrayList(Arrays.asList(
            42, "Wilson",
            "Wilkinson", "Abraham", "Dagobert"
        ));
        //... the rest of the code is the same as the previous test
```

The problem here is that Java collections can contain any type of element. You cannot ever be sure that a collection, such as `ArrayList`, contains only the types that you expect. Even if you use generics (that we will learn about in this chapter), the chances of such a bug are smaller, but it is still there. Don't ask me how; I cannot tell you. This is the nature of the bugs—you cannot tell how they work until you zap them. The thing is that you have to be prepared for such an exceptional case.

Handling exceptions

Exceptional cases should be handled in Java using exceptions. The `ClassCastException` is there and it happens when the sort tries to compare `String` to `Integer` using `StringComparator`, and to do that, it tries to cast an `Integer` to `String`.

When an exception is thrown by the program using the `throw` command, or by the Java runtime, the execution of the program stops at that point, and instead of executing the next command, it continues where the exception is caught. It can be in the same method, or in some calling method up in the call chain. To catch an exception, the code throwing the exception should be inside a `try` block, and the catch statement following the `try` block should specify an exception that is compatible with the exception thrown.

If the exception is not caught, then the Java runtime will print out the message of the exception along with a stack trace that will contain all the classes, methods, and line numbers on the call stack at the time of the exception. In our case, if we remove the `(expected = ClassCastException.class)` argument of the `@Test` annotation, the test execution will produce the following trace in the output:

```
packt.java189fundamentals.ch03.main.bubble.simple.NonStringElementInCollect
ionException: There are mixed elements in the collection.

	at
packt.java189fundamentals.ch03.main.bubble.simple.StringComparator.compare(
StringComparator.java:13)
	at
packt.java189fundamentals.ch03.main.bubble.BubbleSort.sort(BubbleSort.java:
17)
	at
packt.java189fundamentals.ch03.main.bubble.simple.BubbleSortTest.canNotSort
MixedElements(BubbleSortTest.java:108)
	at
java.base/jdk.internal.reflect.NativeMethodAccessorImpl.invoke0(Native
Method)
	at
java.base/jdk.internal.reflect.NativeMethodAccessorImpl.invoke(NativeMethod
AccessorImpl.java:62)
	at
java.base/jdk.internal.reflect.DelegatingMethodAccessorImpl.invoke(Delegati
ngMethodAccessorImpl.java:43)
	at java.base/java.lang.reflect.Method.invoke(Method.java:564)
	at
org.junit.runners.model.FrameworkMethod$1.runReflectiveCall(FrameworkMethod
.java:50)
	at
```

```
org.junit.internal.runners.model.ReflectiveCallable.run(ReflectiveCallable.
java:12)
        at
org.junit.runners.model.FrameworkMethod.invokeExplosively(FrameworkMethod.j
ava:47)
        at
org.junit.internal.runners.statements.InvokeMethod.evaluate(InvokeMethod.ja
va:17)
        at org.junit.runners.ParentRunner.runLeaf(ParentRunner.java:325)
        at
org.junit.runners.BlockJUnit4ClassRunner.runChild(BlockJUnit4ClassRunner.ja
va:78)
        at
org.junit.runners.BlockJUnit4ClassRunner.runChild(BlockJUnit4ClassRunner.ja
va:57)
        at org.junit.runners.ParentRunner$3.run(ParentRunner.java:290)
        at org.junit.runners.ParentRunner$1.schedule(ParentRunner.java:71)
        at
org.junit.runners.ParentRunner.runChildren(ParentRunner.java:288)
        at org.junit.runners.ParentRunner.access$000(ParentRunner.java:58)
        at org.junit.runners.ParentRunner$2.evaluate(ParentRunner.java:268)
        at org.junit.runners.ParentRunner.run(ParentRunner.java:363)
        at org.junit.runner.JUnitCore.run(JUnitCore.java:137)
        at
com.intellij.junit4.JUnit4IdeaTestRunner.startRunnerWithArgs(JUnit4IdeaTest
Runner.java:68)
        at
com.intellij.rt.execution.junit.IdeaTestRunner$Repeater.startRunnerWithArgs
(IdeaTestRunner.java:47)
        at
com.intellij.rt.execution.junit.JUnitStarter.prepareStreamsAndStart(JUnitSt
arter.java:242)
        at
com.intellij.rt.execution.junit.JUnitStarter.main(JUnitStarter.java:70)
Caused by: java.lang.ClassCastException: java.base/java.lang.Integer cannot
be cast to java.base/java.lang.String
        at
packt.java189fundamentals.ch03.main.bubble.simple.StringComparator.compare(
StringComparator.java:9)
        ... 24 more
```

This stack trace is not really long. In the production environment, in an application that runs on an application server, the stack trace may contain a few hundred elements. In this trace, you can see that IntelliJ was starting the test execution involved JUnit runner, until we get through the test to the comparator, where the actual exception was thrown.

The problem with this approach is that the real issue is not the class casting failure. The real issue is that the collection contains mixed elements. It is only realized by the Java runtime when it tries to cast two incompatible classes. Our code can be smarter. We can amend the comparator:

```
public class StringComparator implements Comparator {

    @Override
    public int compare(Object first, Object second) {
        try {
            final String f = (String) first;
            final String s = (String) second;
            return f.compareTo(s);
        } catch (ClassCastException cce) {
            throw new NonStringElementInCollectionException(
                "There are mixed elements in the collection.", cce);
        }
    }
}
```

This code catches the `ClassCastException` and throws a new one. The advantage of throwing a new exception is that you can be sure that this exception is thrown from the comparator and that the problem really is that there are mixed elements in the collection. Class casting problems may happen at other places of the code as well. Some application code may want to catch the exception and want to handle the case; for example, sending an application-specific error message and not dumping only a stack trace to the user. This code can catch `ClassCastException` as well, but it cannot be sure what the real cause of the exception is. On the other hand, `NonStringElementInCollectionException` is definite.

The `NonStringElementInCollectionException` is an exception that does not exist in the JDK. We will have to create it. Exceptions are Java classes, and our exception looks as follows:

```
package packt.java189fundamentals.ch03.main.bubble.simple;

public class NonStringElementInCollectionException extends RuntimeException
{
    public NonStringElementInCollectionException(String message, Throwable
cause) {
        super(message, cause);
    }
}
```

Java has the notion of checked exceptions. It means that any exception that is not extending `RuntimeException` (directly or indirectly) should be declared in the method definition. Suppose our exception was declared as follows:

```
package packt.java189fundamentals.ch03.main.bubble.simple;

public class NonStringElementInCollectionException extends Exception {
    public NonStringElementInCollectionException(String message, Throwable
cause) {
        super(message, cause);
    }
}
```

Then, we could declare the `compare` method as follows:

```
public int compare(Object first, Object second) throws
NonStringElementInCollectionException
```

The problem is that the exception a method throws is part of the method signature, and this way, `compare` will not override the `compare` method of the interface, and that way, the class will not implement the `Comparator` interface. Thus, our exception has to be a runtime exception.

There can be a hierarchy of exceptions in an application, and often, novice programmers create huge hierarchies of them. If there is something you can do, it does not mean that you should do it. Hierarchies should be kept as flat as possible, and this is especially true for exceptions. If there is an exception in the JDK that describes your exceptional case, then use the ready-made exception. This works just as well as for any other class—if it is ready, do not implement it again.

It is also important to note that throwing an exception should only be done in exceptional cases. It is not to signal some normal operational condition. Doing that hinders readability of the code and also consumes CPU. Throwing an exception is not an easy task for the JVM.

It is not only an exception that can be thrown. The `throw` command can throw, and the `catch` command can catch anything that extends the `Throwable` class. There are two subclasses of `Throwable`—`Error`, and `Exception`. An `Error` is thrown if some error happened during the execution of the Java code. The two most infamous errors are `OutOfMemoryError` and `StackOverflowError`. If any of these happen, you cannot do anything reliably to catch them.

There is also `InternalError` and `UnknownError` in the JVM, but since JVM is fairly stable, you will hardly ever meet these errors.

This way, we handled this special case when some programmer accidentally writes 42 among the names, but will it be nicer if the error was identified during compile time? To do that, we will introduce generics.

Just a last thought before we go there. What class behavior do we test with the `canNotSortMixedElements` unit test? The test is inside the `BubbleSortTest` test class, but the functionality is in the comparator implementation, `StringComparator`. This test checks something that is out of the scope of the unit test class. I can use it for demonstration purposes, but this is not a unit test. The real functionality of the sort implementation can be formalized this way—whatever exception the comparator throws is thrown by the sort implementation. You can try to write this unit test, or read on; we will have it in the next section.

The `StringComparator` class does not have a test class because `StringComparator` is part of the test and we will never write a test for a test. Otherwise, we will sink into an endless rabbit hole.

Generics

The generics feature was introduced into Java in version 5. To start with an example, our `Sortable` interface until now was this:

```
public interface Sortable {
    Object get(int i);
    int size();
}
```

After introducing generics, it will be as follows:

```
package packt.java189fundamentals.ch03.generic;

public interface Sortable<E> {
    E get(int i);
    int size();
}
```

The E identifier denotes a type. It can be any type. It says that a class is a sortable collection if it implements the interface, namely the two methods—size and get. The get method should return something that is of type E, whatever E is. This may not make too much sense up until now, but you will soon get the point. After all, generics is a difficult topic.

The Sort interface will become the following:

```
package packt.java189fundamentals.ch03.generic;

public interface Sort<E> {
    void sort(Sortable<E> collection);
}
```

And SortSupport becomes the following:

```
package packt.java189fundamentals.ch03.generic;


import packt.java189fundamentals.ch03.Swapper;

import java.util.Comparator;

public interface SortSupport<E> {
    void setSwapper(Swapper swap);

    void setComparator(Comparator<E> compare);
}
```

This still does not provide much more clarification than the previous version without generics, but, at least, it does something. In the actual class implementing the Sort interface, Comparator should accept the same type that Sortable uses. It is not possible that Sortable works on Strings and we inject a comparator for Integers.

The implementation of BubbleSort is as follows:

```
package packt.java189fundamentals.ch03.main.bubble.generic;

// ... imports were removed from printout ...

public class BubbleSort<E> implements Sort<E>, SortSupport<E> {
    private Comparator<E> comparator = null;
    private Swapper swapper = null;

    @Override
    public void sort(Sortable<E> collection) {
        var n = collection.size();
        while (n > 1) {
```

```
            for (int j = 0; j < n - 1; j++) {
                if (comparator.compare(collection.get(j),
                        collection.get(j + 1)) > 0) {
                    swapper.swap(j, j + 1);
                }
            }
            n--;
        }
    }

    @Override
    public void setComparator(Comparator<E> comparator) {
        this.comparator = comparator;
    }

    @Override
    public void setSwapper(Swapper swapper) {
        this.swapper = swapper;
    }
}
```

The real power of generics will come when we write the tests. The first test does not change much, although, with the generics, it is more definite:

```
    @Test
    public void canSortStrings() {
        var actualNames = new ArrayList<>(List.of(
            "Johnson", "Wilson",
            "Wilkinson", "Abraham", "Dagobert"
        ));
        var expectedResult = List.of(
            "Abraham", "Dagobert",
            "Johnson", "Wilkinson", "Wilson"
        );
        Sortable<String> names =
            new ArrayListSortable<>(actualNames);
        var sort = new BubbleSort<String>();
        sort.setComparator(String::compareTo);
        sort.setSwapper(new ArrayListSwapper<>
        (actualNames));
        sort.sort(names);
        Assert.assertEquals(expectedResult,
        actualNames);
    }
```

When we define `ArrayList`, we will also declare that the elements of the list will be strings. When we allocate the new `ArrayList`, there is no need to specify again that the elements are strings because it comes from the actual elements there. Each of them is a string; therefore, the compiler knows that the only thing that can come between the < and < characters is `String`.

The two characters < and <, without the type definition in-between, is called a **diamond operator**. The type is inferred. If you get used to generics, this code brings you more information on the types that the collections work on and the code becomes more readable. The readability and the extra information is not the only point.

As we know that the `Comparator` argument is `Comparator<String>` now, we can use the advanced features of Java available since Java 8 and can pass the `String::compareTo` method reference to the comparator setter.

The second test is the important one for us now. This is the test which ensures that `Sort` does not interfere with the exception that the comparator throws:

```
@Test
public void throwsWhateverComparatorDoes() {
    final ArrayList<String> actualNames =
        new ArrayList<>(List.of(
            42, "Wilson"
        ));
    final var names = new ArrayListSortable<>
    (actualNames);
    final var sort = new BubbleSort<>();
    final var exception = new RuntimeException();
    sort.setComparator((a, b) -> {
        throw exception;
    });
    final Swapper neverInvoked = null;
    sort.setSwapper(neverInvoked);
    try {
        sort.sort(names);
    } catch (Exception e) {
        Assert.assertSame(exception, e);
        return;
    }
    Assert.fail();
}
```

The thing is, it does not even compile. The compiler says that it cannot infer the type of `ArrayList<>` on the fourth line. When all the arguments of the `asList` method were strings, the method returned a list of `String` elements and therefore the new operator was known to generate `ArrayList<String>`. This time, there is an integer, and thus, the compiler cannot infer that `ArrayList<>` is for `String` elements.

To change the type definition from `ArrayList<>` to `ArrayList<String>` is not a cure. In that case, the compiler will complain about the value `42`. This is the power of generics. When you use classes that have type parameters, the compiler can detect when you provide a value of the wrong type. To get the value into `ArrayList` to check that the implementation really throws an exception, we will have to conjure the value into it. We can try to replace the value `42` with an empty `String` and then add the following line, which will still not compile:

```
actualNames.set(0,42);
```

The compiler will still know that the value you want to set in `ArrayList` is supposed to be `String`. To get the array with the `Integer` element, you will have to explicitly unlock the safety handle and pull the trigger, shooting yourself:

```
((ArrayList)actualNames).set(0,42);
```

We don't do that, even for the sake of the test. We do not want to test the JVM that it recognizes that an `Integer` cannot be cast to a `String`. That test is done by the different Java implementation. What we really test is that whatever exception the comparator throws the sort will throw the same exception.

Now, the test looks like this:

```
@Test
public void throwsWhateverComparatorDoes() {
    final var actualNames =
        new ArrayList<>(List.of(
            "", "Wilson"
        ));
    final var names = new ArrayListSortable<>(actualNames);
    final var sort = new BubbleSort<>();
    final var exception = new RuntimeException();
    sort.setComparator((a, b) -> {
        throw exception;
    });
    final Swapper neverInvoked = null;
    sort.setSwapper(neverInvoked);
    try {
        sort.sort(names);
```

```
        } catch (Exception e) {
            Assert.assertSame(exception, e);
            return;
        }
        Assert.fail();
    }
```

Now, we changed the declaration of the variable `actualNames` to `var` so that type is inferred from the right-hand side expression. In this case, it is `ArrayList<String>`, and the generic `String` parameter is inferred from the list created calling `List.of()`. This method also has generic parameters and thus we could write `List.<String>of()`. In this call, however, this generic parameter is inferred from the arguments. All arguments are strings, thus the returned list is `List<String>`. In the previous example that did not compile, the created list had the type `List<Object>`. This was incompatible with the declaration on the left-hand side, and the compiler complained about it. If we use `var` for the variable declaration, the compiler cannot detect this error at this point and we will have a `List<Object>` variable instead of `List<String>`.

We set the Swapper to be `null` because it is never invoked. When I first wrote this code, that was evident to me. A few days later, I read the code and I stopped. *Why is swapper null?* Then I remembered in a second or two. But anytime, when reading and understanding the code hicks up, I tend to think about refactoring. I can add a comment to the line saying `//never invoked`, but comments tend to remain there even when functionality changes. I learned it the hard way in 2006, when a wrong comment prevented me from seeing how the code was executing. I was reading the comment while debugging, instead of the code, and bug fixing took two days while the system was down. Instead of a comment, I tend to use constructs that make the code express what happens. The extra variable may make the class file a few bytes bigger, but it is optimized out by the JIT compiler so the final code does not run slower.

The comparator that throws an exception was provided as a lambda expression. Lambda expressions can be used in cases where an anonymous class or named class would be used having only one simple method. Lambda expressions are anonymous methods stored in variables or passed in arguments for later invocation. We will discuss the details of lambda expressions in `Chapter 8`, *Extending our E-Commerce Application*.

For now, we will go on implementing `QuickSort`, and to do that, we will use the TDD methodology.

Test-Driven Development

TDD is a code-writing approach where the developers first write a test based on the specification and then write the code. This is just the opposite of what the developer community has been used to. The conventional approach that we followed was to write the code and then write tests for it. To be honest, the real practice was to write the code and test it with adhoc tests and no unit tests at all. Being a professional, you will never do that, by the way. You always write tests. (And now, write it down a hundred times—I will always write tests.)

One of the advantages of TDD is that the tests do not depend on the code. As the code does not exist at the creation of the test, developers cannot rely on the implementation of the unit and, thus, it cannot influence the test creation process. This is generally good. Unit tests should be black-box tests as much as possible.

A black-box test is a test that does not take into account the implementation of the tested system. If a system is refactored, implemented in a different way, but the interface it provides to the external world is the same, then the black-box tests should run just fine. A white-box test depends on the internal working of the system tested. When the code changes the white-box test, the code may also need tuning to follow the change. The advantage of a white-box test can be the simpler test code. Not always. The gray-box test is a mixture of the two.

Unit tests are supposed to be black-box tests, but, many times, it is not simple to write a black-box test. Developers will write a test that they think is black-box, but many times, this belief proves to be false. When the implementation changes, something is refactored and the test does not work anymore, and it needs to be corrected. It just happens that knowing the implementation, the developers, especially those who wrote the unit, will write a test that depends on the internal working of the code. Writing the test before the code is a tool to prevent this. If there is no code, you cannot depend on it.

TDD also says that the development should be an iterative approach. You write only one test at the start. If you run, it fails. Of course, it fails! As there is no code yet, it has to fail. Then, you will write the code that fulfills this test. Nothing more, only the code that makes this test pass. Then, you will go on writing a new test for another part of the specification. You will run it and it fails. This proves that the new test tests something that was not developed yet. Then, you will develop the code to satisfy the new test and, possibly, you will also modify a block of code that you have already written in the previous iterations. When the code is ready, the tests will pass.

Many times, developers are reluctant to modify the code. This is because they are afraid of breaking something that was already working. When you follow TDD, you should not, and at the same time, you need not be afraid of this. There are tests for all features that were already developed. If some of the code modification breaks some functionality, the tests will immediately signal the error. The key is that you run the tests as often as possible when the code is modified.

Implementing QuickSort

Quicksort, as we have already discussed, is made of two major parts. One is partitioning and the other one is doing the partitioning recursively until the whole array is sorted. To make our code modular and ready to demonstrate the JPMS module-handling feature, we will develop the partitioning and the recursive sorting into separate classes and in a separate package. The complexity of the code will not justify this separation.

The partitioning class

The partitioning class should provide a method that moves the elements of the collection based on a pivot element, and we will need to know the position of the pivot element after the method finishes. The signature of the method should look something like this:

```
public int partition(Sortable<E> sortable, int start, int end, E pivot);
```

The class should also have access to `Swapper` and `Comparator`. In this case, we defined a class and not an interface; therefore, we will use the constructor injection.

These constructs, like setters and constructor injectors, are so common and happen so frequently that IDEs support the generation of these. You will need to create the `final` fields in the code and use the *code generation* menu to create the constructor.

The partitioning class will look like the following:

```
public class Partitioner<E> {

    private final Comparator<E> comparator;
    private final Swapper swapper;

    public Partitioner(Comparator<E> comparator, Swapper swapper) {
        this.comparator = comparator;
        this.swapper = swapper;
    }
```

```
    public int partition(Sortable<E> sortable, int start, int end, E pivot)
{
        return 0;
    }
}
```

This code does nothing, but that is how TDD starts. We will create the definition of a requirement providing the skeleton of the code and the test that will call it. To do that, we will need something that we can partition. The simplest choice is an `Integer` array. The `partition` method needs an object of type `Sortable<E>`, and we will need something that wraps the array and implements this interface. We name that class `ArrayWrapper`. This is a general-purpose class. It is not only for the test. Because of that, we create it as production code, and as such, we put it in the `main` directory and not in the `test` directory. As this wrapper is independent of the implementation of `Sort`, the proper position of this class is in a new `SortSupportClasses` module. We will create the new module as it is not part of the interface. Implementations depend on the interface, but not on the support classes. There can also be some application that uses our libraries and may need the interface module and some of the implementation, but still does not need the support classes when they deliver the wrapping functionality themselves. After all, we cannot implement all possible wrapping functionality. The SRP also holds for the modules.

Java libraries tend to contain unrelated functionality implementations. This is no good. For the short run, it makes the use of the library simpler. You will only need to specify one dependency in your POM file, and you will have all the classes and APIs that you need. In the long run, the application gets bigger, carrying a lot of classes that are part of some of the libraries, but the application never uses them.

To add the new module, the module directory has to be created along with the source directories and the POM file. The module has to be added to the parent POM and it also has to be added to the `dependencyManagement` section so that the test code of the `QuickSort` module can use it without specifying the version. The new module depends on the interface module, so this dependency has to be added to the POM of the support classes.

The `ArrayWrapper` class is simple and general:

```
package packt.java189fundamentals.ch03.support;

import packt.java189fundamentals.ch03.generic.Sortable;

public class ArrayWrapper<E> implements Sortable<E> {
    private final E[] array;

    public ArrayWrapper(E[] array) {
        this.array = array;
```

```
    }

    public E[] getArray() {
        return array;
    }

    @Override
    public E get(int i) {
        return array[i];
    }

    @Override
    public int size() {
        return array.length;
    }
}
```

The `ArraySwapper` class, which we also need, comes into the same module. It is just as simple as the wrapper:

```
package packt.java189fundamentals.ch03.support;

import packt.java189fundamentals.ch03.Swapper;

public class ArraySwapper<E> implements Swapper {
    private final E[] array;

    public ArraySwapper(E[] array) {
        this.array = array;
    }

    @Override
    public void swap(int k, int r) {
        final E tmp = array[k];
        array[k] = array[r];
        array[r] = tmp;
    }
}
```

Having these classes, we can create our first test:

```
package packt.java189fundamentals.ch03.qsort.phase1;

// ... imports deleted from print ...

public class PartitionerTest {
```

Before creating the `@Test` method, we will need two helper methods that make assertions. Assertions are not always simple, and in some cases, they may involve some coding. The general rule is that the test and the assertions in it should be as simple as possible; otherwise, they are just a possible source of programming errors. Additionally, we created them to avoid programming errors, not to create new ones.

The `assertSmallElements` method asserts that all elements before `cutIndex` are smaller than `pivot`:

```
private void assertSmallElements(Integer[] array, int cutIndex, Integer
pivot) {
    for (int i = 0; i < cutIndex; i++) {
        Assert.assertTrue(array[i] < pivot);
    }
}
```

The `assertLargeElements` method makes sure that all elements following `cutIndex` are at least as large as `pivot`:

```
private void assertLargeElements(Integer[] array, int cutIndex, Integer
pivot) {
    for (int i = cutIndex; i < array.length; i++) {
        Assert.assertTrue(pivot <= array[i]);
    }
}
```

The test uses a constant array of `Integers` and wraps it into an `ArrayWrapper` class:

```
@Test
public void partitionsIntArray() {
    final var partitionThis = new Integer[]{0, 7, 6};
    final var swapper = new ArraySwapper<> \
    (partitionThis);
    final var partitioner =
            new Partitioner<Integer>(
                    (a, b) -> a < b ? -1 : a > b ? +1 : 0,
                     swapper);
    final Integer pivot = 6;
    final int cutIndex = partitioner.partition(
       new ArrayWrapper<>(partitionThis), 0, 2, pivot);
    Assert.assertEquals(1, cutIndex);
    assertSmallElements(partitionThis, cutIndex, pivot);
    assertLargeElements(partitionThis, cutIndex, pivot);
}
```

There is no `Comparator` for the `Integer` type in the JDK, but it is easy to define one as a lambda function. Now, we can write the `partition` method, as follows:

```
public int partition(Sortable<E> sortable,
                     int start,
                     int end,
                     E pivot) {
    var small = start;
    var large = end;
    while (large > small) {
        while(comparator.compare(sortable.get(small), pivot) < 0
                && small < large) {
            small++;
        }
        while(comparator.compare(sortable.get(large), pivot) >= 0
                && small < large) {
            large--;
        }
        if (small < large) {
            swapper.swap(small, large);
        }
    }
    return large;
}
```

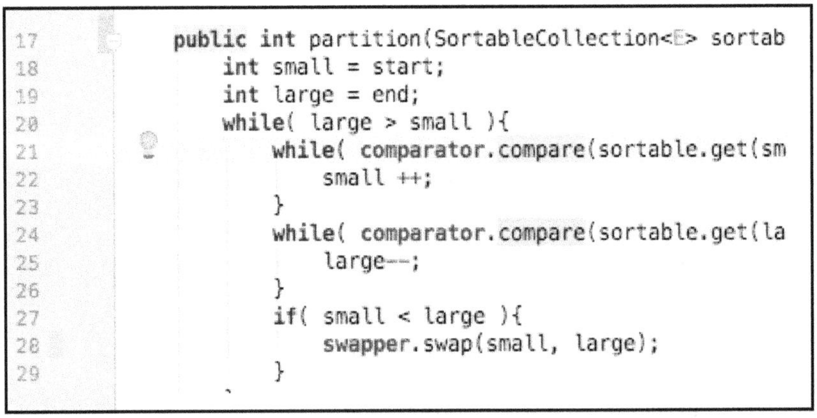

```
    public int partition(SortableCollection<E> sortab
        int small = start;
        int large = end;
        while( large > small ){
            while( comparator.compare(sortable.get(sm
                small ++;
            }
            while( comparator.compare(sortable.get(la
                large--;
            }
            if( small < large ){
                swapper.swap(small, large);
            }
```

If we run the test, it runs fine. However, if we run the test with coverage, then the IDE tells us that the coverage is only 92%. The test covered only 13 of the 14 lines of the `partition` method.

There is a red rectangle on the gutter at line **17**. This is because the test array is already partitioned. There is no need to swap any element in it when the pivot value is `6`. It means that our test is good, but not good enough. What if there is an error on that line?

To amend this problem, we will extend the test, changing the test array from `{0, 7, 6 }` to `{0, 7, 6, 2}`. Run the test and it will fail. Why? After some debugging, we will realize that we invoke the method `partition` with the fixed parameter `2` as the last index of the array. But, we made the array longer. Why did we write a constant there in the first place? It is a bad practice. Let's replace it with `partitionThis.length-1`. Now, it says that `cutIndex` is `2`, but we expected `1`. We forgot to adjust the assertion to the new array. Let's fix it. Now it works.

The last thing is to rethink the assertions. The less code the better. The assertion methods are quite general, and we will use it for one single test array. The assertion methods are so complex that they deserve their own test. But, we do not write code to test a test. Instead, we can simply delete the methods and have the final version of the test as follows:

```
@Test
public void partitionsIntArray() {
    final var partitionThis = new Integer[]{0, 7, 6, 2};
    final var swapper = new ArraySwapper<>(partitionThis);
    final var partitioner =
            new Partitioner<Integer>(
        (a, b) -> a < b ? -1 : a > b ? +1 : 0, swapper);
    final var pivot = 6;
    final var cutIndex = partitioner.partition(
            new ArrayWrapper<>(partitionThis),
            0,
            partitionThis.length - 1,
            pivot);
    Assert.assertEquals(2, cutIndex);
    final var expected = new Integer[]{0, 2, 6, 7};
    Assert.assertArrayEquals(expected, partitionThis);
}
```

And then again, is this a black-box test? What if the partitioning returns `{2, 1, 7, 6}`? It fits the definition. We can create more complex tests to cover such cases. But a more complex test may also have a bug in the test itself. As a different approach, we can create tests that may be simpler but rely on the internal structure of the implementation. These are not black-box tests and thus not ideal unit tests. I will go for the second one, but I will not argue if someone chooses the other.

Recursive sorting

We will implement the quicksort with an extra class that is in the `qsort` package along with the partitioning class, which is as follows:

```
package packt.java189fundamentals.ch03.qsort;

// ... imports are deleted from print ...
public class Qsort<E> {
    final private Comparator<E> comparator;
    final private Swapper swapper;
// ... constructor setting fields deleted from print ...
    public void qsort(Sortable<E> sortable, int start, int end) {
        if (start < end) {
            final var pivot = sortable.get(start);
            final var partitioner = new Partitioner<E>(comparator,
swapper);
            var cutIndex = partitioner.partition(sortable, start, end,
pivot);
            if (cutIndex == start) {
                cutIndex++;
            }
            qsort(sortable, start, cutIndex - 1);
            qsort(sortable, cutIndex, end);
        }
    }
}
```

The method gets `Sortable<E>` and two index parameters. It does not sort the whole collection; it sorts only the elements between the `start` and the `end` index.

It is always important to be extremely precise with the indexing. Usually, there is no problem with the start index in Java, but a lot of bugs source from how the `end` index is interpreted. In this method, the value of `end` can mean that the index is already not part of the to-be-sorted interval. In that case, the `partition` method should be invoked with `end-1` and the first recursive call with `end-1` as the last parameter. It is a matter of taste. The important thing is to be precise and define the interpretation of index parameters.

If there is only one `(start == end)` element, then there is nothing to be sorted and the method returns. This is the end criterion of the recursion. The method also assumes that the `end` index is never smaller than the `start` index. As this method is used only inside the library that we are developing at the moment, such an assumption is not too risky to make.

If there is something to be sorted, then the method takes the first element of the to-be-sorted interval and uses it as a pivot and calls the `partition` method. When the partition is done, the method recursively calls itself for the two halves.

This algorithm is recursive. This means that the method calls itself. When a method call is executed, the processor allocates some memory in an area called **stack** and it stores the local variables there. This area that belongs to the method in the stack is called the **stack frame**. When the method returns, this area is released and the stack is restored, simply moving the stack pointer where it was before the call. This way, a method can continue its execution after calling another method; the local variables are there.

When a method calls itself, it is not different. The local variables are local to the actual call of the method. When the method calls itself, it allocates space for the local variables again on the stack. In other words, these are new *instances* of the local variables.

We use recursive methods in Java, and in other programming languages when the definition of the algorithm is recursive, it is extremely important to understand that when the processor code runs; it is not recursive anymore. On that level, there are instructions, registers, and memory loads and jumps. There is nothing like a function or method and therefore, on that level, there is nothing like recursion.

If you get that, it is easy to understand that any recursion can be coded as a loop.

As a matter of fact, it is also true the other way around—every loop can be coded as recursion, but that is not really interesting until you start functional programming.

The problem with the recursion in Java, and in many other programming languages, is that it may run out of stack space. For quicksort, this is not the case. You can safely assume that the stack for method calling in Java is a few hundreds of levels. Quicksort needs a stack that is approximately log_2n deep, where n is the number of elements to be sorted. In the case of one billion elements, this is 30, that should just fit.

Why is the stack not moved or resized? That is because the code that runs out of the stack space is usually bad style. They can be expressed in more readable form in the form of some loop. An even more robust stack implementation would only lure the novice programmer to do some less readable recursive coding.

There is a special case of recursion named tail recursion. A tail recursive method calls itself as the last instruction of the method. When the recursive call returns the code, the calling method does nothing else but release the stack frame that was used for this method invocation. In other words, we will keep the stack frame during the recursive call just to throw it right away afterward. Why not throw it away before the call? In that case, the actual frame will be reallocated because this is just the same method that is kept, and the recursive call is transformed into a jump instruction. This is an optimization that Java does not do. Functional languages are doing it, but Java is not really a functional language and therefore tail-recursive functions should rather be avoided and transformed to a loop in the Java source level.

Non-recursive sorting

To demonstrate that even non-tail recursive methods can be expressed in a non-recursive way, here is the quicksort that way:

```
public class NonRecursiveQuickSort<E> {
// ... same fields and constructor as in Qsort are
deleted from print ...

    private static class StackElement {
        final int begin;
        final int fin;

        public StackElement(int begin, int fin) {
            this.begin = begin;
            this.fin = fin;
        }
    }

    public void qsort(Sortable<E> sortable, int
    start, int end) {
        final var stack = new
    LinkedList<StackElement>();
        final var partitioner = new Partitioner<E>
        (comparator, swapper);
        stack.add(new StackElement(start, end));
        var i = 1;
        while (!stack.isEmpty()) {
            var it = stack.remove(0);
            if (it.begin < it.fin) {
                final E pivot =
                sortable.get(it.begin);
                var cutIndex =
          partitioner.partition(sortable, it.begin,
```

```
                  it.fin, pivot);
24.                     if( cutIndex == it.begin ){
25.                         cutIndex++;
26.                     }
27.                     stack.add(new StackElement(it.begin,
                         cutIndex - 1));
28.                     stack.add(new StackElement(cutIndex,
                         it.fin));
29.                 }
30.             }
31.         }
32. }
```

This code implements a stack on the Java level. While it seems that there is still something scheduled to be sorted in `stack`, it fetches it from the stack and does the sort partitioning, and schedules the two parts for being sorted.

This code is more complex than the previous one and you have to understand the role of the `StackElement` class and how it works. On the other hand, the program uses only one instance of the `Partitioner` class and it is also possible to use a thread pool to schedule the subsequent sorts instead of handling the tasks in a single process. This may speed up the sort when it is executed on a multi-CPU machine. However, this is a bit more complex task and this chapter contains a lot of new things without multitasking; therefore, we will look at multithreaded code in two chapters later only.

In the very first version of the sort, I was coding it without the three lines that compare `cutIndex` against the interval start and increments it in the `if` branch (lines 24-26). It is needed a lot. But, the unit tests we created in this book do not discover the bug if we miss those lines. I recommend that you just delete those lines and try to write some unit tests that fail. Then, try to understand what the special case is when those lines are vital and try to modify your unit test so that it is the simplest possible that still discovers that bug. (Finally, put the four lines back and see if the code works.) Additionally, find some architectural reason why not to put this modification into the method `partition`. That method could just return `large+1` in the case of `large == start`.

Implementing the API class

Having done all this, the last thing we will need is to have `QuickSort` as a simple class (all the real work was already done in different classes):

```
public class QuickSort<E> extends AbstractSort<E> {
    public void sort(Sortable<E> sortable) {
        final var n = sortable.size();
        final var qsort = new Qsort<E>(comparator,swapper);
        qsort.qsort(sortable, 0, n-1);
    }
}
```

Do not forget that we also need a test! But, in this case, that is not much different than that of `BubbleSort`:

```
    @Test
    public void canSortStrings() {
        final var actualNames = new String[]{
                "Johnson", "Wilson",
                "Wilkinson", "Abraham", "Dagobert"
        };
        final var expected = new String[]{"Abraham",
                "Dagobert", "Johnson", "Wilkinson", "Wilson"};
        var sort = new QuickSort<String>();
        sort.setComparator(String::compareTo);
        sort.setSwapper(new ArraySwapper<>(actualNames));
        sort.sort(new ArrayWrapper<>(actualNames));
        Assert.assertArrayEquals(expected, actualNames);
    }
```

This time, we used `String` array instead of `ArrayList`. This makes this test simpler and, this time, we already have the support classes.

You may recognize that this is not a unit test. In the case of `BubbleSort`, the algorithm was implemented in a single class. Testing that single class is a unit test. In the case of `QuickSort`, we separated the functionality into separate classes, and even into separate packages. A real unit test of the `QuickSort` class will disclose the dependency of that class on other classes. When this test runs, it involves the execution of `Partitioner` and also `Qsort`; therefore, it is not really a unit test.

Should we bother about that? Not really. We want to create unit tests that involve a single unit to know where the problem is when a unit test fails. If there were only integration tests, a failing test case would not help a lot in pointing out where the problem is. All it says is that there is some problem in the classes that are involved in the test. In this case, there are only a limited number of classes (three) that are involved in this test, and they are tied together. They are actually tied together and related to each other so closely that in the real production code, I would have implemented them in a single module. I separated them here to demonstrate how to test a single unit and also to demonstrate Java module support that needs a bit more than a single class in a JAR file.

Creating modules

Module handling, also known as project **Jigsaw,** or **JPMS**, is a feature that was made available only in Java 9. It was a long-planned feature. First, it was planned for Java 7, but it was so complex that it got postponed to Java 8 and then to Java 9. Finally, JPMS was included in the release 9 of Java. The same time Oracle introduced the notion of long-term and also short-term support releases. A short-term release is supported only until the next version of the language is released. The long-term releases, on the other hand, are supported for a longer time, many times even years after the new version or even new long-term supported version is released. Before Java 9, all releases were long-term support releases. Oracle was creating with new minor versions if there was any significant bug that affected the stability or the security of the applications. There were even new versions created for Java 1.6 when Java 1.8 was available.

That time ORACLE declared that Java 9 and 10 will not be long-term supported releases. However, Java 11, or Java 18.9, numbered according to the new versioning scheme, is a long-term support release and as such, it is the first long-term supported release that has **JPMS** implemented.

Why modules are needed

We have already seen that there are four levels of access in Java. A method or field can be `private`, `protected`, `public`, or `default` (also known as package private) when no modifier is supplied inside a class. When you develop a complex library to be used in several projects, the library itself will contain many classes in many packages. There will certainly be classes and methods, fields in those that are supposed to be used solely inside the library by other classes from different packages. These classes are not to be used by the code outside the library. Making them anything less visible than `public` will render them unusable inside the library. Making them `public` will make them visible from outside. This is not good.

In our code, the Maven module `quick` compiled into a JAR can only be used if the method sort can invoke `qsort`. But, we do not want `qsort` to be used directly from outside. In the next version, we may want to develop a version of the sort that uses `qsort` from the `NonRecursiveQuickSort` class, and we do not want complaining customers whose code does not compile or work because of a minor library upgrade. We can document that the internal methods and classes, which are public are not for use, but in vain. Developers using our library do not read the documentation. This is also why we do not write excessive comments. Nobody will read it, not even the processor executing the code.

What is a Java module?

A Java module is a collection of classes in a JAR or in a directory that also contains a special class named `module-info`. If there is this file in a JAR or directory, then it is a module, otherwise, it is just a collection of classes that are on the `classpath` (or not). Java 8, and the earlier versions will just ignore that class as it is never used as code. This way, using older Java, causes no harm, and backwards compatibility is maintained.

To create such a JAR is a bit tricky. The `module-info.class` file should have bytecode that conforms to Java 9 bytecode or later, but the other classes should contain older version bytecodes.

The module information defines what the module exports and what it requires. It has a special format. For example, we can place `module-info.java` in our `SortInterface` Maven module:

```
module packt.java189fundamentals.SortInterface{
    exports packt.java189fundamentals.ch03;
    exports packt.java189fundamentals.ch03.generic;
}
```

This means that any class that is `public` and inside the `packt.java189fundamentals.ch03` package can be used from outside. This package is exported from the module, but other classes from other packages are not visible from the outside of the module, even if they are `public`. The naming requirement is the same as in the case of packages—there should be a name that is not likely to collide with other module names. The reverse domain name is a good choice, but it is not a must, as you can see in this book. There is no top-level domain `packt`, yet.

We should also modify the parent POM to ensure that the compiler we use is Java 9 or later configuring the Maven compiler plugin at `project/build/plugins/`:

```
<plugin>
    <groupId>org.apache.maven.plugins</groupId>
    <artifactId>maven-compiler-plugin</artifactId>
    <version>3.7.0</version>
    <configuration>
        <source>1.10</source>
        <target>1.10</target>
    </configuration>
    <dependencies>
        <dependency>
            <groupId>org.ow2.asm</groupId>
            <artifactId>asm</artifactId>
            <version>6.1.1</version>
        </dependency>
    </dependencies>
</plugin>
```

Older versions would be confused with the `module-info.java` file. (By the way, even the early access version of Java 9 I used for the first edition of this book sometimes gave me a hard time.)

We also create a `module-info.java` file in the Maven module, `quick`, which is as follows:

```
module packt.java189fundamentals.quick {
    exports packt.java189fundamentals.ch03.quick;
    requires packt.java189fundamentals.SortInterface;
    }
```

This module exports another package and requires the `packt.java189fundamentals.SortInterface` module that we have just created. Now, we can compile the modules and the created JARs in the `./quick/target` and `./SortInterface/target` directories, are now Java modules.

To test the functionality of module support, we will create another Maven module called `Main`. It has only one class, called `Main`, with a `public static void main` method:

```
package packt.java189fundamentals.ch03.main;

// ... imports are deleted from print ...

public class Main {
    public static void main(String[] args) throws IOException {
        final var fileName = args[0];
        BufferedReader br = null;
        try {
            br = new BufferedReader(new InputStreamReader(new
FileInputStream(new File(fileName))));
            final var lines = new LinkedList<String>();
            String line;
            while ((line = br.readLine()) != null) {
                lines.add(line);
            }
            String[] lineArray = lines.toArray(new String[0]);
            var sort = new FQuickSort<String>();
            sort.setComparator((a, b) -> ((String) a).compareTo((String)
b));
            sort.setSwapper(new ArraySwapper<>(lineArray));
            sort.sort(new ArrayWrapper<>(lineArray));
            for (final String outLine : lineArray) {
                System.out.println(outLine);
            }
        } finally {
            if (br != null) {
                br.close();
            }
        }
    }
}
```

It takes the first argument (without checking that there is one, which we should not use in a production code) and uses that as a file name. Then, it reads the lines of the file into a `String` array, sorts it, and prints it to the standard output.

As the module support only works for modules, this Maven module also has to be a Java module and has a `module-info.java` file:

```
module packt.java189fundamentals.Main{
    requires packt.java189fundamentals.quick;
    requires packt.java189fundamentals.SortInterface;
    requires packt.java189fundamentals.SortSupportClasses;
}
```

Additionally, we will have to create a `module-info.java` file for the support module; otherwise, we will not be able to use it from our module.

After compiling the modules using `mvn install`, we can run it to print the lines of a file sorted. For example, we can print out the lines of the parent POM sorted, that does not make much sense, but it is fun. Here is the Windows command file that starts the Java code:

```
set MODULE_PATH=Main/target/Main-1.0.0-SNAPSHOT.jar;
set MODULE_PATH=%MODULE_PATH%SortInterface/target/SortInterface-1.0.0-
SNAPSHOT.jar;
set MODULE_PATH=%MODULE_PATH%quick/target/quick-1.0.0-SNAPSHOT.jar;
set
MODULE_PATH=%MODULE_PATH%SortSupportClasses/target/SortSupportClasses-1.0.0
-SNAPSHOT.jar
java -p %MODULE_PATH% -m
packt.java189fundamentals.Main/packt.java189fundamentals.ch03.main.Main
pom.xml
```

The JAR files get on the module path, which is given to the Java execution using the command-line option `-p`. To start the `public static void main()` method of a class that is in a module, it is not enough anymore to specify the fully qualified name of the class. We have to use the `-m` option followed by a `module/class` formatted specification of the module and the class.

Now, if we try to access `Qsort` directly inserting the following line, `Qsort<String> qsort = new Qsort<>(String::compareTo,new ArraySwapper<>(lineArray));` into the `main` method, Maven will complain because the module system hides it from our `Main` class.

The module system also supports the `java.util.ServiceLoader`-based class-loading mechanism, which we will not discuss in this book. This is an old technology that is rarely used in an enterprise environment when Spring, Guice, or some other dependency injection framework is used. If you see a `module-info.java` file that contains the `uses` and `provides` keywords, then first consult with the Java documentation about the `ServiceLoader` class at `http://docs.oracle.com/javase/8/docs/api/java/util/ServiceLoader.html`, and then the Java 9 language documentation on module support (`http://openjdk.java.net/projects/jigsaw/quick-start`).

Summary

In this chapter, we developed a general sorting algorithm implementing quicksort. We modified our project to be a multi-module Maven project and also to use Java module definitions. We were using JUnit to develop unit tests, and we developed the code using TDD. We converted the code from old-style Java to new using generics, and we used exception handling. These are the basic tools that are needed for the coming chapters, where we will develop a guessing game. First, we will develop a simpler version, and in the subsequent chapter, we will develop a version that uses parallel computing and multiple processors.

4
Mastermind - Creating a Game

In this chapter, we will start to develop a simple game. The game is Mastermind, for two players. Player one selects four differently colored pins out of six possible colors and arranges them on a board in a row hidden from the other player. The other player tries to guess the colors of the pins and their positions. On each guess, player one guesses the number of matching colors and the pins matching both color and position. The program will act as both player one and player two. Our code will play alone. However, what remains for us to play with is the most important thing—the code.

This example is complex enough to deepen the **Object-Oriented** (**OO**) principles and how we design classes and model the real world. We have already used the classes provided in the Java runtime. This time, we will use collections and discuss this important area. These classes and interfaces are widely used and available in the JDK and are as important for a professional Java developer as the language itself.

The build tool this time is Gradle.

In this chapter, we will cover the following:

- Java collections
- Dependency injection
- How to comment our code and create JavaDoc documentation
- How to create integration tests

The game

Mastermind (`https://en.wikipedia.org/wiki/Mastermind_(board_game)`) is an old game. The plastic version ubiquitous in every house with children was invented in 1970. I got a board around 1980 as a Christmas gift, and a program for solving the game puzzle in the BASIC language was one of the first programs that I created, in around 1984.

The game board contains holes in several rows in four columns. There are plastic pins of six different colors that can be inserted into the holes. Each pin has one color. They are usually red, green, blue, yellow, black, and white. There is a special row that is hidden from one of the players (the guesser).

To play the game, one of the players (hider) has to select four pins from a set of pins. The selected pins should have different colors. The pins are placed in the hidden row, one by one, each into a position.

The guesser tries to find out what colors are in which position, guessing. Each guess selects four pins and places them in a row. The hider tells the guesser how many pins are in correct position and how many have a color that is on the table but are not in the correct position:

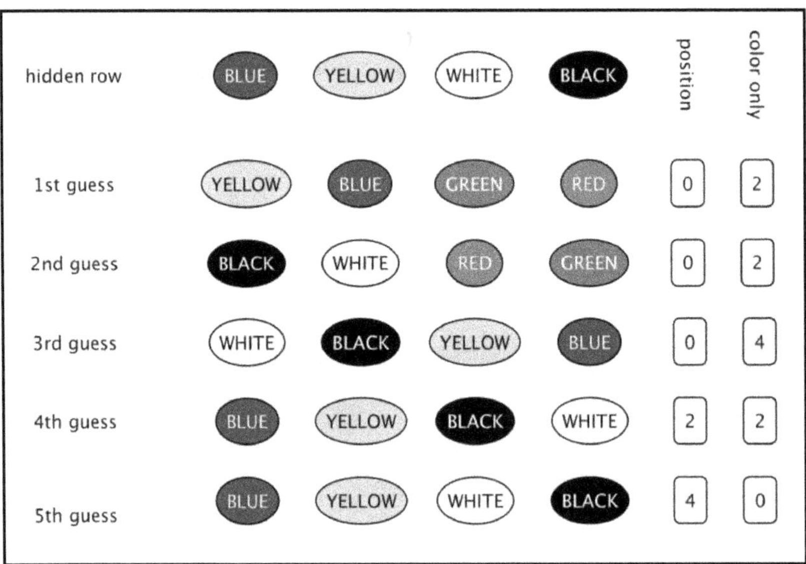

A sample play may go like this:

1. The hider hides four pins with the colors blue, yellow, white, and black.
2. The guesser guesses yellow, blue, green, and red.

3. The hider tells the guesser that there are two colors matching, but none of them are in the correct position in the hidden row. The hider says this because yellow and blue are in the hidden row but not in the positions as the guesser guessed. They are actually swapped, but this information the hider keeps a secret. All they say is that there are two colors matching, none in the correct position.
4. The next guess is ...

The game finishes when the guesser finds the correct colors in the correct order. The same game can also be described with textual notation—`B` for blue, `Y` for yellow, `G` for green, `W` for white, `R` for red, and `b` for black (luckily, we have upper and lower case letters on the computer):

```
RGBY 0/0

GRWb 0/2
YBbW 0/2
BYGR 0/4
RGYB 2/2
RGBY 4/0
```

Guess what! This is the actual output of the program that we'll develop in this chapter.

We also played the game, allowing a position to be empty. This essentially is the same as having a seventh color. When we found that the game is too simple, even with seven colors, we changed the rules to allow colors to appear at different positions. These are all valid variations of the game.

In this chapter, we will use six colors and no color repetitions in the hidden row. The other versions of the game are a bit more complex to program, but they are essentially the same, and solving those variations would not add to our learning experience.

The model of the game

When we develop a piece of code with an OO mindset, we try to model the real world and map real-world objects to objects in the program. You certainly have heard object orientation explained with the very typical examples of geometric objects, or the car and the motor thing to explain composition. Personally, I believe that these examples are too simple to get a good understanding. They may be good for starters, but we are already in the fourth chapter of this book. The Mastermind game is much better. It is a bit more complex than just rectangles and triangles, but not as complex as a telecom billing application or an atomic power plant control.

What are the real-world objects that we have in this game? We have a table and we have pins of different colors. There are two Java classes that we certainly will need. What is in a table? There are rows each having four positions. Perhaps we will need a class for a row. A table will have rows. We will also need something that hides the secret. This also may be a row, and each row may also hold the information about how many positions and how many colors are matching. In the case of the secret row, this information is obvious—4 and 0.

What is a pin? Each pin has a color and, generally, that is it. There are no other features of a pin, except that it can be inserted into a hole on the table, but this is a real-life feature we will not model. Essentially, a pin is a color and nothing else. This way, we can eliminate the pin class from our model early on, even before we have created it in Java. Instead, we have colors.

What is a color? This is something that may be hard to immerse into the first time. We all know well what a color is. It is a mixture of different frequencies of lights, as our eyes perceive it. We can have paints and prints in different colors, and so on. There are many things that we do not model in this program. It is really hard to tell what we model about color in our code because these features are so obvious that we take it for granted in real life; we can tell that two colors are different. This is the only feature we need. To do this, the simplest class of Java can be used:

```
public class Color {
}
```

If you have two variables of the type `Color`, you can tell whether they are the same or not. You can use object identity comparing `a` and `b` using the expression `a == b`, or you can use the `equals()` method inherited from the `Object` class, `a.equals(b)`. It is tempting to encode the colors with letters or use `String` constants to denote them. It may be easier first, but there are serious drawbacks later. When the code becomes complex, it leads to bugs; it will be easy to pass something also encoded as a `String` instead of a color, and only unit tests may save the day. This is better than the compiler already complaining in the IDE when you type the wrong argument.

When we play the game, the pins are in small boxes. We pull pins out of the boxes. How do we get the colors in the program? We need something from where we can fetch colors. Or looking at it the other way, we need something that can give us colors. We will call it `ColorManager`. Now, `ColorManager` knows how many different colors we have, and any time we need a color, we can ask for it.

Again, there is a temptation to design `ColorManager` so that it can serve a color by its serial number. If we have four colors, we could ask for color numbers 0, 1, 2, or 3. But then again, it would just implicitly encode the colors as integer numbers, which we agreed we will not do. We should find the minimum feature that we will need to model the game.

To describe the structure of the classes, professional developers usually use **Unified Modeling Language** (**UML**) class diagrams. UML is a diagram notation that is standardized and is almost exclusively used to visualize software architecture. There are many diagram types in UML to describe the static structure and the dynamic behavior of a program. This time, we will look at a very simplified class diagram:

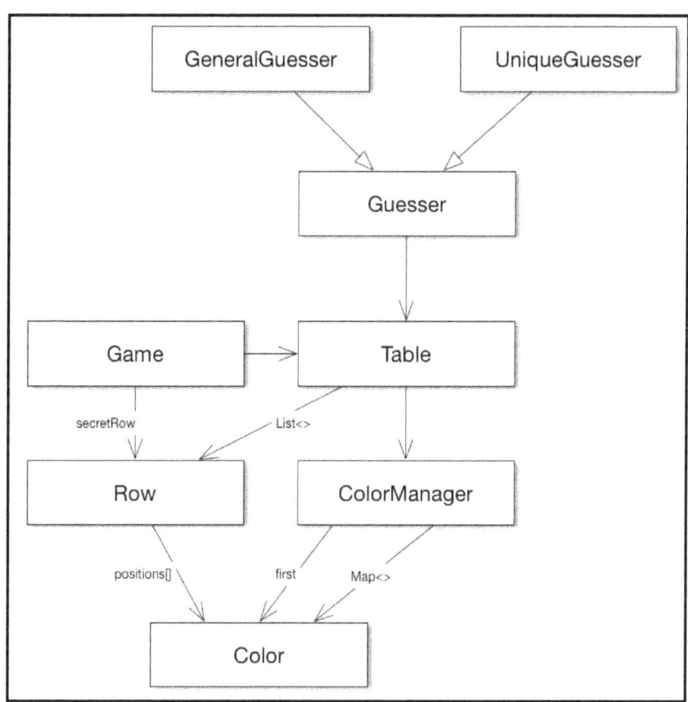

We have no room to get into the details of UML class diagrams. Rectangles denote the classes, normal arrows denote the relations when a class has a field of the other class type, and a triangle-headed arrow means that a class extends another. The arrow points to the direction of the class being extended.

A **Game** class contains a secret **Row** class and a **Table** class. **Table** has a **ColorManager** class and a `List<>` of **Row** classes. **ColorManager** has a first color and has a `Map<>` of **Color** classes. We have not discussed why that is the design; we will get there, and the diagram helps us to do so. A **Row** class is essentially an array of **Color** classes.

The player has one function—they have to guess many times until they find the hidden secret. To get to the model of **ColorManager**, we will have to design the algorithm of **Guesser**.

When the player makes the first guess, any combination of colors is just as good as any other. Later, the guesses should consider the responses that were given for previous guesses. It is a reasonable approach to try only color variations that can be the actual secret. The player selects a variation and looks at all previous guesses, assuming that the selected variation is the secret. If the responses to the rows they already made are the same for this variation as for the unknown secret in the game, then it is reasonable to try this variation. If there is any difference in the responses, then this variation is certainly not the variation that was hidden.

There are more complex approaches to this game that have a special strategy of selecting one of the color variations from the set of the possible guesses that match the answers. We do not discuss those algorithms here. When we find a color variation that can be the solution, we will use that one.

To follow this approach, the guesser has to generate all possible color variations, one after the other, and compare them against the table. The guesser code will not create and store all the possible variations ahead. It has to know where it was and has to be able to calculate the next variation coming. This assumes an order of the variations. For a short while, let's forget that no color may appear twice in a variation. A simple ordering can be made the same way as we sort decimal numbers. If we have a three-digit number, then the first one is 000, the next one is 001, and so on until 009, always fetching the next digit for the last position. After that, 010 comes. We increased a digit next to the last one and we set the last one to 0 again. Now, we have 011, 012, and so on. You know, how we count numbers. Now, replace the digits with colors and we have only six and not ten. Or, we have as many as we want when we instantiate a `ColorManager` object.

This leads to the functionality of `ColorManager`. It has to do the following two things:

- Give the first color to the caller
- Give the next color that follows a given color (we will name the method `nextColor`)

The latter functionality should also signal when there is no next color. This will be implemented using another method, named `thereIsNextColor`.

It is a convention to start the method names that return a Boolean value with `is`. That would lead to the name following this convention—`isThereNextColor`; or this one—`isNextColor`. Either of these names explains the functionality of the method. If I ask the question `isThereNextColor`, the method will answer me `true` or `false`. But, this is not how we will use the method. We will talk in simple sentences. We will use short sentences. We will avoid unnecessary, gibberish expressions. We will also program that way. Most probably, the caller will use this method in an `if` statement. They will write the following:

```
if( thereIsNextColor(currentColor)){...}
```

They will not write this:

```
if( isThereNextColor(currentColor)){...}
```

I think the first version is more readable, and readability comes first. Last, but not least, nobody will blame you if you follow the old convention, and if that is the company standard, you have to anyway.

To do all this, `ColorManager` also has to create the color objects and should store them in a structure that helps the operations to be performed:

```
package packt.java189fundamentals.example.mastermind;

import java.util.HashMap;
import java.util.Map;

public class ColorManager {
    final protected int nrColors;
    final protected Map<Color, Color> successor = new HashMap<>();
    private Color first;

    public ColorManager(int nrColors) {
        this.nrColors = nrColors;
        createOrdering();
    }

    protected Color newColor(){
        return new Color();
    }

    private Color[] createColors() {
        Color[] colors = new Color[nrColors];
```

```
22.         for (int i = 0; i < colors.length; i++) {
23.             colors[i] = newColor();
24.         }
25.         return colors;
26.     }
27.
28.     private void createOrdering() {
29.         Color[] colors = createColors();
30.         first = colors[0];
31.         for (int i = 0; i < nrColors - 1; i++) {
32.             successor.put(colors[i], colors[i + 1]);
33.         }
34.     }
35.     public Color firstColor() {
36.         return first;
37.     }
38.
39.     boolean thereIsNextColor(Color color) {
40.         return successor.containsKey(color);
41.     }
42.
43.     public Color nextColor(Color color) {
44.         return successor.get(color);
45.     }
46. }
```

The structure we use is a `Map`. Now, `Map` is an interface defined in the Java runtime and has been available since the very early releases of Java. A `Map` has keys and value, and for any key, you can easily retrieve the value assigned to the key.

You can see on the line, where the `successor` variable is defined (line 8), that we define the type of the variable as an interface, but the value is an instance of a class. Obviously, the value cannot be an instance of an interface because such beasts do not exist. But, why do we define the variable to be an interface? The reason is abstraction and coding practice. If we need to change the implementation we use for some reason, the variable type may still remain the same, and there is no need to change the code elsewhere. It is also a good practice to declare the variable to be an interface so that we will not have the temptation to use some special API of the implementation that is not available in the interface just by convenience. When it is really needed, we can change the type of the variable and use the special API. After all, there is a reason that API is there, but the mere temptation to use some special thing just because it is there is hindered. This helps to write simpler and cleaner programs.

`Map` is only one of the interfaces defined in the Java runtime belonging to the Java collections. There are many other interfaces and classes. Although the JDK and all the classes are many and almost nobody knows all the classes that are there, collections is a special area that a professional developer should be knowledgeable about. Before getting into details on why `HashMap` is used in this code, we will have an overview of the collection classes and interfaces. This will help us also understand the other collections used in this program.

Java collections

Collections are interfaces and classes that help us store more than one object. We have already seen arrays, which can do that. We have also seen `ArrayList` in the previous chapters. We did not discuss in detail what other possibilities there are in the JDK. Here, we will go into more detail but leave the streams and the functional methods for later chapters, and we will also refrain from going into details. That is rather the task of a reference book.

Using the implementation of the collection classes and interfaces reduces the programming effort. First of all, you do not need to program something that is already there. Secondly, these classes are highly optimized, both in implementation and in their features. They have very well-designed APIs and the code is fast and uses a small memory footprint. However, their code was written a long time ago and is not in a good style, being very hard to read and understand.

When you use a collection from the JDK, it is more likely that you are interoperable with some library. If you cook your own version of linked lists, it is not likely that you will find a ready-made solution that will sort your list. If you use the `LinkedList` class in the JDK standard class library, you will get a ready-made solution from the `Collections` class, right from the JDK. It is also worth mentioning that the Java language itself supports these classes. For example, you can easily iterate through the elements of a `Collection` with a shortened special syntax of the `for` command.

The collections in the JDK contain interfaces that define the behavior of the different collection types, implementation classes, and algorithms that perform certain actions such as sorting. Many times, these algorithms work on different implementation versions, getting the same result, but optimized for the implementation-specific class.

You can use the API given by the interface, and if you change the implementation in your code, you will get an optimized version fitting the implementation.

The following diagram shows the relations between the different `Collection` interfaces:

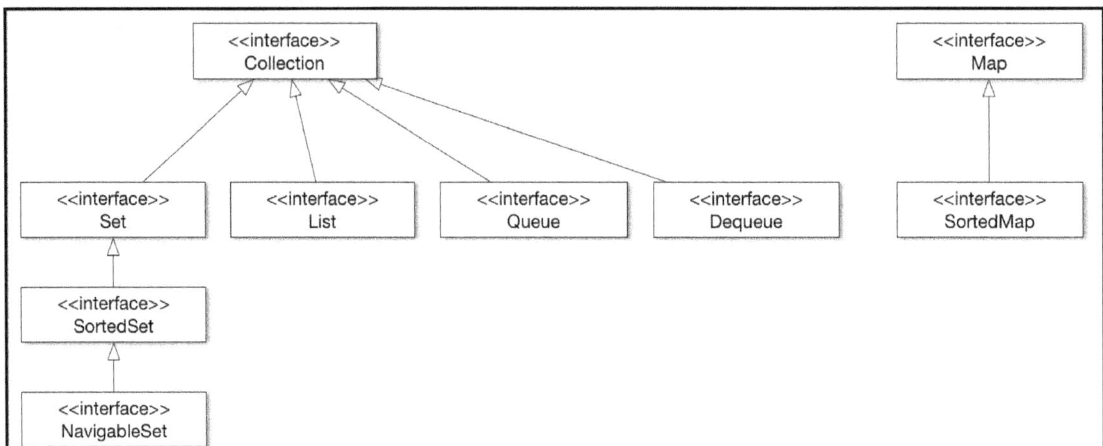

The `Collection` interfaces can be categorized into two bags. One bag contains the interfaces that extend the `Collection` interface, and the other one contains `Map`, and a `SortedMap` extending `Map`. This way, `Map` is not really a collection, as it does not simply contain other objects, but pairs as values and keys.

Interface collection

`Collection` is the top of the interface hierarchy. This interface defines the methods that all implementations should provide, no matter whether they implement the `Set`, `SortedSet`, `List`, `Queue`, or `Deque` interface directly. As `Collection` simply says that an object that implements the `Collection` interface is only an object that collects other objects together, the methods it defines are like adding a new object to the collection, clearing all elements from there, checking that an object is already a member of the collection, and iterating through the elements.

For an up-to-date definition of the interface, consult the Java API documentation (`https://download.java.net/java/early_access/jdk11/docs/api/`). You can consult the online API any time, and it is recommended that you do so.

The Java language itself directly supports the interface. You can iterate through the elements of the `Collection` with the enhanced `for` loop syntax, the same way as you can iterate over the elements of an array where the collection should be an expression that results in an object that implements the `Collection` interface:

```
for( E element : collection ){...}
```

In the preceding code, `E` is either an object or the generic type of the elements of the `Collection`.

The `Collection` interface is not directly implemented in the JDK. Classes implement one of the subinterfaces of `Collection`.

Set

The `Set` is a special collection that cannot contain duplicate elements. When you want to add an object to a set that already has that object or one, which is equal to the actual one, then the `add` method will not add the actual object. The `add` method will return `false`, indicating the failure.

You can use `Set` in your program when you need a collection of unique elements where you simply want to check that an element is a member of a set or not, whether an object belongs to a certain group or not.

As we will return to our program code, we will see that the `UniqueGuesser` class has to implement an algorithm that checks that a color in a guess is present only once. This algorithm is the ideal candidate for a `Set` to be used:

```
private boolean isNotUnique(Color[] guess) {
    final var alreadyPresent = new HashSet<Color>();
    for (final var color : guess) {
        if (alreadyPresent.contains(color)) {
            return true;
        }
        alreadyPresent.add(color);
    }
    return false;
}
```

The code creates a set, which is empty when the method starts. After that, it checks for each color (notice the enhanced `for` loop over the array elements) if it was already present before. To do that, the code checks whether the `color` is already in the set. If it is there, the guess is not unique as we have found a color that is present at least twice. If the `color` was not in the set, then the guess can still be unique in colors. To be able to detect that later, the code puts the color into the set.

The actual implementation of `Set` that we use is `HashSet`. In the JDK, there are many classes implementing the `Set` interface. The most widely used is `HashSet`. It is also worth mentioning `EnumSet`, `LinkedHashSet`, and `TreeSet`. The last one also implements the `SortedSet` interface, thus we will detail it there.

To understand what `HashSet` (and later, `HashMap`) are and how they work, we will have to discuss what hashes are. They play very important and central roles in many applications. They do their job under the hood in the JDK, but there are some very important constraints that programmers have to follow, or else really weird and extremely hard to find bugs will make their life miserable. I dare to say that violation of the hash contract in `HashSet` and `HashMap` are the cause of the second most difficult to find bugs next to multithreading issues.

Thus, before going on with the different collection implementations, we will visit this topic. We are already one-level deep from our example in this detour discussing collections, and now we will go even one level deeper. I promise this is the last in-depth level of detours.

Hash functions

A hash is a mathematical function that assigns a number to an element. Sounds terrible, doesn't it? Say you work as a university admin and you have to tell whether Wilkinson is a student in your class. You can store the names on small papers in envelopes, one for each starting letter. Instead of searching through the 10,000 students, you can look at the papers in the envelope titled W. This very simple hash function assigns the first letter of the name to the name (or the ordinal number of the letter, as we said that a hash function results a number). This is not really a good hash function because it puts only a few elements, if any, into the envelope denoted X and many into A, for example.

A good hash function returns each possible ordinal number with similar probability. In hash tables, we usually have more buckets (envelopes, in the previous example) than the number of elements to be stored. Therefore, when an element is searched for, it is likely that there is only one element there. At least that is what we would like to have. If there are multiple elements in a single bucket, it is called collision. A good hash function has as few collisions as possible.

For backwards compatibility, there is a `Hashtable` class in the JDK. This was one of the first hash table implementations in Java right in the very first version, and because Java is backward compatible, it was not thrown away. The `Map` interface was introduced in version 1.2 only. `Hashtable` has many drawbacks and its use is not recommended. (Even the name violates Java naming conventions.) We do not discuss this class in this book. Whenever we talk about hash tables, we are referring to the actual array that is inside the implementation of `HashSet`, `HashMap`, or any other collection that uses some hash-indexed table.

Hash tables are arrays that use the result of the hash function to index the array. The array elements are called buckets. Hash table implementations try to avoid the situation where there are more than one elements in the same bucket. To do that, the table is resized from time to time when the buckets get full above a certain limit. When more than 70% of the buckets already contain an element, then the table size is doubled. Even with such a threshold and the resizing of the array, it cannot be guaranteed that there will never be more than one element in a single bucket. Therefore, the implementations do not usually store single elements in the buckets, but a linked list of elements. Most of the time, the list will contain only one element, but when there is a collision, two or more elements have the same hash value, and then the list can store the elements.

When the bucket array is resized, each element has to be placed again. This operation may take considerable time and, during this time, the individual elements are moved between the buckets.

During this operation, the hash table cannot reliably be used and this may be some source of issues in a multithreaded environment. In single-thread code, you do not meet this problem. When you call the `add()` method, the hash table (set or map) decides that the table has to be resized. The `add()` method calls the resizing method and does not return until it is finished. Single-thread code has no possibility to use the hash table during this period—the one and single thread is executing the resizing itself. In a multithreaded environment, it may happen that one thread invokes `add()` that starts a resize and another thread also calls `add()` while the hash table is reorganized. Hash table implementations in the JDK in such cases will throw `ConcurrentModificationException`.

`HashSet` and `HashMap` use the hash function provided by the `Object` that is stored in the collection. The `Object` class implements the `hashCode()` and `equals()` methods. You can override them, and if you do, you should override both in a consistent manner. First, we will see what they are and then how to override them consistently.

The equals method

The documentation of `Set` says, sets contain no pair of elements `e1` and `e2` so that `e1.equals(e2)`. The `equals()` method returns `true` if the `e1` and `e2` are in some way equal. It may be different from two objects being identical. There can be two distinct objects that are equal. For example, we could have a color implementation that has the name of the colors as an attribute and two color objects may return `true`, calling the `equals()` method on one of them and passing the argument as the other when the two strings are equal. The default implementation of the `equals()` method is in the code of the `Object` class and this returns `true` if, and only if, `e1` and `e2` are exactly the same and single object.

It seems to be obvious, but my experience shows that it cannot be stressed enough that the implementation of `equals()` in an object has to be as follows:

- **Reflexive**: This means that an object always equals itself
- **Symmetric** (commutative): This means if `e1.equals(e2)` is `true`, then `e2.equals(e1)` should also be `true`
- **Transitive**: This means if `e1.equals(e2)` and `e2.equals(e3)`, then `e1.equals(e3)`
- **Consistent**: This means that the return value should not change if the objects were not changed between the invocations

The hashCode method

The `hashCode()` method returns an `int`. The documentation says that any class redefining this method should provide the following implementation:

- Consistently return the same value if the object was not modified
- Result the same `int` value for two objects that are equal (the `equals()` method returns `true`)

The documentation also mentions that this is not a requirement to result different `int` values for objects that are not equal, but it is desirable to support the performance of the hash implementing collections.

If you violate any of these rules in the implementation of `equals()` and `hashCode()`, then the JDK classes using them may fail. You can be sure that `HashSet`, `HashMap`, and similar classes were fully debugged, seeing that you added an object to a set and then the set reporting that if it is not there, will be a bewildering experience. However, only until you find out that the two objects being equal and stored in the set have different `hashCode()` values, `HashSet` and `HashMap` will look for the object only in the bucket that is indexed by the `hashCode()` value.

It is also a common mistake to store an object in a `HashSet` or `HashMap` and then modify it. The object is in the collection, but you cannot find it because the `hashCode()` returns a different value because it was modified. Objects stored in a collection should not be modified unless you know what you are doing.

Many times, objects contain fields that are not interesting from the equality point of view. The `hashCode()` and `equals()` methods should be idempotent to those fields and you can alter those fields even after storing the object in a `HashSet` or in `HashMap`. (Idempotent means that you can change the value of those fields however you want, and the result of the methods will not change.)

As an example, you may administer triangles in objects maintaining the coordinates of the vertices and the color of the triangle. However, you do not care about the color for equality, only that the two triangles are at the exact same location in the space. In that case, the `equals()` and `hashCode()` methods should not take the field color into account. This way, we can paint our triangles; they will still be found in `HashSet` or `HashMap`, no matter what the color field is.

Implementing equals and hashCode

Implementing these methods is fairly simple. As this is a very common task, the IDEs support the generation of these methods. These methods are tied together so much that the menu items in the IDEs are not separate; they allow you to generate these methods at once.

Asking the IDE to generate the `equals()` method will result in something like the following code:

```
@Override
public boolean equals(Object o) {
  if (this == o) return true;
  if (o == null || getClass() != o.getClass()) return false;
  MyObjectJava7 that = (MyObjectJava7) o;
  return Objects.equals(field1, that.field1) &&
  Objects.equals(field2, that.field2) &&
  Objects.equals(field3, that.field3);
}
```

For this sample, we have three `Object` fields named `field1`, `field2`, and `field3`. The code with any other types and fields will look very similar.

First, the method checks for object identity. One `Object` always `equals()` itself. If the reference passed as the argument is `null` and not an object, or they are of different classes, then this generated method will return `false`. In other cases, the static method of the `Objects` class (note the plural) will be used to compare each of the fields.

The `Objects` utility class was introduced in Java 7. The static methods, `equals()` and `hash()`, support the override of the `Object equals` and `hashCode()` methods. `hashCode()` creation before Java 7 was fairly complex and required the implementation of modulo arithmetic with some magic numbers that are hard to explain just looking at the code without knowing the mathematics behind it.

This complexity is now hidden behind the following `Objects.hash` method:

```
@Override
 public int hashCode() {
     return Objects.hash(field1, field2, field3);
 }
```

The generated method simply calls the `Objects::hash` method, passing the important fields as arguments.

HashSet

Now, we know essentially a lot of things about hashes, so we can bravely discuss the `HashSet` class. `HashSet` is an implementation of the `Set` interface that internally uses a hash table. Generally, that is it. You store objects there and you can see if an object is already there or not. When there is a need for a `Set` implementation, almost always `HashSet` is the choice. Almost...

EnumSet

`EnumSet` can contain elements from a certain enumeration. Recall that enumerations are classes that have fixed a number of instances declared inside the `enum` itself. As this limits the number of the different object instances, and this number is known during compilation time, the implementation of the `EnumSet` code is fairly optimized. Internally, `EnumSet` is implemented as a bit field and is a good choice where bit field manipulations would be the choice were we programming in a low-level language.

LinkedHashSet

`LinkedHashSet` is a `HashSet` that also maintains a doubly linked list of the elements it holds. When we iterate through a `HashSet`, there is no guaranteed order of the element. When `HashSet` is modified, the new elements are inserted into one of the buckets and, possibly, the hash table gets resized. This means that the elements get rearranged and get into totally different buckets. Iteration over the elements in `HashSet` just takes the buckets and the elements in it as they are in some order that is arbitrary from the caller's point of view.

`LinkedHashSet`, however, iterates over the elements using the linked list it maintains, and the iteration is guaranteed to happen in the order the elements were inserted. This way, the `LinkedHashSet` is a compound data structure that is a `HashSet` and a `LinkedList` at the same time.

SortedSet

`SortedSet` is an interface that guarantees that the classes implementing it will iterate over the set in a sorted order. The order may be the natural ordering of the objects if the objects implement the `Comparable` interface, or a `Comparator` object may drive it. This object should be available when the instance of the class implementing the `SortedSet` is created; in other words, it has to be a constructor parameter.

NavigableSet

`NavigableSet` extends the `SortedSet` interface with methods that let you do a proximity search in the set. This essentially lets you search for an element that is in the search and is any of the following:

- Less than the searched object
- Less than or equal to the searched element
- Greater than or equal to the searched object

TreeSet

`TreeSet` is an implementation of `NavigableSet` and so is also a `SortedSet` and, as a matter of fact, it is also a `Set`, as the `SortableSet` documentation implies there are two types of the constructor, each having multiple versions. One requires some `Comparator`, while the other one relies on the natural ordering of the elements.

List

`List` is an interface that requires the implementing class to keep track of the order of the elements. There are also methods that access an element by index and iteration defined by the `Collection` interface that guarantees the order of the elements. The interface also defines the `listIterator` method that returns an `Iterator` also implementing the `ListIterator` interface. This interface provides methods that let the caller insert elements to the list while iterating through it and also going back and forth in the iteration. It is also possible to search for a certain element in the `List`, but most implementations of the interface provide poor performance while the search is simply going through all elements until the element searched for is found. There are many classes implementing this interface in the JDK. Here, we will mention two.

LinkedList

This is a doubly-linked list implementation of the `List` interface that has a reference to the previous and also to the next element in the list for each element. The class also implements the `Deque` interface. It is fairly cheap to insert or delete an element from the list because it needs only the adjustment of few references. On the other hand, the access to an element by index will need iteration from the start of the list, or from the end of the list; whichever is closer to the specified indexed element.

ArrayList

This class is an implementation of the `List` interface that keeps the references to the elements in an array. That way, it is fairly fast to access an element by index. On the other hand, inserting an element to `ArrayList` can be costly. It needs moving all references above the inserted element one index higher, and it may also require resizing the backing array in case there is no room in the original one to store the new element. Essentially, this means allocating a new array and copying all references to it.

The reallocation of the array may be optimized if we know how large the array will grow and will call the `ensureCapacity()` method. This will resize the array to the size provided as an argument, even if the currently used slots are less numbered.

My experience is that novice programmers use `ArrayList` when they need a list without considering the algorithmic performance of the different implementations. I do not actually know why there is this popularity of `ArrayList`. The actual implementation used in a program should be based on the proper decision and not habit.

Queue

A `Queue` is a collection that usually stores elements for later use. You can put elements into a queue and you can pull them out. An implementation may specify the given order, that may be **first in first out** (**FIFO**) or **last in first out** (**LIFO**), or some priority-based ordering.

On a queue, you can invoke the `add()` method to add an element, `remove()` to remove the head element, and the `element()` method to access the head element without removing it from the queue. The `add()` method will throw an exception when there is a capacity problem and the element cannot be added to the queue. When the queue is empty, and there is no head element, the `element()` and `remove()` methods throw exceptions.

As exceptions can only be used in exceptional cases, and the calling program may handle these situations in the normal course of the code, all these methods have a version that just returns some special value signaling the situation. Instead of `add()`, a caller may call `offer()` to offer an element for storage. If the queue cannot store the element, it will return `false`. Similarly, `peek()` will try to get access to the head element or return `null` if there is none, and `poll()` will remove and return the head element or just return `null` if there is none.

Note that these methods returning `null` just makes the situation ambiguous when the implementation, such as `LinkedList`, allows `null` elements. Never store a `null` element in a queue or else you will not be able to tell whether the queue is empty or that just the first element is `null`.

Deque

`Deque` is an interface that is a double-ended queue. It extends the `Queue` interface with the methods that allow access to both ends of the queue to add, look at, and remove elements from both ends.

For the `Queue` interface, we need six methods. `Dequeue`, having two manageable ends, needs 12 methods. Instead of `add()`, we have `addFirst()` and `addLast()`. Similarly, we can use `offerFirst()` and `offerLast()`, `peekFirst()` and `peekLast()`, and `pollFirst()` and `pollLast()`. For some reason, the methods that implement the functionality of the `element()` method in the `Queue` interface are named `getFirst()` and `getLast()` in the `Dequeue` interface.

Since this interface extends the `Queue` interface, the methods defined there can also be used to access the head of the queue. In addition to these, this interface also defines the `removeFirstOccurrence()` and `removeLastOccurrence()` methods, which can be used to remove a specific element inside the queue. We cannot specify the index of the element to remove and we also cannot access an element based on an index. The `removeFirst()/LastOccurrence()` methods' argument is the object that is to be removed. If we need this functionality, we can use `Deque` even if we add and remove elements from one end of the queue.

Why are there these methods in `Deque` and not in `Queue`? These methods have nothing to do with the double-headedness of `Deque`. The reason is that methods could not be added to interfaces after they were released. If we add a method to an interface, we break the backwards compatibility because all classes that implement that interface have to implement the new method. Java 8 introduced default methods that eased this constraint, but the `Queue` interface was defined in Java 1.5 and the `Deque` interface was defined in Java 1.6. There was no way at that time to add the new methods to the already existing interfaces.

Map

A `Map` pairs keys and values. If we want to approach a `Map` from the `Collection` point of view, then a `Map` is a collection of key/value pairs. You can put key/value pairs into a `Map` and you can get a value based on a key. Keys are unique in the same way as elements in a `Set`. If you look at the source code of the different implementations of the `Set` interface, you may see that some of them are implemented as a wrapper around a `Map` implementation where the values are simply discarded.

The interface defines a lot of methods. The two most important methods are `put()` and `get()`. The `put(key,value)` method can be used to store a key/value pair in the map. If there is a pair that has a key that `equals()` the key we want to set in the pair, then the old value will be replaced. In this case, the return value of `put()` is the old object, otherwise, it returns `null`. Note that a returned `null` value may also indicate that the value associated with the key was `null`.

The `get(key)` method returns the value stored with the specified key. Again, the method `equals()` is used to check the equality of the key provided and the one used in the map. If the map does not have any associated value with the key provided as an argument, then this method returns `null`. This may also mean that the actual value associated with the key is the `null` reference.

To distinguish between the two cases when there is no value stored for a given key and when the value stored is `null`, there is another method named `contains()`. This method returns `true` if this map contains a mapping for the specified key.

There are many other methods in the `Map` interface that you can find in the JavaDoc documentation of the JDK.

Using `Map` is easy and alluring. Many languages, such as Python, Go, JavaScript, and Perl, support this data structure on the language level. However, using a `Map` when an array would be sufficient is a bad practice that I have seen many times, especially in scripting languages. Java is not prone to that novice programmer error, but you may still find yourself in a situation when you want to use a `Map`, and still, there is a better solution. It is a general rule that the simplest data structure should be used that is sufficient for the implementation of the algorithm.

HashMap

`HashMap` is a hash table-based implementation of the `Map` interface. Because the implementation uses a hash table, the `get()` and `put()` methods usually perform very fast, constant, and time-independent of the actual number of elements in the map. If the map size grows and the number of table elements is not enough to store the elements ergonomically, putting a new element into this type of map may force the implementation to resize the underlying array. In this case, each element that is already in the array has to be placed again in the new, increased size array. In those cases, the `put()` operation may consume significant time, proportional to the number of elements in the map.

When an element is to be stored in this map, then `hashCode()` method is called on the key object and the return value used to decide which bucket of the underlying hash table should store the new element. The buckets contain a simple binary tree structure. If the bucket is empty, storing the element in this structure is as simple as if the element were stored in the bucket directly. On the other hand, when two or more elements have the same `hashCode()` value, then they can also be stored in the map in the same bucket, though efficiency is a bit degrading.

Because of the possible collisions of the `hashCode()` values, the time needed for a `get()` or a `put()` method call may be a wee bit longer than otherwise.

This implementation of the `Map` interface is the most frequently used in Java programs; the implementation is fine-tuned and the use can be configured. The simplest way is to create a `HashMap` calling the default constructor. If we happen to know how many elements there will be on the map, then we can specify it, passing an `int` to the constructor. In this case, the constructor will allocate an array, which has a size not smaller than the capacity we required, and the size is a power of two.

There is a third constructor where we can define a `float` load factor. The default value for the load factor is `0.75`. When the number of elements in the map is more than the size of the hash table size multiplied by the load factor, then the next `put()` call will double the size of the underlying hash table. This early resizing tries to avoid `hashCode()` collisions to become too frequent. If we store instances of some special class where we are sure that the `hashCode()` is extremely good, then we can set the load factor closer to `1.0`. If we do not care for the speed too much and we do not want the underlying hash table to increase too much, we can even use a value larger than `1.0`. In this case, however, I would consider using some different data structures.

In most cases, the choice when we need a `Map` is `HashMap`. Usually, we should not really worry too much about these implementation details. In some rare cases, though, when the memory use or performance is degrading, we should know the implementation intricacies of the map we use.

IdentityHashMap

`IdentityHashMap` is a special `Map` that implements the `Map` interface per se, but as a matter of fact, the implementation violates the contract of the `Map` interface that the documentation defines. It does it for a good reason. The implementation uses a hash table just as `HashMap`, but to decide the equality of the key found in the bucket comparing with the key element provided as the argument to the get method, it uses `Object` reference (== operator) and not the method `equals()`, which is required by documentation of `Map` interface.

The use of this implementation is reasonable when we want to distinguish different `Object` instances as keys that otherwise equal each other. Using this implementation for performance reasons is almost certainly a wrong decision. Also, note that there is no `IdentityHashSet` implementation in the JDK. Probably, such a collection is so rarely used that its existence in the JDK would cause more harm than good, alluring novice programmers to misuse.

Dependency injection

In the previous chapter, we briefly already discussed **dependency injection** (**DI**). Before going on with our example, we will dig into it in a bit more detail. We will do so because the programming structure we will create heavily builds on this principle.

Objects usually do not work on their own. Most of the time, the implementation depends on the services of other classes. For example, when we want to write something to the console, we use the `System` class and we use the `final` field `out` and the `println()` method through that object. Another example is how, when we manage the table of guesses, we need `Color` objects and `ColorManager`.

When writing to the console, we may not realize the dependency because the class, being part of the JDK class library, is available all the time, and all we need to do is write `System.out.println()`. It may be as obvious as being able to walk because we have legs. No matter how simple this seems, we depend on our legs to walk, and, similarly, we depend on the `System` class when we want to write to the console.

When we just write `System.out.println()`, the dependency is wired into the code. We cannot send the output somewhere else unless we change the code. This is not very flexible, and in many cases, we need a solution that can work with different output, a different color manager, or a different type of whatever service our code depends on.

The first step to do that has a field that has a reference to the object that gives our class the service. In the case of output, the type of the field can be of the `OutputStream` type. If we use this field in the code and not something that is wired into the code directly, then we have the possibility to use different dependencies. For example, we can send the output into a file and not to the console. We do not need to change the code where the writing happens. All we have to do is to assign a different value to the field referencing the `OutputStream` during object creation.

This is already the next step, that is, how this field gets the value.

One of the solutions is to use DI. In this approach, some external code prepares the dependencies and injects them into the object. When the first call to a method of the class is issued, all the dependencies are already filled and ready to be used.

In this structure, we have four different actors:

- The `client` object is the one that gets the injected `service` objects during the process
- The `service` object or objects are injected into the `client` object
- Injector is the code that performs the injection
- Interfaces define the service that the client needs

If we move the logic of the creation of the `service` objects from the client code, the code becomes shorter and cleaner. The actual competency of the `client` class should hardly ever cover the creation of the `service` objects. For example, a `Game` class contains a `Table` instance, but a game is not responsible for creating the `Table`. It is given to it to work with it, just as in real life that we model.

The creation of `service` objects is sometimes as simple as issuing the `new` operator. Sometimes, `service` objects also depend on other `service` objects and also act as clients in the process of DI. In this case, the creation of the `service` objects may be a lot of lines. The structure of the dependencies can be expressed in a declarative fashion that describes which `service` object needs other `service` objects and also what implementation of the service interfaces are to be used. DI injectors work with such declarative descriptions. When there is a need for an object that needs `service` objects that themselves need other `service` objects, the injector creates the service instances in the appropriate order using the implementations that match the declarative descriptions. The injector discovers all the dependencies transitively and creates a transitive closure graph of the dependencies.

The declarative description of the needed dependencies can be XML, or a special language developed especially for the DI, or it can even be Java itself using a specially designed fluent API (`https://blog.jooq.org/2012/01/05/the-java-fluent-api-designer-crash-course/`). XML was first used in DI injectors. Later, **Groovy**-based **Domain-Specific Language** (`https://martinfowler.com/books/dsl.html`) came into the picture as a Java-fluent API approach. We will use only the last one, with it being the most modern, and we will use **Spring** and **Guice DI** containers, since they are the most well-known injector implementations.

Implementing the game

Collections without examples are boring. Fortunately, we have our game where we use a few collection classes and also other aspects that we will examine in this chapter.

ColorManager

We jumped into the pool filled with collection classes from the implementation of the `ColorManager` class. Let's refresh our memory with the part of the class that is interesting for us now—the constructor:

```
package packt.java189fundamentals.example.mastermind;

import java.util.HashMap;
import java.util.Map;

public class ColorManager {
    final protected int nrColors;
    final protected Map<Color, Color> successor = new HashMap<>();
```

```
        private Color first;

        public ColorManager(int nrColors) {
            this.nrColors = nrColors;
            createOrdering();
        }

        protected Color newColor(){
            return new Color();
        }

        private Color[] createColors() {
            Color[] colors = new Color[nrColors];
            for (int i = 0; i < colors.length; i++) {
                colors[i] = newColor();
            }
            return colors;
        }

        private void createOrdering() {
            Color[] colors = createColors();
            first = colors[0];
            for (int i = 0; i < nrColors - 1; i++) {
                successor.put(colors[i], colors[i + 1]);
            }
        }
        // ...
    }
```

We use `HashMap` to keep the colors in an ordered list. At first, the choice of `HashMap` seems to be strange. It's very true that, during the coding of `ColorManager`, I also considered `List`, which seemed to be a more obvious choice. If we had a `List<Color> colors` variable, then the `nextColor` method would be something like this:

```
public Color nextColor(Color color) {
     if (color == Color.none)
          return null;
     else
          return colors.get(colors.indexOf(color) + 1);
 }
```

The constructor will be much simpler, as shown in the following piece of code:

```
final List<Color> colors = new ArrayList<>();
     public ColorManager(int nrColors) {
          this.nrColors = nrColors;
          for (int i = 0; i < nrColors; i++) {
               colors.add(new Color());
```

```
        }
        colors.add(Color.none);
    }
    public Color firstColor() {
        return colors.get(0);
    }
```

Why did I choose the more complex solution and the more complex data structure? The reason is performance. When the `nextColor()` method is invoked, the list implementation first finds the element checking all the elements in the list and then fetches the next element. The time is proportional to the number of colors. When our number of colors increases, the time will also increase to just get the next color having one.

At the same time, if we focus on the actual method that we want to implement, `nextColor(Color)`, instead of the verbal expression of the task we want to solve (to get the colors in a sorted order), then we will easily come to the conclusion that `Map` is more reasonable. What we need is exactly a `Map`—having one element, we want another related to the one we have. The key and the value is also `Color`. Getting the next element is practically constant time using `HashMap`. This implementation is probably faster than the one based on `ArrayList`.

The problem is that it is only probably faster. When you consider refactoring code to have better performance, your decision should always be based on measurements. If you implement code that you only think is faster, practice shows, you will fail. In the best case, you will optimize code to be blazingly fast and runs during the application server setup. At the same time, optimized code is usually less readable. Something for something. Optimization should never be done prematurely. Code for readability first. Then, assess the performance, and in case there is a problem with the performance, profile the execution and optimize the code where it hurts the most on the overall performance. Micro-optimizations will not help. Did I do premature optimization selecting the `HashMap` implementation instead of `List`? If I actually implemented the code using `List` and then refactored it, then yes. If I was thinking about the `List` solution and then it came to me that `Map` solution is better without prior coding, then I did not. Such considerations will become easier as you gather more experience.

The class color

We have already looked at the code for the class code and it was the simplest class in the world. In reality, as it is in the Packt code repository, the code is a bit more complex:

```
/**
 * Represents a color in the MasterMind table.
 */
public class Color {
    /**
     * A special object that represents a
     * value that is not a valid color.
     */
    public static final Color none = new Color();
}
```

We have a special color constant named `none` that we use to signal a reference that is of type `Color` but is not a valid `Color`. In professional development, we used the `null` value for a long time to signal invalid reference, and because we are backwards compatible, we still use it. However, it is recommended to avoid the `null` reference wherever possible.

Tony Hoare (`https://en.wikipedia.org/wiki/Tony_Hoare`), who invented the `null` reference in 1965, admitted once that this was a mistake that cost billions of dollars in the IT industry.

The problem with the `null` value is that it takes the control away from the class, and thus, opens encapsulation. If a method returns `null` in some situation, the caller is strictly required to check the nullity and act according to that. For example, you cannot call a method on a `null` reference (at least you can't do that in Java) and you cannot access any field. If the method returns, a special instance of the object these problems are less serious. If the caller forgets to check the special return value and invokes methods on the special instance, the methods invoked still have the possibility to implement some exception or error handling. The class has the control encapsulated and can throw a special exception that may give more information about the error caused by the programmatic mistake by the caller not checking the special value.

JavaDoc and code comments

There is also another difference between what we presented here earlier and the listing. This is the commenting of the code. Code comments are part of the program, which is ignored, and filtered out by the compiler. These comments are solely for those who maintain or use the code.

In Java, there are two different comments. The code enclosed between `/*` and `*/` are comments. The start and the end of the comment do not need to be on the same line. The other type of comment start with the `//` characters and end at the end of the line.

To document the code, the JavaDoc tool can be used. JavaDoc is part of the JDK and it is a special tool that reads the source code and extracts HTML documentation about the classes, methods, fields, and other entities that have a comment starting with the `/**` characters. The documentation will contain the JavaDoc comments in a formatted way and also the information that is extracted from the program code.

The documentation also appears as online help in the IDE when you move the mouse over a method call or class name, if there is any. The JavaDoc comment can contain HTML codes, but it generally should not. If really needed, you can use `<p>` to start a new paragraph or the `<pre>` tags to include some preformatted code sample into the documentation, but nothing more gives real benefit. Documentation should be as short as possible and contain as little formatting as possible.

There are special tags that can appear in the JavaDoc documentation. These are prefilled by the IDEs when you start to type a JavaDoc as `/**` and then press *Enter*. These are inside the comment and start with the `@` character. There are a predefined set of tags—`@author`, `@version`, `@param`, `@return`, `@exception`, `@see`, `@since`, `@serial`, and `@deprecated`. The most important tags are `@param` and `@return`. They are used to describe the method arguments and the return value. Although we are not there yet, let's peek ahead to the `guessMatch` method from the `Guesser` class:

```
/**
 * A guess matches if all rows in the table matches the guess.
 *
 * @param guess to match against the rows
 * @return true if all rows match
 */
private boolean guessMatch(Color[] guess) {
    for (Row row : table.rows) {
        if (!row.guessMatches(guess)) {
            return false;
        }
    }
```

```
        return true;
    }
```

The name of the parameter is automatically generated by the IDE. When you create the documentation, write something that is meaningful and not a tautology. Many times, novice programmers feel the urge to write JavaDoc, and that something has to be written about the parameters. They create documentation like this:

```
    * @param guess is the guess
```

Really? I would never have guessed. If you do not know what to write there to document the parameter; it may happen that you were choosing the name of the parameter excellent.

The documentation of our preceding example will look as follows:

```
packt.java189fundamentals.example.mastermind.Guesser
private boolean guessMatch(Color[] guess)

A guess matches if all rows in the table matches the guess.

Params: guess – to match against the rows
Returns: true if all rows match
```

Focus on what the method, class, and interface do and how JavaDoc can be used. Do not explain how it works internally. JavaDoc is not the place for the explanation of the algorithm or the coding. Its aim is to help use the code. However, if somebody happens to explain how a method works, it is not a disaster. Comments can easily be deleted.

There is, however, a comment that is worse than nothing: outdated documentation that is not valid anymore. When the contract of the element has changed, but the documentation does not follow the change and is misleading the user who wants to call the method, interface, or class, it will face serious bugs and will be clueless.

From now on, JavaDoc comments will not be listed in print to save trees, and electrons in the eBook version, but they are there in the repository and can be examined.

Row

Now, we have a `Color` class and even instances when we need a `ColorManager`. This is the time to store `Color` objects in `Row` objects. The `Row` class is a bit longer, but not too complex. We look at the code in small fragments in this section with explanations in-between:

```
package packt.java189fundamentals.example.mastermind;

public class Row {
    final Color[] positions;
    protected int matchedPositions;
    protected int matchedColors;
```

A `Row` contains three fields. One is the `positions` array. Each element of the array is a `Color`. The `matchedPositions` is the number of positions that are matched, and `matchedColors` is the number of colors that match a color in the hidden row but are not in the same position in the hidden row:

```
public static final Row none = new Row(Guesser.none);
```

`none` is a constant that contains a special `Row` instance that we will use wherever we would use `null`. The constructor gets the colors in an array that should be in the row:

```
public Row(Color[] positions) {
    this.positions = Arrays.copyOf(positions, positions.length);
}
```

The constructor makes a copy of the original array. This is an important piece of code that we'll examine a little. Let's reiterate that Java passes arguments by value. It means that when you pass an array to a method, you will pass the value of the variable that holds the array. However, an array in Java is an object just as well as anything else (except primitives such as `int`). Therefore, what the variable contains is a reference to an object that happens to be an array. If you change the elements of the array, you actually change the elements of the original array. The array reference is copied when the argument passes, but the array itself, and the elements, are not.

The `java.util.Arrays` utility class provides a lot of useful tools. We can easily code the array copying in Java, but why reinvent the wheel? In addition to that, arrays are a continuous area of memory that can very effectively be copied from one place to another using low-level machine code. The `copyOf` method that we invoke calls the `System.arraycopy` method, which is a native method and as such executes native code.

Note that there is no guarantee that `Arrays.copyOf` invokes the native implementations and that this will be extremely fast in case of large arrays. The very version I was testing and debugging was doing it that way, and we can assume that a good JDK does something similar, effective, and fast.

After we copied the array, it is not a problem if the caller modifies the array that was passed to the constructor. The class will have a reference to a copy that will contain the same elements. However, note that if the caller changes any of the objects that are stored in the array (not the reference in the array, but the object itself that is referenced by an array element), then the same object is modified. `Arrays.copyOf` does not copy the objects that are referenced by the array, only the array elements. In our case, we have `Color` instances in the array and because this class has no field at all, it is inherently immutable, with no instance of it can be changed.

The row is created along with the colors, and so we used a `final` field for the `Color` array named `positions`. The matches, however, cannot be known when a row is created; therefore, they cannot be `final`. One of the players creates the `Row` and, after that, the other player will tell the two `int` values later. We need a setter to set these fields. We do not create two setters for the two values, however, because they are always defined at the same time in the game together:

```
public void setMatch(int matchedPositions, int matchedColors) {
    if (matchedColors + matchedPositions > positions.length) {
        throw new IllegalArgumentException(
                "Number of matches can not be more that the position.");
    }
    this.matchedColors = matchedColors;
    this.matchedPositions = matchedPositions;
}
```

The `setMatch` method does not only set the values but also checks that the values are consistent. The sum of the two values cannot be more than the number of the columns. This check ensures that the caller, who uses the API of the `Row` class, does not use it inconsistently. If this API is used only from inside our code, this assertion should not be part of the code. A good coding style, in that case, will ensure that the method is never invoked inconsistently using unit tests. When we create an API to be used out of our control, we should check that the use is consistent. Failing to do so, our code may behave weirdly when used inconsistently. When the caller sets matches to values that do not match any possible guess, the game may never finish and the caller may have a hard time figuring out what is going on. This figuring out will probably need the debug execution of our code. That is not the task of the user of the library. Always try to create code that does not need debugging from the consumer of the API.

If we throw an exception in this case, the program stops where the bug is. There is no need to debug the library.

The following method decides if a guess, given as an argument, matches the actual row:

```
public boolean guessMatches(Color[] guess) {
    return nrMatchingColors(guess) == matchedColors &&
            nrMatchingPositions(guess) == matchedPositions;
}
```

This method checks that the answers to the guess in the row can be valid if the current guess was in the hidden row. The implementation is fairly short and simple. A guess matches a row if the number of the colors matching and the number of positions matching are the same as the number given in the row. There is, of course, some extra code in the implementation of the `nrMatchingColors()` and `nrMatchingPositions()` methods, but this method is indeed simple. Do not be shy in writing short methods! Do not think that a one-line method that essentially contains one statement is useless. Wherever we use this method, we could also write the expression, which is right after the return statement, but we do not for two reasons. The first and most important reason is that the algorithm, which decides that a row matches a guess, belongs to the implementation of the class `Row`. If ever the implementation changes, the only location where the code is to be changed is here. The other reason is also important, and that is readability. In our codebase, we call this method from the `abstract class Guesser`. It contains an `if` statement with the following expression:

```
if (!row.guessMatches(guess)) {
```

Would it be more readable in the following way?

```
if( !(nrMatchingColors(guess) == matchedColors &&
nrMatchingPositions(guess) ==
matchedPositions)) {
```

I am certain that the majority of programmers understand the intention of the first version easier. I would even recommend implementing the `doesNotMatchGuess` method to improve the readability of the code even more:

```
public int nrMatchingColors(Color[] guess) {
    int count = 0;
    for (int i = 0; i < guess.length; i++) {
        for (int j = 0; j < positions.length; j++) {
            if (i != j && guess[i] == positions[j]) {
                count++;
            }
        }
    }
```

```
        return count;
    }
```

The number of matching colors is the number of the colors that appear both in the row and in the guess, but not in the same position. The definition, and how we calculate it, is fairly simple and unambiguous if no color can appear twice in the hidden row. If a color may appear multiple times in the hidden row, this implementation will count all occurrences of that color in the guess as man times as it appears in the hidden row. If we, for example, have a hidden `RRGB` row and the guess is `bYRR`, the calculation will say 4. It is a matter of agreement between the players how they count in this case. The important aspect is that they use the same algorithm, which should be true in our case, because we will ask the program to play both players, and also because we defined at the start of the chapter that no color can appear more than once in the hidden row.

Because we will program the code ourselves, we can trust that it will not cheat.

Counting the colors that are OK, and also on the position where they are supposed to be, is even simpler:

```
    public int nrMatchingPositions(Color[] guess) {
        int count = 0;
        for (int i = 0; i < guess.length; i++) {
            if (guess[i] == positions[i]) {
                count++;
            }
        }
        return count;
    }
```

The last method in this class is the one that returns the number of the columns:

```
    public int nrOfColumns() {
        return positions.length;
    }
```

This method tells the number of columns in the `Row`. This method is needed in the `Game` class that controls the flow of a whole game. As this class is in the same package as `Row`, it can access the field positions. I created the code to get the number of columns as `row.positions.length`. But then, I was reading the code the next day and told myself—this is ugly and unreadable! What I am interested in here is not some mysterious positions' length; it is the number of columns. And the number of columns is the responsibility of the `Row` class and not the business of any other class. If I start to store the positions in a `List`, which does not have `length` (it has method `size()`), it is the sole responsibility of `Row` and should not affect any other code. So, I created the `nrOfColumns()` method to improve the code and to have proper encapsulation.

The `Row` class has another constructor that clones a row from another one:

```
protected Row(Row cloneFrom) {
    this(cloneFrom.positions);
    setMatch(cloneFrom.matchedPositions, cloneFrom.matchedColors);
}
```

This is used by extending the `PrintableRow` class. This class makes it possible that, during test runs, we can print out the table, the guesses, and generally how the game goes.

The `PrintableRow` class looks like this:

```
package packt.java189fundamentals.example.mastermind;

public class PrintableRow extends Row {
    public PrintableRow(Row row) {
        super(row);
    }

    public Color position(int i) {
        return positions[i];
    }

    public int matchedPositions() {
        return matchedPositions;
    }

    public int matchedColors() {
        return matchedColors;
    }
}
```

The first versions of these methods were in the `Row` class and then moved to the new `PrintableRow` class. During the refactoring, I used to cut and paste functionality of the IDE. I could also use the refactoring support that can move methods directly from one class to another. There is one IDE functionality that should not be used—copy and paste.

When you write code, please never use copy and paste. You can use cut and paste to move code fragments around. The danger is in the copy paste use. Many developers claim that their use of actual copy and paste is not copy paste programming. Their reasoning is that they change the pasted code so much that it has practically nothing to do with the original code. Really? In that case, why did you need the copied code when you started the modification of it? Why not start from scratch? That is because if you use the IDE's copy and paste functionality then, no matter what, you do copy paste programming. Face it and do not try to lie to yourself.

`PrintableRow` is pretty neat and separates the output concern from the core functionality. When you need an instance, it is not a problem that you have a `Row` instance already in hand. The constructor will essentially clone the original class and return a printable version, calling the cloning constructor defined in the parent class. During the development of this class, I created the cloning code in the `PrintableRow` class. However, this functionality placement violates encapsulation. Even though `PrintableRow` extends the `Row` class and, as such, it is not an eternal sin to know the inner working of the parent class, it is better not to depend on it if possible. Thus, the newly `protected` constructor was created in the parent class and invoked from the child.

A piece of code is never finished and never perfect. In a professional environment, programmers tend to finish polishing the code when it is good enough. There is no code that cannot be made better, but there is a deadline. The software has to be passed on to the testers and users and has to be used to help the economy. After all, that is the final goal of a professional developer—have a code that supports the business. A code that never runs is worth nothing. I do not want you to think that the examples that I provided here were created perfect up-front. I do not even dare say that they are perfect now in the second edition of this book. The reason for that is (did you read carefully?) because they are not perfect. As I said, a code is never perfect. When I first created `Row`, it contained the printing methods in an inner class. I did not like it. The code was smelly. So, I decided to move the functionality to the `Row` class. However, I still did not like the solution. Then, I went to bed, slept, worked, and returned to it a few days later. What I could not create the day before now seemed obvious—these methods have to be moved to a subclass. Now comes another dilemma. Should I present this final solution or should I have here the different versions? In some cases, I will just present the final version. In other cases, like this, there are things to learn from the development step. In these cases, I present not only the code but part of its evolution on how it was created. I admit, sometimes, I create code that even makes me facepalm myself a day later. Who doesn't?

Table

The Mastermind table is a simple class that has only one very simple functionality:

```
public class Table {
    final ColorManager manager;
    final int nrColumns;
    final List<Row> rows;
```

```
    public Table(int nrColumns, ColorManager manager) {
        this.nrColumns = nrColumns;
        this.rows = new LinkedList<>();
        this.manager = manager;
    }
    public void addRow(Row row) {
        rows.add(row);
    }
}
```

There is one thing to mention, which is nothing new, but worth repeating. The `rows` variable is declared as `final` and it gets the value in the constructor. This is a `List<Row>` type variable. The fact that it is `final` means that it will hold the same list object during its lifetime. The length, members, and other features of the list may and will change. We will add new rows to this list. Final object variables reference an object, but it does not guarantee that the object itself is immutable. It is only the variable that does not change.

When you do a code review and explain to your colleagues what a class does, and you find yourself starting the explanation *this class is very simple* many times, it means the code is good. Well, it may still be wrong in other aspects, but at least the class' granularity seems to be okay.

Guesser

The `Guesser` abstract class and the `UniqueGuesser` and `GeneralGuesser` subclasses are the most interesting classes of the program. They actually perform the task that is the core of the game. Given a `Table` with a hidden row, the guesser has to create new guesses.

To do this, a `Guesser` needs to get a `Table` when it is created. This is passed as a constructor argument. The only method it should implement is `guess`, which returns a new guess based on the table and in its actual state.

We want to implement a guesser that assumes that all colors in the hidden row are different, and also one that does not make this assumption; we will implement three classes to do this. `Guesser` is an abstract class that implements only the logic that is independent of the assumptions. These methods will be inherited by both actual implementations, `UniqueGuesser` and `GeneralGuesser`, which implement the guessing functionality if each color is or isn't unique in a row, respectively.

Let's go through the actual code of the class:

```
package packt.java189fundamentals.example.mastermind;

public abstract class Guesser {
    protected final Table table;
    private final ColorManager manager;
    protected final Color[] lastGuess;
    public static final Color[] none = new Color[]{Color.none};

    public Guesser(Table table) {
        this.table = table;
        this.lastGuess = new Color[table.nrColumns];
        this.manager = table.manager;
    }
```

The state of the guesser is the last guess it made. Although this is on the last row of the table, it is more of an internal matter of the guesser. The guesser has all the possible guesses, one after the other; `lastGuess` is the one where it left off last time and it should continue from there when it is invoked again.

`none` in this class is just an object that we try to use instead of `null`, whenever we need to return something that is a reference to a `Guess` but is not really a guess.

Setting the first guess very much depends on the assumption of color uniqueness:

```
abstract protected void setFirstGuess();
```

The first guess should not contain duplicated colors in case the hidden row is not allowed to contain any, therefore the method in this class is abstract.

The next method is an internal one that is overridden in the concrete classes:

```
protected Color[] nextGuess() {
    if (lastGuess[0] == null) {
        setFirstGuess();
        return lastGuess;
    } else {
        return nextNonFirstGuess();
    }
}
```

The `nextGuess` method is an internal one that generates the next guess, which just comes as we order the possible guesses. It does not check anything against the `Table`; it only generates the next guess almost without thinking. The implementation on how we do the first guess and how we do the consecutive guesses are different. Thus, we implement these algorithms in different methods and invoke them from here.

The `nextNonFirstGuess` method represents the next guess in the special case when the guess is not the first one:

```
private Color[] nextNonFirstGuess() {
    int i = 0;
    boolean guessFound = false;
    while (i < table.nrColumns && !guessFound) {
        if (manager.thereIsNextColor(lastGuess[i])) {
            lastGuess[i] = manager.nextColor(lastGuess[i]);
            guessFound = true;
        } else {
            lastGuess[i] = manager.firstColor();
            i++;
        }
    }
    if (guessFound) {
        return lastGuess;
    } else {
        return none;
    }
}
```

Look back a few pages where we detailed how the algorithm works. We made the statement that this way of working is very much like the way we count with decimal numbers. By now, you have enough Java knowledge and programming skill to understand what the method does. It is more interesting to know why it is coded that way.

Hint—as always, to be readable.

There is the temptation to eliminate the `guessFound` variable. Would it not be simpler to return from the middle of the method when we find the blessed guesses? If we did, there would be no need to check the `guessFound` value before returning the `none` value. The code would not get there if we returned from the middle of the loop.

Yes, it would be simpler to write. But, we create code to be readable and not writable. You can say that *yes, but less code is more readable*. Not in this case! Returning from a loop degrades the readability. Not to mention, the `return` statements are scattered around in the method at different stages of execution.

Also, returning from the loop represents an implicit end condition for the loop. In our case, the head of the loop clearly states how long we iterate in the loop—until we reached in the counting the total width of the table or we have a guess found.

When somebody writes code optimized in that way, it is similar to a toddler who makes his/her first steps and then looks proudly at his/her mother. Okay, boy/girl, you are great. Now, go on and start walking. When you are the postman, walking will be boring. That will be your profession. So, slide aside the pride and write boring code. Professionals write boring code. Won't it be slow?

No! It will not be slow. First of all, it is not slow until the profiler proves that the code does not meet the business requirements. If it does, it is fast enough, no matter how slow it is. Slow is good as long as it is okay for the business. After all, Just in Time compiler (JIT) should have some task optimizing the code to run.

The following method checks whether the guess matches the previous guesses and their results on the `Table`:

```
private boolean guessMatch(Color[] guess) {
    for (Row row : table.rows) {
        if (!row.guessMatches(guess)) {
            return false;
        }
    }
    return true;
}
```

As we have the guess matching already implemented in the class `Row`, all we have to do is invoke that method for each row in the table. If all rows match, then the guess can be good for the table. If any of the former guesses do not match, then this guess goes down the drain.

As we check the negated expression of matching, we created an English version of the negated method.

In situations like this, it could be enough to create the `guessDoesNotMatch` version of the method. However, the logical execution of the code is more readable if the method is not negated. Therefore, it is more error-prone to write the `guessDoesNotMatch` method alone. Instead, we will implement the original, readable version, and the aux method to be nothing more than a negation.

After all the aux methods, the next and final method we are implementing is the public one, `guess()`:

```
public Row guess() {
    Color[] guess = nextGuess();
    while (guess != none && guessDoesNotMatch(guess)) {
        guess = nextGuess();
```

```
        }
        if (guess == none) {
            return Row.none;
        } else {
            return new Row(guess);
        }
    }
```

It just calls `nextGuess()` again and again until it finds one guess that matches the hidden row, or there are no more guesses. If it finds a proper guess, it encapsulates it to a `Row` object and it returns it so that it can later be added to the `Table` by the `Game` class. This algorithm is the same in both cases, having unique and non-unique colors in a row.

UniqueGuesser

The `UniqueGuesser` class has to implement `setFirstGuess` (all concrete classes extending an abstract class should implement the abstract methods of the parents), and it can and will override the protected `nextGuess` method:

```
package packt.java189fundamentals.example.mastermind;

import java.util.HashSet;

public class UniqueGuesser extends Guesser {


    public UniqueGuesser(Table table) {
        super(table);
    }

    @Override
    protected void setFirstGuess() {
        int i = lastGuess.length - 1;
        for (var color = table.manager.firstColor();
             i >= 0;
             color = table.manager.nextColor(color)) {
            lastGuess[i--] = color;
        }
    }
```

The `setFirstGuess` method selects the first guess in such a way that any possible color variations that come after the first one create the guesses one after the other, if we follow the algorithm.

The aux `isNotUnique` method returns true if the guess contains duplicate colors. It is not interesting to see how many. If all colors are the same, or only one color appears twice, it does not matter. The guess is not unique and does not fit our guesser. This method tells us that.

Note that this method was already listed when we discussed the `Set` JDK interface:

```
private boolean isNotUnique(Color[] guess) {
    final var alreadyPresent = new HashSet<Color>();
    for (final var color : guess) {
        if (alreadyPresent.contains(color)) {
            return true;
        }
        alreadyPresent.add(color);
    }
    return false;
}
```

To do this, it uses a `Set`, and any time a new color is found in the `guess` array, the color is stored in the set. If the set contains the color when we find it in the array, it means that the color was already used before; the guess is not unique.

Also, notice that in this case, I coded the loop in a way that we return from the middle of the loop. The *don't return from the middle of a loop/method* rule is not set in stone. In this case, I felt that returning from the middle of the loop gives better readability rather than introducing a new `boolean`. The loop is short and whoever reads the code can easily spot the `return` just two lines below the loop head.

The last method that we have to implement in this concrete class is `nextGuess()`:

```
@Override
protected Color[] nextGuess() {
    Color[] guess = super.nextGuess();
    while (isNotUnique(guess)) {
        guess = super.nextGuess();
    }
    return guess;
}
```

The overriding `nextGuess()` method is simple. It asks the super `nextGuess()` implementation to make guesses but throws away those that it does not like.

GeneralGuesser

The `GeneralGuesser` class also has to implement the constructor and `setFirstGuess`, but generally, that is it. It does not need to do anything else:

```
package packt.java189fundamentals.example.mastermind;

public class GeneralGuesser extends Guesser {

    public GeneralGuesser(Table table) {
        super(table);
    }

    @Override
    protected void setFirstGuess() {
        int i = 0;
        for (Color color = table.manager.firstColor();
             i < lastGuess.length;
            ) {
            lastGuess[i++] = color;
        }
    }
}
```

The algorithm is extremely simple. It just puts the first color into each column of the `lastGuess` array. `Guess` could not be simpler. Everything else is inherited from the `abstract class Guesser`.

The Game class

An instance of the `Game` class contains a `Row` holding the secret color values and also contains a `Table`. When there is a new guess, the `Game` instance stores the guess into the `Table` and also sets the number of positions and colors matching the secret row:

```
package packt.java189fundamentals.example.mastermind;

public class Game {

    final Table table;
    final private Row secretRow;
    boolean finished = false;
    final int nrOfColumns;

    public Game(Table table, Color[] secret) {
        this.table = table;
```

```
            this.secretRow = new Row(secret);
            this.nrOfColumns = secretRow.nrOfColumns();
        }

        public void addNewGuess(Row row) {
            if (isFinished()) {
                throw new IllegalArgumentException(
                    "You can not guess on a finished game.");
            }
            final int positionMatch =
                secretRow.nrMatchingPositions(row.positions);
            final int colorMatch =
                secretRow.nrMatchingColors(row.positions);
            row.setMatch(positionMatch, colorMatch);
            table.addRow(row);
            if (positionMatch == nrOfColumns) {
                finished = true;
            }
        }

        public boolean isFinished() {
            return finished;
        }
    }
```

Think about what I wrote earlier about short methods. When you download the code from the Packt repository to play with it, try to make it look more readable. You can, perhaps, create and use a method named `boolean itWasAWinningGuess(int positionMatch)`.

Creating an integration test

We have created unit tests in the previous chapter and there are unit tests for the functionalities implemented in the classes of this chapter as well. We will just not print these unit tests here, but you can find them in the Packt code repository. Instead of listing the unit tests, we will look at an integration test.

Integration tests need the invocation of many classes working together. They check that the functionality can be delivered by the whole application, or at least a larger part of the application, and do not focus on a single unit. They are called integration tests because they test the integration between classes. The classes alone are all OK. They should not have any problem as it was already verified by the unit tests. Integration focuses on how they work together.

If we want to test the `Game` class, we will either have to create mocks that mimic the behavior of the other `Game` classes, or we will just write an integration test. Technically, an integration test is very similar to a unit test. In most cases, the very same JUnit framework is used to execute the integration tests. This is the case for the integration test of this game.

The build tool, however, needs to be configured to execute the integration tests only when it is required. Usually, integration test executions need more time, and sometimes resources, such as an external database that may not be available at each and every developer desktop. Unit tests run every time the application is compiled, so they have to be fast. To separate the unit and integration tests, there are different techniques and configuration options, but there is no such more or less de-facto standard, such as the directory structure introduced by Maven (later adapted by Gradle).

In our case, the integration test does not need any extra resources and does not take enormous time to run. It plays a game from the start to the end and plays the role of both the players. It is very much like somebody playing chess with themselves, making a step and then turning the table. It is an interesting question in those games who wins.

The aim of this code is twofold. On one hand, we want to see that the code runs and plays a whole game. If the game finishes, then it is just OK. This is a very weak assertion, and real integration tests perform lots of assertions (one test tests only one assertion, though). We will focus on the other aim—delivering some joy and visualizing the game on the console in text format so that the reader does not get bored.

To do that, we will create a utility class that prints out a color and assigns letters to the `Color` instances on the fly.

WARNING: There are several limitations in this class that we have to talk about after we look at the code. I'd say that this code is here only to demonstrate what *not to do*, to establish some reasoning for the next chapter, and why we need to refactor the code we created in this one. Read it with care!

This is the `PrettyPrintRow` class:

```
package packt.java189fundamentals.example.mastermind;

import java.util.HashMap;
import java.util.Map;

public class PrettyPrintRow {

    private static final Map<Color, Character>
            letterMapping = new HashMap<>();
    private static final String letters = "RGBYWb";
    private static int counter = 0;

    private static char colorToChar(Color color) {
        if (!letterMapping.containsKey(color)) {
            letterMapping.put(color, letters.charAt(counter));
            counter++;

        }
        return letterMapping.get(color);
    }
```

This is the heart of this class. When a color is to be printed, it gets a letter assigned unless it already has one. As the `Map` containing the assignments in each and every game that is running in the JVM will use the same mapping, a new `Game` is started. It allocates new `Color` objects and will soon run out of the six characters that we allocated here in the `String` constant.

If the `Game` instances run in parallel, then we are in even more trouble. The class is not thread-safe at all. If two threads concurrently call the `colorToChar` method for the same `Color` instance (which is not likely because each `Game` uses its own color, but note that **not likely** in programming is very much like a famous last words quote on a tombstone), then both threads may see that there is no letter assigned to the color at the same time and both will assign the letter (the same letter or two different letters, based on luck) and increase the counter once or twice. At least, what we can say is that the execution is nondeterministic.

You may recall that I said violating the hash contract is the second most difficult to find a bug in after multithread issues. Such a nondeterministic code is exactly that—a multithread issue. There is no prize for finding the most difficult bug. When the application does not run, and a bug affects the production system for hours or days, no business person will be happy, and they will not be amazed after you find the bug. It may be an intellectual challenge, and many programmers experience debugging something like that, but the real value is not creating the bugs in the first place.

As a summary, this code can only be used once in a JVM (under the same classloader) by a single thread. For this chapter, it is just okay, though a smelly and shameful code. Later, it will be a good example for the next chapter, in which we will see how to refactor the application so that it will not need such a hacking to print out the colors.

Code smell is a term coined by Kent Back, according to Martin Fowler (`http://martinfowler.com/bliki/CodeSmell.html`). It means that some code looks not good, nor apparently bad, but some constructs make the developer feel that it may not be good. As it is defined on the web page, *A code smell is a surface indication that usually corresponds to a deeper problem in the system.* The term is widely accepted and has been used in software development for the last 10 years.

The rest of the code is plain and simple:

```
        public static String pprint(Row row) {
            var string = "";
            final var pRow = new PrintableRow(row);
            for (int i = 0; i < pRow.nrOfColumns(); i++) {
                string += colorToChar(pRow.position(i));
            }
            string += " ";
            string += pRow.matchedPositions();
            string += "/";
            string += pRow.matchedColors();
            return string;
        }
    }
```

The integration test, or rather the demonstration code (as it does not contain any assertions other than it runs without exception), defines six colors and four columns. This is the size of the original game. It creates a color manager, and then it creates a table and a secret. The secret could be just any random color selection from the six colors that are available (there are 360 different possibilities tested in the `UniqueGuesserTest` unit test available from the Packt code repository). As we know that the `Guesser` implementation starts from one end of the color set and creates the new guesses systematically, we want to set a secret that it will guess last. This is not because we are evil, but rather because we want to see that our code really works.

The directory structure of the code is very similar to the one we used in the case of the Maven build tool, as can be seen on the following screenshot created on a Windows machine:

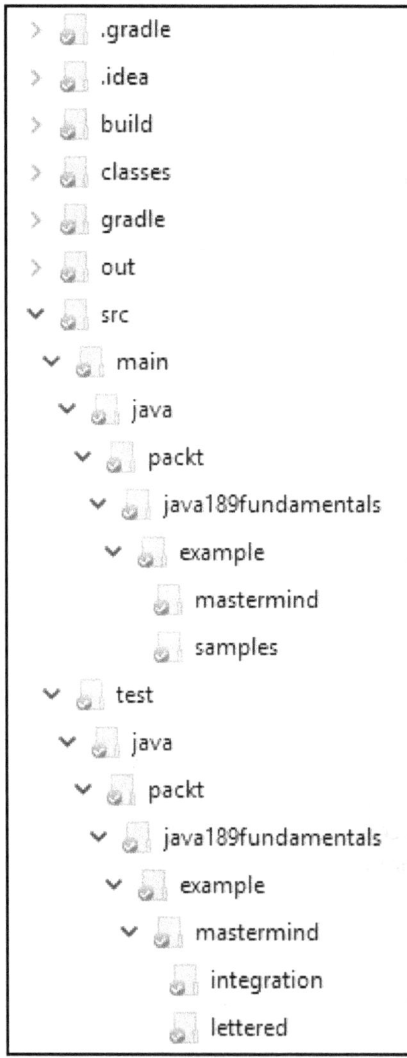

The source code is under the `src` directory, and the `main` and `test` source code files are separated into two subdirectory structures. The compiled files will be generated in the `build` directory when we use Gradle.

The code of the integration test class is as follows:

```
package packt.java189fundamentals.example.mastermind.integration;


import org.junit.Assert;
import org.junit.Test;
import packt.java189fundamentals.example.mastermind.*;

public class IntegrationTest {

    final int nrColors = 6;
    final int nrColumns = 4;
    final ColorManager manager = new ColorManager(nrColors);

    private Color[] createSecret() {
        Color[] secret = new Color[nrColumns];
        int count = 0;
        Color color = manager.firstColor();
        while (count < nrColors - nrColumns) {
            color = manager.nextColor(color);
            count++;
        }
        for (int i = 0; i < nrColumns; i++) {
            secret[i] = color;
            color = manager.nextColor(color);
        }
        return secret;
    }

    @Test
    public void testSimpleGame() {
        Table table = new Table(nrColumns, manager);
        Color[] secret = createSecret();
        System.out.println(PrettyPrintRow.pprint(new Row(secret)));
        System.out.println();
        Game game = new Game(table, secret);

        Guesser guesser = new UniqueGuesser(table);
        while (!game.isFinished()) {
            Row guess = guesser.guess();
            if (guess == Row.none) {
                Assert.fail();
            }
```

```
                game.addNewGuess(guess);
                System.out.println(PrettyPrintRow.pprint(guess));
            }
        }
    }
```

The easiest way to run the test is starting it from inside the IDE. When the IDE imports the project based on the build file, be it a Maven `pom.xml` or Gradle `build.gradle`, IDE usually provides a run button or menu to start the code. Running the game will print out the following piece of code that we worked so hard on in this chapter:

```
RGBY 0/0

GRWb 0/2
YBbW 0/2
BYGR 0/4
RGYB 2/2
RGBY 4/0
```

Summary

In this chapter, we programmed a table game—Mastermind. We not only programmed the model of the game but also created an algorithm that can guess. We revisited some OO principles and discussed why the model was created the way it was. We created the model of the game and at the same time we learned about Java collections, integration tests, and JavaDoc. In the next chapter, we will build on this knowledge and we will enhance the game to run on multiple processors.

5
Extending the Game - Run Parallel, Run Faster

In this chapter, we will extend the Mastermind game. As it is now, it can guess the secret that was hidden and it also can hide the pegs. The test code can even do both at the same time. It can play against itself, leaving us only with the fun of programming. What it cannot do is make use of all the processors that we have in today's notebooks and servers. The code runs synchronous and utilizes only a single processor core.

We will alter the code extending the guessing algorithm in order to slice up the guessing into subtasks and execute the code in parallel. In so doing, we will get acquainted with Java concurrent programming. This will be a huge topic, with many subtle twists and turns lurking in the shadows. We will get into those details that are the most important and will form a firm base for further studies whenever you need concurrent programs.

As the outcome of the game is the same as it was, only faster, we have to assess what faster is. To do that, we will utilize a new feature introduced in Java 9—the micro-benchmarking harness.

In this chapter, we will cover the following topics:

- The meaning of processes, threads, and fibers
- Multithreading in Java
- Issues with multithread programming and how to avoid them
- Locking, synchronization, and blocking queues
- Microbenchmarking

How to make Mastermind parallel

The old algorithm was to go through all the variations and try to find a guess that matches the current state of the table. Assuming that the currently examined guess is the secret, will we get the same answers for the guesses that are already on the table as the answers that are actually on the table? If yes, then the current guess can be the secret, and it is just as good a guess as any other guesses.

A more complex approach can implement the min-max algorithm (`https://en.wikipedia.org/wiki/Minimax`). This algorithm does not simply get the next possible guess, but also looks at all the possible guesses and selects the one that shortens the outcome of the game the most. If there is a guess that can be followed by three more guesses in the worst case, and there is another for which this number is only two, then min-max will choose the latter. It is a good exercise to implement the min-max algorithm for those readers who are interested. In the case of the six colors and four columns for the pegs, the min-max algorithm solves the game in no more than five steps. The simple algorithm we implemented also solves the game in five steps. However, we do not go in that direction.

Instead, we want to have a version of the game that utilizes more than one processor. How can you transform the algorithm into a parallel one? There is no simple answer to this. When you have an algorithm, you can analyze the calculations and parts of the algorithm, and you can try to find dependencies. If there is a calculation, *B,* that needs the data, which is the result of another calculation, *A*, then it is obvious that *A* can only be performed when *B* is ready. If there are parts of the algorithm that do not depend on the outcome of the others, then they can be executed in parallel.

For example, the quick-sort has two major tasks for partitioning and then sorting of the two parts. It is fairly obvious that the partitioning has to finish before we start sorting the two partitioned parts. However, the sorting tasks of the two parts do not depend on each other; they can be done independently. You can give them to two different processors. One will be happily sorting the part containing the smaller elements, while the other one will carry the larger ones.

If we recall the non-recursive quick-sort implementation, you can see that we scheduled the sorting tasks into a stack and then performed the sorting by fetching the elements from the stack in a `while` loop:

```
public class NonRecursiveQuickSort<E> {
// ... same fields and constructor as in Qsort are deleted from print ...

    private static class StackElement {
        final int begin;
```

```
        final int fin;

        public StackElement(int begin, int fin) {
            this.begin = begin;
            this.fin = fin;
        }
    }

    public void qsort(Sortable<E> sortable, int start, int end) {
        final var stack = new LinkedList<StackElement>();
        final var partitioner = new Partitioner<E>(comparator, swapper);
        stack.add(new StackElement(start, end));
        var i = 1;
        while (!stack.isEmpty()) {
            var it = stack.remove(0);
            if (it.begin < it.fin) {
                final E pivot = sortable.get(it.begin);
                var cutIndex = partitioner.partition(sortable, it.begin,
it.fin, pivot);
                if( cutIndex == it.begin ){
                    cutIndex++;
                }
                stack.add(new StackElement(it.begin, cutIndex - 1));
                stack.add(new StackElement(cutIndex, it.fin));
            }
        }
    }
}
```

Instead of executing the sort right there in the core of the loop, we could pass the tasks to asynchronous threads to perform it and go back for the next waiting task. We just do not know how. Yet. That is why we are here in this chapter.

Processors, threads, and processes are complex and abstract things, and they are hard to imagine. Different programmers have different techniques to imagine parallel processing and algorithms. I can tell you how I do it. There is no guarantee that this will work for you. Others may have different techniques in their mind. As a matter of fact, I just realized that as I write this, I have actually never told this to anyone before. It may seem childish, but anyway, here goes.

When I imagine algorithms, I imagine people. One processor is one person. This helps me overcome the freak fact that a processor can perform billions of calculations in a second. I actually imagine a bureaucrat wearing a brown suit and doing the calculations. When I create a code for a parallel algorithm, I imagine many of them working behind their desks. They work alone and they do not talk. It is important that they do not talk to each other. They are very formal. When there is a need for information exchange, they stand up with a piece of paper they have written something on, and they bring it to each other. Sometimes, they need a piece of paper for their work. Then, they stand up, go to the place where the paper is, take it, bring it back to their desk, and go on working. When they are ready, they go back and bring the paper back. If the paper is not there when they need it, they queue up and wait until someone who has the paper brings it there.

How does this help with the Mastermind game?

I imagine a boss who is responsible for the guesses. There is a table on the wall in the office with the previous guesses and the results for each row. The boss is too lazy to come up with new guesses so he gives this task to subordinates. When a subordinate comes up with a guess, the boss checks whether the guess is valid. He does not trust the subordinates, and if the guess is good, he makes it an official guess, putting it on the table along with the result.

The subordinates deliver the guesses written on small post-it notes, and they put them in a box on the table of the boss. The boss looks at the box from time to time, and if there is a note, the boss takes it. If the box is full and a subordinate wants to put a paper there, the subordinate stops and waits until the boss takes at least one note so that there is some room in the box for a new note. If the subordinates queue up to deposit guesses in the box, they all wait their turn.

The subordinates should be coordinated; otherwise, they will just come up with the same guesses. Each of them should have an interval of guesses. For example, the first one should check the guesses from 1234 up until 2134, the second should check from 2134 up until 3124, and so on, if we denote the colors with numbers.

Will this structure work? Common sense says that it will. However, bureaucrats, in this case, are metaphors, and metaphors are not exact. Bureaucrats are human, even when they do not seem to be, much more than threads or processors. They sometimes behave extremely strangely, doing things that normal humans don't really do often. However, we can still use this metaphor if it helps us to imagine how parallel algorithms work.

We can imagine that the boss goes on holiday and does not touch the heap of paper piling up on the table. We can imagine that some of the workers are producing results much faster than the others. As this is only imagination, the speedup can be 1,000 times (think of a time-lapse video). Imagining these situations may help us discover special behavior that rarely happens, but that may cause problems. As the threads work in parallel, a significant number of subtle differences may greatly influence general behavior.

In an early version, as I coded the parallel Mastermind algorithm, the bureaucrats started working and filled the box of the boss with guesses before the boss could put any of them on the table. As there were no guesses on the table, the bureaucrats simply found all possible variations in their interval possibly constituting a good guess. The boss gained nothing by the help of the parallel helpers; the boss had to select the correct ones from all possible guesses, while the guessers were just idle.

Another time, the bureaucrats were checking guesses against the table while the boss was putting a guess on it. Sticking to our metaphor, some of the bureaucrats freaked out, saying that it is not possible to check a guess against a table if someone is changing it. More precisely, executing the code in a bureaucratic thread threw `ConcurrentModificationException` when the `List` of the table was modified.

Another time, I tried to avoid the overly speedy work of bureaucrats, and I limited the size of the box where they could put their papers containing the guesses. When the boss finally discovered the secret, and the game finished, the boss told the bureaucrats that they could go home. The boss did that by creating a small paper with the instruction—you can go home and put it on the tables of the bureaucrats. What did the bureaucrats do? They kept waiting for the box to have space for the paper because while waiting there, they were not reading the table for any change! (Until the process was killed. This is kind of equivalent on macOS and on Linux as ending the process from the task manager on Windows.)

Such coding errors happen and, to avoid as many as possible, we have to do at least two things. Firstly, we have to understand how Java multithreading works and, secondly, have a code as clean as possible. For the second, we will clean up the code even more and then we will look at how the parallel algorithm described earlier can be implemented in Java, running on the JVM instead of utilizing bureaucrats.

Refactoring

When we finished the previous chapter, we had the classes of the Mastermind game designed and coded in a nice and perfectly object-oriented way that did not break any of the *OO* principles. Did we? Absurd. There is no code, except for a few trivial examples, that cannot be made to look nicer or better. Usually, when we develop code and finish the coding, it looks great. It works, the tests all run, and documentation is ready. From the professional point of view, it really is perfect. Well, it is good enough. The big question that we have not tested yet is maintainability. What is the cost of altering the code?

That is not an easy question, especially because it is not a definite one. Alter to what? What is the modification we want to make? We do not know that when we create the code in the first place. If the modification is to fix a bug, then it is obvious that we did not know that beforehand. If we knew, we would not have introduced the bug in the first place. If this is a new feature, then there is a possibility that the function was foreseen. However, usually, this is not the case. When a developer tries to predict the future, and what features the program will need in the future, they usually fail. It is the task of the customer to know the business. Features that are needed are driven by the business in the case of professional software development. After all, that is what it means to be professional.

Even though we do not exactly know what needs to be altered later in the code, there are certain things that may give hints to experienced software developers. Usually, the *OO* code is easier to maintain than the *ad hoc* code, and there is a code aroma that it is possible to detect. For example, take a look at the following code lines:

```
while (guesser.guess() != Row.none) {
. . .
while (guesser.nextGuess() != Guesser.none) {
. . .
public void addNewGuess(Row row) {
. . .
Color[] guess = super.nextGuess();
```

We may sense the odor of something strange. (Each of these lines is in the code of the application as we finished it in `Chapter 4`, *Mastermind - Creating a Game*.) The return value of the `guess()` method is compared to `Row.none`, which is a `Row`. In the next example line, we compare the return value of the `nextGuess()` method to `Guesser.none`, which should be a guess rather than a `Guesser`. When we add a new guess to something in the next example line, we actually add a `Row`. Finally, we can realize that the method `nextGuess()` returns a guess that is not an *object* with its own declared class. A guess is just an array of `Colors`. These things are messy. How do we go about improving the quality of the code?

Should we introduce another layer of abstraction creating a `Guess` class? Will it make the code more maintainable? Or will it only make the code more complex? It is usually true that the fewer code lines we have, the less possibility we have for bugs. However, sometimes, the lack of abstraction will make the code complex and tangled. What is the case in this situation? What is a general way to decide?

The more experience you have, the easier you will tell by looking at the code and acutely knowing what modifications you want to make. Many times, you will not bother making the code more abstract, and many other times, you will create new classes without hesitation. When in doubt, create the new classes and see what comes out. The important thing is not to ruin the already existing functionality. You can do that only if you have sufficient unit tests.

When you want to introduce some new functionality or fix a bug, but the code is not appropriate, you will have to modify it first. When you modify the code so that the functionality does not change, the process is named **refactoring**. You change a small part of the code in a limited time, and then you build it. If it compiles and all unit tests run, then you can go on. The hint is to run the build frequently. It is like building a new road near an existing one. Once every few miles, you should meet the old line. Failing to do so, you will end up somewhere in the middle of the desert going in totally the wrong direction, and all you can do is return to the starting point—your old to-be-refactored code. Effort wasted.

It is not only safety that compels us to run the build frequently; it is also time limitation. Refactoring does not directly deliver revenue. The functionality of the program is tied directly to income. Nobody will pay us for infinite refactoring work. Refactoring has to stop sometime and it is usually not the time when there is nothing to be refactored anymore. The code will never be perfect, but you may stop when it is good enough. And, many times, programmers are not satisfied with the quality of the code, and when they are forced to stop by some external factor (usually called the project manager), the code should compile and tests should run so that the new feature and bug fixing can be performed on the actual code base.

Refactoring is a huge topic and there are many techniques that can be followed during such an activity. It is so complex that there is a whole book about it by Martin Fowler (`http://martinfowler.com/books/refactoring.html`), that will soon have a second edition.

In our case, the modification we want to apply to our code is to implement a parallel algorithm. The first thing we will modify is the `ColorManager`. When we wanted to print guesses and rows on the terminal, we implemented it with some bad tricks. Why not have color implementations that can be printed? We can have a class that extends the original `Color` class and has a method that returns something that represents that color. Do you have any candidate name for that method? It is the `toString()` method. It is implemented in the `Object` class and any class can freely override it. When you concatenate an object to a string, automatic type conversion will call this method to convert the object to `String`. By the way, it is an old trick to use `""+object` instead of `object.toString()` to avoid a `null` pointer exception. Needless to say, we do not use tricks.

The `toString()` method is also invoked by the IDEs when the debugger wants to display the value of some object, so it is generally recommended to implement `toString()` if, for no other reason, then to ease development. If we have a `Color` class that implements `toString()`, then the `PrettyPrintRow` class becomes fairly straightforward and is less deceptive:

```
public class PrettyPrintRow {

    public static String pprint(Row row) {
        var string = "";
        var pRow = new PrintableRow(row);
        for (int i = 0; i < pRow.nrOfColumns(); i++) {
            string += pRow.pos(i);
        }
        string += " ";
        string += pRow.full();
        string += "/";
        string += pRow.partial();
        return string;
    }
}
```

We removed the problem from the printing class, but you may argue that the issue is still there, and you are right. Very often, when there is a problem in a class design, the way to the solution is to move the problem from the class to another. If it is still a problem there, then you may split the design more and more and, at the final stage, you will realize that what you have is an issue and not a problem.

To implement a `LetteredColor` class is also straightforward:

```
package packt.java189fundamentals.mastermind.lettered;

import packt.java189fundamentals.mastermind.Color;

public class LetteredColor extends Color {

    private final String letter;
    public LetteredColor(String letter){
        this.letter = letter;
    }

    @Override
    public String toString(){
        return letter;
    }
}
```

Again, the problem was pushed forward. But, in reality, this is not a problem. It is an *OO* design. Printing is not responsible for assigning a `String` to colors for their representation. And the color implementation itself is also not responsible for that. The assignment has to be performed where the color is made, and then the `String` has to be passed to the constructor of the `LetteredColor` class. The `color` instances are created in `ColorManager`, so we have to implement this in the `ColorManager` class. Or not? What does `ColorManager` do? It creates the colors and...

When you come to an explanation or description of a class that lists the functionalities, you may immediately see that the **single responsibility principle** was violated. `ColorManager` should manage the colors. Managing is providing a way to get the colors in a definite order and getting the first and the next when we know one color. We should implement the other responsibility—the creation of a color in a separate class.

A class that has the sole function of creating an instance of another class is called `factory`. That is almost the same as using the `new` operator but, unlike `new`, the factories can be used in a more flexible manner. We will see that immediately. The `ColorFactory` interface contains a single method, as follows:

```
package packt.java189fundamentals.mastermind;

public interface ColorFactory {
    Color newColor();
}
```

Interfaces that define only one method are named functional interfaces because their implementation can be provided as a lambda expression or as a method reference at the place where you would use an object that is an instance of a class that implements the functional interface. For example, the `SimpleColorFactory` implementation creates the following `Color` objects:

```
package packt.java189fundamentals.mastermind;

public class SimpleColorFactory implements ColorFactory {
    @Override
    public Color newColor() {
        return new Color();
    }
}
```

Where we use `new SimpleColorFactory()` in our code, we can just as well write `Color::new` or `() -> new Color()`.

It is very much like how we create an interface, and then an implementation, instead of just writing `new Color()` in the code in `ColorManager`. `LetteredColorFactory` is a bit more interesting:

```
package packt.java189fundamentals.mastermind.lettered;

import packt.java189fundamentals.mastermind.Color;
import packt.java189fundamentals.mastermind.ColorFactory;

public class LetteredColorFactory implements ColorFactory {

    private static final String letters =
"0123456789ABCDEFGHIJKLMNOPQRSTVWXYZabcdefghijklmnopqrstvwxzy";
    private int counter = 0;

    @Override
    public Color newColor() {
        Color color = new LetteredColor(letters.substring(counter, counter
+ 1));
        counter++;
        return color;
    }
}
```

Now, here, we have the functionality that assigns `String` objects to the `Color` objects when they are created. It is very important that the `counter` variable that keeps track of the already created colors is not `static`. The similar variable in the previous chapter was `static`, and it meant that it could run out of characters whenever newer `ColorManager` objects created too many colors. It actually did happen during the unit test execution when each test created `ColorManager` objects and new `Color` instances. The printing code tried to assign new letters to the new colors. The tests were running in the same JVM under the same classloader, and the unfortunate `static` variable had no clue as to when it could just start counting from zero for the new tests.

The drawback of this factory solution, on the other hand, is that somebody, somewhere, has to instantiate the factory, and it is not the `ColorManager`. `ColorManager` already has a responsibility, and it is not to create a color factory. The `ColorManager` has to get the `ColorFactory` in its constructor:

```
package packt.java189fundamentals.mastermind;

import java.util.HashMap;
import java.util.Map;

public class ColorManager {
    protected final int nrColors;
    protected final Map<Color, Color> successor = new HashMap<>();
    private final ColorFactory factory;
    private Color first;

    public ColorManager(int nrColors, ColorFactory factory) {
        this.nrColors = nrColors;
        this.factory = factory;
        createOrdering();
    }

    private Color[] createColors() {
        var colors = new Color[nrColors];
        for (int i = 0; i < colors.length; i++) {
            colors[i] = factory.newColor();
        }
        return colors;
    }

    private void createOrdering() {
        var colors = createColors();
        first = colors[0];
        for (int i = 0; i < nrColors - 1; i++) {
            successor.put(colors[i], colors[i + 1]);
        }
```

```
    }

    public Color firstColor() {
        return first;
    }

    public boolean thereIsNextColor(Color color) {
        return successor.containsKey(color);
    }

    public Color nextColor(Color color) {
        return successor.get(color);
    }

    public int getNrColors() {
        return nrColors;
    }
}
```

You may also notice that I could not resist refactoring the `createColors` method into two methods to follow the single responsibility principle.

Now, the code that creates a `ColorManager` has to create a factory and pass it to the constructor. For example, the unit test's `ColorManagerTest` class will contain the following method:

```
@Test
public void thereIsAFirstColor() {
    var manager = new ColorManager(NR_COLORS, Color::new);
    Assert.assertNotNull(manager.firstColor());
}
```

This is the simplest way ever to implement a factory defined by a functional interface. Just name the class and reference the `new` operator as if it was a method by creating a method reference.

The next thing we will refactor is the `Guess` class, which, actually, we did not have so far. A `Guess` class contains the pegs of the guess, and can calculate the number of full (color as well as position) and partial (color present but in the wrong position) matches. It can also calculate the next `Guess` that comes after this guess. This functionality was implemented in the `Guesser` class so far, but this is not really the functionality for how we select the guesses when checking the guesses already made on the table. If we follow the pattern we set up for the colors, we may implement this functionality in a separate class named `GuessManager`, but, as for now, it is not needed. Again, the required level of abstraction is largely a matter of taste; this thing is not black or white.

It is important to note that a `Guess` object can only be made at once. If it is on the table, the player is not allowed to change it. If we have a `Guess` that is not yet on the table, it is still just a `Guess` identified by the colors and orders of the pegs. A `Guess` object never changes after it was created. Such objects are easy to use in multithread programs and are called immutable objects. Because this is a relatively longer class, we will examine the code in several fragments throughout this book:

```
package packt.java189fundamentals.mastermind;

import java.util.Arrays;
import java.util.HashSet;

public class Guess {
    public final static Guess none = new Guess(new Color[0]);
    private final Color[] colors;
    private boolean uniquenessWasNotCalculated = true;
    private boolean unique;

    public Guess(Color[] colors) {
        this.colors = Arrays.copyOf(colors, colors.length);
    }
```

The constructor is creating a copy of the array of colors that are passed as an argument. Because a `Guess` is immutable, this is extremely important. If we just keep the original array, any code outside of the `Guess` class could alter the elements of the array, essentially changing the content of `Guess` that is not supposed to be changing.

The next part of the code is two simple getters:

```
public Color getColor(int i) {
    return colors[i];
}

public int nrOfColumns() {
    return colors.length;
```

```
}
```

The next method is the one that calculates the `nextGuess`:

```
public Guess nextGuess(ColorManager manager) {
    final var colors = Arrays.copyOf(this.colors, nrOfColumns());

    int i = 0;
    var guessFound = false;
    while (i < colors.length && !guessFound) {
        if (manager.thereIsNextColor(getColor(i))) {
            colors[i] = manager.nextColor(colors[i]);
            guessFound = true;
        } else {
            colors[i] = manager.firstColor();
            i++;
        }
    }
    if (guessFound) {
        return new Guess(colors);
    } else {
        return Guess.none;
    }
}
```

In this method, we start to calculate the `nextGuess`, starting with the color array that is contained in the actual object. We need a work array, which is modified, so we will copy the original. The final new object could, this time, use the array we use during the calculation. To allow that, we would need a separate constructor that does not create a copy of the `Color` array. It is a possible extra code. We should consider creating that only if we see that that is the bottleneck in the code and we are not satisfied with the actual performance. In this application, it is not the bottleneck either, and we are satisfied with the performance, as you will see later when we discuss benchmarking.

The next method just checks whether the passed `Guess` has the same number of colors as the actual one:

```
private void assertCompatibility(Guess guess) {
    if (nrOfColumns() != guess.nrOfColumns()) {
        throw new IllegalArgumentException("Can not compare different
length guesses");
    }
}
```

This is just a safety check used by the next two methods that calculate the matches:

```
public int nrOfPartialMatches(Guess guess) {
    assertCompatibility(guess);
    int count = 0;
    for (int i = 0; i < nrOfColumns(); i++) {
        for (int j = 0; j < nrOfColumns(); j++) {
            if (i != j &&
                    guess.getColor(i) == this.getColor(j)) {
                count++;
            }
        }
    }
    return count;
}

public int nrOfFullMatches(Guess guess) {
    assertCompatibility(guess);
    int count = 0;
    for (int i = 0; i < nrOfColumns(); i++) {
        if (guess.getColor(i) == this.getColor(i)) {
            count++;
        }
    }
    return count;
}
```

The next `isUnique()` method checks whether there is any color more than once in the `Guess`. As the `Guess` is immutable, it may not happen that a `Guess` is unique on one occasion and not unique at another time. This method should return the same result whenever it is called on a specific object. Because of that, it is possible to cache the result. This method does this, saving the return value to an instance variable.

You may say that this is premature optimization. Yes, it is. I decided to do it for one reason. It is a demonstration of a locally saved result and, based on that, you can try to modify the `nextGuess()` method to do the same. The `isUnique()` method is as follows:

```
public boolean isUnique() {
    if (uniquenessWasNotCalculated) {
        final var alreadyPresent = new HashSet<Color>();
        unique = true;
        for (final var color : colors) {
            if (alreadyPresent.contains(color)) {
                unique = false;
                break;
            }
            alreadyPresent.add(color);
```

```
            }
            uniquenessWasNotCalculated = false;
        }
        return unique;
    }
```

Methods that return the same result for the same arguments are called idempotent. Caching the return value for such a method can be very important if the method is called many times and the calculation is using a lot of resources. When the method has arguments, caching the result is not simple. The `object` method has to remember the result for all arguments that were already calculated, and this storage has to be effective. If it takes more resources to find the stored result than the calculation of it, then the use of cache not only uses more memory but also slows down the program. If the method is called for several arguments during the lifetime of the object, then the storage memory may just grow too large. The elements that will no longer be needed have to be purged. However, we cannot know which elements of the cache are not needed later. We are not fortune tellers, so we will have to guess. (Just like fortune tellers.)

As you can see, caching can get complex. To do that professionally, it is almost always better to use some readily available cache implementation. The caching we use here is only the tip of the iceberg. Or, it is even only the sunshine glimpsing on it.

The rest of the class is fairly standard and something we have talked about in detail—a good check of your knowledge is to understand how the `equals()`, `hashCode()`, and `toString()` methods are implemented this way. I implemented the `toString()` method to help me debug, but it is also used in the example output that will soon follow. Here are the methods:

```
    @Override
    public boolean equals(Object o) {
        if (this == o) return true;
        if (o == null || !(o instanceof Guess)) return false;
        var guess = (Guess) o;
        return Arrays.equals(colors, guess.colors);
    }

    @Override
    public int hashCode() {
        return Arrays.hashCode(colors);
    }

    @Override
    public String toString() {
        if (this == none) {
            return "none";
```

```
        } else {
            String s = "";
            for (int i = colors.length - 1; i >= 0; i--) {
                s += colors[i];
            }
            return s;
        }
    }
```

Mainly, this is all the modification I needed while I developed the parallel algorithm. After these changes, the code looks much better and nicely describes the functionality so that we can focus on the main topic of this chapter—how to execute code in Java in parallel.

The parallel execution of the code in Java is done in threads. You may know that there is a `Thread` object in Java runtime, but without understanding what a thread in the computer is, it makes no sense. In the following subsections, we will learn what these threads are, how to start a new thread, how to synchronize data exchange between threads, and finally, put all of this together and implement the Mastermind game parallel guessing algorithm.

Processes

When you power on your computer, the program that starts is the operating system (OS). The OS controls the machine hardware and the programs that you can run on the machine. When you start a program, the OS creates a new process. It means that the OS allocates a new entry in a table (array) where it administers the processes and fills in the parameters that it knows, and needs to know, about the process. For example, it registers what memory segment the process is allowed to use, what the ID of the process is, which user started it, and which other process was used to start it. You cannot start a process just out of thin air. When you double-click on an EXE file, you actually tell the file explorer, which is a program running as a process, to start the EXE file as a separate process. The explorer calls the system via an API and kindly asks the OS to do that. The OS will register the explorer process as the parent of the new process. The OS does not actually start the process at this point, but creates all the data that it needs subsequently to start it and, when there is some free CPU resource, then the process gets started, and, after that, it gets paused very soon, restarted and then paused, and so on. You will not notice it because the OS will start it again and again and is always pausing the process repeatedly. It needs to do this to provide run possibilities for all processes. That way, we experience all processes running at the same time. In reality, processes do not run at the same time on a single processor, but they get time slots to run often so we feel like they were running all the time.

If you have more than one CPU in the machine, then processes can actually run at the same time—as many processes as there are CPUs. As the integration gets more advanced today, desktop computers have CPUs that contain multiple cores that function almost like separate CPUs. On my machine, I have four cores, each capable of executing two threads simultaneously; so, my macOS is almost like an 8 CPU machine. When I started working, an 8-CPU computer was a million dollar machine.

Processes have separate memories. They are allowed to use one part of the memory and, if a process tries to use a part that does not belong to it, the processor will stop doing so. The OS will kill the process.

Just imagine how frustrated the developers of the original Unix must have been that they named the program to stop a process as `kill`. Stopping a process is called killing it. It is like medieval times, when they cut off the hand of a felon. You touch the wrong part of the memory and get killed. I would not like to be a process.

Memory handling by the OS is very complex, in addition to separating the processes from each other. When there is not enough memory, the OS writes part of the memory to disk, freeing up the memory and reloading that part when it is needed again. This is a very complex, low-level implemented and highly-optimized algorithm supported by special hardware operations. It is the responsibility of the OS.

Threads

When I said that the OS executes the processes in time slots, I simplified how this really happens. Every process has one or more threads, and threads are executed. A thread is the smallest execution managed by an *external* scheduler. Older OSes did not have the notion of a thread and were executing processes. As a matter of fact, the first thread implementations were simply duplicates of processes that were sharing the memory.

You may hear the term *lightweight process* if you read something old. It means a thread.

The important thing is that the threads do not have their own memory. They use the memory of the process. In other words, the threads that run in the same process have indistinguishable access to the same memory segment.

The possibility of implementing parallel algorithms that make use of the multiple cores in a machine extremely powerful, but, at the same time, it may lead to bugs:

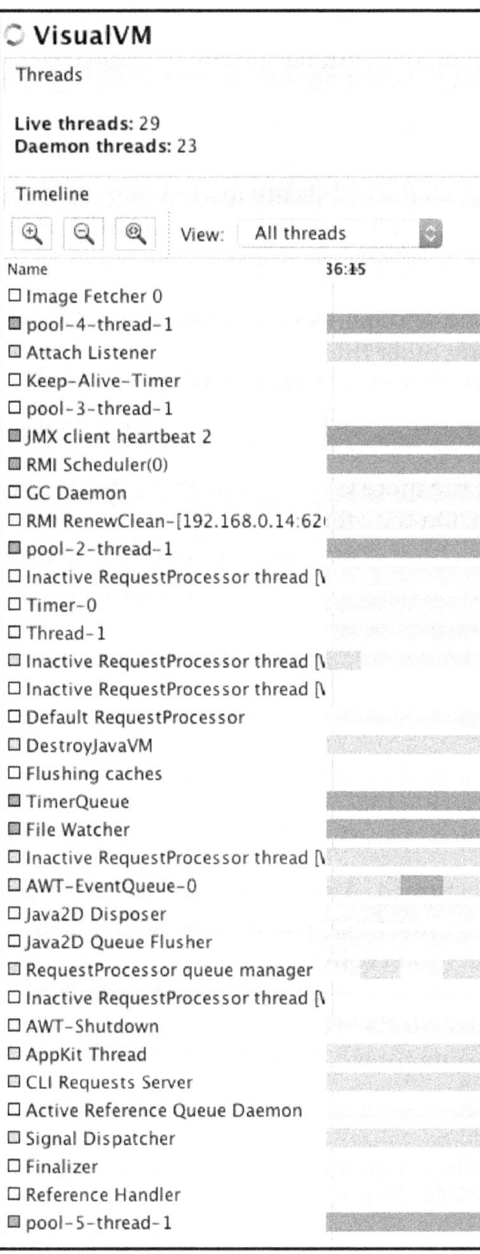

Imagine that two threads increment the same long variable. The increment first calculates the incremented value of the lower 32 bits and then the upper, if there were any overflow bits. These are two or more steps that may be interrupted by the OS. It may happen that one thread increments the lower 32 bits, it remembers that there is something to do to the upper 32 bits, starts the calculation, but has no time to store the result before it gets interrupted. Then, another thread increments the lower 32 bits, the upper 32 bits, and then the first thread just saves the upper 32 bits that it has calculated. The result gets garbled. On an older 32-bit Java implementation, it was extremely easy to demonstrate this effect. On a 64-bit Java implementation, all the 64 bits are loaded into registers and saved back to the memory in one step so it is not that easy to demonstrate this multithread, but it does not mean that there are none.

When a thread is paused and another thread is started, the OS has to perform a context switch. It means that, among other things, the CPU registers have to be saved and then set to the value that they should have for the other thread. A context switch is always saving the state of the thread and loading the previously saved state of the thread to be started. This is on a CPU register level. This context switch is time-consuming; therefore, the more context switches there are, the more CPU resources are used for the thread administration instead of letting them run. On the other hand, if there are not enough switches, some threads may not get enough time slots to execute, and the program hangs.

Fibers

Java version 11 does not have fibers, but there are some libraries that support limited fiber handling, and also there is a JDK project (`http://openjdk.java.net/projects/loom/`) that aims to have a later JVM version that supports fibers. Therefore, sooner or later, we will have fibers in Java and, hence, it is important to understand and know what they are.

A fiber is a finer unit than a thread. A program code executing in a thread may decide to give up the execution and tell the fiber manager to just execute some other fiber. What is the point and why is it better than using another thread? The reason is that this way, fibers can avoid part of the context switch. A context switch cannot be avoided totally because a different part of the code that starts to execute it may use the CPU registers in a totally different way. As it is the same thread, the context switching is not the task of the OS, but the application.

The OS does not know whether the value of a register is used or not. There are bits in the registers, and no one can tell, seeing only the processor state, whether those bits are relevant for the current code execution or just happen to be there in that way. The program generated by a compiler does know which registers are important and which are those that can just be ignored. This information changes from place to place in the code, but when there is a need for a switch, the fiber passes the information of what is needed to be switched at that point to the code that does the switching.

The compiler calculates this information, but Java does not support fibers in the current version. The tools that implement fibers in Java analyze and modify the bytecode of the classes to do this after the compilation phase.

Golang's goroutines are types of fibers and that is why you can easily start many thousands, or even millions, of goroutines in Go, but you are advised to limit the number of threads in Java to a lower number. They are not the same thing.

Even though the term *lightweight process* is slowly disappearing and is being used by less and less, fibers are frequently still referred to as lightweight threads.

java.lang.Thread

Everything in Java (well, almost) is an object. If we want to start a new thread, we will need an object and, therefore, a class that represents the thread. This class is `java.lang.Thread`, which is built into the JDK. When you start a Java code, the JVM automatically creates a few `Thread` objects and uses them to run different tasks that are needed by it. If you start up **VisualVM**, you can select the **Threads** tab of any JVM process and see the actual threads that are in the JVM. For example, the VisualVM as I started has 29 live threads. One of them is the thread named `main`. This is the one that starts to execute the `main` method (surprise!). The `main` thread started most of the other threads. When we want to write a multithread application, we will have to create new `Thread` objects and start them. The simplest way to do that is to initiate `new Thread()` and then call the `start()` method on the thread. It will start a new `Thread` that will just finish immediately as we did not give it anything to do. The `Thread` class, as it is in the JDK, does not do our business logic. The following are the two ways of specifying the business logic:

- Creating a class that implements the `Runnable` interface and passing an instance of it to a `Thread` object
- Creating a class that extends the `Thread` class and overrides the `run` method

The following block of code is a very simple demonstration program:

```
package packt.java189fundamentals.thread;

public class SimpleThreadIntermingling {
    public static void main(String[] args) {
        Thread t1 = new MyThread("t1");
        Thread t2 = new MyThread("t2");
        t1.start();
        t2.start();
        System.out.print("started ");

    }

    static class MyThread extends Thread {
        private final String name;

        MyThread(String name) {
            this.name = name;
        }

        @Override
        public void run() {
            for (int i = 1; i < 1000; i++) {
                System.out.print(name + " " + i + ", ");
            }
        }
    }
}
```

The preceding code creates two threads and starts them one after the other. When the start method is called, it schedules the thread object to be executed and then returns. As a result, the new thread will soon start executing asynchronously while the calling thread continues its execution. The two threads and the `main` thread run parallel in the following example and create an output that looks something like this:

```
started t2 1, t2 2, t2 3, t2 4, t2 5, t2 6, t2 7, t2 8, t1 1, t2 9, t2 10,
t2 11, t2 12,...
```

The actual output changes from run to run. There is no definite order of the execution, or how the threads get access to the single screen output. There is not even a guarantee that in each and every execution, the message `started` is printed before any of the thread messages.

To get a better understanding of this, we look at the state diagram of threads. A Java thread can be in one of the following states:

- `NEW`
- `RUNNABLE`
- `BLOCKED`
- `WAITING`
- `TIMED_WAITING`
- `TERMINATED`

These states are defined in the `enumThread.State`. When you create a new thread object, it is in the `NEW` state. At this moment, the thread is nothing special, it is just an object but the OS execution scheduling does not know about it. In some sense, it is only a piece of memory allocated by the JVM.

When the start method is invoked, the information about the thread is passed to the OS and the OS schedules the thread so that it can be executed by it when there is an appropriate time slot. Doing this is a resourceful action and that is the reason why we do not create and, especially, do not start new `Thread` objects only when required. Instead of creating new `Threads`, we will keep the existing threads for a while, even if they are not needed at the moment, and reuse an existing one if there is one suitable.

A thread in the OS can also be in a running state, as well as runnable, when the OS schedules and executes it. At the moment, the Java JDK API does not distinguish between the two for good reason. It would be useless. When a thread is in the `RUNNABLE` state, asking from inside the thread itself if it is actually running will result in an obvious answer—if the code just returned from the `getState()` method implemented in the `Thread` class, then it runs. If it were not running, it would not have returned from the call in the first place. Going even further, the invocation of the method `getState()` is also impossible inside a non-running `Thread`. If the `getState()` method were called from another thread, then the result concerning the other thread by the time the method returns would be meaningless. The OS may have stopped, or started, the queried thread several times by then.

A thread is in a `BLOCKED` state when the code executing in the thread tries to access a resource that is not currently available. To avoid constant polling of resources, the OS provides an effective notification mechanism so that the threads get back to the `RUNNABLE` state when the resource they need becomes available.

A thread is in the `WAIT` or `TIMED_WAITING` state when it waits for some other thread or lock. `TIMED_WAITING` is the state when the waiting started, calling a version of a method that has a timeout.

Finally, the `TERMINATED` state is reached when the thread has finished its execution. If you append the following lines to the end of our previous example, then you will get a `TERMINATED` printout and an exception is thrown up to the screen complaining about an illegal thread state, which is because you cannot start an already terminated thread:

```
System.out.println();
System.out.println(t1.getState());
System.out.println();
t1.start();
```

Instead of extending the `Thread` class to define what to execute asynchronously, we can create a class that implements the `Runnable` interface. Doing that is more coherent with the *OO* programming approach. The something that we implement in the class is not a functionality of a thread. It is more of a something that can be executed. It is something that can just run.

If the execution is asynchronous in a different thread, or if it is executed in the same thread that was calling the run method, this is a different concern that is to be separated. If we do it that way, we can pass the class to a `Thread` object as a constructor argument. Calling `start` on the `Thread` object will start the run method of the object we passed. This is not the gain. The gain is that we can also pass the `Runnable` object to an `Executor` (dreadful name, huh!). `Executor` is an interface, and implementations execute `Runnable` (and also `Callable`, see later) objects in `Thread` objects in an efficient way. Executors usually have a pool of `Thread` objects that are prepared and in the `BLOCKED` state. When the `Executor` has a new task to execute, it gives it to one of the `Thread` objects and releases the lock that is blocking the thread. The `Thread` gets into the `RUNNABLE` state, executes the `Runnable`, and gets blocked again. It does not terminate and, thus, can be reused to execute another `Runnable` later. That way, `Executor` implementations avoid the resource-consuming process of thread registration in the OS.

Professional application code never creates a new `Thread`. Application code uses a framework to handle the parallel execution of the code or uses `Executor` implementations provided by some `ExecutorService` to start `Runnable` or `Callable` objects.

Pitfalls

We have already discussed many of the problems that we may face when developing a parallel program. In this section, we will summarize them with the usual terminology used for the problems. Terminology is not only interesting, but it is also important when you talk to colleagues so that you understand one another.

Deadlocks

Deadlock is the most infamous parallel programming pitfall and, for this reason, we will start with this one. To describe the situation, we will follow the metaphor of bureaucrats.

The bureaucrat has to stamp a paper. To do that, he needs the stamp and the paper. First, he goes to the drawer where the stamp is and takes it. Then, he walks to the drawer where the paper is and takes the paper. He inks the stamp, and presses on the paper. Then, he returns the stamp and the paper to their places. Everything is peachy; we are on cloud 9.

What happens if another bureaucrat takes the paper first and then the stamp second? They may soon end up as one bureaucrat with the stamp in hand waiting for the paper, and another one with the paper in hand waiting for the stamp. And, they may just stay there, frozen forever, and then more and more start to wait for these locks, and the paper never gets stamped, and the whole system sinks into a frozen anarchy.

To avoid such situations, the locks have to be ordered and the locks should always be acquired in the same order. In the preceding example, the simple agreement that the ink pad is acquired first and the stamp second solves the problem. Whoever acquired the stamp can be sure that the ink pad is free, or will soon be free.

Race conditions

We talk about race conditions when the result of a calculation may be different based on the speed and CPU access of the different parallel running threads. Let's take a look at the following two methods:

```
    void method1(){
1         a = b;
2         b = a+1;
          }
     void method2(){
3         c = b;
4         b = c+2;
          }
```

The order of the lines can be 1234, 1324, 1342, 3412, 3142, or 3142. Any execution order of the four lines may happen that assures that **1** runs before **2** and **3** runs before **4**, but there are no other restrictions. Assuming that the value of `b` is zero at the start, the value of `b`, is either 1 or `2£` at the end of the execution of the segments. This is almost never what we want. We prefer it if the behavior of our program is not stochastic except, perhaps when implementing a random generator.

Note that the implementation of the parallel Mastermind game also faces something that is a kind of race condition. The actual guesses very much depend on the speed of the different threads, but this is irrelevant from the point of view of the final result. We may have different guesses in different runs and, that way, the algorithm is not deterministic. What is guaranteed is that we find the final solution.

Overused locks

In many situations, it may happen that the threads are waiting on a lock, which protects a resource from concurrent access. If the resource cannot be used by multiple threads simultaneously, and there are more threads, then the threads are starving. However, in many cases, the resource can be organized in a way so that the threads can get access to some of the services that the resource provides, and the locking structure can be less restrictive. In that case, the lock is overused and the situation can be mended without allocating more resource for the threads. It may be possible to use several locks that control access to the different functionality of the resource.

Starving

Starving is the situation when several threads are waiting for a resource trying to acquire a lock and some threads get access to the lock only after an extremely long period of time, or never. When the lock is released and there are threads waiting for it, then one of the threads can get the lock. There is usually no guarantee that a thread gets the lock if it waits long enough. Such a mechanism would require intensive administration of the threads, sorting them in the waiting queue. As locking should be a low latency and high-performance action, even a few CPU clock cycles are significant; therefore, the locks do not provide this type of fair access by default. Not wasting time with fairness in thread scheduling is a good approach, in case the locks have only one thread waiting. The main goal of locks is not scheduling the waiting threads, but rather preventing parallel access to resources.

It is like a shop. If there is somebody at the cashier, you wait. It is a lock that's built in implicitly. It is not a problem if people do not queue up for the cashier, so long as there is almost always one free. However, when there are several people waiting in front of the cashiers, then having no queue and the waiting order will certainly lead to very long waiting time for someone who is slow to get access to the cashier. Generally, the solution of fairness and creating a queue of waiting threads (customers) is not a good solution. The good solution is to eliminate the situation that leads to waiting queues. You can employ more cashiers, or you can do something totally different that makes the peak load smaller. In a shop, you can give a discount to drive customers who come in at off-peak hours. In programming, several techniques can be applied, usually, depending on the actual business we code, and the fair scheduling of locks is usually a workaround.

ExecutorService

`ExecutorService` is an interface in the JDK. An implementation of the interface can execute a `Runnable` or `Callable` class in an asynchronous way. The interface only defines the API for the implementation and does not require that the invocation is asynchronous. In reality, that is why we use such a service. Invoking the `run` method of a `Runnable` interface in a synchronous way is simply calling a method. We do not need a special class for that.

The `Runnable` interface defines one `run` method. It has no arguments, returns no value, and does not throw an exception. The `Callable` interface is parameterized and the only method it defines, `call`, has no argument, but returns a generic value and may also throw `Exception`. In a code, we implement `Runnable` if we just want to run something, and `Callable` when we want to return something. Both of these interfaces are functional interfaces; therefore, they are good candidates to be implemented using lambda.

To have an instance of an implementation of an `ExecutorService`, we can use the utility class `Executors`. Very often, when there is an `XYZ` interface in the JDK, there can be an `XYZs` (plural) utility class that provides a factory for the implementations of the interface. If we want to start the `t1` task many times, we can do so without creating a new `Thread`. We should use the following executor service:

```
public class ThreadIntermingling {
    public static void main(String[] args) throws InterruptedException,
ExecutionException {
        final var es = Executors.newFixedThreadPool(2);
        final var t1 = new MyRunnable("t1");
        final var t2 = new MyRunnable("t2");
        final Future<?> f1 = es.submit(t1);
        final Future<?> f2 = es.submit(t2);
        System.out.print("started ");
        var o = f1.get();
        System.out.println("object returned " + o);
        f2.get();
        System.out.println();
        es.submit(t1);
        es.shutdown();
    }

    static class MyRunnable implements Runnable {
        private final String name;

        MyRunnable(String name) {
            this.name = name;
        }

        @Override
        public void run() {
            for (int i = 1; i < 10; i++) {
                System.out.print(name + " " + i + ", ");
            }
        }
    }
}
```

This time, we do not get an exception when we submit the task `t1` the second time. In this example, we are using a fixed size thread pool that has two `Thread` slots. As we want to start only two threads simultaneously, it is enough. There are implementations that grow and shrink the size of the pool dynamically. A fixed size pool should be used when we want to limit the number of threads or we know from some other information source the number of threads *a priori*. In this case, it is a good experiment to change the size of the pool to one and see that the second task will not start in this case until the first one finishes. The service will not have another thread for `t2` and will have to wait until the one and only `Thread` in the pool becomes available.

When we submit the task to the service, it returns even if the task cannot currently be executed. The tasks are put in a queue and will start execution as soon as there are adequate resources to start them. The `submit` method returns a `Future<?>` object, as we can see in the preceding sample.

It is like a service ticket. You bring your car to the repair mechanic, and you get a ticket. You are not required to stay there until the car is fixed, but, at any time, you can ask whether the car is ready. All you need is the ticket. You can also decide to wait until the car is ready. A `Future` object is something similar. You do not get the value that you need. It will be calculated asynchronously. However, there is a `Future` promise that it will be there and your ticket to access the object you need is the `Future` object.

When you have a `Future` object, you can call the `isDone()` method to see whether it is ready. You can start waiting for it to call `get()` with, or without, a timeout. You can also cancel the task executing it, but, in that case, the outcome may be questionable. Just like, in the case of your car, if you decide to cancel the task, you may get back your car with the motor disassembled. Similarly, canceling a task that is not prepared for it may lead to resource loss, opened and inaccessible database connections (this is a painful memory for me, even after 10 years), or just a garbled unusable object. Prepare your tasks to be canceled or do not cancel them.

In the preceding example, there is no return value for `Future` because we submitted a `Runnable` object and not a `Callable` one. In that case, the value passed to the `Future` is not to be used. It is usually `null`, but that is nothing to depend on.

The final and most important thing that many developers miss, even me, after not writing multithread Java API using the code for years, is shutting down the `ExecutorService`. The `ExecutorService` is created and it has `Thread` elements. The JVM stops when all non-daemon threads are stopped. "It ain't over till the fat lady sings."

A thread is a daemon thread if it was set to be a daemon (invoking `setDaemon(true)`) before it was started. A thread that is automatically a daemon thread of the one starting it is also a daemon thread. Daemon threads are stopped by the JVM when all other threads are finished and the JVM wants to finish. Some of the threads the JVM executes itself are daemon threads, but it is likely that there is no practical use of creating daemon threads in an application program.

Not shutting down the service simply prevents the JVM from stopping. The code will hang after the `main` method finishes. To tell the `ExecutorService` that there is no need for the threads it has, we will have to `shutdown` the service. The call will only start the shutdown and return immediately. In this case, we do not want to wait. The JVM does anyway. If we need to wait, we will have to call `awaitTermination`.

Completable future

Java version 1.8 introduced a new implementation of the interface `Future`—`CompletableFuture`. The `java.util.concurrent.CompletableFuture` class can be used to asynchronously execute programs defining callbacks to handle the results. As Java 1.8 also introduced lambda expressions, the callbacks can be described using them:

```
public static void main(String[] args) throws ExecutionException,
InterruptedException {
    var future = CompletableFuture.supplyAsync(() ->
            {
                var negative = true;
                var pi = 0.0;
                for (int i = 3; i < 100000; i += 2) {
                    if (negative)
                        pi -= (1.0 / i);
                    else
                        pi += (1.0 / i);
                    negative = !negative;
                }
                pi += 1.0;
                pi *= 4.0;
                return pi;
            }
    ).thenAcceptAsync(piCalculated -> System.out.println("pi is " +
piCalculated));
    System.out.println("All is scheduled");
    future.get();
}
```

The completable future class implements the `Future` interface, but it also provides other methods that are handy when we need to describe the execution of asynchronous code. The extra methods are defined in the `CompletionStage` interface, which is a somewhat strange name at first, but we will understand what it really means soon.

We have already seen one of the many methods defined in this interface—`thenAcceptAsync()`. The preceding code creates a completable future that is defined by a lambda expression. The static method `supplyAsync()` accepts a `Supplier` as an argument. The threading system of Java will invoke this supplier later. The return value of this method is a `CompletableFuture` and it is used to create another `CompletableFuture` using the method `thenAcceptAsync()`. This second `CompletableFuture` is attached to the first one. It will start only when the first one has finished. The argument to the `thenAcceptAsync()` is a consumer that will consume the result of the first `CompletableFuture` provided by the `Supplier`. The structure of the code can be described with the following pseudo-code:

```
CompletableFuture.supplyAsync( supply_value ).thenAcceptAsync(
consume_the_value )
```

It says to start the `Supplier` represented by `supply_value` and, when it is done, to feed this value to the consumer represented by `consume_the_value`. The sample code calculates the value of pi and supplies this value. The `consume_the_value` part prints the value to the output. When we run the code, then the text `All is scheduled` will probably be printed to the output first and the calculated value of pi only after it.

There are many other methods implemented by the class. When the completable future does not produce any value or we just do not need to consume the value, then we should use the `thenRunAsync(Runnable r)` method.

If we want to consume the value and also want to create a new value from it, then we should use the `thenApplyAsync()` method. The argument to this method is a `Function` that gets the result of the completable future after that runs and the result is the value for the completable future `thenApplyAsync()` returns.

There are many other methods that execute code after the completable future is completed. These all serve the purpose of specifying some callback after the first completable future is complete. The execution of the code of the completable future may throw an exception. In that case, the completable future is completed; it does not throw an exception. The exception is caught and stored in the completable future object and it is thrown only when we want to access the result calling the `get()` method. The method `get()` throws an `ExecutionException` encapsulating the original exception. The `join()` method throws the original exception.

Methods such as `thenAcceptAsync()` have their synchronous pairs, for example, `thenAccept()`. If this is called, then the passed code will be executed either:

- Use the same thread that was used to execute the original completable future in case the completable future on which this code relies has not finished yet; or
- Use the normal caller thread if the completable future was already finished

In other words, if we look again at the pseudo code:

```
var cf = CompletableFuture.supplyAsync( supply_value );
cf.thenAccept( consume_the_value )
```

But this time it is `thenAccept()` and not `thenAcceptAsync()`, so either the thread that executes the code presented by `supply_value` continues executing `consume_the_value` after it finished with `supply_value`, or, if the execution of `supply_value` is already finished when the method `thenAccept()` is invoked, then it will simply execute as follows:

```
consume_the_value( cf.get() )
```

In this instance, the code `consume_the_value` is simply executed synchronously. (Note that if an exception happens, it will be stored and not directly thrown.)

The best use case for the use of `CompletableFuture` is when we have an asynchronous calculation and we need callback methods handling the result.

ForkJoinPool

The `ForkJoinPool` is a special `ExecutorService` that has methods to execute `ForkJoinTask` objects. These classes are very handy when the task that we want to perform can be split into many small tasks and then the results, when they are available, aggregated. Using this executor, we need not care about the size of the thread pool and shutting down the executor. The size of the thread pool is adjusted to the number of processors on the given machine in order to have optimal performance. As the `ForkJoinPool` is a special `ExecutorService` that is designed for short running tasks, it does not expect any task to be there longer or being needed when there are no more tasks to run. Therefore, it is executed as a daemon thread; when the JVM shuts down, the `ForkJoinPool` automatically stops.

To create a task, a programmer should extend either `java.util.concurrent.RecursiveTask` or `java.util.concurrent.RecursiveAction`. The first one is to be used when there is some return value from the task, the second when there is no computed value returned. They are called recursive because, many times, these tasks split the problem they have to solve smaller problems and invoke these tasks asynchronously through the fork/join API.

A typical problem to be solved using this API is quicksort. In `Chapter 3`, *Optimizing the Sort - Making Code Professional*, we created two versions of the quicksort algorithm, one using recursive calls and one without. We can also create a new one, which, instead of calling itself recursively, schedules the task to be executed, perhaps by another processor. Scheduling is the task of the `ForkJoinPool` implementation of `ExecutorService`.

You may revisit the code of `Qsort.java` in `Chapter 3`, *Optimizing the Sort - Making Code Professional*. Here is the version that is using `ForkJoinPool` without some of the obvious code, including the constructor and the `final` field definitions:

```
public void qsort(Sortable<E> sortable, int start, int end) {
    ForkJoinPool pool = new ForkJoinPool();
    pool.invoke(new RASort(sortable, start, end));
}

private class RASort extends RecursiveAction {

    final Sortable<E> sortable;
    final int start, end;

    public RASort(Sortable<E> sortable, int start, int end) {
        this.sortable = sortable;
        this.start = start;
        this.end = end;
```

```
    }

    public void compute() {
        if (start < end) {
            final E pivot = sortable.get(start);
            int cutIndex = partitioner.partition(sortable, start, end,
pivot);
            if (cutIndex == start) {
                cutIndex++;
            }
            RecursiveAction left = new RASort(sortable, start, cutIndex -
1);
            RecursiveAction right = new RASort(sortable, cutIndex, end);
            invokeAll(left, right);
            left.join();
            right.join();
        }
    }
}
```

After the array is split by the pivot element, two `RecursiveAction` objects are created. They store all the information that is needed to sort the left-hand and the right-hand side of the array. When `invokeAll()` is invoked, these actions get scheduled. The `invokeAll()` method is inherited by the preceding code from the `ForkJoinClass` class through `RecursiveAction`, which itself is extended in this code.

Good reading material is available on the API and on the application of Oracle's Javadoc documentation.

Variable access

Now that we can start threads and create code that runs parallel, it is time to talk a little bit about how these threads can exchange data between one another. At first glance, it seems fairly simple. The threads use the same shared memory; therefore, they can read and write all the variables that the Java access protection allows them. This is true, except that some threads may just decide not to read the memory. After all, if they have just recently read the value of a particular variable, why read it again from the memory to the registers if it was not modified? Who would have modified it? Let's see the following short example:

```
package packt.java189fundamentals.thread;

public class VolatileDemonstration implements Runnable {
    private final Object o;
    private static final Object NON_NULL = new Object();
```

```
        @Override
        public void run() {
            while( o == null );
            System.out.println("o is not null");
        }

        public VolatileDemonstration() throws InterruptedException {
            new Thread(this).start();
            Thread.sleep(1000);
            this.o = NON_NULL;
        }

        public static void main(String[] args) throws InterruptedException {
            VolatileDemonstration me = new VolatileDemonstration();
        }
    }
```

What will happen? You may expect that the code starts up, starts the new thread, and then, when the `main` thread sets the object to something that is not `null`, will it stop? It will not.

It may stop on some Java implementations, but, in most of them, it will just keep spinning. The reason for that is that the JIT compiler optimizes the code. It sees that the loop does nothing and also that the variable will just never be non-null. It is allowed to assume that because the variables not declared to be `volatile` are not supposed to be modified by different threads, the JIT is eligible to optimize. If we declare the `Object o` variable to be `volatile`, then the code will stop. You also have to remove the `final` keyword because a variable cannot be `final` and `volatile` at the same time.

In case you try to remove the call to sleep, the code will also stop. This, however, does not fix the issue. The reason is that JIT optimization kicks in only after about 5,000 loops of the code execution. Before that, the code runs naive and stops before optimization will eliminate the extra, and regularly not needed, access to the non-volatile variable.

If this is so gruesome, then why don't we declare all variables to be volatile? Why does Java not do that for us? The answer is speed. To understand it deeper, we will use our metaphor with the office, and the bureaucrats.

The CPU heartbeat

These days, CPUs run on 2 to 4 GHz frequency processors. It means that a processor gets 2 to 4 times 10^9 clock signals to do something every second. A processor cannot perform any atomic operation faster than this, and also there is no reason to create a clock that is faster than what a processor can follow. It means that a CPU performs a simple operation, such as incrementing a register, in half or quarter of a nanosecond. This is the heartbeat of the processor, and if we think of the bureaucrat as humans, and who they are, then it is equivalent to one second, approximately, as their heartbeat. In our imagination, this slows down the operation of the computer to an understandable speed.

Processors have registers and caches on the chip on different levels; L1, L2, and sometimes L3; there is the memory, SSD, disk, magnetic disk, network, and tapes that may be needed to retrieve data.

Accessing data that is in the L1 cache takes approximately 0.5 ns. You can grab a paper that is on your desk—half a second. Accessing data that is in the L2 cache takes 7 ns. This is a paper in the drawer. You have to push the chair back a bit, bend it in a sitting position, pull out the drawer, take the paper, push the drawer back, raise and put the paper on the desk; it takes 10 seconds, give or take.

Main memory read is 100 ns. The bureaucrat stands up, goes to the shared file storage by the wall, waits while other bureaucrats are pulling their papers or putting theirs back, selects the drawer, pulls it out, takes the paper, and walks back to the desk. This takes two minutes. This is volatile variable access every time you write a single word on a document and it has to be done twice, once to read, and once to write, even if you happen to know that the next thing you will do is just fill in another field of the form on the same paper.

Modern architectures, where there are no multiple CPUs, but rather single CPUs with multiple cores, are a bit faster. One core may check the other core's caches to see whether there was any modification on the same variable. This accelerates volatile access to 20 ns or so, which is still a magnitude slower than non-volatile.

Although the rest is less focused on multithread programming, it is worth mentioning here, because it gives a good understanding of the different time magnitudes.

Reading a block from an SSD (4 K block usually) takes 150,000 ns. In human speed, that is a little bit more than 5 days. Reading or sending something to a server over the network on the Gb local ethernet is 0.5 ms, which is like waiting for almost a month for the metaphoric bureaucrat. If the data over the network is on a spinning magnetic disk, then seek time adds up (the time until the disk rotates so that the part of the magnetic surface gets under the reading head) to 20 ms. It is, approximately, a year in human terms for the imagined little bureaucrats running up and down in our computational environment.

If we send a network packet over the Atlantic on the internet, it takes approximately 150 ms. It is like 14 years, and this was only one single package; if we want to send data over the ocean, this would constitute thousands of years in historic times. If we count one minute for a machine to boot, it is equivalent to the time span of our whole civilization.

We should consider these numbers when we want to understand what the CPU is doing most of the time. It waits. Additionally, this metaphor also helps to calm your nerves when you think about the speed of a real-life bureaucrat. They are not that slow after all if we consider their heartbeat, which implies that they have a heart. However, let's get back to real life, CPUs, L1 and L2 caches, and volatile variables.

Volatile variables

Let's modify the declaration of the `o` variable in our sample code as follows:

```
private volatile Object o = null;
```

The preceding code runs fine and stops after a second or so. Any Java implementation has to guarantee that multiple threads can access `volatile` fields and the value of the field is consistently updated. This does not mean that volatile declaration will solve all synchronization issues, but guarantees that the different variables and their value change relations are consistent. For example, let's consider that we have the following two fields incremented in a method:

```
private int i=0,j=0;
 public void method(){
     i++; j++;
 }
```

In the preceding code, reading `i` and `j` in a different thread may never result in `i>j`. Without the `volatile` declaration, the compiler is free to reorganize the execution of the increment operations and thus, it will not guarantee that an asynchronous thread reads consistent values.

Synchronized block

Declaring variables is not the only tool for ensuring consistency between threads. There are other tools in the Java language, and one of them is the synchronized block. The `synchronized` keyword is part of the language and it can be used in front of a method or a program block, which is inside a method, constructor, or initializer block.

Every object in the Java program has a monitor that can be locked and unlocked by any running thread. When a thread locks a monitor, it is said that the thread holds the lock, and no two threads can hold the lock of a monitor at a time. If a thread tries to lock a monitor that is already locked, it gets `BLOCKED` until the monitor is released. A synchronized block starts with the `synchronized` keyword, and then an object instance specified between parentheses, and then blocking takes place. The following small program demonstrates the `synchronized` block:

```
package packt.java189fundamentals.thread;

public class SynchronizedDemo implements Runnable {
    public static final int N = 1000;
    public static final int MAX_TRY = 1_000_000;

    private final char threadChar;
    private final StringBuffer sb;

    public SynchronizedDemo(char threadChar, StringBuffer sb) {
        this.threadChar = threadChar;
        this.sb = sb;
    }

    @Override
    public void run() {
        for (int i = 0; i < N; i++) {
            synchronized (sb) {
                sb.append(threadChar);
                sleep();
                sb.append(threadChar);
            }
        }
    }

    private void sleep() {
        try {
            Thread.sleep(1);
        } catch (InterruptedException ignored) {
        }
    }

    public static void main(String[] args) {
        boolean failed = false;
        int tries = 0;
        while (!failed && tries < MAX_TRY) {
            tries++;
            StringBuffer sb = new StringBuffer(4 * N);
            new Thread(new SynchronizedDemo('a', sb)).start();
```

```
            new Thread(new SynchronizedDemo('b', sb)).start();
            failed = sb.indexOf("aba") != -1 || sb.indexOf("bab") != -1;
        }
        System.out.println(failed ? "failed after " + tries + " tries" :
"not failed");
    }
}
```

The code starts two different threads. One of the threads appends `aa` to the `StringBuffer` named `sb`. The other one appends `bb`. This appending is done in two separate stages, with a sleep in between. The sleep is needed to avoid JIT that optimizes the two separate steps into one. Each thread executes the `append` 1,000 times, each time appending `a` or `b` twice. As the two `append` one after the other, and they are inside a `synchronized` block, it cannot happen that an `aba` or `bab` sequence gets into the `StringBuffer`. While one thread executes the synchronized block, the other thread cannot execute it.

If I remove the synchronized block, then the JVM I used to test Java HotSpot (TM) 64-Bit Server VM (build 9-ea+121, mixed mode and also 18.3 build 10+46, mixed mode for the second edition of the book) prints out the failure with a try count of around several hundred. (Have a look at the `SynchronizedDemoFailing` class in the code base available from Packt.)

It clearly demonstrates what synchronization means, but it also draws our attention to another important phenomenon. The error only occurs around every few hundred thousand executions. It is extremely rare, even though this example was furnished to demonstrate such a mishap. If a bug appears so rarely, it is extremely hard to reproduce and, even more, to debug and fix. Most of the synchronization errors manifest in mysterious ways and fixing them is usually the result of meticulous code review rather than debugging. Therefore, it is extremely important to clearly understand the true nature of Java multithread behavior before starting a commercial multithread application.

The `synchronized` keyword can also be used in front of a method. In this case, the object to acquire the lock of is `this` object. In the case of a `static` method, synchronization is executed on the whole class.

Wait and notify

There are five methods implemented in the `Object` class that can be used to get further synchronization functionality—`wait`, with three different timeout argument signatures, `notify`, and `notifyAll`. To call `wait`, the calling thread should have the lock of the `Object` on which `wait` is invoked. It means that you can only invoke `wait` from inside a synchronized block and, when it is called, the thread gets `BLOCKED` and releases the lock. When another thread calls `notifyAll` on the same `Object`, the thread gets into the `RUNNABLE` state. It cannot continue execution immediately as it cannot get the lock on the object. The lock is held at that moment by the thread that just called `notifyAll`. However, sometime after the other thread releases the lock, in other words, it gets out of the `synchronized` block, the waiting thread can acquire it and can continue the execution.

If there are more threads waiting on an object, all of them get out of the `BLOCKED` state. The `notify` method wakes only one of the waiting threads. There is no guarantee as to which thread is awoken.

The typical use of `wait`, `notify`, and `notifyAll` is when one or more threads are creating objects that are consumed by another thread, or threads. The storage where the objects travel between the threads is a kind of queue. The consumer waits until there is something to read from the queue, and the producer puts the objects into the queue one after the other. The producer notifies the consumers when it puts something in the queue. If there is no room left in the queue, the producer has to stop and wait until the queue has some space. In this case, the producer calls the `wait` method. To wake the producer up, the consumer calls `notifyAll` when it reads something.

The consumer consumes the objects from the queue in a loop and only calls `wait` if there is nothing to be read from the queue. When the producer calls `notifyAll`, and there is no consumer waiting, the notification is just ignored. It flies away, but this is not a problem; consumers are not waiting. When the consumer consumes an object and calls `notifyAll`, and there is no producer waiting, the situation is the same. It is not a problem.

It cannot happen that the consumer consumes, calls `notifyAll`, and, after the notification was up in the air, unable to locate a waiting producer, so a producer starts to wait. This cannot happen because the whole code is in a `synchronized` block and it ensures that no producer is in the critical section. This is the reason why `wait`, `notify`, and `notifyAll` can only be invoked when the lock of the `Object` class is acquired.

If there are many consumers executing the same code and they are equally good at consuming the objects, then it is an optimization to call `notify` instead of `notifyAll`. In that case, `notifyAll` will just wake all consumer threads. However, only the lucky one will recognize that they were woken up; the others will see that somebody else already got away with the bait.

I recommend that you practice at least once to implement a blocking queue that can be used to pass objects between threads. Do it only as practice and never use your practice code in production. Starting with Java 1.5, there are implementations of the `BlockingQueue` interface. Use one that fits your needs. We will do that too, in our example code.

Feel fortunate that you can code in Java 11. I started using Java professionally when it was 1.4 and, on one occasion, I had to implement a blocking queue. Life just gets better and easier all the time with Java.

In professional code, we usually avoid using `synchronized` methods or blocks and `volatile` fields as well as the `wait` and `notify` methods, and `notifyAll` too, if possible. We can use asynchronous communication between threads or pass the whole multithreading to the framework for handling. The `synchronized` and `volatile` keywords cannot be avoided in some special cases when the performance of the code is important, or we cannot find a better construct. Sometimes, the direct synchronization of specific code and data structures is more efficient than the approach delivered by JDK classes. It should be noted, however, that those classes also use these low-level synchronization constructs, so it is not magic how they work. To learn from a professional code, you can look into the code of the JDK classes before you want to implement your own version. You will realize that it is not that simple to implement these queues; the code of the classes is not complex without good reason. If you find the code simple, it means that you are senior enough to know what not to reimplement. Or, perhaps, you do not even realize what code you read.

Lock

Locks are incorporated in Java; every `Object` has a lock that a thread may acquire when it enters a `synchronized` block. We discussed that already. In some programming code, there are situations when this kind of structure is not optimal.

In some situations, the structure of locks may be lined up to avoid deadlock. It may be needed to acquire lock *A* before *B*, and to acquire *B* before *C*. However, *A* should be released as soon as possible, to allow access to a resource protected by lock *D*, also needing lock *A* before it. In complex and highly parallel structures, the locks are frequently structured as trees. A thread should climb down along the tree to a leaf representing the resource to acquire the lock. In the act of climbing, the thread gets hold of a lock on a node, then a lock on a node below it, and then releases the lock above, just like a real climber descending (or climbing up if you imagine the tree with the leaves at the top, which is more realistic; nevertheless, graphs usually show trees upside down).

You cannot leave a `synchronized` block remaining in another that is inside the first one. Synchronized blocks are nested. The `java.util.concurrent.Lock` interface defines methods to handle that situation and the implementations are also there in the JDK to be used in our code. When you have a lock, you can call the `lock()` and `unlock()` methods. The actual order is in your hands and you can write the following line of code to get the locking sequence:

```
a.lock(); b.lock(); a.unlock(); c.lock()
```

With great freedom, however, comes great responsibility. The locks and unlocks are not tied to the execution sequence of the code, unlike in the case of a synchronized block, and it may be very easy to create code that, in some cases, just loses a lock without unlocking it, rendering some resources unusable. The situation is similar to a memory leak. You will allocate (lock) something and forget to release (unlock) it. After a while, the program will run out of resources.

My personal recommendation is to avoid using locks if possible and to instead use higher-level constructs and asynchronous communications between threads, such as blocking queues.

Condition

The `java.util.concurrent.Condition` interface is similar to the built-in `wait()`, `notify()`, and `notifyAll()` objects in functionality. Any implementation of `Lock` should create new `Condition` objects and return them as a result to the invocation of the `newCondition()` method. When the thread has a `Condition`, it can call `await()`, `signal()`, and `signalAll()` when the thread has the lock that created the condition object.

The functionality is very similar to the `Object` methods mentioned. The big difference is that you can create many `Condition` objects for a single `Lock` and they will work independently of one another, but not independent of the `Lock`.

ReentrantLock

`ReentrantLock` is the simplest implementation of the `Lock` interface in the JDK. There are two ways to create this type of lock—with and without a fairness policy. If the `ReentrantLock(Boolean fair)` constructor is called with `true` as an argument, then the lock will be assigned to the thread that is waiting for the lock the longest time in case there are many threads waiting. This will avoid a thread being made to wait for an inordinate amount of time and starving. On the other hand, handling the locks this way needs more administration from the `ReentrantLock` code and runs a bit slower. (Never be afraid of slow code until you have measured it.)

ReentrantReadWriteLock

This class is an implementation of `ReadWriteLock`. `ReadWriteLock` is a lock that can be used for parallel read access and exclusive write access. It means that several threads can read the resource protected by the lock, but when a thread writes the resource, no other thread can get access to it, not even read it during that period. A `ReadWriteLock` is simply two `Lock` objects returned by the `readLock()` and `writeLock()` methods. To get read access on `ReadWriteLock`, the code has to invoke `myLock.readLock().lock()`, and get access to the write lock, `myLock.writeLock().lock()`. Acquiring one of the locks and releasing it in the implementation is coupled with the other lock. To acquire a write lock, no thread should have an active read lock, for example.

There are several intricacies involved in the use of the different locks. For example, you can acquire a read lock, but you cannot get a write lock so long as you have the read lock. You have to release the read lock first to acquire a write lock. This is just one of the simple details, but this is the one that novice programmers have trouble with many times. Why is it implemented this way? Why should the program get a write lock, which is more expensive—in the sense of the higher probability of locking other threads—when it is still unsure that it wants to write the resource? The code wants to read it and, based on the content, it may later decide that it wants to write it.

The issue is not with the implementation. The developers of the library decided this rule, not because they just liked it that way or because they were aware of parallel algorithms and deadlock possibilities. When two threads have `readLock` and each decides to upgrade the lock to `writeLock`, then they would intrinsically create a deadlock. Each would hold the `readLock` while waiting for the `writeLock` and none of them would get ever it.

On the other end, you can downgrade a `writeLock` to a `readLock` without risking that in the meantime, somebody acquires a `writeLock` and modifies the resource.

Atomic variables

Atomic classes enclose primitive values into objects and provide atomic operations on them. We discussed race conditions and volatile variables. For example, if we have an `int` variable to be used as a counter and we want to assign a unique value to objects that we work with, we can increment the value and use the result as a unique ID. However, when multiple threads use the same code, we cannot be sure about the value we read after the increment. It may happen that another thread also incremented the value in the meantime. To avoid that, we will have to enclose the increment and assign the incremented value to an object in a `synchronized` block. This can also be done using `AtomicInteger`.

If we have a variable of `AtomicInteger`, then calling `incrementAndGet` increments the value of `int` enclosed in the class and returns the incremented value. Why do it instead of using a synchronized block? The first answer is that if the functionality is there in the JDK, then using it results in fewer lines of code than implementing it again. Developers maintaining the code you create are expected to know the JDK libraries. On the other hand, studying your code for them takes time, and time is money.

The other reason is that these classes are highly optimized and, very often, they implement the features using platform-specific native code that greatly outperforms the version we can implement using synchronized blocks. Worrying about performance too early is not good, but parallel algorithms and synchronization between threads are usually used when performance is crucial; thus, there is a good chance that the performance of the code using the atomic classes is important. Having said all that, the main reason is still readability and simplicity.

In the `java.util.concurrent.atomic` package, there are several classes, `AtomicInteger`, `AtomicBoolean`, `AtomicLong`, and `AtomicReference` among them. They all provide methods that are specific to the encapsulated value.

The `compareAndSet()` method is implemented by every atomic class. This is a conditional value-setting operation that has the following format:

```
boolean compareAndSet(expectedValue, updateValue);
```

When it is applied to an atomic class, it compares the actual value with the one `expectedValue`, and, if they are the same, then it sets the value to `updateValue`. If the value was updated, the method returns `true` and it does all this in an atomic action. Needless to say, if the condition does not hold and the update is not performed, the returned value is `false`.

You may ask the question that if this method is in all of these classes, why is there no `Interface` defining this method? The reason for this is that the argument types are different based on the encapsulated type, and these types are primitives. As primitives cannot be used as generic types yet, it is not possible to define an interface.

In case of `AtomicXXXArray`, the method has an extra first argument, which is the index of the array element handled in the call.

The variables encapsulated are handled the same way as volatile, as far as the reordering and access by multiple threads running on different processor cores are concerned. The actual implementation of the atomic classes may use special hardware codes that can provide better performance than the naive implementation in Java and therefore the atomic classes may have better performance than the same functionality implemented in vanilla Java code using volatile variables and synchronized blocks.

The general advice is to consider using atomic classes if there is one usable, and you will find yourself creating a synchronized block for check-and-set, atomic increment, or addition operations.

BlockingQueue

`BlockingQueue` is an interface that extends the standard `Queue` interface with methods that are suitable for use by multithread applications. Any implementation of this interface provides methods that allow different threads to put an element into the queue, pull elements off the queue, and wait for elements that are in the queue.

When there is a new element to be stored in the queue, you can `add()` it, `offer()` it, or `put()` it. These are the names of the methods that store elements and they do the same thing, just a bit differently. The `add()` method throws an exception if the queue is full and there is no room for the element. The `offer()` method does not throw an exception but returns either `true` or `false`, depending on whether the operation is successful. If it can store the element in the queue, it returns `true`. There is also a version of `offer()` that specifies a timeout. That version of the method waits and returns only `false` if it cannot store the value in the queue during the period. The `put()` method is the simplest version; it waits until it can do its job.

When talking about the available room in a queue, do not get puzzled and confuse it with general Java memory management. If there is no more memory, and the garbage collector is also unable to release any, you will certainly get an `OutOfMemoryError`. An exception is thrown by `add()`, and the `false` value is returned by `offer()` when the queue limits are reached. Some of the `BlockingQueue` implementations can limit the number of elements that can be stored in a queue simultaneously. If that limit is reached, then the queue is full and cannot accept more elements.

There are four different ways of fetching elements from a `BlockingQueue` implementation. In this direction, the special case is when the queue is empty. In that case, the `remove()` method throws an exception instead of returning the element, the `poll()` method returns `null` if there is no element, and the `take()` method just waits until it can return an element.

Finally, there are two methods inherited from the `Queues` interface that do not consume the element from the queue, but just *look at* it. The `element()` method returns the head of the queue or throws an exception if the queue is empty. The `peek()` method returns `null` if there is no element in the queue. The following table summarizes the operations borrowed from the documentation of the interface:

	Throws exception	**Special value**	**Blocks**	**Times out**
Insert	`add(e)`	`offer(e)`	`put(e)`	`offer(e, time, unit)`
Remove	`remove()`	`poll()`	`take()`	`poll(time, unit)`
Examine	`element()`	`peek()`	`not applicable`	`not applicable`

LinkedBlockingQueue

This is an implementation of the `BlockingQueue` interface, which is backed up by a linked list. The size of the queue is not limited by default (to be precise, it is `Integer.MAX_VALUE`), but it can optionally be limited in a constructor argument. The reason to limit the size in this implementation is to aid the use when the parallel algorithm performs better with a limited size queue. The implementation itself does not have any restriction on the size other than `Integer.MAX_VALUE`, which is fairly big.

LinkedBlockingDeque

This is the simplest implementation of the `BlockingQueue` and also its `BlockingDeque` subinterface. As we discussed in the previous chapter, a `Deque` is a double-ended queue that has `add`, `remove`, and `offer` method types, among others, in the form of `xxxFirst` and `xxxLast` to carry out the act with one or other end of the queue. The `Deque` interface defines `getFirst` and `getLast`, instead of consistently naming `elementFirst` and `elementLast`, so this is something you should get used to. After all, the IDEs help with automatic code completion so this should not really be a big problem.

ArrayBlockingQueue

`ArrayBlockingQueue` implements the `BlockingQueue` interface, hence the `Queue` interface. This implementation manages a queue with fixed-size elements. The storage in the implementation is an array and the elements are handled in a *FIFO* manner—first-in, first-out. This is the class that we will also use in the parallel implementation of Mastermind for the communication between the boss and the subordinate bureaucrats.

LinkedTransferQueue

The `TransferQueue` interface is extending `BlockingQueue` and the only implementation of it in the JDK is `LinkedTransferQueue`. A `TransferQueue` comes in handy when a thread wants to hand over some data to another thread and needs to be sure that the other thread takes the element. This `TransferQueue` has a `transfer()` method that puts an element on the queue but does not return until some other thread calls `remove()`, thereby removing it (or calls `poll()`, thereby polling it). That way, the producing thread can be sure that the object put on the queue is in the hands of another processing thread and does not wait in the queue. The `transfer()` method also has a format, `tryTransfer()`, in which you can specify a timeout value. If the method times out, the element is not put into the queue.

IntervalGuesser

We discussed the different Java language elements and JDK classes that are all available to implement parallel algorithms. Now, we will see how to use these approaches to implement the parallel guesser for the Mastermind game.

Before we start, I have to admit that this task is not a typical concurrent, parallel programming tutorial task. Tutorials talking about concurrent programming techniques tend to select problems for their examples that are easy to solve using a parallel code and that scale well. A problem scales well if the parallel algorithm running on *N* processor practically runs *N* times faster than the non-parallel solution. My personal opinion is that those examples paint the sky blue without stormy clouds. However, when you face concurrent programming in real life, those clouds are there and you will see thunder and lightning, and, if you are not experienced, you will get your feet wet.

Real-life problems frequently do not scale ideally. We have already visited an example that scales well, though not ideally—quicksort. This time, we will develop a parallel algorithm for something that more closely resembles real-life problems. Solving the mastermind game on N processor will not speed up the solution *N* times and the code is not trivial. This example will show you what real-life problems look like and, even though it will not teach you all of the possible issues, you will not be shocked when you see one of them for the first time in a commercial environment.

One of the most important classes in this solution is `IntervalGuesser`. This is the class that effects the creation of the guesses. It creates the guesses between a start and an end guess and sends them to a `BlockingQueue`. The class implements `Runnable`, so it can run in a separate `Thread`. The purist implementation will separate the `Runnable` functionality from the interval guessing, but, as the whole class is hardly more than 50 lines, it is a forgivable sin implementing the two functionalities in a single class:

```
public class IntervalGuesser extends UniqueGuesser implements Runnable {
    private final Guess start;

    private final Guess end;
    private Guess lastGuess;
    private final BlockingQueue<Guess> guessQueue;

    public IntervalGuesser(Table table,
                           Guess start,
                           Guess end,
                           BlockingQueue<Guess> guessQueue) {
        super(table);
        this.start = start;
        this.end = end;
        this.lastGuess = start;
        this.guessQueue = guessQueue;
        nextGuess = start;
    }

    @Override
    public void run() {
        Thread.currentThread()
            .setName("guesser [" + start + "," + end + "]");
        var guess = guess();
        try {
            while (guess != Guess.none) {
                guessQueue.put(guess);
                guess = guess();
            }
        } catch (InterruptedException ignored) {
        }
    }


    @Override
    protected Guess nextGuess() {
        var guess = super.nextGuess();
        if (guess.equals(end)) {
            guess = Guess.none;
        }
```

```
            lastGuess = guess;
            return guess;
        }

        public String toString() {
            return "[" + start + "," + end + "]";
        }
    }
```

Implementation is very simple, since most of the functionality is already implemented in the abstract `Guesser` class. The more interesting code is the one that invokes the `IntervalGuesser`.

ParallelGamePlayer

The `ParallelGamePlayer` class implements the `Player` interface that defines the `play` method:

```
    @Override
    public void play() {
        final var table = new Table(NR_COLUMNS, colorManager);
        final var secret = new RandomSecret(colorManager);
        final var secretGuess = secret.createSecret(NR_COLUMNS);
        final var game = new Game(table, secretGuess);
        final var guessers = createGuessers(table);
        final var finalCheckGuesser = new UniqueGuesser(table);
        startAsynchronousGuessers(guessers);
        try {
            while (!game.isFinished()) {
                final var guess = guessQueue.take();
                if (finalCheckGuesser.guessMatch(guess)) {
                    game.addNewGuess(guess);
                }
            }
        } catch (InterruptedException ie) {

        } finally {
            stopAsynchronousGuessers(guessers);
        }
    }
```

This method creates a `Table`, a `RandomSecret` that creates the guess used as a secret in a random way, a `Game` object, `IntervalGuesser` objects, and a `UniqueGuesser`.

The `IntervalGuesser` objects are the bureaucrats; the `UniqueGuesser` is the boss who crosschecks the guesses that the `IntervalGuesser` objects create. We create the interval guessers in a separate method, `createGuessers()`:

```
private IntervalGuesser[] createGuessers(Table table) {
    final var colors = new Color[NR_COLUMNS];
    var start = firstIntervalStart(colors);
    final IntervalGuesser[] guessers = new IntervalGuesser[nrThreads];
    for (int i = 0; i < nrThreads - 1; i++) {
        Guess end = nextIntervalStart(colors);
        guessers[i] = new IntervalGuesser(table, start, end, guessQueue);
        start = end;
    }
    guessers[nrThreads - 1] = new IntervalGuesser(table, start, Guess.none,
guessQueue);
    return guessers;
}


private Guess firstIntervalStart(Color[] colors) {
    for (int i = 0; i < colors.length; i++) {
        colors[i] = colorManager.firstColor();
    }
    return new Guess(colors);
}

private Guess nextIntervalStart(Color[] colors) {
    final int index = colors.length - 1;
    int step = NR_COLORS / nrThreads;
    if (step == 0) {
        step = 1;
    }
    while (step > 0) {
        if (colorManager.thereIsNextColor(colors[index])) {
            colors[index] = colorManager.nextColor(colors[index]);
            step--;
        } else {
            return Guess.none;
        }
    }
    Guess guess = new Guess(colors);
    while (!guess.isUnique()) {
        guess = guess.nextGuess(colorManager);
    }
    return guess;
}
```

The interval guessers are created in a way that each will have its unique range of color variations so that, together, they cover all possible color guesses. The `firstIntervalStart()` method returns the guess that contains the *first* color at all positions. The `nextIntervalStart()` method returns the color set that starts the next range, advancing the colors so that each guesser will have the same number of guesses to check at the end (plus or minus one).

The `startAsynchronousGuessers()` method starts off the asynchronous guessers and then reads the guesses in a loop from them and puts them on the table if they are OK until the game finishes. At the end of the method, in the `finally` block, the asynchronous guessers are stopped.

The start and stop methods for the asynchronous guessers employ `ExecutorService`:

```
private void startAsynchronousGuessers(IntervalGuesser[] guessers) {
    executorService = Executors.newFixedThreadPool(nrThreads);
    for (IntervalGuesser guesser : guessers) {
        executorService.execute(guesser);
    }
}

private void stopAsynchronousGuessers(IntervalGuesser[] guessers) {
    executorService.shutdown();
    guessQueue.drainTo(new LinkedList<>());
}
```

The code is quite straightforward. The only thing that needs a bit of explanation is the `drainTo()` call. This method drains the unused guesses that the worker threads still have into a linked list that we immediately throw away (we do not keep any reference to it). This is required in order to help any `IntervalGuesser`, which may be waiting with a suggested guess in hand, trying to put it into the queue. When we drain the queue, the guesser thread returns from the `put()` method in the `guessQueue.put(guess);` line in `IntervalGuesser` and can catch the interrupt. The rest of the code does not contain anything that would be radically different from what we have already seen.

The final question that we still want to discuss in this chapter is, how much time did we gain by making the code parallel?

Microbenchmarking

Microbenchmarking is measuring the performance of a small code fragment. When we want to optimize our code, we will have to measure it. Without measurement, code optimization is like shooting blindfolded. You will not hit the target, but you likely will shoot somebody else.

Shooting is a good metaphor because you should usually not do it, but when you really have to, then you have no choice. If there is no performance issue and the software meets requirements, then any optimization, including speed measurement, is a waste of money. This does not mean that you are encouraged to write slow and sloppy code. When we measure performance, we compare it against a requirement, and the requirement is usually at the user level, something like "the response time of the application should be less than 2 seconds". To do such a measurement, we usually create load tests in a test environment and use different profiling tools, in case the measured performance is not satisfactory, that tell us what is consuming the most time and where we should optimize. Many times, it is not only Java code, but configuration optimization, using a larger database connection pool, more memory, and similar things.

Microbenchmarking is a different story. It is about the performance of a small Java code fragment and, as such, closer to Java programming.

It is rarely used and, before starting to execute a microbenchmark for an actual commercial environment, we will have to think twice. Microbenchmark is a luring tool to optimize something small without knowing whether it is worth optimizing that code at all. When we have a huge application that has several modules running on several servers, how can we be sure that improving a special part of the application drastically improves performance? Will it pay back in increased revenue, generating so much profit that it covers the costs incurred in performance testing and development? Statistically, you can almost be certain that such an optimization, including microbenchmarking, will not pay off.

I once maintained the code of a senior colleague. He created a highly optimized code to recognize configuration keywords that were present in a file. He created a program structure that represented a decision tree based on the characters in the key string. If there was a keyword in the configuration file that was misspelled, the code threw an exception at the very first character, where it could decide that the keyword could not be correct. To insert a new keyword, it needed to get through the code structure to find the occasion in the code where the new keyword was initially different from already existing ones and extend the deeply nested `if/else` structures. To read the list of keywords handled was possible from the comments that listed all the keywords that he did not forget to document. The code was working amazingly fast, probably saving a few milliseconds of the servlet application's start up time. The application was started up only after system maintenance every few months.You feel the irony, don't you? Seniority is not always the number of years. Those more fortunate can save their inner child.

So, when should microbenchmarking be used? I can see two areas:

- You have identified the code segment that consumes most of the resources in your application and the improvement can be tested by microbenchmarks
- You cannot identify the code segment that will consume most of the resources in an application, but you suspect it

The first is the usual case. The second is when you develop a library, and you just do not know all the applications that will use it. In this case, you will try to optimize the part that you think is the most crucial for most of the imagined, suspected applications. Even in that case, it is better to take some sample applications that are created by users of your library and collect some statistics regarding use.

Why should we talk about microbenchmarking in detail? What are the pitfalls? Benchmarking is an experiment. The first program I wrote was a TI calculator code and I could just count the number of steps the program made to factor two large (10 digits those days were large) prime numbers. Even at that time, I was using an old mechanical Russian stopwatch to measure the time, being lazy to calculate the number of steps. Experimenting and measuring were easier.

Today, you cannot manually calculate the number of steps the CPU makes, even if you wanted to. There are so many small factors that may change the performance of the applications that are beyond the control of the programmer, which makes it impossible to calculate the steps. We have the measurement left for us, and we will acquire all the problems associated with measurements.

What is the biggest problem? We are interested in something, say *X*, and we usually cannot measure that. So, we will measure *Y* instead and hope that the values of *Y* and *X* are coupled together. We want to measure the length of the room, but instead, we measure the time it takes for the laser beam to travel from one end to the other. In this case, the length, *X*, and the time, *Y*, are strongly coupled. Many times, *X* and *Y* only correlate more or less. Most of the time, when a person carries out a measurement, the *X* and *Y* values bear no relation to each other at all. Still, people bet their houses, and more, on decisions backed by such measurements.

Microbenchmarking is no different. The first question is, how do we measure the execution time? The small code runs short times and `System.currentTimeMillis()` may just return the same value when the measurement starts and when it ends, because we are still in the same millisecond. Even if the execution is 10 ms, the error of the measurement is still at least 10%, purely because of the quantification of the time as we measure. Luckily, there is `System.nanoTime()`. But is there? Just because the name says it returns the number of nanoseconds from a specific start time does not necessarily mean it really can.

It very much depends on the hardware and the implementation of the method in the JDK. It is called nano because this is the precision that we cannot certainly reach. If it was microseconds, then some implementation may be limited by the definition, even if, on the specific hardware, there is a more precise clock. However, this is not only about the level of accuracy of an available hardware clock; it is about the precision of the hardware.

Let's remember the heartbeat of the bureaucrats, and the time needed to read something from memory. Calling a method, such as `System.nanoTime()`, is like asking the bellboy in a hotel to run down from the second floor to the lobby and peek out to look at the clock on the tower on the other side of the road, come back, and tell precisely what time it was when we asked. Nonsense. We should know the precision of the clock on the tower and the speed of the bellboy running from the floor to the lobby and back. This is a bit more than just calling `System.nanoTime()`. This is what a microbenchmarking harness does for us.

The **Java Microbenchmarking Harness** (**JMH**) is available for some time as a library. It is developed by Oracle and used to tune the performance of several core JDK classes. This is good news for those who develop the Java platform for a new hardware, but also for developers because it means that the JMH is, and will be, supported by Oracle.

> *"JMH is a Java harness to build, run, and analyze nano/micro/milli/macro benchmarks written in Java and other languages targeting the JVM."*

(Quote from the official site of JMH, `http://openjdk.java.net/projects/code-tools/jmh/`).

You can run `jmh` as a separate project independent from the actual project you measure, or you can just store the measurement code in a separate directory. The harness will compile against the production class files and will execute the benchmark. The easiest way, as I see it, is to use the Gradle plugin to execute JMH. You can store the benchmark code in a directory called `jmh` (the same level as `main` and `test`) and create a `main` class that can start the benchmark.

The Gradle build script is extended to include the following lines:

```
buildscript {
    repositories {
        jcenter()
    }
    dependencies {
        classpath "me.champeau.gradle:jmh-gradle-plugin:0.2.0"
    }
}
apply plugin: "me.champeau.gradle.jmh"

jmh {
    jmhVersion = '1.13'
    includeTests = true
}
```

And the `MicroBenchmark` class is as follows:

```
public class MicroBenchmark {

    public static void main(String... args)
        throws RunnerException {
        var opt = new OptionsBuilder()
            .include(MicroBenchmark.class.getSimpleName())
            .forks(1)
            .build();

        new Runner(opt).run();
    }

    @Benchmark
    @Fork(1)
    public void playParallel(ThreadsAndQueueSizes t3qs) {
        int nrThreads = Integer.valueOf(t3qs.nrThreads);
        int queueSize = Integer.valueOf(t3qs.queueSize);
        new ParallelGamePlayer(nrThreads, queueSize).play();
    }

    @Benchmark
```

```
    @Fork(1)
    public void playSimple() {
        new SimpleGamePlayer().play();
    }

    @State(Scope.Benchmark)
    public static class ThreadsAndQueueSizes {
        @Param(value = {"1", "4", "8"})
        String nrThreads;
        @Param(value = {"-1", "1", "10", "100", "1000000"})
        String queueSize;
    }
}
```

`ParallelGamePlayer` is created to play the game with -1, 1, 4, and 8 `IntervalGuesser` threads, and, in each case, there is a test running with a queue of length 1, 10, 100, and 1 million. These are 16 test executions. When the number of threads is negative, then the constructor uses `LinkedBlockingDeque`. There is another separate measurement that measures the non-parallel player. The test was executed with unique guesses and secrets (no color used more than once), ten colors, and six columns.

When the harness starts, it does all the calibrations automatically and runs the tests for many iterations to let the JVM start up. You may recall the code that just never stopped unless we used the `volatile` modifier on the variable that was used to signal the code to stop. That happened because the JIT compiler optimized the code. This is done only when the code has already run a few thousand times. The harness makes these executions in order to warm the code up and ensure that the measurement is done when the JVM is already at full speed.

Running this benchmark takes approximately 15 minutes on my machine. During the execution, it is recommended to stop all other processes and let the benchmark use all available resources. If there is anything using resources during the measurement, then it will be reflected in the result:

```
Benchmark        (nrThreads) (queueSize)  Score    Error
playParallel               1          -1  15,636  ± 1,905
playParallel               1           1  15,316  ± 1,237
playParallel               1          10  15,425  ± 1,673
playParallel               1         100  16,580  ± 1,133
playParallel               1     1000000  15,035  ± 1,148
playParallel               4          -1  25,945  ± 0,939
playParallel               4           1  25,559  ± 1,250
playParallel               4          10  25,034  ± 1,414
playParallel               4         100  24,971  ± 1,010
playParallel               4     1000000  20,584  ± 0,655
playParallel               8          -1  24,713  ± 0,687
```

```
playParallel              8          1    24,265   ± 1,022
playParallel              8         10    24,475   ± 1,137
playParallel              8        100    24,514   ± 0,836
playParallel              8    1000000    16,595   ± 0,739
playSimple              N/A        N/A   18,613    ± 2,040
```

The actual output of the program is a bit more verbose; it was edited for printing purposes. The `Score` column shows how many times the benchmark can run in a second. The `Error` column shows that the measurement has less than 10% scattering.

The fastest performance we have is when the algorithm runs on eight threads, which is the number of threads the processor can independently handle on my machine. It is interesting that limiting the size of the queue did not help performance. I actually expected it to be different. Using a one million length array as a blocking queue has a huge overhead and it is not a surprise that, in this case, the execution is slower than when we have only 100 elements in the queue. List-based queue handling with unlimited links, on the other hand, is fairly fast and clearly shows that the extra speed at the limited queue for 100 elements does not come from the fact that the limit prevents the `IntervalThreads` from running too far.

When we start one thread, we expect similar results to when we run the serial algorithm. The fact that the serial algorithm beats the parallel algorithm running on one thread is not a surprise. The thread creation and the communication between the main thread and the extra single thread have overheads. The overheads are significant, especially when the queue is unnecessarily large.

Summary

In this chapter, we have learned a lot of things. First of all, we refactored the code to be ready for further development that uses parallel guessing. We got acquainted with processes and threads, and we even mentioned fibers. After that, we looked at how Java implements threads and how to create code that runs on multiple threads. Additionally, we saw the different means that Java provides to programmers requiring parallel programs, starting threads, or just starting tasks in already existing threads.

Perhaps the most important part of this chapter that you should remember is the metaphor of bureaucrats and the different speeds. This is extremely important when you want to understand the performance of concurrent applications. I hope that this is a catchy picture, one that is easy to remember.

There was a huge topic about the different synchronization means that Java provides, and you have also learned about the pitfalls that programmers can fall into when programming concurrent applications.

Last, but by no means least, we created the concurrent version of the Mastermind guesser and also measured that it is indeed faster than the version that uses only one processor (at least on my machine). We used the Java microbenchmark harness with the Gradle build tool and talked a little about how to perform microbenchmarking.

This was a long chapter and not an easy one. I may tend to think that this is the most complex and theoretical chapter. If you understood half of it at first read, you can be proud. On the other hand, be aware that this is only a solid base from which to start experimenting with concurrent programming and there is a long way to go before being recognized as experienced and professional in this area. And, moreover, this chapter is not an easy one. But, first of all, be proud of yourself at the end of this chapter.

In the following chapters, we will learn more about web and web programming. In the very next chapter, we will develop our little game so that it can run on a server and the player can play with it using a web browser. This will establish the basic knowledge for web programming. Later, we will build on this, developing web-based service applications, reactive programming, and all the tools and areas that will make you a professional Java developer.

6
Making Our Game Professional - Do it as a Web App

In this chapter, we will program a web application. We will build on what we have achieved already and create a web version of the Mastermind game. This time, it will not only run alone, guessing and answering the number of positions and matched colors, but also communicate with the user, asking for the answers to the guesses. This will be a real game that you can play with. Web programming is extremely important for Java developers. Most of the programs are web applications. The universal client available on the internet is the web browser. The thin-client, web browser-based architecture is widely accepted in enterprises as well. There are only a few exceptions when the architecture has something apart from the web client. If you want to become a professional Java developer, you must be familiar with web programming. And it is fun as well!

There are many technical topics that we will visit during the development. First of all, we will discuss networking and web architecture. This is the concrete base of the whole building. It is not too sexy, just like when you construct a building. You spend a lot of money and effort digging trenches, and then you bury the concrete and end up, at the end of this phase, with what you seemingly had before—flat ground, except that there is the base. Building without this base, the house would either collapse soon after or during the process of building. Networking is just as important for web programming. There are a lot of topics that seemingly have nothing to do with programming. Still, it is the base of the building and, when you program web applications, you will also discover the fun aspect of it.

We will also talk a bit about HTML, CSS, and JavaScript, but not too much. We cannot avoid them because they are also important for web programming, but they are topics that you can learn from somewhere else as well. In case you are not an expert in some of these areas, there are usually other experts in enterprise project teams who can extend your knowledge. (In the case of networking, there is no mercy.) In addition to that, JavaScript is a topic so complex and huge that it deserves a whole book, to begin with. There are only a very small number of experts who have a deep understanding of both Java and JavaScript. I understand the general structure of the language and the environment it runs in, but I cannot keep up with the new frameworks that are released every week these days, focusing as I do on other areas.

You will learn how to create Java applications that run on an application server, this time in Jetty, and we will see what a servlet is. To have a jump start, we will create a web *hello world* application. Then, we will create the servlet version of Mastermind. Note that we hardly ever program servlets directly without the aid of a framework that implements the code to handle parameters, authentication, and many other things that are not application-specific. We will still stick to a naked servlet in this chapter because it is not possible to effectively use frameworks, such as Spring, without first understanding what a servlet is. To be an engineer, you have to get your hands dirty first. Spring will come in the next chapter.

We will mention **JavaServer Pages** (**JSP**), only because you may meet some legacy application, which was developed using that technology, but modern web applications do not use JSP. Still, JSP is a part of the servlet standard and is available for use. There are other technologies that were developed in the recent past but do not seem to be future-proof these days. They are still usable, but appear only in legacy applications, and choosing them for a new project is fairly questionable. We will talk about these technologies shortly in a separate section.

By the end of this chapter, you will understand how basic web technology works and what the major architectural elements are, and you will be able to create simple web applications. This is not enough to be a professional Java web developer but will be a good grounding for the next chapter, where we will have a look at the professional frameworks used in today's enterprises for real application developments.

Web and network

Programs run on computers, and computers are connected to the internet. This network was developed in the last 60 years, first to provide military data communication that is resilient to rocket attacks, before being extended to be an academic network, and later becoming a commercial network used by anyone and available almost ubiquitously all over the world.

The design of the network and research into the same started as a response to Gagarin's orbiting of the Earth in the sixties. Sending Gagarin to space and orbiting the Earth was a demonstration that Russia could send a rocket anywhere on the globe, possibly with atomic explosives. It meant that any data network that needed some central control was not resilient to such an attack. It was not feasible to have a network with a central location as a single point of failure. Therefore, research was started to create a network that continues to operate, even if any part of it is brought down.

IP

The network delivers data packets between any two computers connected to it. The protocol used on the network is IP, which is simply an abbreviation of Internet Protocol. Using IP, a computer can send a data packet to another. The package contains a header and the data content. The header contains the internet addresses of the sender and the target machine, other flags, and information about the package. Since the machines are not connected to each other directly, routers forward the packets. It is like post offices sending letters to each other until they get into the hands of the postman you know, who can directly deliver it to your mailbox. To do that, the routers use the information in the header. The algorithm and organization of how the routers interact are complex and something we do not need to know in order to be Java professionals.

If you ever need to program in order to send IP packets directly, you should look at `java.net.DatagramPacket`, as the rest is implemented in the JDK, in the operating system, and on the firmware of the network card. You can create a data packet; sending it and changing the modulated voltage on the network card or emitting photons to the fiber is not your concern.

IP currently has two versions. The old version still in use is IPv4. The new version that coexists with the old one is IPv6, or IPng (*ng* stands for *new generation*). The major difference that may concern a Java developer is that version 4 uses 32-bit addresses and version 6 uses 128-bit addresses. When you see a version-4 address, you will see something like `192.168.1.110`, which contains the four bytes in a decimal format separated by dots. IPv6 addresses are expressed as `2001:db8:0:0:0:0:2:1`, as eight 16-bit numbers expressed in hexadecimal separated by colons.

The web is a bit more complex than sending data packets. If sending a data packet is akin to sending a one-page letter, then a web page download is like discussing a contract in a paper mail. There should be an agreement in the initial paper mail as to what to send, what to answer, and so on until the contract is signed. On the internet, that protocol is called the **Transmission Control Protocol** (**TCP**). While it is highly unlikely (but possible) that you will meet IP routing issues, being a Java developer, you certainly will face TCP programming. Therefore, we will cover how TCP works shortly. Be aware that this is very brief. Really. You will not become a TCP expert reading the next section, but you will get a glimpse of the most important issues that affect web programming.

TCP/IP

The TCP protocol is implemented in the operating system and provides a higher level of interface than IP. When you program TCP, you do not deal with datagrams. Instead, you have a channel of byte streams where you can put bytes to be delivered to the other computer, and you can read bytes from the channel that were sent by the other computer, exactly in the order as they were sent. This is a kind of connection between two computers and, what's more, between two programs.

There are other protocols that are implemented over IP and that are not connection-oriented. One of them is **User Datagram Protocol** (**UDP**). It is used for services when there is no need for connections. It is also used when the data may be lost and it is more important that the data gets to the destination in a timely manner than not losing any of the packets (video streaming, telephony). Another application of the protocol is when the data amount is small and it can be requested again if lost; the cost of requesting again is cheaper than using the more complex TCP protocol. A typical example of this last type of use is a DNS request, which we will detail in the next section.

The TCP software layer implemented in the operating system deals with the intricacies of the packet handling. Resending a lost package, reordering packages that arrive in a different order than they were originally supposed to, and deleting extra packages that may arrive multiple times, is all done automatically by this layer. This layer is popularly referred to as the **TCP stack**.

Since the TCP is a connected protocol, there is a need for something that tells the TCP stack which stream a datagram belongs to when it arrives. The stream is identified by two ports. A port is a 16-bit integer. One identifies the program that initiates the connection, called the source port. The other one identifies the target program—the destination port. These are contained in each and every TCP packet that's delivered. When a machine runs a **Secure Shell** (**SSH**) server as well as a web server, these applications use different ports. These ports are usually `22` and `80`. When a package comes that contains the destination port number `22` in the TCP header, the TCP stack knows that the data in the packet belongs to the stream handled by the SSH server. Likewise, if the destination port is `80`, then the data goes to the web server.

When we program a server, we usually have to define the port number; otherwise, clients cannot find the server program. Web servers are usually listening on port `80`, and clients try to connect to that port. The client port is usually not important and not specified; it is allocated by the TCP stack automatically.

To connect from a client code to a server is easy—this just requires a few lines of code. Sometimes, it is only one line of code. However, under the hood, there is a lot of work that the TCP stack does that we should care about because it takes time to build up a TCP connection and it can greatly influence the performance of our application.

To have a connection, the TCP stack sends a datagram to the destination. This is not enough to have a connection, but this is the first step to establish a connection. This packet is empty, and the name of it is SYN. After sending this packet, the client starts to wait for the server to answer. If there is no server, or if it is too busy to answer, or if it simply cannot give an answer to this specific client for any reason, then sending any further packages would be network traffic waste.

When the server receives the SYN package, it replies with an SYN-ACK package. Finally, after receiving the SYN-ACK package, the client sends a package called ACK. If the packets go through the Atlantic, this is approximately 45 ms for each package, which is equivalent to 45 million seconds in bureaucrat time. This is almost one and a half years. We need three of those to set up the connection, and this is only the connection build-up; we have not sent any data so far.

When a TCP connection is established, the client does not start sending data without self-control. It starts sending just a few packages and then waits to see what happens. If the packages arrive and the server acknowledges them, it then sends more, with this volume increasing once it can see that the connection and the server are able to accept a higher volume of packages. Sending data that the server is not prepared for, and that it cannot handle, would not only be useless but also a waste of network resources. TCP is designed to optimize network usage. The client sends some data, and then it waits for an acknowledgment. The TCP stack automatically manages this. If the acknowledgment arrives, it sends more packets. If the carefully designed optimization algorithm, implemented in the TCP stack, believes that it is good to send more, it sends a bit more data than during the first step. If there are negative acknowledgments telling the client that the server could not accept some of the data and had to throw it away, then the client will reduce the number of packets it sends without acknowledgment. But first, it starts slow and cautious.

This is called TCP slow start, and we have to be aware of it. Although it is a low-level networking feature, it has consequences that we have to consider in our Java code—we use database connection pools instead of creating a new connection to the database each time there is a need for some data; we try to have as few connections to web servers as possible, using techniques such as *keep-alive, SPDY* protocol, or *http/2* (also replacing SPDY).

As for now, it is enough that TCP is connection-oriented, where you build up a connection to a server, send and receive bytes, and finally close the connection. When you have a network performance problem, you have to look at the issues I detailed previously (and ask a network expert).

DNS

The TCP protocol creates a channel using the IP addresses of machines. When you type a URL in the browser, it usually does not contain IP numbers. It contains machine names. The name is converted to IP numbers using a distributed database called **Domain Name System** (**DNS**). This database is distributed, and when a program needs to convert a name to an address, it sends a DNS request to one of the DNS servers it knows. These servers send queries to one another, or tell the client whom to ask, until the client knows the IP address assigned to the name. The servers and the client also cache the recently requested names, so answering is fast. On the other hand, when the IP address of a server changes this name, not all clients will immediately see the address assignment over the globe. The DNS lookup can be easily programmed, and there are classes and methods in JDK that support this, but usually, we do not need to worry about that; when we program, it is done automatically in web programming.

The HTTP protocol

The **Hypertext Transfer Protocol** (**HTTP**) is built on top of the TCP. When you type a URL in a browser, the browser opens a TCP channel to the server (after DNS lookup, of course) and sends an HTTP request to the web server. The server, after receiving the request, produces a response and sends it to the client. After that, the TCP channel may be closed or kept alive for further HTTP request-response pairs.

Both the request and the response contain a header and an optional (possibly zero-length) body. The header is in text format, and is separated from the body by an empty line.

More precisely, the header and the body are separated by four bytes—`0x0D`, `0x0A`, `0x0D`, and `0x0A`, which are two `CR`, `LF` line separators. The HTTP protocol uses carriage return and line feed to terminate lines in the header and, thus, an empty line is two `CRLF` following each other.

The start of the header is a status line plus header fields. The following is a sample HTTP request:

```
GET /html/rfc7230 HTTP/1.1
Host: tools.ietf.org
Connection: keep-alive
Pragma: no-cache
Cache-Control: no-cache
Upgrade-Insecure-Requests: 1
User-Agent: Mozilla/5.0 (Macintosh; Intel Mac OS X 10_11_6)
AppleWebKit/537.36 (KHTML, like Gecko) Chrome/52.0.2743.116 Safari/537.36
Accept:
text/html,application/xhtml+xml,application/xml;q=0.9,image/webp,*/*;q=0.8
DNT: 1
Referer: https://en.wikipedia.org/
Accept-Encoding: gzip, deflate, sdch, br
Accept-Language: en,hu;q=0.8,en-US;q=0.6,de;q=0.4,en-GB;q=0.2
```

And this is the response:

```
HTTP/1.1 200 OK
Date: Tue, 04 Oct 2016 13:06:51 GMT
Server: Apache/2.2.22 (Debian)
Content-Location: rfc7230.html
Vary: negotiate,Accept-Encoding
TCN: choice
Last-Modified: Sun, 02 Oct 2016 07:11:54 GMT
ETag: "225d69b-418c0-53ddc8ad0a7b4;53e09bba89b1f"
Accept-Ranges: bytes
Cache-Control: max-age=604800
```

```
Expires: Tue, 11 Oct 2016 13:06:51 GMT
Content-Encoding: gzip
Strict-Transport-Security: max-age=3600
X-Frame-Options: SAMEORIGIN
X-Xss-Protection: 1; mode=block
X-Content-Type-Options: nosniff
Keep-Alive: timeout=5, max=100
Connection: Keep-Alive
Transfer-Encoding: chunked
Content-Type: text/html; charset=UTF-8

<!DOCTYPE html PUBLIC "-//W3C//DTD XHTML 1.0 Transitional//EN"
  "http://www.w3.org/TR/xhtml1/DTD/xhtml1-transitional.dtd">
<html xmlns="http://www.w3.org/1999/xhtml" xml:lang="en" lang="en">
<head profile="http://dublincore.org/documents/2008/08/04/dc-html/">
  <meta http-equiv="Content-Type" content="text/html; charset=utf-8" />
    <meta name="robots" content="index,follow" />
```

The request does not contain a body. The status line is as follows:

```
GET /html/rfc7230 HTTP/1.1
```

It contains the so-called method of the request, the object that is requested, and the protocol version used by the request. The remainder of the request of the header contains header fields that have the format `label: value`. Some of the lines are wrapped in the printed version, but there is no line break in a header line.

The response specifies the protocol it uses (usually the same as the request), the status code, and the message format of the status:

```
HTTP/1.1 200 OK
```

After this, the response header fields come with the same syntax as in the request. One important header field is the content type:

```
Content-Type: text/html; charset=UTF-8
```

It specifies that the response body (truncated in the printout) is HTML text.

The actual request was sent to `https://tools.ietf.org/html/rfc7230`, which is the standard that defines the 1.1 version of HTTP. You can easily look into the communication yourself, starting up the browser, and opening the developer tools. Such a tool is built into every browser these days. You can use it to debug the program behavior on the network application level by looking at the actual HTTP requests and responses on the byte level. The following screenshot shows how the developer tool shows this communication:

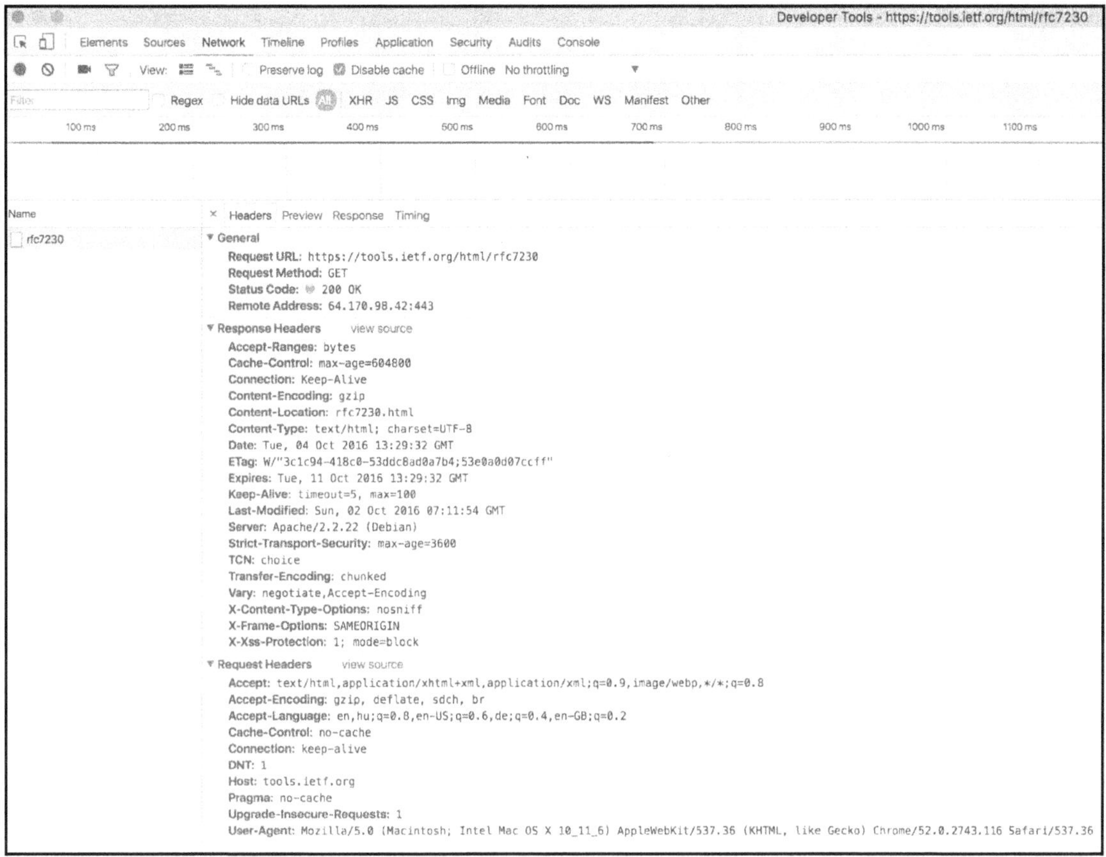

HTTP methods

The method that is the first word in the status line of the request tells the server what to do with the request. The standard defines different methods, such as `GET`, `HEAD`, `POST`, `PUT`, `DELETE`, and others.

The client uses the `GET` method when it wants to get the content of a resource. In the case of a `GET` request, the body of the request is empty. This is the method used by the browser when we download a web page. JavaScript programs use this method many times when they want to get some information from the server, but do not want to send much information to the server.

When the client uses `POST`, the intention is usually to send data to the server. The server replies and, very often, there is also a body in the reply. However, the main purpose of the request/reply communication is to send information from the client to the server. This is the opposite of the `GET` method in one way.

The `GET` and `POST` methods are the most frequently used methods. Although there is a general guideline to use `GET` to retrieve data and `POST` to send data to the server, it is only a recommendation, and there is no clean separation of the two cases. Many times, `GET` is used to send data to the server. After all, it is an HTTP request with a status line and header fields, and although there is no body in the request, the object (part of the URL) that follows the method in the status line is still able to deliver parameters. Very often, it is also easy to test a service that responds to a `GET` request because you only need a browser to type in the URL with the parameters, and then look at the response in the browser developer tools.

You should not be surprised if you see an application that uses `GET` requests to execute operations that modify the state on a web server. However, not being surprised does not mean approval. You should be aware that, in most cases, these are not good practices. When we send sensitive information using the `GET` request, the parameters in the URL are available to the client in the address line of the browser. When we send using `POST`, the parameters are still reachable by the client (after all, the information the client sends is generated by the client and, as such, cannot be unavailable), but are not that easy for a simple security-unaware user to copy and paste the information and then forward it, perhaps, to a malevolent third party. The decision between using `GET` and `POST` should always consider practicalities and security issues.

The `HEAD` method is identical to a `GET` request, but the response will not contain a body. This is used when the client is not interested in the actual response. It may happen that the client already has the object and wants to see whether it was changed. The `Last-Modified` header will contain the time when the resource was last changed, and the client can decide whether it has a newer one or needs to ask for the resource in a new request.

The `PUT` method is used when the client wants to store something on the server, and `DELETE` is used when the client wants to erase some resource. These methods are used only by applications usually written in JavaScript and not directly by the browser.

There are other methods defined in the standard, but these are the most important and frequently used ones.

Status codes

The response starts with the status code. These codes are also defined, and there are a limited number of codes usable in a response. The most important is `200`, which says everything is OK; the response contains what the request wanted. The codes are always in the range from `100` to `599`, and contain three digits. They are grouped according to the first digit as follows:

- `1xx`: These codes are information codes. They are rarely used but can be very important in some cases. For example, `100` means continue. A server can send this code when it gets a `POST` request and the server wants to signal the client to send the body of the request because it can process it. Using this code, and the client then waiting for this code, may save a lot of bandwidth if properly implemented on the server and also on the client.
- `2xx`: These codes mean success. The request is answered properly, or the requested service was implemented. There are codes such as `200`, `201`, and `202` defined in the standard and there is a description about when to use one or the other.
- `3xx`: These codes mean redirection. One of these codes is sent when the server cannot directly service the request but knows the URL that can. The actual codes can distinguish between a permanent redirect (when it is known that all future requests should be sent to the new URL) and a temporary redirect (when any later request should be sent here and possibly served or redirected), but the decision is kept on the server side.
- `4xx`: These are error codes. The most famous code is `404`, which means Not Found, that is, the server is not able to respond to the request because the resource is not found. `401` means that the resource to serve the request may be available but it requires authentication. `403` is a code that signals that the request was valid, but is still refused to be served by the server.
- `5xx`: These codes are server error codes. When a response holds one of these error codes, the meaning is that there is an error on the server. This error may be temporary, for example, when the server is processing too many requests and cannot respond to a new request with a calculation-intensive response (this is usually signaled by error code `503`) or when the feature is not implemented (code `501`). The general error code `500` is interpreted as Internal Error, which means that no information, whatsoever, is available about what was going wrong on the server, but it was not going well, and hence no meaningful response is forthcoming.

HTTP/2

After almost 20 years since the last release of HTTP, the newest version of HTTP was released in 2015. This new version of the protocol has several enhancements vis-à-vis previous versions. Some of these enhancements also affect the way server applications will be developed.

The first and most important enhancement is that the new protocol will make it possible to send several resources parallel in a single TCP connection. The keep-alive flag was already available to avoid the recreation of the TCP channel, but it does not help when a response is created slowly. In the new protocol, other resources can also be delivered in the same TCP channel, even before a request is fully served. This requires complex package handling in the protocol. This is hidden from the server application programmer as well as the browser programmer. The application server, the servlet container, and the browser implement this transparently.

HTTP/2 will always be encrypted. Therefore, it will not be possible to use `http` as a protocol in the browser URL. It will always be `https`.

The feature that will require changes in servlet programming to leverage the advantages of the new version of the protocol is Server push. Version 4.0 of the servlet specification includes support for HTTP/2. The specification is available from `https://javaee.github.io/servlet-spec/downloads/servlet-4.0/servlet-4_0_FINAL.pdf`.

Server push is an HTTP response to a request that will come in the future. How can a server answer a request that is not even issued? Well, the server anticipates. For example, the application sends an HTML page that has references to many small pictures and icons. The client downloads the HTML page, builds the DOM structure, analyzes it, and realizes that the pictures are needed, and sends the request for the pictures. The application programmer knows what pictures are there and may code the server to send the pictures even before the browser requests it. Every response of this nature includes a URL that this response is for. When the browser wants the resource, it realizes that it is already there and does not issue a new request. In `HttpServlet`, the program should access `PushBuilder` via the request's new `getPushBuilder()` method and use that to push down resources to the client.

Cookies

Cookies are maintained by the browser and are sent in the HTTP request header by using the `Cookie` header field. Each cookie has a name, value, domain, path, expiration time, and some other parameters. When a request is sent to a URL that matches the domain, the path of a non-expired cookie, the client sends the cookie to the server. Cookies are usually stored in small files on the client by the browser or in a local database. The actual implementation is the business of the browser, and we need not worry about it. It is just text information, which is not executed by the client. It is only sent back to the server when certain rules (mainly domain and path) match. Cookies are created by servers and are sent to the client in HTTP responses using the `Set-Cookie` header field. Thus, essentially, the server tells the client, "Hey, here is this cookie, whenever you come to me next time, show me this piece of information so I will know it is you". Cookies can also be created by JavaScript client code. However, because the JavaScript code also comes from the server, these cookies can also be considered as coming from the server.

Cookies are usually designed to remember clients. Advertisers and online shops that need to remember who they are talking to heavily use it. But this is not the only use. These days, any application that maintains user sessions uses cookies to chain up the HTTP requests that come from the same user. When you log in to an application, the username and password you use to identify yourself are sent to the server only once and, in subsequent requests, only a special cookie is sent to the server to identify the already logged-in user. This use of cookies emphasizes why it is important to use cookie values that cannot be easily guessed. If the cookie used to identify a user is easily guessable, then an attacker could just create a cookie and send it to the server mimicking the other user. Cookie values, for this purpose, are usually long, random strings.

Cookies are not always sent back to the server where they originate. When the cookie is sent, the server specifies the domain of the URL where the cookie should be sent back. This is used when a different server from the one providing the services requiring authentication does the user authentication.

Applications sometimes encode values into cookies. This is not necessarily bad, though in most actual cases, it is. When encoding something into a cookie, we should always consider the fact that the cookie travels through the network. Cookies with encoded data can grow huge as more and more data is encoded in it. They can create an unnecessary burden on the network. Usually, it is better to send just a unique, otherwise meaningless, random key, and store the values in a database, be it on disk or in the memory.

Client server and web architecture

The applications we have developed so far were running on a single JVM. We already have some experience with concurrent programming, and this is something that will come in handy now. When we program a web application, part of the code will run on the server and a part of the application logic will execute in the browser. The server part will be written in Java, the browser part will be implemented in HTML, CSS, and JavaScript. Since this is a Java book, we will focus mainly on the server part, but we should still be aware of the fact that much of the functionality can, and should be, implemented to run in the browser. The two programs communicate with each other over the IP network, that is, the internet, or, in the case of an enterprise internal application, the company network.

Today, a browser can execute powerful applications, implemented in JavaScript. New browser versions also support WebAssembly. This technology executes the code in a virtual machine that has a just-in-time compiler, just like the Java virtual machine has and, therefore, the code execution is as fast as a native application. There have already been showcase installations of the graphical games that run inside the browser. Languages such as C, Rust, and GO can be compiled to WebAssembly and we can expect that other languages will also be available. This means that the programming methodology of the browsers will be replaced, and more and more functionality will be implemented in the client application. That way, the applications will become more and more like the conventional old client-server applications, the difference now being that the client will run in the sandbox of the browser and the communication is a HTTP protocol.

A few years ago, such applications required the client application to be implemented in Delphi, C++, or Java, using the windowing capabilities of the client operating system.

Originally, the client-server architecture meant that the functionality of the application was implemented on the client, and the program was using general services only from the server. The server provided database access and file storage but nothing more. Later, the three-tier architecture put the business functionality on the servers that used other servers for database and other general services, and the client application implemented the user interface and limited business functionality.

When web technology started to penetrate enterprise computing, the web browser started to replace the client applications in many use cases. Previously, the browser could not run complex JavaScript applications. The application was executed on the web server and the client displayed the HTML that the server created as a part of the application logic. Every time something was changed on the user interface, the browser started a communication with the server, and, in an HTTP request-response pair, the browser content was replaced. A web application was essentially a series of form filling and form data sending operations to the server, and the server responded with HTML-formatted pages, presumably containing new forms.

JavaScript interpreters were developed and became more and more effective and standardized. Today, modern web applications contain HTML (which is a part of the client code and is not generated by the server on the fly), CSS, and JavaScript. When the code is downloaded from the web server, the JavaScript starts to execute and communicate with the server. It is still HTTP requests and responses, but the responses do not contain HTML code. It contains pure data, usually in the JSON format. This data is used by the JavaScript code and some of the data, if needed, is displayed on the web browser display also controlled by JavaScript. This is functionally equivalent to a three-tier architecture, with several small but very important differences.

The first difference is that the code is not installed on the client. The client downloads the application from a web server, and the only thing that is installed is the modern browser. This removes a lot of the enterprise maintenance burdens and costs.

The second difference is that the client is not able to access the resources of the client machine, or has only limited access. Thick client applications could save anything in a local file or access a local database. For a browser application, this is very limited, for security reasons. At the same time, this is a handy limitation because clients are not, and should not, be a trusted part of the architecture. The disk in the client computer is expensive to back up. It can be stolen with a notebook and encrypting it is costly. There are tools to protect client storage, but, most of the time, storing the data on the server only is a more viable solution.

It is also a common program design error to trust the client application. The client physically controls the client computer and, although it can be made technically very difficult, the client can still overcome the security limitations of the client device and client code. If it is only the client application that checks the validity of some functionality or data, then the physical security provided by the physical control of the server is not used. Whenever data is sent from the client to the server, the data has to be checked in terms of validity, no matter what the client application is. Actually, since the client application can be changed, we just don't really know what the client application really is.

In this chapter and, as a matter of fact, throughout this book, we focus on Java technologies; therefore, the sample application will barely contain any client technology. I could not help but create some CSS. On the other hand, I definitely avoided JavaScript. Therefore, I have to emphasize again that the example is designed to demonstrate the programming of the server side and still providing something that really works. A modern application would use REST and JSON communications and would not play around creating HTML on the fly on the server side. Originally, I wanted to create a JavaScript client and REST server application, but the focus was moved so much from server-side Java programming that I dropped this idea. On the other hand, you can extend the application to be one like that.

Writing a servlet

Servlets are Java classes that are executed in a web server that implements the servlet container environment. The first web servers could only deliver static HTML files to the browsers. For each URL, there was an HTML page on the web server and the server delivered the content of this file, in response to a request sent by the browser. Very soon, there was a need to extend the web servers to be able to initiate a program that calculates the content of the response, on the fly, when the request is processed.

The first standard to do that was a defined **Common Gateway Interface** (**CGI**). It started a new process to respond to a request. The new process got the request on its standard input, and the standard output was sent back to the client. This approach wastes a significant amount of resources. Starting a new process, as you learned in the previous chapter, is way too costly just to respond to an HTTP request. Even starting a new thread seems to be unnecessary, but with that, we are running a bit ahead of ourselves.

The next approach was FastCGI, executing the external process continually and reusing it. The approaches following FastCGI all use in-process extensions. In these cases, the code calculating the response runs inside the same process as the web server. Such standards or extension interfaces were ISAPI for the Microsoft IIS server, NSASPI for the Netscape server, and the Apache module interface. Each of these made it possible to create a **dynamically loaded library** (**DLL** on Windows, or shared object **SO** files on Unix systems) to be loaded by the web server during startup and to map certain requests to be handled by the code implemented in these libraries.

When somebody programs PHP, for example, the Apache module extension is the PHP interpreter that reads the PHP code and acts upon it. When somebody programs ASP pages for the Microsoft IIS, the ISAPI extension implementing the ASP page interpreter is executed (well, this is a bit sloppy and oversimplified to say, but works as an example).

To Java, the interface definition is a servlet defined in JSR369 as of version 4.0.

JSR stands for Java Specification Request. These are requests for modification of the Java language, library interfaces, and other components. The requests go through an evaluation process and, when they are accepted, they become a standard. The process is defined by the Java Community Process (JCP). JCP is also documented and has different versions. The current version is 2.10 and can be found at `https://jcp.org/en/procedures/overview`.

A servlet program implements the servlet interface. Usually, this is affected by extending the `HttpServlet` class. This class is an abstract implementation of the `Servlet` interface. This abstract class implements methods, such as `doGet()`, `doPost()`, `doPut()`, `doDelete()`, `doHead()`, `doOption()`, and `doTrace()`, free to be overridden by the actual class extending it. If a servlet class does not override one of these methods, sending the corresponding HTTP method, `GET`, `POST`, and so on, will return the `405 Not Allowed` status code.

Hello world servlet

Before getting into the technical details, let's create an extremely simple *hello world* servlet. To do it, we will set up a Gradle project with the build file, `build.gradle`, the servlet class in the `src/main/java/packt/java9/by/example/mastermind/servlet/HelloWorld.java` file, and, last but not least, we have to create the file `src/main/webapp/WEB-INF/web.xml`. The `gradle.build` file will look like the following:

```
apply plugin: 'java'
apply plugin: 'war'
apply from:
'https://raw.github.com/gretty-gradle-plugin/gretty/master/pluginScripts/gr
etty.plugin'

repositories {
    jcenter()
}
targetCompatibility = "1.10"
sourceCompatibility = "1.10"
dependencies {
    providedCompile "javax.servlet:javax.servlet-api:3.1.0"
    testCompile 'junit:junit:4.12'
    compile 'org.slf4j:slf4j-api:1.7.7'
    compile 'ch.qos.logback:logback-classic:1.0.11'
    compile 'com.google.inject:guice:4.1.0'
}
```

The Gradle build file uses two plugins, `java` and `gretty`. We have already used the `java` plugin in the previous chapter. The `gretty` plugin adds tasks such as `appRun` that load the Jetty servlet container and start up the application. The `gretty` plugin also uses the `war` plugin, which compiles web applications into a Web Archive (WAR) packaging format.

The WAR packaging format is practically the same as JAR; it is a zip file and contains a `lib` directory that contains all the JAR files that the web application depends on. The classes of the application are in the directory, `WEB-INF/classes`, and there is a `WEB-INF/web.xml` file that describes servlet URL mapping, which we will explore in detail soon.

Since we want to develop an extremely simple servlet, we add the servlet API as a dependency to the project. This is, however, not a `compile` dependency. The API is available when the servlet runs in the container. Still, it has to be available when the compiler compiles our code; therefore, a *dummy* implementation is provided by the artifact specified as `providedCompile`. Because it is specified that way, the build process will not package the library into the generated WAR file. The generated file will contain nothing that is specific to Jetty or any other servlet container.

The servlet container will provide the actual implementation of the servlet library. When the application is deployed and started in a Jetty, the Jetty-specific implementation of the servlet library will be available on the classpath. When the application is deployed to a Tomcat, the Tomcat-specific implementation will be available.

We create a class in our project, as follows:

```
package packt.java11.mastermind.servlet;

import javax.servlet.ServletException;
import javax.servlet.http.HttpServlet;
import javax.servlet.http.HttpServletRequest;
import javax.servlet.http.HttpServletResponse;
import java.io.IOException;
import java.io.PrintWriter;

public class HelloWorld extends HttpServlet {

    private String message;

    public void init() throws ServletException {
        message = "Hello World";
    }

    public void doGet(HttpServletRequest request,
                      HttpServletResponse response)
            throws ServletException, IOException {
```

```
        response.setContentType("text/html");
        PrintWriter out = response.getWriter();
        out.println("<h1>" + message + "</h1>");
    }

    public void destroy() {
    }
}
```

When the servlet is initiated, the `init` method is invoked. When the servlet is taken out of service, the `destroy` method is called. These methods can be overridden to provide a more fine-grained control than the constructor and other finalization possibilities. A servlet object may be put into service more than once and, after calling `destroy`, the servlet container may invoke `init` again; thus, this cycle is not strictly tied to the life cycle of the object. Usually, there is not much that we do in these methods, but sometimes, you may need some code in them.

Also, note that a single servlet object may be used to serve many requests, even at the same time; thus, the servlet classes and methods in it should be thread-safe. The specification demands that a servlet container uses only one servlet instance in case the container runs in a non-distributed environment. In case the container runs on the same machine in several processes, each executing a JVM, or even on different machines, there can be many servlet instances that handle the requests. Generally, the servlet classes should be designed such that they do not assume that only one thread is executing them, but, at the same time, they should also not assume that the instance is the same for the different requests. We simply cannot know.

What does this mean in practice? You should not use instance fields that are specific to a certain request. In the preceding example, the field initialized to hold the message holds the same value for each and every request; essentially, the variable is almost a final constant. It is used only to demonstrate some functionality for the `init` method.

The `doGet` method is invoked when the servlet container gets an HTTP request with the `GET` method. The method has two arguments. The first one represents the request, and the second one represents the response. The `request` can be used to collect all the information that comes in the request. In the preceding example, there is nothing like that. We do not use any of the inputs. If a request comes to our servlet, then we answer the `Hello, World` string, no matter what. Later, we will see examples when we read the parameters from the request. The `response` gives methods that can be used to handle the output.

In the example, we fetch `PrintWriter`, which is to be used to send characters to the body of the HTTP response. This is the content that appears in the browser. The mime type we send is `text/html`, and this is set by calling the `setContentType` method. This will get into the HTTP header field, `Content-Type`. The standard and the JavaDoc documentation of the classes define all the methods that can be used, and also how these should be used.

Finally, we have a `web.xml` file that declares the servlets that are implemented in our code. This is, just as the name of the file indicates, an XML file. It declaratively defines all the servlets that are included in the archive and also other parameters. In the following example, the parameters are not defined, only the servlet and the mapping to the URL. Since we have only one single servlet in this example, the WAR file, it is mapped to the root context. Each and every `GET` request that arrives to the servlet container and to this archive will be served by this servlet:

```
<web-app version="2.5" xmlns="http://java.sun.com/xml/ns/javaee"
         xmlns:xsi="http://www.w3.org/2001/XMLSchema-instance"
         xsi:schemaLocation="http://java.sun.com/xml/ns/javaee
http://java.sun.com/xml/ns/javaee/web-app_2_5.xsd">

    <servlet>
        <display-name>HelloWorldServlet</display-name>
        <servlet-name>HelloWorldServlet</servlet-name>
        <servlet-class>packt.java11.mastermind.servlet.HelloWorld</servlet-
class>
    </servlet>
    <servlet>
        <display-name>Mastermind</display-name>
        <servlet-name>Mastermind</servlet-name>
        <servlet-class>packt.java11.mastermind.servlet.Mastermind</servlet-
class>
    </servlet>

    <servlet-mapping>
        <servlet-name>HelloWorldServlet</servlet-name>
        <url-pattern>/hello</url-pattern>
    </servlet-mapping>
    <servlet-mapping>
        <servlet-name>Mastermind</servlet-name>
        <url-pattern>/master</url-pattern>
    </servlet-mapping>

</web-app>
```

JavaServer Pages

I promised you that I would not bore you with JavaServer Pages (JSP) because that is a technology of the past. Even though it is the past, it is still not history as there are many programs running that still use JSP.

JSP pages are web pages that contain HTML and Java code combined. When an HTTP request is served by a JSP page, the servlet container reads the JSP page, executes the Java parts, takes the HTML parts as they are, and, in this way, mixing the two together, creates an HTML page that is sent to the browser:

```
<%@ page language="java"
         contentType="text/html; charset=UTF-8"
         pageEncoding="UTF-8"%>
<html>
<body>
<% for( int i = 0 ; i < 5 ; i ++ ){ %>
  hallo<br/>
<% } %>
</body>
</html>
```

The preceding page will create an HTML page that contains the text `hallo` five times, each in a new line separated by the tag `br`. Behind the scenes, the servlet container converts the JSP page to a Java servlet, then compiles the servlet using the Java compiler, and then runs the servlet. It does it every time there is a change to the source JSP file; therefore, it is very easy to incrementally craft some simple code using JSP. The code that is generated from the preceding JSP file is 138 lines long (on the Tomcat 8.5.5 version), which is simply long and boring to list here, but the part that may help to understand how the Java file generation works only comprises a few lines.

If you want to see all the lines of the generated servlet class, you can deploy the application into a Tomcat server and look at the `work/Catalina/localhost/hello/org/apache/jsp/` directory. It is a little-known fact among developers that this code is actually saved to disk and is available. It occasionally helps when you need to debug some JSP pages.

Here are a few lines of interest that were generated from the preceding code:

```
out.write("n");
      out.write("<html>n");
      out.write("<body>n");
 for( int i = 0 ; i < 5 ; i ++ ){
      out.write("n");
      out.write("  hallo<br/>n");
 }
      out.write("n");
      out.write("</body>n");
      out.write("</html>n");
```

The JSP compiler moves the inside of the JSP code out and the outside in. In the JSP code, Java is surrounded by HTML, and, in the generated servlet Java source code, the HTML is surrounded by Java. It is like when you want to mend clothes: the first thing is to turn the dress inside out.

It is not only the Java code that you can mix into HTML in the JSP pages but also the so-called tags. Tags are collected into tag libraries, implemented in Java, and packaged into JAR files, and they should be available on the classpath to be used. The JSP page using the tags from a particular library should declare the use:

```
<%@ taglib prefix="c"
         uri="http://java.sun.com/jsp/jstl/core" %>
```

The tags look like HTML tags, but they are processed by the JSP compiler and executed by the code implemented in the `taglib` library. JSP may also refer to the value of the Java objects that are available within the scope of the JSP. To do this inside the HTML page, the JSP expression language could be used.

JSP was originally created to ease the development of a web application. The main advantage is the fast startup of development. There is no need for tedious configuration, setup, and other auxiliary tasks during development, and when there is any change to the JSP page, there is no need to compile the whole application again—the servlet container generates the Java code, compiles it to the class file, loads the code into memory, and executes. JSP was a competitor of Microsoft ASP pages, which mixed HTML with VisualBasic code.

As the application starts to expand, using JSP technology causes more problems than it solves. The code that mixes the business logic and the view of the application, how it is rendered in the browser, becomes messy. Developing JSP requires frontend technology knowledge. A Java developer is expected to know some frontend technology, but is rarely a design expert and CSS guru. The modern code also contains JavaScript, many times embedded in the HTML page. After all, the big advantage of JSP is that it contains code that runs on the server as well as on the client-side code. The developers follow the paradigm many times, so do not be surprised to see some legacy code that contains Java, HTML, CSS, and JavaScript all mixed in a JSP file. Since Java and JavaScript are syntactically similar sometimes, it is not obvious to see what is executed on the server and what is executed on the client. I have even seen code that created JavaScript code from Java code in a JSP file. That is a total mix of different responsibilities and a mess that is nearly impossible to maintain. This led to the total deprecation of JSP as of today.

The deprecation of JSP is not official. It is my expert opinion. You may meet some experienced developers who are still in love with JSP, and you may find yourself in projects where you are required to develop programs in JSP. It is not shameful doing that. Some people do worse for money.

To mend the messy situation, there were technologies that advocated the separation of the server code and the client functionality more and more. These technologies include Wicket, Vaadin, JSF, and different Java templating engines, such as Freemarker, Apache Velocity, and Thymeleaf. These latter technologies can also be interesting when you generate textual output from Java, even when the code is not web-related at all.

These technologies, with discipline, helped control the development and maintenance costs of moderate and large web projects, but the basic problem of the architecture was still there: no clear separation of concerns.

Today, modern applications implement the code of a web application in separate projects: one for the client, using HTML, CSS, and JavaScript, and a separate one to implement server functionality in Java (or in something else, but we focus here on Java). The communication between the two is the REST protocol, which we will cover in subsequent chapters.

HTML, CSS, and JavaScript

HTML, CSS, and JavaScript are client-side technologies. These are extremely important for web applications, and a professional Java developer should have some knowledge of them. The developers who are experts in both areas are called full-stack developers these days, though I find the name a bit misleading. A certain understanding is inevitable.

HTML is the textual representation of a structured text. The text is given as characters, as in any text file. Tags represent the structure. A start tag starts with a < character, then the name of the tag, then, optionally, `name="value"` attributes, and finally a closing > character. An end tag starts with </, then the name of the tag, and then >. Tags are enclosed in hierarchies; thus, you should not close a tag sooner than the one that was opened later. First, the tag that was opened last has to be closed, then the next, and so on. This way, any actual tag in the HTML has a level, and all tags that are between the start and end tags are *below* this tag. Some tags that cannot enclose other tags or text do not have end tags and stand on their own. Consider the following sample:

```
<html>
  <head>
    <title>this is the title</title>
  </head>
</html>
```

The tag `head` is under `html`, and `title` is under `head`. This can be structured into a tree, as follows:

```
html
+ head
  + title
    + "this is the title"
```

The browser stores the HTML text in a tree structure, and this tree is the object model of the web page document, thus the name, **Document Object Model** (**DOM**) tree.

The original HTML concept mixed formatting and structure and, even with the current version of HTML5, we still have tags such as `b`, `i`, and `tt` that suggest to the browser to display the text between the start and end tags in bold, italics, and teletype, respectively.

As the name HTML, standing for Hypertext Markup Language, suggests, the text can contain references to other web pages in the form of hyperlinks. These links are assigned to texts using the `a` tag (standing for anchor) or to some form that may consist of different fields, and when the submit button of the form is pressed, the content of the fields is sent to the server in a `POST` request. When the form is sent, the content of the fields is encoded in the so-called `application/x-www-form-urlencoded` form.

The HTML structure always tried to promote the separation of structure and formatting. To do so, formatting was moved to styles. Styles defined in **Cascading Style Sheets** (**CSS**) provide much more flexibility for formatting than HTML; the format of a CSS is more effective for formatting. The aim to create CSS was that the design can be decoupled from the structure of the text.

If I had to choose one of the three, I would opt for CSS as the one that is least important for Java server-side web developers and, at the same time, the most important for the users (things should look nice).

JavaScript is the third pillar of client-side technologies. JavaScript is a fully functional, interpreted programming language executed by the browser. It can access the DOM tree, and read and modify it. When the DOM tree is modified, the browser automatically displays the modified page. JavaScript functions can be scheduled and registered to be invoked when an event occurs. For example, you can register a function to be invoked when the document is fully loaded, when the user presses a button, clicks on a link, or just hovers the mouse over some section. Although JavaScript was first only used to create funny animations on the browser, today it is possible, as well as standard practice, to program fully functional clients using the capabilities of the browser. There are really powerful programs written in JavaScript, even such power-hungry applications as PC emulators.

Last, but by no means least, us Java developers must keep an eye on the new WebAssembly technology that I described earlier.

In this book, we focus on Java and use the client-side technologies as much as is needed for demonstration technologies. However, being a Java web developer professional, you have to learn these technologies as well, to some extent at least, so as to understand what a client can do and to be able to cooperate with the professionals responsible for frontend technologies.

Mastermind servlet

Playing the Mastermind game via the web is a bit different from what it used to be. Until now, we did not have any user interaction, and our classes were designed accordingly. For example, we could add a new guess to the table, along with the partial and full matches calculated by the program. Now, we have to separate the creation of a new guess, add it to the game, and set the full and partial matches. This time, we have to display the table first, and the user has to calculate and provide the number of matches.

We have to modify some of the classes to be able to do that. We need to add a new method to `Game.java`:

```
public Row addGuess(Guess guess, int full, int partial) {
    assertNotFinished();
    final Row row = new Row(guess, full, partial);
    table.addRow(row);
    if (itWasAWinningGuess(full)) {
```

```
            finished = true;
        }
        return row;
    }
```

Until now, we had only one method that was adding a new guess, and since the program knew the secret, it was immediately calculating the value of `full` and `partial`. The name of the method could be `addNewGuess`, overloading the original method, but this time, the method is used not only to add a new guess but also to add old guesses to rebuild the table. That is because we rebuild the actual state of the game from the information the browser sends to the server every time the player gives an answer for the next guess. The state of the game is stored in the client and it is sent up in the HTTP request to the server.

When the program starts, there are no guesses. The program creates one, the first one. Later on, when the user tells the program the full and partial matches, the program needs the `Game` structure with `Table` and `Row` objects containing `Guess` objects and the `full` and `partial` match values. These were already available, but when the new HTTP hit comes in, we have to pull it from somewhere. Programming a servlet, we have to store the state of the game somewhere and restore it when a new HTTP request hits the server.

Storing state

Storing the state can be done in two places. One place, which we will first do in our code, is the client. When the program creates a new guess, it adds it to the table and sends an HTML page that contains not only the new guess but also all the previous guesses and the `full` and `partial` match values that the user gave for each of the rows. To send the data to the server, the values are stored in the fields of a form. When the form is submitted, the browser gathers the information in the fields, creates an encoded string from the content of the fields, and puts the content into the body of a `POST` request.

The other possibility for storing the actual state is on the server. The server could store the state of the game, and it could reconstruct the structure when it creates a new guess. The problem, in this case, is knowing which game to use. If the state is stored on the server, then it should store many games, at least one for each user. The users may use the application concurrently. It does not necessarily mean strong concurrency along the lines of what we examined in the previous chapter.

Even if the users are not served at the same time in multiple threads, there can be games that are active. There can be multiple users playing multiple games and, while serving an HTTP request, we should know which user we are serving.

Servlets maintain sessions that can be used for this purpose, as we will see in the next section.

Deciding where to store the state of an application is an important architectural question. When making the decision, you should consider reliability, trust, security, which itself also depends on trust, performance, and possibly other factors.

HTTP session

When a client sends requests from the same browser to the same servlet, the series of requests belong to one session. To know that the requests belong to the same session, the servlet container automatically sends a cookie named `JSESSIONID` to the client, and this cookie has a long, random, hard-to-guess value (`tkojxpz9qk9xo7124pvanc1z`, as I run the application in Jetty). The servlet maintains a session store that contains the `HttpSession` instances. The key string that travels in the value of the `JSESSIONID` cookie identifies the instance. When an HTTP request arrives at the servlet, the container attaches the session to the request object from the store. If there is no session for the key, then one is created, and the code can access the session object by calling the `request.getSession()` method.

An `HttpSession` object can store attributes. The program can call the `setAttribute(String,Object)`, `getAttribute(String)`, and `removeAttribute(String)` methods to store, retrieve, or delete an attribute object. Each attribute is assigned to a `String` and can be any `Object`.

Although the session attribute store essentially looks as simple as a `Map<String, ?>` object, it is not. The values stored in the session can be moved from one node to another when the servlet container runs in a clustered or other distributed environment. To do that, the values are serialized; therefore, the values stored in the session should be `Serializable`. Failing to do so is a very common novice error. During development, executing the code in a simple development Tomcat or Jetty container practically never serializes the session to disk and never loads it from the serialized form. This means that the values set using `setAttribute` will be available by calling `getAttribute`. We run into trouble the first time the application gets installed in a clustered environment. As soon as an HTTP request arrives on different nodes `getAttribute` may return `null`. The method `setAttribute` is called on one node and, during the processing of the next request, `getAttribute` on a different node cannot deserialize the attribute value from the disk shared among the nodes. This is usually, and sadly, the production environment.

Although currently, the session can store reliably only objects of classes that implement the `Serializable` interface, we should be aware that Java serialization will change some time in the future. Serialization is a low-level functionality and having it wired into a language was not a good decision by the time Java was created. At least it seems now that it was not. There is nothing to be afraid of in regards serialization—servlet standard and implementations will handle the situation properly. On the other hand, it is counter-intuitive to use serialization in your own code other than those provided by the frameworks.

You, as a developer, should also be aware that serializing and deserializing an object is a heavy operation that costs several CPU cycles. If the structure of the application uses only a part of the client state serving most of the HTTP requests, then this is a waste of CPU to create the whole state in memory from a serialized form and then serializing it again. In such cases, it is more advisable to store only a key in the session and use some database (SQL or NoSQL) or some other service to store the actual data referenced by the key. Enterprise applications almost exclusively use this structure.

Storing state on the client

First, we will develop our code by storing the state on the client. The form needed to send the user input and the number of new full and partial matches also contains all the previous colors for all the guesses and answers given at that time by the user. To do so, we create a new helper class to format the HTML code. This is something that is done in a modern enterprise environment using templates, JSP files, or just totally avoided using pure REST and a one-page application in the enterprise environment. Nevertheless, here, we will use the old technology in order to demonstrate the gears that rotate under the hood of modern engines:

```
package packt.java11.mastermind.servlet;

import packt.java11.mastermind.Color;
import packt.java11.mastermind.Table;

import javax.inject.Inject;
import javax.inject.Named;

public class HtmlTools {
    @Inject
    Table table;

    @Inject
```

```
@Named("nrColumns")
private int NR_COLUMNS;

public String tag(String tagName, String... attributes) {
    StringBuilder sb = new StringBuilder();
    sb.append("<").append((tagName));
    for (int i = 0; i < attributes.length; i += 2) {
        sb.append(" ").
                append(attributes[i]).
                append("=\"").
                append(attributes[i + 1]).
                append("\"");
    }
    sb.append(">");
    return sb.toString();
}

public String inputBox(String name, String value) {
    return tag("input", "type",
            "text", "name", name, "value", value, "size", "1");
}

public String colorToHtml(Color color, int row, int column) {
    return tag("div",
            "class", "color" + color) +
            tag("/div") +
            tag("div",
                    "class", "spacer") +
            tag("/div");
}

public String paramNameFull(int row) {
    return "full" + row;
}

public String paramNamePartial(int row) {
    return "partial" + row;
}

public String paramNameGuess(int row, int column) {
    return "guess" + row + column;
}

public String tableToHtml() {
    StringBuilder sb = new StringBuilder();
    sb.append("<html><head>");
    sb.append("<link rel=\"stylesheet\"")
            .append(" type=\"text/css\" href=\"colors.css\">");
```

```
        sb.append("<title>Mastermind guessing</title>");
        sb.append("<body>");
        sb.append(tag("form",
                "method", "POST",
                "action", "master"));

        for (int row = 0; row < table.nrOfRows(); row++) {
            for (int column = 0; column < NR_COLUMNS; column++) {
                final String html =
                        colorToHtml(table.getColor(row, column),
                                row, column);
                sb.append(html);
            }
            if (row < table.nrOfRows() - 1) {
                sb.append("" + table.getFull(row));
                sb.append(tag("div", "class", "spacer"))
                        .append(tag("/div"));
                sb.append("" + table.getPartial(row));
            } else {
                sb.append(inputBox(paramNameFull(row), "" +
table.getFull(row)));
                sb.append(inputBox(paramNamePartial(row), "" +
table.getPartial(row)));
            }
            sb.append("<p>");
        }
        return sb.toString();
    }
}
```

Except for the `@Inject` annotation, the rest of the code is simple and straightforward. We will focus on `@Inject` in the very near future. What we have to focus on is the HTML structure the code generates. The generated page will look something like this:

```
<html>
    <head>
        <link rel="stylesheet" type="text/css" href="colors.css">
        <title>Mastermind guessing</title>
        <body>
            <form method="POST" action="master">
                <input type="hidden" name="guess00" value="3">
                <div class="color3"></div>

                <div class="spacer"></div>

                <input type="hidden" name="guess01" value="2">
                <div class="color2"></div>
```

```
                    <div class="spacer"></div>

                    <input type="hidden" name="guess02" value="1">
                    <div class="color1"></div>

                    <div class="spacer"></div>

                    <input type="hidden" name="guess03" value="0">
                    <div class="color0"></div>

                    <div class="spacer"></div>

                    <input type="text"
                           name="full0" value="0" size="1">
                    <input type="text"
                           name="partial0" value="2" size="1">


                    <input type="hidden" name="guess10" value="5">
                    <div class="color5"></div>


    ...deleted content that just looks almost the same...



                    <input type="submit" value="submit">
                </form>
            </body>
        </head>
    </html>
```

The form contains the colors in `div` tags, and it also contains the *letter* of the color in hidden fields. These input fields are sent to the server when the form is submitted, just like any other field, but they do not appear on the screen and the user cannot edit them. The full and partial matches are displayed in the text input fields. Since it is not possible to display the `Color` objects in an HTML text, we use `LetteredColor` and `LetteredColorFactory`, which assign single letters to colors. The first six colors are simply numbered as `0`, `1`, `2`, `3`, `4`, and `5`. A CSS file can control how the colors will look on the browser window.

You may remember that we covered how and where to implement the display of individual colors. First, we created a special printing class that was assigning letters to already existing colors, but that was only usable in a very limited environment (unit tests, mainly). Now, we have the issue again. We have the lettered color, but now we need real colors because this time, we have a client display that is capable of displaying colors.

The real power of modern web technology shines here. The content and the format can be separated from each other. The pegs of different colors are listed in HTML as `div` tags. They have a formatting class, but the actual look is defined in a CSS file that is responsible for nothing else but the look:

```
.color0 {
    background: red;
    width : 20px;
    height: 20px;
    float:left
}
.color1 {
    background-color: green;
    width : 20px;
    height: 20px;
    float:left
}
... .color2 to .color5 is deleted, content is the same except different
colors ...

.spacer {
    background-color: white;
    width : 10px;
    height: 20px;
    float:left
}
```

Dependency injection with Guice

The servlet class is very simple, as demonstrated in the following code:

```
package packt.java11.mastermind.servlet;

import com.google.inject.Guice;
import com.google.inject.Injector;
import org.slf4j.Logger;
import org.slf4j.LoggerFactory;

import javax.servlet.ServletException;
import javax.servlet.http.HttpServlet;
import javax.servlet.http.HttpServletRequest;
import javax.servlet.http.HttpServletResponse;
import java.io.IOException;

public class Mastermind extends HttpServlet {
```

```
    private static final Logger log =
            LoggerFactory.getLogger(Mastermind.class);

    public void doGet(HttpServletRequest request,
                      HttpServletResponse response)
            throws ServletException, IOException {
        doPost(request, response);
    }

    public void doPost(HttpServletRequest request,
                       HttpServletResponse response)
            throws ServletException, IOException {
        Injector injector =
                Guice.createInjector(new MastermindModule());
        MastermindHandler handler =
                injector.getInstance(MastermindHandler.class);
        handler.handle(request, response);
    }
}
```

Because many threads use servlets concurrently, and thus we cannot use instance fields holding data for a single hit, the servlet class does nothing else but create a new instance of a `MastermindHandler` class and invoke its `handle` method. Since there is a new instance of `MastermindHandler` for each request, it can store objects in fields specific to the request. To create a handler, we use the Guice library created by Google.

We have already talked about dependency injection. The handler needs a `Table` object to play, a `ColorManager` object to manage the colors, and a `Guesser` object to create a new guess, but creating these or fetching some prefabricated instances from somewhere is not the core functionality of the handler. The handler has to do one thing—handle the request; the instances needed to do this should be injected from outside. This is done by a `Guice` injector.

To use Guice, we have to list the library among the dependencies in `build.gradle`. The actual content of the file was already listed before the `HelloWorld` servlet.

Then, we have to create an `injector` instance that will do the injection. The injector is created with the following line in the servlet:

```
Injector injector = Guice.createInjector(new MastermindModule());
```

The instance of `MastermindModule` specifies what to inject where. This is essentially a configuration file in the Java format. Other dependency injector frameworks used, and continue to use, XML and annotations to describe the injection binding and what to inject where, but Guice solely uses Java code. The following is the DI configuration code:

```
public class MastermindModule extends AbstractModule {
    @Override
    protected void configure() {
        bind(int.class)
                .annotatedWith(Names.named("nrColors"))
                .toInstance(6);
        bind(int.class)
                .annotatedWith(Names.named("nrColumns"))
                .toInstance(4);
        bind(ColorFactory.class)
                .to(LetteredColorFactory.class);
        bind(Guesser.class)
                .to(UniqueGuesser.class);
    }
```

The methods used in the `configure` method are created in a fluent API manner so that the methods can be chained one after the other, and so that the code can be read almost like English sentences. A good introduction to fluent API can be found at `https://blog.jooq.org/2012/01/05/the-java-fluent-api-designer-crash-course/`. For example, the first configuration line could be read in English as:

> *"Bind to the class* `int` *wherever it is annotated with the* `@Name` *annotation having* `"nrColor"` *value to the instance* `6`*."*

The `MastermindHandler` class contains fields that have been annotated with `@Inject` annotation:

```
@Inject
@Named("nrColors")
private int NR_COLORS;
@Inject
@Named("nrColumns")
private int NR_COLUMNS;
@Inject
private HtmlTools html;
@Inject
Table table;
@Inject
ColorManager manager;
@Inject
Guesser guesser;
```

This annotation is not Guice-specific. `@Inject` is a part of the `javax.inject` package and is a standard part of JDK. JDK does not provide the **dependency injector** (**DI**) framework, but supports the different frameworks so that they can use standard JDK annotations and, in case the DI framework is replaced, the annotations may remain the same and not framework-specific.

When the injector is called to create an instance of `MastermindHandler`, it looks at the class and sees that it has an `int` field annotated with `@Inject` and `@Named("nrColors")`, and finds in the configuration that such a field should have the value 6. It injects the value to the field before returning the `MastermindHandler` object. Similarly, it also injects the values into the other fields and, should it need to create any of the objects to be injected, it does. If there are fields in these objects, then they are also created by injecting other objects and so on.

In this way, the DI framework removes the burden of creating the instances from the programmers' shoulders. This is something fairly boring and is not the core feature of the classes anyway. Instead, it creates all the objects needed to have a functional `MastermindHandler` and links them together via the Java object references. This way, the dependencies of the different objects (`MastermindHandler` needs `Guesser`, `ColorManager`, and `Table`; `ColorManager` needs `ColorFactory`, and `Table` also needs `ColorManager`, and so on) become a declaration, specified using annotations on the fields. These declarations are inside the code of the classes, and it is the right place for them. Where else could we specify what the class needs to properly function than in the class itself?

The configuration in our example specifies that wherever there is a need for `ColorFactory`, we will use `LetteredColorFactory`, and that wherever we need `Guesser`, we will use `UniqueGuesser`. This is separated from the code, and it has to be like that. If we want to change the guessing strategy, we replace the configuration, and the code should work without modifying the classes that use the guesser.

Guice is clever enough and you need not specify that wherever there is a need for `Table`, we will use `Table`—there is no `bind(Table.class).to(Table.class)`. First, I created a line like that in the configuration, but Guice rewarded me with an error message, and now, writing it again in plain English, I feel really stupid. If I need a table, I need a table. Really?

When working with Java 9 or later and where our code uses JPMS, we have to open our code base toward the framework we use. Modules do not allow code from outside to manipulate private classes or object members using reflection. If we do not declare in the module definition file that we want to use Guice and we allow Guice to access the private fields, it will not be able to do that and, that way, it will not work. To open our module to Guice, we have to edit the `module_info.java` file and insert the `opens` keyword, specifying the packages where the classes requiring injection are located.

The MastermindHandler class

We have already started the listing of the `MastermindHandler` class and, since this class is more than a hundred lines, I will not include it here as a whole. The most important method of this class is `handle`:

```
public void handle(HttpServletRequest request,
                   HttpServletResponse response)
        throws ServletException, IOException {

    Game game = buildGameFromRequest(request);
    Guess newGuess = guesser.guess();
    response.setContentType("text/html");
    PrintWriter out = response.getWriter();
    if (game.isFinished() || newGuess == Guess.none) {
        displayGameOver(out);
    } else {
        log.debug("Adding new guess {} to the game", newGuess);
        game.addGuess(newGuess, 0, 0);
        displayGame(out);
    }
    bodyEnd(out);
}
```

We perform three steps. Step 1 is creating the table, and we do it from the request. If this is not the start of the game, there will already be a table, and the HTML form contains all previous guess colors and the answers to those. Then, as the second step, we create a new guess based on that. Step 3 is to send the new HTML page to the client.

Again, this is not a modern approach, creating HTML on the servlet code, but demonstrating pure servlet functionality with REST, JSON, and JavaScript, together with some framework, would make this chapter alone a few hundred pages long, and it would definitely divert our attention away from Java.

Printing HTML text to a `PrintWriter` is not something that should be new to you at this point in this book; therefore, we will not list that code here. You can download the working example from the Packt GitHub repository. Instead of printing, we will focus on the servlet parameter handling.

The request parameters are available via the `getParameter()` method, which returns the string value of a parameter. This method assumes that any parameter, be it `GET` or `POST`, appears only once in the request. In case there are parameters that appear multiple times, the value should have been a `String` array. In such a case, we should use `getParameterMap()`, which returns the whole map with the `String` keys and `String[]` values. Even though we do not have multiple values for any key this time, and we also know the values of the keys coming as `POST` parameters, we will still use the latter method. The reason for this is that we will later use the session to store these values, and we want to have a method that is reusable in that case.

To get to that stage, we convert the request's `Map<String,String[]>` to `Map<String,String>`:

```
private Game buildGameFromRequest(HttpServletRequest request) {
    return buildGameFromMap(toMap(request));
}

private Map<String, String> toMap(HttpServletRequest request) {
    log.debug("converting request to map");
    return request.getParameterMap().entrySet().
            stream().collect(
            Collectors.toMap(
                    Map.Entry::getKey,
                    e -> e.getValue()[0]));
}
```

Then, we use that map to recreate the game:

```
private Game buildGameFromMap(Map<String, String> params) {
    var secret = new Guess(new Color[NR_COLUMNS]);
    var game = new Game(table, secret);
    for (int row = 0;
         params.containsKey(html.paramNameGuess(row, 0));
         row++) {
```

```
        Color[] colors = getRowColors(params, row);
        Guess guess = new Guess(colors);
        var full = Integer.parseInt(params.get(html.paramNameFull(row)));
        var partial =
Integer.parseInt(params.get(html.paramNamePartial(row)));
        log.debug("Adding guess to game");
        game.addGuess(guess, full, partial);
    }
    return game;
}
```

The conversion from `String` to `int` is done via the method `parseInt()`. This method throws `NumberFormatException` when the input is not a number. Try to run the game, use the browser, and see how Jetty handles the case when the servlet throws an exception. How much valuable information do you see in the browser that can be used by a potential hacker? Fix the code so that it asks the user again if any of the numbers are not well-formatted!

Storing state on the server

The application state should usually not be saved on the client. There may be some special case in addition to the one where you write educational code and want to demonstrate how not to do it. Generally, the state of the application related to the actual use is stored in the session object or in some database. This is especially important when the application asks the user to enter a lot of data and does not want the user to lose the work if there is some hiccup in the client computer.

You spend a lot of time selecting the appropriate items in an online shop, choosing the appropriate items that work together, creating a configuration of your new model airplane, and, all of a sudden, there is a blackout in your home. If the state was stored on the client, you'd have had to start from scratch. If the state is stored on the server, the state is saved to disk; the servers are duplicated, fed by battery-backed power supplies, and, when you reboot, your client machine and the power comes back in your home, you log in, and miraculously, the items are all there in your shopping basket. Well, it is not a miracle; it is web programming.

In our case, the second version will store the state of the game in the session. This will let the user have the game restored so long as the session is there. If the user quits and restarts the browser, the session gets lost and a new game can start.

Since there is no need to send the actual colors and matching in hidden fields this time, the HTML generation is modified a bit, and the generated HTML will also be simpler:

```
<html>
<head>
    <link rel="stylesheet" type="text/css" href="colors.css">
    <title>Mastermind guessing</title>
<body>
<form method="POST" action="master">
    <div class="color3"></div>
    <div class="spacer"></div>
    <div class="color2"></div>
    <div class="spacer"></div>
    <div class="color1"></div>
    <div class="spacer"></div>
    <div class="color0"></div>
    <div class="spacer"></div>
0
    <div class="spacer"></div>
2
    <div class="color5"></div>
...
    <div class="spacer"></div>
    <div class="color1"></div>
    <div class="spacer"></div>
    <input type="text" name="full2" value="0" size="1">
    <input type="text" name="partial2" value="0" size="1">
    <input type="submit" value="submit">
</form></body></head></html>
```

The number of full and partially matching colors is displayed as a simple number, so this version does not allow *cheating* or modification of the previous results. (These are the numbers `0` and `2` after the `div` tags that have the CSS class `spacer`.)

The `handle` method in `MastermindHandler` also changes, as shown in the following code:

```
public void handle(HttpServletRequest request,
                   HttpServletResponse response)
        throws ServletException, IOException {

    Game game = buildGameFromSessionAndRequest(request);
    Guess newGuess = guesser.guess();
    response.setContentType("text/html");
    PrintWriter out = response.getWriter();
    if (game.isFinished() || newGuess == Guess.none) {
        displayGameOver(out);
    } else {
        log.debug("Adding new guess {} to the game", newGuess);
```

```
            game.addGuess(newGuess, 0, 0);
            sessionSaver.save(request.getSession()); // note the added line
            displayGame(out);
        }
        bodyEnd(out);
    }
```

The variable `sessionSaver` is a field that has the type `SessionSaver` and it is injected into the class by the Guice injector. `SessionSaver` is a class that we create. This class will convert the current `Table` into something that is stored in the session, and it also recreates the table from the data stored in the session. The `handle` method uses the `buildGameFromSessionAndRequest` method to restore the table and to add the full and partial match answers that the user just gave in the request. When the method creates a new guess and fills it in the table, and also sends it to the client in the response, it saves the state in the session by calling the `save()` method via the `sessionSaver` object.

The `buildGameFromSessionAndRequest` method replaces the other version, which we named `buildGameFromRequest`:

```
    private Game buildGameFromSessionAndRequest(HttpServletRequest request) {
        var game =
    buildGameFromMap(sessionSaver.restore(request.getSession()));
        var params = toMap(request);
        int row = getLastRowIndex(params);
        log.debug("last row is {}", row);
        if (row >= 0) {
            var full = Integer.parseInt(params.get(html.paramNameFull(row)));
            var partial =
    Integer.parseInt(params.get(html.paramNamePartial(row)));
            log.debug("setting full {} and partial {} for row {}", full,
    partial, row);
            table.setPartial(row, partial);
            table.setFull(row, full);
            if (full == table.nrOfColumns()) {
                game.setFinished();
            }
        }
        return game;
    }
```

Note that this version has the same illness of using the `parseInt()` method from the `Integer` class in JDK, which throws an exception.

The GameSessionSaver class

This class has three public methods:

- `save()`: This saves a table to the user session
- `restore()`: This gets a table from the user session
- `reset()`: This deletes any table that may be in the session

The code of the class is as follows:

```
public class GameSessionSaver {
    private static final String STATE_NAME = "GAME_STATE";
    @Inject
    private HtmlTools html;
    @Inject
    Table table;
    @Inject
    ColorManager manager;

    public void save(HttpSession session) {
        var params = convertTableToMap();
        session.setAttribute(STATE_NAME, params);
    }

    public void reset(HttpSession session) {
        session.removeAttribute(STATE_NAME);
    }

    public Map<String, String> restore(HttpSession session) {
        return (Map<String, String>)
                Optional.ofNullable(session.getAttribute(STATE_NAME))
                        .orElse(new HashMap<>());
    }

    private Map<String, String> convertTableToMap() {
        var params = new HashMap<String, String>();
        for (int row = 0; row < table.nrOfRows(); row++) {
            for (int column = 0;
                 column < table.nrOfColumns();
                 column++) {
                params.put(html.paramNameGuess(row, column),
                        table.getColor(row, column).toString());
            }
            params.put(html.paramNameFull(row),
                    "" + table.getFull(row));
            params.put(html.paramNamePartial(row),
                    "" + table.getPartial(row));
```

```
            }
            return params;
        }
    }
```

When we save the session and convert the table to a map, we use a `HashMap`. The implementation, in this case, is important. The `HashMap` class implements the `Serializable` interface; therefore, we can be safe putting it into the session. This alone does not guarantee that everything in `HashMap` is `Serializable`. The keys and the values in our case are Strings and, fortunately, the `String` class also implements the `Serializable` interface. This way, the converted `HashMap` object can be safely stored in the session.

Also note that, although serialization can be slow, storing `HashMap` in a session is so frequent that it implements its own serialization mechanism. This implementation is optimized and avoids serialization being dependent on the internal structure of the map.

It is time to think about why we have the `convertTableToMap()` method in this class and `buildGameFromMap()` in the class `MastermindHandler`. Converting the game and the table in it to a `Map` and the other way round should be implemented together. They are just two directions of the same conversion. On the other hand, the implementation of the `Table` to `Map` direction should use a `Map` version that is `Serializable`. This is very much related to session handling. Converting a `Map` object, in general, to a `Table` object is one level higher, restoring the table from wherever it was stored—client, session, database, or in the moisture of the cloud. Session storage is only one possible implementation, and methods should be implemented in the class that meets the abstraction level. The best solution could be to implement these in a separate class. You have homework!

The `reset()` method is not used from the handler. This is invoked from the `Mastermind` class, that is, the servlet class to reset the game when we start it:

```
public void doGet(HttpServletRequest request,
                  HttpServletResponse response)
        throws ServletException, IOException {
    var sessionSaver = new GameSessionSaver();
    sessionSaver.reset(request.getSession());
    doPost(request, response);
}
```

Without this, playing the game against the machine once would just display the finished game every time we want to start it again until we exit the browser and restart it or explicitly delete the `JSESSIONID` cookie somewhere in the advanced menu of the browser. Calling `reset` does not delete the session. The session remains the same, and thus the value of the `JSESSIONID` cookie too, but the game is deleted from the session object that the servlet container maintains.

Running the Jetty web servlet

Since we have included the Jetty plugin in our Gradle build, the targets of the plugin are available. To start Jetty is as easy as typing the following:

```
gradle appRun
```

This will compile the code, build the WAR file, and start the Jetty servlet container. To help us remember, it also prints the following on the command line:

```
Running at http://localhost:8080//hello
```

We can open this URL and see the opening screen of the game with the colors that the program created as a first guess:

Now, it is time to have some fun and play with our game, giving answers to the program. Do not make it easy for the code! Refer to the following screenshot:

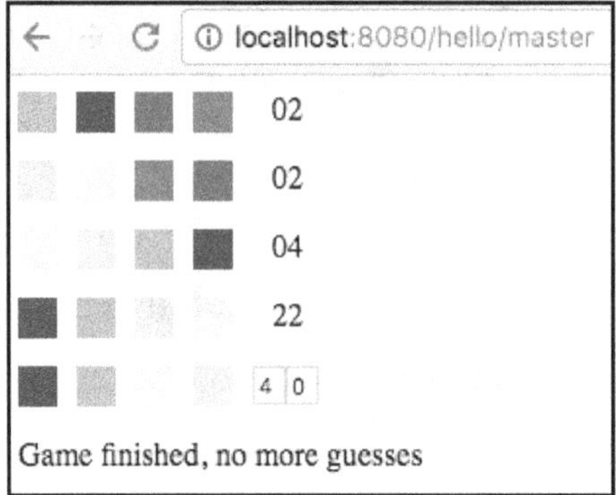

At the same time, if you look at the console where you have typed `gradle appRun`, you will see that the code is printing out log messages, as shown in the following screenshot:

```
$ gradle appRun
Starting a Gradle Daemon, 1 busy and 1 incompatible Daemons could not be reused, use --status for details
WARNING: An illegal reflective access operation has occurred
WARNING: Illegal reflective access by org.codehaus.groovy.reflection.CachedClass (file:/C:/Users/peter_verhas/.gradle/caches/modules-2/files-2.1/org.codehaus
.groovy/groovy/2.4.15/74b7e0b99526c569e3a59cb84dbcc6204d601ee6/groovy-2.4.15.jar) to method java.lang.Object.finalize()
WARNING: Please consider reporting this to the maintainers of org.codehaus.groovy.reflection.CachedClass
WARNING: Use --illegal-access=warn to enable warnings of further illegal reflective access operations
WARNING: All illegal access operations will be denied in a future release
14:04:41 INFO  Jetty 9.2.24.v20180105 started and listening on port 8080
14:04:41 INFO  ch06 runs at:
14:04:41 INFO    http://localhost:8080/ch06

> Task :appRun
Press any key to stop the server.

14:04:42.015 [qtp131037934-15] DEBUG packt.java11.mastermind.Table - table is created with 4 columns and packt.java11.mastermind.ColorManager@7b2fccd7 colorM
anager
14:04:42.023 [qtp131037934-15] DEBUG p.j.m.servlet.MastermindHandler - converting request to map
14:04:42.031 [qtp131037934-15] DEBUG p.j.m.servlet.MastermindHandler - last row is -1
14:04:42.031 [qtp131037934-15] DEBUG p.j.m.servlet.MastermindHandler - last row is -1
14:04:42.034 [qtp131037934-15] DEBUG p.j.m.servlet.MastermindHandler - Adding new guess 0123 to the game
14:04:42.034 [qtp131037934-15] DEBUG packt.java11.mastermind.Table - Size of thetable 1
14:04:42.034 [qtp131037934-15] DEBUG packt.java11.mastermind.Table - Fetching color #0 from row 0
14:04:42.035 [qtp131037934-15] DEBUG packt.java11.mastermind.Table - Size of thetable 1
14:04:42.036 [qtp131037934-15] DEBUG packt.java11.mastermind.Table - Fetching color #1 from row 0
14:04:42.037 [qtp131037934-15] DEBUG packt.java11.mastermind.Table - Size of thetable 1
14:04:42.037 [qtp131037934-15] DEBUG packt.java11.mastermind.Table - Fetching color #2 from row 0
14:04:42.039 [qtp131037934-15] DEBUG packt.java11.mastermind.Table - Size of thetable 1
14:04:42.039 [qtp131037934-15] DEBUG packt.java11.mastermind.Table - Fetching color #3 from row 0
14:04:42.045 [qtp131037934-15] DEBUG packt.java11.mastermind.Table - Size of thetable 1
14:04:42.046 [qtp131037934-15] DEBUG packt.java11.mastermind.Table - Fetching color #0 from row 0
14:04:42.075 [qtp131037934-15] DEBUG packt.java11.mastermind.Table - Size of thetable 1
14:04:42.075 [qtp131037934-15] DEBUG packt.java11.mastermind.Table - Fetching color #1 from row 0
14:04:42.075 [qtp131037934-15] DEBUG packt.java11.mastermind.Table - Size of thetable 1
14:04:42.075 [qtp131037934-15] DEBUG packt.java11.mastermind.Table - Fetching color #2 from row 0
14:04:42.076 [qtp131037934-15] DEBUG packt.java11.mastermind.Table - Size of thetable 1
14:04:42.076 [qtp131037934-15] DEBUG packt.java11.mastermind.Table - Fetching color #3 from row 0
<===========--> 87% EXECUTING [38s]
> :appRun
> IDLE
```

These printouts come through the logger that we have in our code. In the previous chapters, we used the `System.out.println()` method calls to send informational messages to the console. This is a practice that should not be followed in any program that is more complex than a *hello world*.

Logging

There are several logging frameworks available for Java, and each has advantages and disadvantages. There is one built into the JDK in the `java.util.logging` package and accessing the logger is supported by the `System.getLogger()` method in the `System.Logger` and `System.LoggerFinder` classes. Even though `java.util.logging` has been available in Java since JDK 1.4, a lot of programs use other logging solutions. In addition to the built-in logging, we have to mention `log4j`, `slf4j`, and Apache Commons Logging. Before getting into the details of the different frameworks, let's discuss why it is important to use logging instead of just printing to the standard output.

Configurability

The most important reason is configurability and ease of use. We use logging to record information about the operation of the code. This is not the core functionality of the application, but it is inevitable to have a program that can be operated. There are messages we print out to the log, which can be used by the operating personnel to identify environmental issues. For example, when an `IOException` is thrown and it gets logged, the operation may look at the logs and identify that a disk got full. They may delete files, or add a new disk and extend the partition. Without the logs, the only information would be that the program does not work.

The logs are also used many times to hunt down bugs. Some of the bugs do not manifest in the test environment and are very difficult to reproduce. In such a case, the logs that print out detailed information about the execution of the code are the only source of finding the root cause of some error.

Since logging needs CPU, IO bandwidth, and other resources, it should be carefully examined regarding what and when to log. This examination and the decisions could be done during programming and, as a matter of fact, that is the only possibility if we used `System.out.println` for logging. If we need to find a bug, we should log a lot. If we log a lot, the performance of the system will go down. The conclusion is that we should only log as and when required. If there is a bug in the system that cannot be reproduced, the developers ask the operation to switch on debug logging for a short period of time. Switching on and off different parts of logging is not possible when `System.out.println` is used. When the debug level log is switched on, performance may go down for a while but, at the same time, the logs become available for analysis.

At the same time, the analysis is simpler when we have to find the log lines that are relevant (and you do not know beforehand which are relevant) if there is a small (several hundred megabytes) log file rather than a lot of 2 GB compressed log files to find the lines in.

Using a logging framework, you can define loggers that identify the source of the log messages and log levels. A string usually identifies the logger, and it is common practice to use the name of the class from which the log message is created. This is such a common practice that the different log frameworks provide factory classes that get the class itself, instead of its name, to get a logger.

The possible logging levels may be slightly different in different logging frameworks, but the most important levels are as follows:

- `FATAL`: This is used when the log message concerns an error that prevents the program from continuing its execution.
- `ERROR`: This is used when there is a severe error, but the program can still go on functioning even though, most likely, in a limited manner.
- `WARNING`: This is used when there is a condition that is not a direct problem but may later lead to an error if not attended; for example, the program recognizes that a disk is near full, some database connections answer within limits but close to the timeout value, and similar situations.
- `INFO`: This is used to create messages about normal operations that may be interesting to operate and are not an error or warning. These messages may help the operation to debug the operational environment settings.
- `DEBUG`: This is used to log information about the program that is (hopefully) sufficiently detailed to find a bug in the code. The trick is that when we put the log statement into the code, we do not know what bug it could be. If we knew, it would be better to fix it.
- `TRACE`: This is even more detailed information about the execution of the code.

The log frameworks are usually configured using a configuration file. The configuration may limit the logging, switching off certain levels. In a normal operational environment, the first three levels are usually switched on, and `INFO`, `DEBUG`, and `TRACE` are switched on when really needed. It is also possible to switch on and off certain levels only for certain loggers. If we know that the error is certainly in the `GameSessionSaver` class, then we can switch on the `DEBUG` level for that class.

Log files may also contain other information that we did not code directly and that would be very cumbersome to print to the standard output. Usually, each log message contains the precise time when the message was created, the name of the logger, and, in many instances, the identifier of the thread. Imagine if you were forced to put all this into each and every `println` argument; you would probably soon write some extra class to do that. Don't! It has already been done professionally—it is the logger framework.

Loggers can also be configured to send the message to different locations. Logging to the console is only one possibility. Logging frameworks are prepared to send messages to files, databases, Windows Event Recorder, the syslog service, or to any other target. This flexibility, which message to print, what extra information to print, and where to print, is reached by separating the different tasks that the logger framework does into several classes as per the single responsibility principle.

The logger frameworks usually contain loggers that create the logs, formatters that format the message from the original log information, very often adding information such as the thread ID and time stamp, and appenders that append the formatted message to a destination. These classes implement interfaces defined in the logging framework and nothing but the size of the book stops us from creating our own formatters and appenders.

When a log is configured, the appenders and formatters are configured, given the class that implements them. Therefore, when you want to send some logs to a special destination, you are not limited to the appenders that are provided by the authors of the framework. There are a lot of independent open source projects for different logging frameworks providing appenders for different targets.

Performance

The second reason for using a logging framework is performance. Although it is not good to optimize for performance before we profile the code (premature optimization), using a methodology that is known to be slow and inserting several lines into our performance-critical code, invoking slow methods is not really professional either. Using a well-established, highly optimized framework in a way that is an industry best practice should not be questionable.

Using `System.out.println()` sends the message to a stream and returns only when the IO operation is done. Using real logging handles the information to the logger and lets the logger do the logging asynchronously, and it does not wait for completion.

It is really a drawback that log information may be lost if there is a system failure, but this is usually not a serious issue considering how rarely that happens and what is on the other side of the wage—performance. What do we lose if there is a missing debug log line when the disk got full, rendering the system unusable in any case?

There is one exception to this—audit logging—when some log information about the system's transactions has to be saved for legal reasons so that the operation and the actual transactions can be audited. In such a case, the log information is saved in a transactional manner, making the log part of the transaction. Because that is a totally different type of requirement, audit logging is not usually done with any of these frameworks.

Also, `System.out.println()` is not synchronized and, hence, different threads may just garble the output. Log frameworks pay attention to this issue.

Log frameworks

The most widely used logging framework is **Apachelog4j**. It currently has a second version that is a total rewrite of the first version. It is very versatile and has many appenders and formatters. The configuration of log4j can be in XML or the properties file format, and it can also be configured through API.

The author of log4j version 1 created a new logging framework—**slf4j**. This logging library is essentially a façade that can be used together with any other logging framework. Thus, when you use slf4j in a library you develop, and your code is added to a program as a dependency that uses a different logging framework, it is easy to configure slf4j to send the logs to the loggers of the other framework. Thus, the logs will be handled together and not in a separate file, which is desirable for reducing the cost of operation. When developing your library code or an application that uses slf4j, there is no need to select another logging framework to slf4j. It has its own simple implementation called backlog.

Apache Commons Logging is also a façade with its own logging implementation, if nothing else fails. The major difference from slf4j is that it is more flexible in configuration and what underlying logging to use, and it implements a runtime algorithm to discover which logging framework is available and is to be used. The industry best practice shows that this flexibility, which also comes with higher complexity and cost, is not needed.

Java logging

Java since version 9 includes a façade implementation for logging. Its application is very simple and we can expect that logging frameworks will very soon start to support this façade. The fact that this façade is built into the JDK has two major advantages:

- The libraries that want to log no longer need to have any dependency on any logging framework or logging façade. The only dependency is the JDK log façade that is there anyway.
- The JDK libraries that log themselves use this façade and thus, they will log into the same log file as the application.

If we use the logging façade provided with JDK, the start of the `ColorManager` class will be changed to the following:

```
package packt.java11.mastermind;

import javax.inject.Inject;
import javax.inject.Named;
import javax.inject.Singleton;
import java.util.HashMap;
import java.util.Map;
import java.lang.System.Logger;

import static java.lang.System.Logger.Level.DEBUG;

@Singleton
public class ColorManager {
    protected final int nrColors;
    protected final Map<Color, Color> successor = new HashMap<>();
    private Color first;
    private final ColorFactory factory;
    private static final Logger log
            = System.getLogger(ColorManager.class.getName());

    @Inject
    public ColorManager(@Named("nrColors") int nrColors,
                        ColorFactory factory) {
        log.log(DEBUG, "creating colorManager for {0} colors", nrColors);
        this.nrColors = nrColors;
        this.factory = factory;
        createOrdering();
    }

    private Color[] createColors() {
        var colors = new Color[nrColors];
```

```
        for (int i = 0; i < colors.length; i++) {
            colors[i] = factory.newColor();
        }
        return colors;
    }

    private void createOrdering() {
        var colors = createColors();
        first = colors[0];
        for (int i = 0; i < nrColors - 1; i++) {
            successor.put(colors[i], colors[i + 1]);
        }
    }

    public Color firstColor() {
        return first;
    }

    public boolean thereIsNextColor(Color color) {
        return successor.containsKey(color);
    }

    public Color nextColor(Color color) {
        return successor.get(color);
    }
}
```

In this version, we do not import the slf4j classes. Instead, we import the `java.lang.System.Logger` class.

Note that we do not need to import the system class, because of the classes from the `java.lang` package are automatically imported. This is not true for the classes that are nested classes in the `System` class.

To get access to the logger, the static method `System.getLogger()` is called. This method finds the actual logger that is available and returns one for the name that we pass as an argument. There is no version of the `getLogger()` method that accepts the class as the argument. If we want to stick to convention, then we have to write `ColorManager.class.getName()` to get the name of the class or we can write the name of the class as a string there. The second approach has the drawback that it does not follow the change of name of the class. Intelligent IDEs, such as IntelliJ, Eclipse, or Netbeans, rename the references to classes automatically, but they have a hard time when the name of the class is used in a string.

The `System.Logger` interface does not declare the convenience methods `error`, `debug`, `warning`, and so on, that are familiar from other logging frameworks and façades. There is only one method named `log()`, and the first argument of this method is the level of the actual log we issue. There are eight levels defined—`ALL`, `TRACE`, `DEBUG`, `INFO`, `WARNING`, `ERROR`, and `OFF`. When creating a log message, we are supposed to use one of the middle six levels. `ALL` and `OFF` are meant to be passed to the `isLoggable()` method only. This method can be used to check whether the actual logging level gets logged or not. For example, if the level is set to `INFO`, then messages sent with `DEBUG` or `TRACE` will not be printed.

The actual implementation is located by the JDK using the service loader functionality. The log implementation has to be in a module that provides the `java.lang.System.LoggerFinder` interface via some implementation. In other words, the module should have a class that implements the `LoggerFinder` interface and the `module-info.java` should declare which class is using the code:

```
provides java.lang.System.LoggerFinder with
                          packt.java11.MyLoggerFinder;
```

The `MyLoggerFinder` class has to extend the `LoggerFinder` abstract class with the `getLogger()` method.

Logging practice

The practice of logging is very simple. If you do not want to spend too much time experimenting with different logging solutions and you do not have a particular requirement, then simply go with slf4j, add the JAR to the dependency list as a compile dependency, and start using logging in the source code.

Since logging is not instance-specific, and loggers implement thread safety, the log objects that we usually use are stored in a `static` field, and since they are used as long as the class is used, the field is also `final`. For example, using the slf4j façade, we can get a logger with the following command:

```
private static final Logger log =
          LoggerFactory.getLogger(MastermindHandler.class);
```

To get the logger, the logger factory is used, which just creates the logger or returns the one that is already available.

The name of the variable is usually `log` or `logger`, but do not be surprised if you see `LOG` or `LOGGER`. The reason for uppercasing the name of the variable is that certain static code analysis checkers treat `static final` variables as constants, as they really are, and the convention in the Java community is to use uppercase names for such variables. It is a matter of taste; very often, `log` and `logger` are used in lowercase.

To create a log item, the `trace()`, `debug()`, `info()`, `warn()`, and `error()` methods create a message with the respective level as the name implies. For example, consider the following line of code:

```
log.debug("Adding new guess {} to the game", newGuess);
```

It creates a debug message. Slf4j has support for formatting using the `{}` literal inside strings. This way, there is no need to append the string from small parts, and in case the actual log item is not sent to the log destination, the formatting will not perform. If we use the `String` concatenation in any form to pass a string as an argument, then the formatting will happen, even if debug logging is not desired as per the example.

The logging methods also have a version that gets only two arguments—a `String` message and `Throwable`. In this case, the logging framework will take care of the output of the exception and the stack trace along with it. If you log something in exception handling code, log the exception and let the logger format it.

Other technologies

We discussed the servlet technology, a bit of JavaScript, HTML, and CSS. When programming in a real professional environment, these technologies are generally used. The creation of the user interface of applications, however, was not always based on these technologies. Older operating system-native GUI applications, as well as Swing, AWT, and SWT, use a different approach to create UI. They build up the UI facing the user from the program code, and the UI is built as a hierarchical structure of components. When web programming started, Java developers had experience with technologies such as these and projects created frameworks that tried to hide the web technology layer.

One technology worth mentioning is Google Web Toolkit, which implements the server as well as the browser code in Java, but since there is no Java environment implemented in the browsers, it transpiles (converts) the client part of the code from Java to JavaScript. The most recent release of the toolkit was created two years ago in 2014 and, since then, Google has released other types of web programming toolkits that support native JavaScript, HTML, and CSS client development.

Vaadin is also a toolkit that you may come across. It lets you write GUI code on the server in Java. It is built on top of GWT and is commercially supported. It may be a good choice in case there are developers available who have experience with GUI development in Java but not in web-native technologies, and the application does not require special usability tuning on the client side. A typical intranet corporate application can select it as a technology.

JavaServer Faces (**JSF**) is a technology that tries to offload the client-side development of the application from the developers providing widgets ready to be used and the server side. It is a collection of several **Java Specification Requests** (**JSR**), and there are several implementations. The components and their relations are configured in XML files and the server creates the client native code. In this technology, there is no transpilation from Java to JavaScript. It is more like using a limited but huge set of widgets, limiting use to those only, and giving up direct programming of the web browser. If they have the experience and knowledge, however, they can create new widgets in HTML, CSS, and JavaScript.

There are many other technologies that were developed to support web applications in Java. The modern approach advocated by most of the big players is to develop the server side and the client side using separate toolsets and methodologies and connect the two using REST communication.

Summary

In this chapter, you learned about the structure of web programming. This was not possible without understanding the basics of TCP/IP networking, which is the protocol of the internet. The application level protocol over that is HTTP, currently in a very new version, 2.0, which is already supported by the servlet standard version 4.0. We created a version of the Mastermind game that, this time, can really be played using the browser, and we started it in a development environment using Jetty. We examined how to store the game state and implemented two versions. Finally, we learned the basics of logging and we looked at other technologies. At the same time, we also looked at the dependency injection implementation Guice from Google, and we studied how it works under the hood, and why and how to use it.

After this chapter, you will be able to start the development of a web application in Java and will understand the architecture of such a program. You will understand what is under the hood when you start learning how to program web applications using the Spring framework, which hides many of the complexities of web programming.

7
Building a Commercial Web Application Using REST

We were playing around until now, but Java is not a toy. We want to use Java for something real and serious, commercial and professional. In this chapter, we will do just that. The example that we will be looking at is not something that is only interesting to play with, such as Mastermind, which we looked at in the previous three chapters, but rather a real commercial application. This isn't a real-life application, actually. You should not expect anything like that in a book. It would be too long and not educational enough. However, the application that we will develop in this chapter could be extended and can be used as a core for a real-life application in case you decide to do so.

In the previous chapter, we created servlets. To do this, we used the servlet specification, and we hand-implemented servlets. This is something you will rarely do these days. In this chapter, we will use a readily available framework instead. This time, we will use Spring, which is the most widely used framework for Java commercial applications, and I dare say it is the de facto standard. It will do all the tedious work that we had to do (at least to understand and learn how a servlet works) in the previous chapter. We will also use Spring for dependency injection (why use two frameworks when one does it all?), and Tomcat.

In the previous chapter, we used Guice as a DI framework and Jetty as a servlet container. These can be perfectly good choices for some projects. For other projects, other frameworks do better. To have the opportunity to look at different tools in this book, we will use different frameworks, even though all of the examples we will show you could be created by simply using Tomcat and Spring exclusively.

The commercial application we will develop will be an ordering system targeting resellers. The interface we will provide to the users will not be a web browser consumable HTML/JavaScript/CSS interface. Instead, it will be a REST interface. The users will, themselves, develop applications that communicate with our system and place orders for different products. The structure of the application will be a microservice architecture, and we will use the SoapUI to test the application, in addition to the standard Chrome developer tool features.

The MyBusiness web shop

Imagine that we have a huge trading and logistics company. There are tens of thousands of different products on the shelves; hundreds of lorries come to our warehouse bringing new goods, and hundreds of lorries deliver goods to our customers. To manage this information, we have an inventory system that keeps track of the goods every minute, of every hour, of every day, so that we know what we actually have in the warehouse. We serve our customers without humans managing the warehouse information. Formerly, there were phones, fax machines, and even telex. Today, all we use is the internet and web services. We do not provide a website for our customers. We have never directly served the end users in our imagined business, but these days, we have a subsidiary that we started off as a separate company to do just that. They have a website, and it is totally independent from us. They are just one of our hundreds of registered partners who each use a web service interface to see the products we have, order products, and track an order's status.

Sample business architecture

Our partners are also large companies with automated administration, with several programs running on several machines. We have no interest in their architecture and the technology they use, but we want to integrate to their operations. We want to serve them in a way that does not require any human interaction for the administration to order goods on either of our sides. To do so, a web service interface is provided that can be utilized, no matter what IT infrastructure they use.

On our side, as we imagine the example, we recently replaced our monolithic application with the microservice architecture, and though there are still some SOAP-based solutions in the system, most of the backend modules communicate using HTTPS and REST protocols. Some of the modules still rely on asynchronous file transfers that are done on a daily basis using FTP, which are started from a Unix `cron` job. The General Ledger system was programmed in COBOL. Fortunately, we do not need to deal with these dinosaurs.

This structure is an imaginary setup, but a realistic one. I made up and described these parts to give you a picture of how you may see mixed technologies in a large enterprise. What I described here is a very simple setup. There are companies that have more than a thousand software modules in their systems using different technologies and totally different interfaces, all interconnected with each other. This is not because they like the mess, but that is the way it becomes after 30 years of continuous IT development. New technologies come and old technologies fade out. The business changes and you cannot stick to the old technologies if you want to stay competitive. At the same time, you just cannot replace the entire infrastructure instantaneously. The result is that we see fairly old technologies still running and, mostly, new technologies. Old technologies get rolled out in time. They do not stay forever, and still, we are sometimes surprised when a dinosaur comes out in front of us.

We have to deal with the two frontend components that we will develop. These are as follows:

- **Product Information**
- **Order Placement and Tracking**

In the following picture, you can see the architectural UML diagram of the structure that we will look at. We will only interact with the frontend components, but it helps to understand how they function and their role if we have the bigger picture:

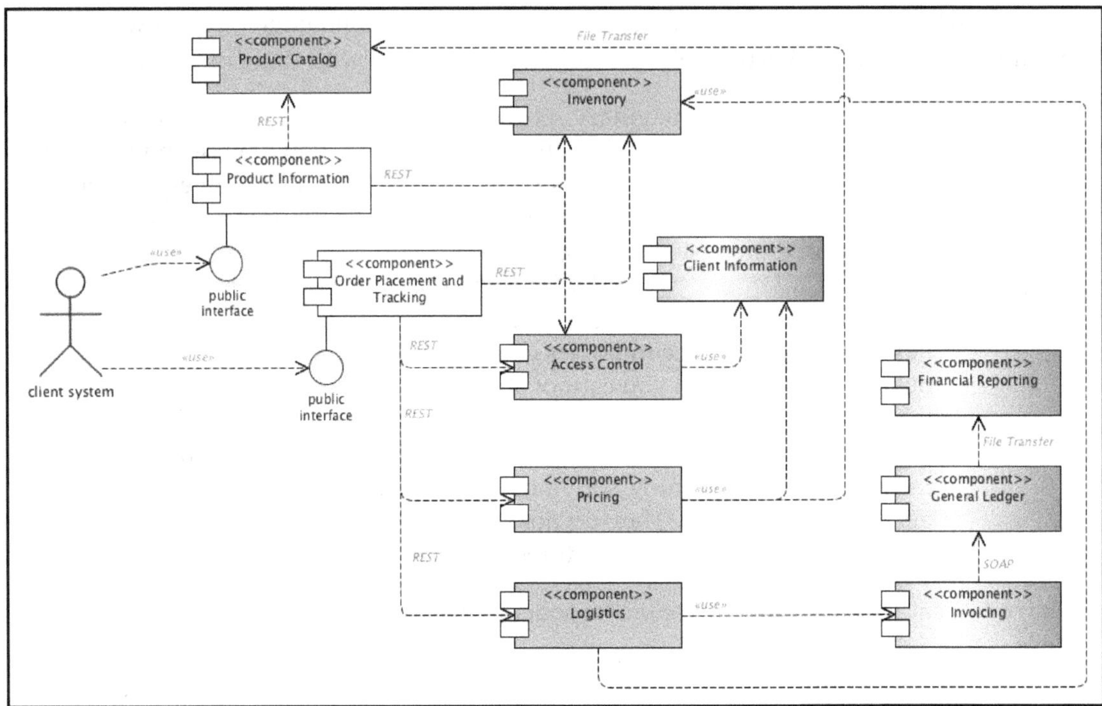

Product Information delivers information about a single product, but it can also deliver a list of products based on query criteria. **Order Placement and Tracking** provides functions so that a customer can place an order, and also lets our clients query the state of past orders.

To provide product information, we need access to the **Product Catalog** module that holds the actual product details.

There can be a lot of other tasks that the **Product Catalog** does, and that is the reason it is a separate module. It can have, for example, a workflow and approval engine that lets product administrators enter product data and managers to check and approve the data. Approval is usually a complex process, considering typos and legal issues (we do not want to trade unlicensed drugs, explosives, and so on), and checking the quality and approval state of the source of the goods. The many complex tasks make it a backend module. In large enterprise applications, the frontend systems rarely do anything else other than the very basic functionality of serving the outside parties. But this is good for us; we can focus on the service that we have to deliver. This is also good for the architecture. It is the same principle as in object-oriented programming—single responsibility.

The **Product Information** module also has to consult with the **Access Control** module to see if a certain product can be delivered to the actual customer, and with the inventory to see if there are any products left, so that we do not offer a product that is out of stock.

The **Order Placement and Tracking** module also needs access to the **Product Inventory** and **Access Control** modules to check whether the order can be fulfilled. At the same time, it also needs services from the **Pricing** module, which can calculate the price for the order, and from the **Logistics** module, which triggers the collection of goods from the inventory locations and shipment to the customer. **Logistics** also has a connection to invoicing, which has a connection to the **General Ledger**, but these are only on the picture to show that the travel of information does not end there. There are many other modules that run the company, all of which are not of interest to us at the moment.

Microservices

The architecture described in the previous chapter is not a clean microservice architecture. You will never meet one in its pure form in any enterprise. It is more like something that we meet in a real company moving from monolithic to microservices.

We will talk about the microservice architecture when the application is developed in the form of many small services that communicate with each other using some simple API, usually over HTTP and REST. The services implement business functions and can be deployed independently. In most cases, it is desirable that the service deployment is automated.

The individual services can be developed using different programming languages, can use different data storage, and can run on different operating systems; thus, they are highly independent of each other. They can be, and usually are, developed by different teams. The important requirement is that they cooperate; thus, the API one service implements is usable by the other services that build upon it.

The microservice architecture is not the Holy Grail of all architectures. It gives different answers to some problems of monolithic architectures, and in most cases, these answers work better when using modern tools. The applications still have to be tested and debugged. The performance has to be managed, and bugs and issues have to be addressed. The difference is that the individual components are not strongly coupled and, that way, the development, deployment, and testing can be separated along different technologies. As microservice architectures in practice separate the modules along networked protocols, debugging may need more network-related work. This may be good, bad, or both at the same time. For the developers, however, the advantage is clear. They can work on a smaller unit independently and can see the result of their work faster.

When developing a single module of a monolithic application, the result can only be seen when the entire application gets deployed. In the case of a large application, that may be rare. A typical deployment cycle in a large corporation developing monolithics is every few months, say three, but it is not rare to see the release only twice or even once a year. Developing microservices, the new module can be deployed as soon as it is ready and tested, so long as it does not break the network interfaces it provides us with and uses from other modules.

If you want to read more on microservices, the first and most authentic source is the article by Martin Fowler (`http://www.martinfowler.com/articles/microservices.html`). Note that this page refers to the Microservices Resource Guide, which lists a lot of microservice information resources.

Service interface design

In this section, we will design the two interfaces that we will implement. When we design interfaces, we focus on the functionality first. Formatting and protocol come later. Interfaces, generally, should be simple and, at the same time, accommodate future changes. This is a hard problem because we cannot see into the future. Business, logistics, and all other experts may see some part of the future—how the world will change and what it will impose on the operation of the company and, especially, on the interface we provide for our partners.

The stability of an interface is of utmost importance because the partners are outside entities. We cannot refactor the code they use. When we change a Java interface in our code, the compiler will complain at all the code locations where the change should be followed. In case of an interface that is used outside of our realm, this is not the case. Even if it is only a Java interface that we publish as open source on *GitHub*, we should be prepared that our users will face issues if we change the library in an incompatible way. In that case, their software will not compile and work with our library. In the case of an ordering system, it means that they will not order from us and we will soon be out of business.

This is one of the reasons why interfaces should be simple. Although this is generally true for most things in life, it is extremely important for interfaces. It is tempting to provide convenience features for the partners because they are easy to implement. In the long run, however, these features may become very expensive as they need maintenance; they should be kept backward compatible. In the long run, they may not gain as much as they cost.

To access product information, we need two functions. One of them lists certain products and another returns the details of a specific product. If it were a Java API, it would look as follows:

```
List<ProductId> query(String query);
ProductInformation byId(ProductId id);
```

Similarly, order placement may look like what's shown in the following code:

```
OrderId placeOrder(Order order);
```

We provide these functions in our application via a web service interface; more specifically, REST using JSON. We will discuss these technologies in a bit more detail, along with the Spring framework and Model View Controller design pattern, but first, let's look at the product information controller to get a feel of what our program will look like:

```
package packt.java11.mybusiness.productinformation;
import ...
@RestController
public class ProductInformationController {
    private final ProductLookup lookup;

    public ProductInformationController(
            @Autowired ProductLookup lookup) {
        this.lookup = lookup;
    }

    @RequestMapping("/pi/{productId}")
    public ProductInformation getProductInformation(
            @PathVariable String productId) {
        return lookup.byId(productId);
```

```
    }

    @RequestMapping("/query/{query}")
    public List<String> lookupProductByTitle(
            @PathVariable String query,
            HttpServletRequest request) {
        return lookup.byQuery(query)
                .stream().map(s -> "/pi/" + s)
                .collect(Collectors.toList());
    }
}
```

If you compare the code of the servlet with the preceding code, you can see that this is much simpler. We do not need to deal with the `HttpServletRequest` object, call an API to get a parameter, or create an HTML output and write it to the response. The framework does this. We annotate the `@RestController` class, telling Spring that this is a controller that utilizes the REST web services; thus, it will create a **JSON** response from the object we return by default. We do not need to care about the conversion of the object to *JSON*, although we can if there really is a need to. The object will be automatically converted to *JSON* using the field names used in the class and the field values of the instance we return. If the object contains more complex structures than just plain `String`, `int`, and `double` values, then the converter is prepared for nested structures and the most common data types.

To have different code handling and different URLs on the servlet, all we need to do is annotate the method with `@RequestMapping`, providing the path part of the URL. The `{productId}` notation inside the mapping string is readable and easy to maintain. Spring just cuts the value from there and puts it in the `productId` variable for us, as requested by the `@PathVariable` annotation.

The actual lookup of the product is not implemented in the controller. This is not the function of the controller. The controller only decides what business logic to invoke and what view to use. The business logic is implemented in a service class. An instance of this service class is injected into the `lookup` field. This injection is also done by Spring. The actual work we have to do is invoke the business logic, which this time, since we have only one, is fairly easy.

Most of these things seem magic without some more details about what the framework does for us. Therefore, before continuing, we will have a look at the building blocks—JSON, REST, MVC, and a bit of the Spring framework.

JSON

JSON stands for **JavaScript Object Notation**. It is defined on the official JSON site (`http://www.json.org/`). This is a textual notation in the same way as the object literals are defined in JavaScript. An object representation starts with the `{` character and ends with the `}` character. The text in-between defines the fields of the objects in the form, `string : value`. The string is the name of the field, and since JSON wants to be language agnostic, it allows any characters to be a part of the name of a field, and thus this string (as well as any string in JSON) should start and end with the `"` characters.

This may seem strange and, in most cases, when you start working with JSON, it is easy to forget and write `{ myObject : "has a string"}` instead of the correct `{ "myObject" : "has a string" }` notation.

Commas separate the fields. You can also have arrays in JSON. They start and end with the `[` and `]` characters, respectively, and they contain comma-separated values. The value in an object field or in an array can be a string, a number, an object, an array, or one of the constants, `true`, `false`, and `null`.

Generally speaking, JSON is a very simple notation which is used to describe data that can be stored in an object. It is easy to write using text editors and easy to read, and thus it is easier to debug any communication that uses JSON than something that uses complex formats. Ways to convert JSON into a Java object and the other way round, are readily available in libraries that we will use in this chapter. A sample JSON object that describes a product from our sample code is also available in the source code of the program, as follows:

```
{"id":"125","title":"Bar Stool",
 "description":"another furniture",
 "size":[20.0,2.0,18.0],"weight":300.0}
```

Note that the formatting of JSON does not require a new line, but at the same time, this is also possible. Program-generated JSON objects are usually compact and not formatted. When we edit an object using a text editor, we tend to format the indentation of the fields in the same way as we usually do in Java programming.

REST

There is no exact definition of the **REST** protocol. It stands for **Representational state transfer**, which probably does not mean anything to someone who has never heard of it. When we program the REST API, we use the HTTP(S) protocol. We send simple requests to the server, and we get simple answers that we program. This way, the client of the web server is also a program (by the way, the browser is also a program) that consumes the response from the server. The format of the response, therefore, is not HTML formatted using CSS and enriched by client-side functions by **JavaScript**, but rather some data descriptive format such as JSON. REST does not set restrictions on the actual format, but these days, JSON is the most widely used format.

The wiki page that describes REST is available at `https://en.wikipedia.org/wiki/Representational_state_transfer`.

REST interfaces are usually made simple. The HTTP requests almost always use the `GET` method. It also makes the testing of REST services simple since nothing is easier than issuing a `GET` request from a browser. Toddlers can do it. `POST` requests are only used when the service performs some transaction or change on the server, and that way, the request is sending data to the server rather than getting some data.

In our application, we will use the `GET` method to query a list of products and get information about a product, and we will only use `POST` to order products. The application that serves these requests will run in a servlet container. You have learned how to create a naked servlet without the use of a framework. In this chapter, we will use the Spring framework, which offloads many of the tasks from the developer. There are many program constructs in servlet programming that are just the same most of the time. They are called boilerplate code. The Spring framework utilizes the Model View Controller design pattern to develop web applications; thus, we will look at it in brief, before discussing Spring in general.

Model View Controller

The **Model View Controller** (**MVC**) is a design pattern. Design patterns are programming constructs—simple structures that give hints on how to solve specific problems. The term design pattern was coined and formally described in the book *Design Patterns, Elements of Reusable Object-Oriented Software*, which was written by Erich Gamma, Richard Helm, Ralph Johnson, and John Vlissides. The book defines a design pattern as a structure with a *name*, a *problem*, and a *solution*. The *name* describes the pattern and gives the vocabulary for the developer community to use when talking about these patterns. It is important that different developers use the same language terminology in order to understand each other. The *problem* describes the situation, that is, the design problem where the pattern can be applied. The *solution* describes classes and objects and the relations between them, which contribute to a good design.

One of them is MVC, which is suitable for programming web applications, but can be used in general for any application that has a user interface. In our case, we do not have a classical user interface because the client is also a program; still, MVC can be and is a good choice to use:

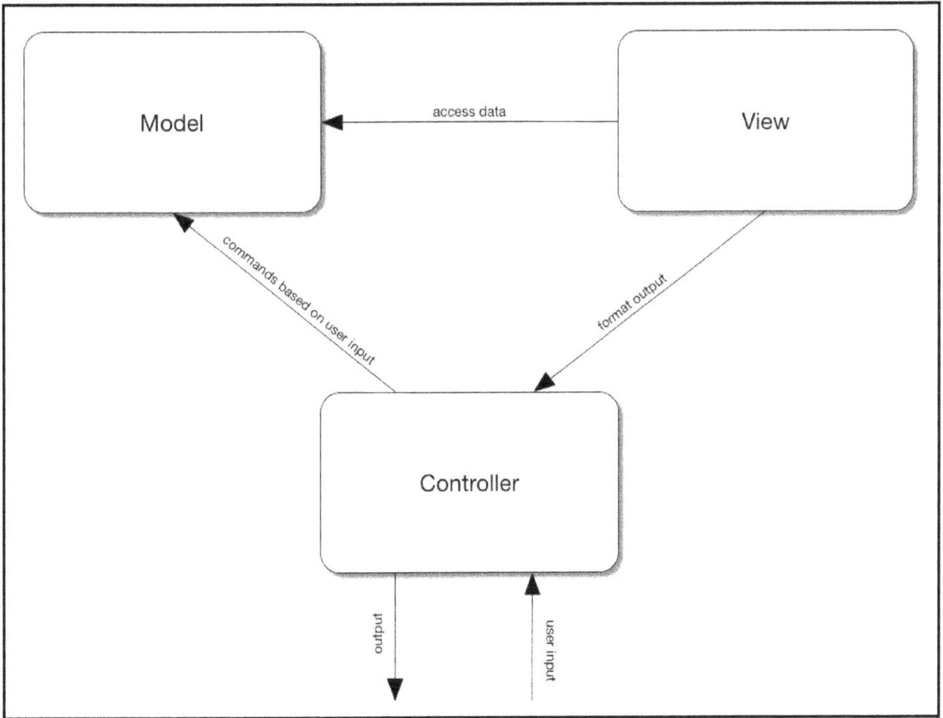

The MVC pattern, as the name also indicates, has three parts—a model, a view, and a controller. This separation follows the single responsibility principle, requiring one part for each distinct responsibility. The controller is responsible for handling the inputs of the system, and it decides what model and view to use. It controls the execution but usually does not do any business logic. The model does the business logic and contains the data. View converts the model data into a representation that is consumable by the client.

MVC is a well-known and widely used design pattern, and it is directly supported by Spring. When you create a web application, you program the controller built into the framework by using annotations. You essentially configure it. You can program the view, but it is more likely that you will use one that is built into the framework. You will want to send data to the client in **XML**, **JSON**, or **HTML**. If you are very exotic, you may want to send **YAML**, but generally, that is it. You do not want to implement a new format that needs to be programmed on the server and, since being new, also on the client.

We create the model, and this time, we also program it. After all, that is the business logic. Frameworks can do many things for us, mainly the things that are the same for most of the applications, but not the business logic. Business logic is the code that distinguishes our code from other programs. That is what we have to program.

On the other hand, that is what we like to do—focus on the business code and avoid all boilerplate provided by the framework.

Now that we know what **JSON**, **REST**, and the general Model View Controller design pattern are, let's look at how these are managed by Spring and how we can put these technologies into action.

Spring framework

The Spring framework is a huge framework with several modules. The first version of the framework was released in 2003, and since then, there have been four major releases delivering new and enhanced features. Currently, Spring is the de facto enterprise framework that's used, perhaps more widely than the de jure standard **EJB 3.0**.

Spring supports dependency injection, **Aspect-Oriented Programming** (**AOP**), and persistence for **SQL** and **NoSQL** databases in a conventional manner and also the Object Relational Mapping way. It has transactional support, messaging, web programming, and many other features. You can configure it using **XML** configuration files, annotations, or by using Java classes.

Architecture of Spring

Spring is not monolithic. You can use a part of it, or only some of the features. You can include some of the modules of Spring that you need and leave out others. Some modules depend on some others, and Gradle, Maven, or some other build tool handles the dependencies.

The following diagram shows you the modules of the Spring framework for version 4:

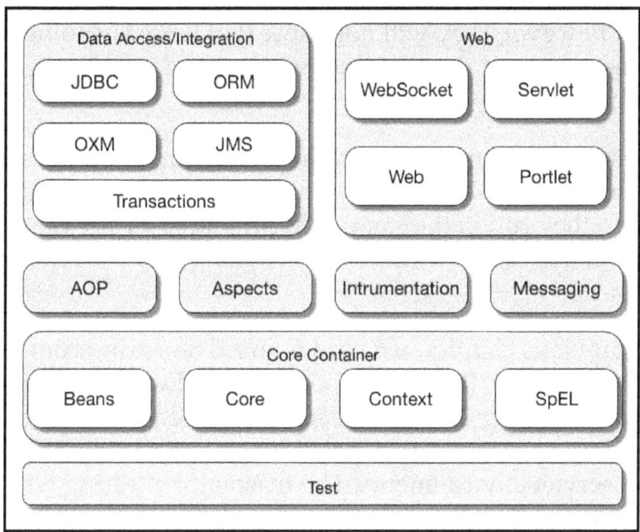

Spring has been constantly developing since its first release, and it is still considered a modern framework. The core of the framework is a dependency injection container similar to the one we saw in the previous chapter. As the framework develops, it also supports AOP and many other enterprise functionalities, such as message-oriented patterns and web programming with an implementation of the Model View Controller, supporting not only servlets but also portlets and WebSockets. Since Spring targets the enterprise application arena, it also supports database handling in many different ways. It supports JDBC using templates, **Object Relational Mapping (ORM)**, and transaction management.

In this sample program, we will use a fairly recent module—Spring boot. This module makes it extremely easy to start writing and running applications, assuming a lot of configurations that are usually the same for many programs. It contains an embedded servlet container that it configures for default settings and configures Spring wherever it is possible so that we can focus on the programming aspect rather than on the Spring configuration.

Spring core

The central element of the core module is the context. When a Spring application starts, the container needs a context in which the container can create different beans. This is very general and true for any dependency injection container. If we programmatically create two different contexts, they may live independent of each other in the same **JVM**. If there is a bean declared as a singleton so that there should only be one single instance of it, then the container will create the single instance for a context when we need it. The objects representing the context have a reference to the object that we have already created. If there are multiple contexts, however, they will not know that there is another context in the JVM that already has an instance, and the container will create a new instance of the singleton bean for the other context.

Usually, we do not use more than one context in a program, but there are numerous examples of there being many contexts in a single JVM. When different servlets run in the same servlet container, they run in the same JVM separated by the class loader, and they may each use Spring. In this case, the context will belong to the servlet and each will have a new context.

In the previous chapter, we used Guice. The Spring context is similar to the Guice injector. In the previous chapter, I was cheating a bit because I was programming Guice to create a new injector for each request. This is far from optimal, and Guice provides an injector implementation that can handle servlet environments. The reason for cheating was that I wanted to focus more on the DI architecture essentials, and I did not want to complicate the code by introducing a complex (well, more complex) implementation of the injector.

The Spring context behavior is defined by the interface `ApplicationContext`. There are two extensions of this interface and many implementations. `ConfigurableApplicationContext` extends `ApplicationContext`, defining setters, and `ConfigurableWebApplicationContext` defines methods that are needed in the web environment. When we program web applications, we usually do not need to interfere directly with the context. The framework configures the servlet container programmatically, and it contains servlets that create the context and invoke our methods. This is all boilerplate code that was created for us.

The context keeps track of the beans that have been created, but it does not create them. To create beans, we need bean factories or at least one factory. A bean factory in Spring is a class that implements the interface `BeanFactory`. This is the topmost interface of the bean factory type hierarchy in Spring. A bean is simply an object, so the bean factory just creates a new instance of a class. However, it also has to register this new object into the context and the bean should also have a name, which is a `String`. This way, the program, and Spring in it, can refer to the bean by its name.

Different beans can be configured in several different ways in Spring. The oldest approach is to create an XML file that describes the different beans, specifying the names, the class that has to be instantiated to create the bean, and fields in case the bean needs other beans to be injected for its creation.

The motivation behind this approach is that this way, the bean wiring, and configuration can be totally independent of the application code. It becomes a configuration file that can be maintained separately.

For example, we may have a large application that works in several different environments. The access to inventory data is available in a multitude of ways in our example. In one environment, the inventory is available by calling SOAP services. In another environment, the data is accessible in an SQL database. In the third environment, it can be available in some NoSQL store. Each of these accesses is implemented as a separate class, implementing a common inventory access interface. The application code only depends on the interface, and it is the container that provides one implementation or the other.

When the configuration of the bean wiring is in XML, then only this XML file is to be edited, and the code can be started with the implementation of the interface that is suitable for the specific environment.

The next possibility is to configure the beans using annotations. In most cases, the reason to use Spring is to separate the object creation from the functionality. In such cases, there may only be one implementation of the beans. Still using Spring, the actual code is cleaner using the framework that was provided for dependency injection. On the other hand, the external XML would move the configuration away from the code that needs configuration. In that case, the annotations that can control bean creation and injections work as declarations inside the code.

The XML configuration in a case when there is only one single implementation that is redundant. Why would I want to specify in an XML configuration that I want an instance of the interface by the single class of my program that implements that interface? It is fairly obvious and it cannot be in any other way, hence that is the only class implementing the interface. We do not like typing things that do not present new information.

To signal that a class can be used as a bean, and to possibly provide a name, we can use the `@Component` annotation. We do not need to provide a name as an argument. In that case, the name will be an empty string, but why have a name if we do not refer to it? Spring scans all the classes that are on the classpath and recognizes the classes that have been annotated, and it knows that they are the candidates to be used for bean creation. When a component needs another bean to be injected, the field can be annotated with `@Autowired` or `@Inject`. The `@Autowired` annotation is a Spring annotation and existed before the `@Inject` annotation was standardized. If you intend to use your code outside of the Spring container, it is recommended that you use standard annotations. Functionally, they are equivalent.

In our code, when Spring creates an instance of the `ProductInformationController` component, it seems that it needs an instance of `ProductLookup`. This is an interface, and thus, Spring starts to look for a class that implements this interface, then it creates an instance of it, possibly first creating other beans, and then the container injects that, setting the field. You can decide to annotate the setter of the field instead of the field itself. In such a case, Spring will invoke the setter, even if the setter is `private`. You can inject dependencies through constructor arguments. The major difference between the setter, field injection, and constructor injection is that you cannot create a bean without dependency in case you use constructor injection. When the bean is instantiated, it should and will have all other beans injected so that it depends on using the constructor injection. At the same time, the dependencies that need to be injected through the setter injection, or directly into a field, could be instantiated later by the container sometime between instantiating the class and readying the bean.

This slight difference may not seem interesting or important until your constructor code becomes more complex than the simple dependency settings or until the dependencies become complex. In the case of a complex constructor, the code should pay attention to the fact that the object is not fully created. This is generally true for any constructor code, but in the case of beans created by a dependency injection container, injecting dependencies through direct field access or via setter injection, it is even more important. It may be advisable to use constructor injection to ensure that the dependencies are there. If a programmer makes a mistake, forgetting that the object is not fully initialized, and uses it in the constructor or a method, which itself is called from a constructor, the dependency is already there. Also, it is cleaner and well-structured to use the constructor to initialize the dependencies and have those fields declared `final`.

On the other hand, constructor injection has its downsides.

If different objects depend on each other and there is a ring in the dependency graph, then Spring will have a hard time if you use constructor dependencies. When class *A* needs class *B* and the other way round, as the simplest circle, then neither *A* nor *B* can be created without the other if the dependency injection is a constructor dependency. In situations like this, the constructor injection cannot be used, and the circle should be broken into at least a single dependency. In situations like this, setter injection is inevitable.

Setter injection may also be better when there are optional dependencies. In most cases, a class may not need all of its dependencies at the same time. Some classes may use a database connection or a NoSQL database handle, but not both at the same time. Although it may also be a code smell and probably a sign of poor OO design, it may happen. It may be a deliberate decision to do that because the pure OO design would result in too deep object hierarchies and too many classes, beyond the maintainable limit. If that is the case, the optional dependencies may be better handled using setter injection. Some are configured and set, and some are left with default values, usually `null`.

Last but not least, we can configure the container using Java classes in case the annotations are not enough. For example, there are multiple implementations of the `ProductLookup` interface, as it is, in our code base. (Don't worry if you did not recognize that; I have not told you about that yet.) There is a `ResourceBasedProductLookup` class that reads properties files from the package and is mainly used to test the application, and there is `RestClientProductLookup`, which is a production-like implementation of the interface. If I have no other configuration except annotating the `lookup` field with `@Autowired`, Spring will not know which implementation to use and will reward the user during startup with the following error message:

```
Error starting ApplicationContext. To display the auto-configuration report
re-run your application with 'debug' enabled.
2023-11-03 07:25:01.217 ERROR 51907 --- [  restartedMain]
o.s.b.d.LoggingFailureAnalysisReporter   :

***************************
APPLICATION FAILED TO START
***************************

Description:

Parameter 0 of constructor in
packt.java9.by.example.mybusiness.productinformation.ProductInformationCont
roller required a single bean, but 2 were found:
        - resourceBasedProductLookup: defined in file
[/.../sources/ch07/productinformation/build/classes/main/packt/java9/by/exa
mple/mybusiness/productinformation/lookup/ResourceBasedProductLookup.class]
        - restClientProductLookup: defined in file
```

```
[/.../sources/ch07/productinformation/build/classes/main/packt/java9/by/exa
mple/mybusiness/productinformation/lookup/RestClientProductLookup.class]

Action:

Consider marking one of the beans as @Primary, updating the consumer to
accept multiple beans, or using @Qualifier to identify the bean that should
be consumed
```

This is a fairly self-explanatory error message; it tells us a lot. Now, it is the time when we can configure the bean in XML, but at the same time, we can also configure it using Java.

Many developers do not get the point the first time. I did not get it either. The whole XML configuration was to separate the configuration from the code. It was to create the possibility that a system administrator changes the configuration and is free to select one or the other implementations of some interface, wiring the application together. Now, Spring tells me that it is better to return to the programmatic way?

At the same time, I could hear concerns for many years that XML is not really any better than Java code. XML writing is essentially programming, except that the tooling and IDE support is not as good for XML as it is for Java code (the latter developed a lot in recent years, although this was for Spring XML configuration).

To understand the concept of returning to Java code from XML, we have to get back to the pure reason and aim of the XML way of configuration.

The main advantage of XML Spring configuration is not that the format is not programmatic, but rather that the configuration code is separated from application code. If we write the configuration in Java and keep those configuration classes to the bare minimum, and they stay as they should, then the separation of application versus configuration code still stands. It is only the format of the configuration that we change from XML to Java. The advantages are numerous. One is that the names of the classes are recognized by the IDE as we edit and we can have autocompleted in Java (note that this also works when using XML in some of the IDEs for utilizing some of the extensions of plugins). In the case of Java, IDE support is ubiquitous. Java is more readable than XML. Well, this is a matter of taste, but most of us like Java more than XML.

System administrators can also edit Java code. When they edit the XML configuration, they usually have to extract it from a JAR or WAR file, edit it, and then package the archive again. In the case of Java editing, they also have to issue a `gradle war` command or something similar. This should not be a showstopper for a system manager who runs Java applications on a server. And again, it is not Java programming. It is only editing some Java code files and replacing some class name literals and string constants.

We follow this approach in our sample application code. We have two configuration files in the application: one for local deployment and testing, and another for production. The `@Profile` annotation specifies which profile the configuration should use. The profile, when the code is executed, can be specified on the command line as a system property, as follows:

```
$ gradle -Dspring.profiles.active=local bootRun
```

The configuration class is annotated with `@Configuration`. The methods that are bean factories are annotated with `@Bean`:

```
package packt.java11.mybusiness.productinformation;

import ...

@Configuration
@Profile("local")
public class SpringConfigurationLocal {

    @Bean
    @Primary
    public ProductLookup productLookup() {
        return new ResourceBasedProductLookup();
    }

    @Bean
    public ProductInformationServiceUrlBuilder urlBuilder() {
        return null;
    }
}
```

The bean factory simply returns a new instance of the `ResourceBasedProductLookup` class that implements the `ProductLookup` interface. This implementation can be used to run the application for local testing when there are no external services to rely on. This implementation reads the product data from local resource files that are packaged into the JAR application.

The production version of the configuration is not much different, but as it may be expected, there are a few more things to configure:

```
package packt.java11.mybusiness.productinformation;
import ...
@Configuration
@Profile("production")
public class SpringConfiguration {

    @Bean
    @Primary
    public ProductLookup productLookup() {
        return new RestClientProductLookup(urlBuilder());
    }

    @Bean
    public ProductInformationServiceUrlBuilder urlBuilder() {
        return new ProductInformationServiceUrlBuilder("http://localhost");
    }
}
```

This version of the `ProductLookup` service class uses an external REST service to retrieve the data that it will present to the clients. To do so, it needs the URLs of these services. Such URLs should usually be configured. In our example, we implement a solution where these URLs can be computed on the fly. I tried to make up a situation where it may be needed in real life, but all the reasoning was contorted and I gave up. The real reason is that this way, we can see code that contains a bean that needs another bean to be injected. For now, note that the `ProductInformationServiceUrlBuilder` instance bean is defined in the same way as the `ProductLookup` bean, and when it has to be injected into the constructor of the `ProductLookup` bean, its defining bean method is used and not the following expression directly:

```
new ProductInformationServiceUrlBuilder("http://localhost");
```

The latter may work, but not in all situations, and we should not use it. For these reasons, we will return when we discuss AOP with Spring in a subsequent section.

Also, note that there is no need to define an interface to define a bean. The type that the bean method returns can also be a class. The context will use the method that fits the needed type, and if there is more than one suitable type and the configuration is not precise enough, as we saw, the container will log an error and will not work.

In the configuration that serves the local profile, we will create a `null` value for `ProductInformationServiceBuilder`. This is because we do not need it when we use local testing. Also, if any method from this class is invoked, it will be an error. Errors should be detected as soon as possible; thus, a `null` value is a simple and reasonable choice. A better choice would be a bean that throws a specific exception if any of the methods were ever invoked. That way, you can see a specific exception and also what method the tested code wanted to invoke instead of a null pointer exception.

The `ProductInformationServiceUrlBuilder` class is very simple:

```
package packt.java11.mybusiness.productinformation;

public class ProductInformationServiceUrlBuilder {
    private final String baseUrl;

    public ProductInformationServiceUrlBuilder(String baseUrl) {
        this.baseUrl = baseUrl;
    }

    public String url(String service) {
        final String serviceUrl;
        switch (service) {
            case "pi":
                serviceUrl = baseUrl + ":8081/product/{id}";
                break;
            case "query":
                serviceUrl = baseUrl + ":8081/query/{query}";
                break;
            case "inventory":
                serviceUrl = baseUrl + ":8083/inventory/{id}";
                break;
            default:
                serviceUrl = null;
                break;
        }
        return serviceUrl;
    }
}
```

This bean also needs a constructor parameter, and we used a string constant in the configuration. This clearly shows us that it is possible to use a simple object to initialize some of the dependencies (what would stop us? It is pure Java after all), but it *may* hinder the working of some Spring features.

Service classes

We have two service classes. These classes serve the controllers with data and implement the business logic, no matter how simple they are. One of the service classes implements calls to REST-based services, while the other one reads data from properties files. The latter can be used to test the application when it's offline. The one that calls REST services is used in the production environment. Both of them implement the `ProductLookup` interface:

```
package packt.java11.mybusiness.productinformation;
import java.util.List;
public interface ProductLookup {
    ProductInformation byId(String id);
    List<String> byQuery(String query);
}
```

`ResourceBasedProductLookup` stores the whole database in a map called products. It is filled from the properties files when one of the service methods is invoked. The `private` method, `loadProducts`, is invoked from each of the service methods when they start, but it only loads the data if it is not loaded yet:

```
package packt.java11.mybusiness.productinformation.lookup;
import ...

@Service
public class ResourceBasedProductLookup implements ProductLookup {
```

The class is annotated using `@Service`. This annotation is practically equivalent to the `@Component` annotation. This is only an alternative name for the same annotation. Spring also handles the `@Component` annotation so that if an annotation interface is annotated using the `@Component` annotation, the annotation can also be used to signal that a class is a Spring component. You can write your own annotation interfaces if you want to signal for better readability, stating that a class is not a simple component but some other special type.

For example, start up your IDE and navigate to the `fromProperties()` method in the `ResourceBasedProductLookup` class:

```
private ProductInformation fromProperties(Properties properties) {
    final ProductInformation pi = new ProductInformation();
    pi.setTitle(properties.getProperty("title"));
    pi.setDescription(properties.getProperty("description"));
    pi.setWeight(Double.parseDouble(properties.getProperty("weight")));
    pi.getSize()[0] = Double.parseDouble(properties.getProperty("width"));
    pi.getSize()[1] = Double.parseDouble(properties.getProperty("height"));
    pi.getSize()[2] = Double.parseDouble(properties.getProperty("depth"));
```

```
        return pi;
    }
```

The `fromProperties()` method creates an instance of `ProductInformation` and fills it in with the parameters given in the `Properties` object.

The `Properties` class is an old and widely used type. Although there are more modern formats and classes, this is still widely used and it is likely that you will meet this class. This is the very reason that we are using it here.

`ProductInformation` is a simple **Data Transfer Object** (**DTO**) that contains no logic—only fields, setters, and getters. It also contains a constant, `emptyProductInformation`, which holds a reference to an instance of the class with empty values.

A `Properties` object is similar to a `Map` object. It contains `String` values that are assigned to `String` keys. There are methods, as we will see in our examples, that help the programmer to load a `Properties` object from a so-called properties file. Such a file usually has the `.properties` extension, and it contains key-value pairs in the following format:

```
key=value
```

For example, the `123.properties` file contains the following:

```
id=123
title=Fundamentals of Java 18.9
description=a new book to learn Java 11
weight=300
width=20
height=2
depth=18
```

The `properties` files are used to store simple configuration values and are almost exclusively used to contain language-specific constants. This is a very contorted use because `properties` files are **ISO Latin-1** encoded files, and in case you need to use some special UTF-8 characters, you have to type them by using the `uXXXX` format or by using the native2ascii converter program. You cannot save them simply as UTF-8. Nevertheless, this is the file the format uses for language-specific strings for program internationalization (also abbreviated as i18n because there are 18 characters between the starting i and the last n in the word internationalization).

To get the `Properties` object, we have to read the files in the project and get them packaged into a JAR file. The Spring class, `PathMatchingResourcePatternResolver`, helps us in doing so.

Gosh, yes, I know! We have to get used to these long names when we use Spring. Anyway, such long and descriptive names are widely used in an enterprise environment and they are needed to explain the functionality of the classes.

We declare a map that will contain all of the products during testing:

```
final private Map<String, ProductInformation> products = new HashMap<>();
```

The key is the product ID, which is a string in our example. The values are `ProductInformation` objects that we fill up using the `fromProperties` method.

The next field signals that the products are not loaded:

```
private boolean productsAreNotLoaded = true;
```

Novice programmers usually use the opposite value with the name `productsAreLoaded`, set to `false` by default. In that case, the only place where we will read a value will negate the value, or the main branch of the `if` command becomes the do nothing part. Neither is a best practice.

```
private void loadProducts() {
    if (productsAreNotLoaded) {
        try {
            Resource[] resources =
                new PathMatchingResourcePatternResolver()
                    .getResources("classpath:products/*.properties");
            for (Resource resource : resources) {
                loadResource(resource);
            }
            productsAreNotLoaded = false;
        } catch (IOException ex) {
            log.error("Test resources can not be read", ex);
        }
    }
}
```

The `getResources()` method returns all of the resources (files) that are on the classpath under the `products` directory that have `.properties` extensions:

```
private void loadResource(Resource resource) throws IOException {
    final int dotPos = resource.getFilename().lastIndexOf('.');
```

```
        final String id = resource.getFilename().substring(0, dotPos);
        Properties properties = new Properties();
        properties.load(resource.getInputStream());
        final ProductInformation pi = fromProperties(properties);
        pi.setId(id);
        products.put(id, pi);
    }
```

The product ID is given by the name of the file. This is calculated using simple string manipulation, cutting off the extension. The `Resource` can also provide an input stream that the `Properties` class's `load` method can use to load all of the properties at once. Finally, we save the new `ProductInformation` object in the map.

We also have a special `noProduct` list that is empty. This is returned if there is no product for the query when we want to search for products:

```
private static final List<String> noProducts = new LinkedList<>();
```

The product lookup service just takes a product from the `Map` and returns it, or if it does not exist, it returns an empty product:

```
@Override
public ProductInformation byId(String id) {
    loadProducts();
    if (products.containsKey(id)) {
        return products.get(id);
    } else {
        return ProductInformation.emptyProductInformation;
    }
}
```

The query is a bit more complex. It implements searching for a product by title. Real-life implementations may implement a more complex logic, but this version is for local testing only; thus, the search by title is enough:

```
@Override
public List<String> byQuery(String query) {
    loadProducts();
    List<String> pis = new LinkedList<>();
    StringTokenizer st = new StringTokenizer(query, "&=");
    while (st.hasMoreTokens()) {
        final String key = st.nextToken();
        if (st.hasMoreTokens()) {
            final String value = st.nextToken();
            log.debug("processing {}={} query", key, value);
            if (!"title".equals(key)) {
                log.error("Search by title is allowed only");
```

```
                return noProducts;
            }
            for (String id : products.keySet()) {
                log.error("key: {} value:{} id:{}", key, value, id);
                ProductInformation pi = products.get(id);
                if (pi.getTitle().startsWith(value)) {
                    pis.add(id);
                }
            }
        }
    }
    return pis;
}
```

The service class that implements the production function is much simpler. Strange, but in most cases, the test code is more complex than the production code:

```
package packt.java11.mybusiness.productinformation.lookup;

import ...
@Component
public class RestClientProductLookup implements ProductLookup {
    private static Logger log =
LoggerFactory.getLogger(RestClientProductLookup.class);

    final private ProductInformationServiceUrlBuilder piSUBuilder;

    public RestClientProductLookup(ProductInformationServiceUrlBuilder
piSUBuilder) {
        this.piSUBuilder = piSUBuilder;
    }
```

The constructor is used to inject the URL builder bean, and this is all the auxiliary code the class has. The rest are the two service methods `byId()` and `byQuery()`. First, we look at the `byId()` method:

```
@Override
public ProductInformation byId(String id) {
    var uriParameters = new HashMap<String, String>();
    uriParameters.put("id", id);
    var rest = new RestTemplate();
    var amount =
        rest.getForObject(piSUBuilder.url("inventory"),
            InventoryItemAmount.class,
            uriParameters);
    log.info("amount {}.", amount);
    if (amount.getAmount() > 0) {
        log.info("There items from {}. We are offering", id);
```

```
            return rest.getForObject(piSUBuilder.url("pi"),
                ProductInformation.class,
                uriParameters);
        } else {
            log.info("There are no items from {}. Amount is {}", id, amount);
            return ProductInformation.emptyProductInformation;
        }
    }
```

The `byId()` method first calls the inventory service to see if there are any products in the inventory. This REST service returns a JSON that has the format `{ amount : nnn }`; thus, we need a class (so simple that we do not list it here) that has the `int amount` field, a setter, and a getter.

The Spring `RestTemplate` provides an easy way to access a REST service. All it needs is the URL template, a type that is used to convert the result, and a `Map` object with the parameters. The URL template string may contain parameters in the same way as the request mapping in the Spring controllers, the name of the parameter being between the `{` and `}` characters. The template class provides simple methods to access REST services. It automatically performs marshaling, sending parameters, and un-marshaling, receiving the response. In the case of a `GET` request, the marshaling is not needed. The data is in the request URL, and the `{xxx}` placeholders are replaced with the values from the map, which are supplied as a third argument. The un-marshaling is readily available for most of the formats. In our application, the REST service sends JSON data and it is indicated in the response `Content-Type` HTTP header. `RestTemplate` converts the JSON to the type provided as an argument. If ever the server decides to send the response in XML, it will also be indicated in the HTTP header, `RestTemplate`, which will handle the situation automatically. As a matter of fact, looking at the code, we cannot tell how the response is encoded. This is also nice because it makes the client flexible and, at the same time, we do not need to deal with such technical details. We can focus on the business logic.

At the same time, the class also provides configuration parameters in the case of marshaling or some other functionality so that it automatically needs that. You can, for example, provide marshaling methods, though I recommend that you use whatever is available by default. In most cases, when a developer thinks that there is a need for a special version of any of these functions, the original design of their code is flawed.

The business logic is very simple. We first ask the inventory if there is a certain product in stock. If there is (more than zero), then we query the product information service and return the details. If there is none, then we return an empty record.

The other service is even simpler. It simply calls the underpinning service and returns the result:

```
@Override
public List<String> byQuery(String query) {
    var uriParameters = new HashMap<String, String>();
    uriParameters.put("query", query);
    var rest = new RestTemplate();
    return rest.getForObject(piSUBuilder.url("query"), List.class,
uriParameters);
}
```

Compiling and running the application

We use `gradle` to compile and run the application. Since the application does not have any specific configuration that would not appear in most similar applications, it is wise to use Spring boot. Spring boot makes it extremely simple to create and run a web application. We need a Java standard `public static void main` method that starts up the application via Spring:

```
package packt.java11.mybusiness.productinformation;

import ...

@SpringBootApplication(scanBasePackageClasses = SpringScanBase.class)
public class Application {

    public static void main(String[] args) {
        SpringApplication.run(Application.class, args);
    }
}
```

This method does nothing except start the `StringApplication` class's `run` method. It passes the original arguments and also the class that the application is in. Spring uses this class to read the annotation. The `@SpringBootApplication` annotation signals that this class is a Spring boot application and provides arguments to configure the packages that contain the application. To do so, you can provide the name of the package that contains the classes, but you can also provide a class in the base package that contains all of the classes that Spring has to be aware of. You may not be able to use the class version of the annotation parameter because the root package may not contain any class, only subpackages. At the same time, providing the name of the root package as `String` will not reveal any typo or misalignment during compile time. Some *IDE* may recognize that the parameter is supposed to be a package name, or it may scan the strings of the program for package names when you refactor or rename a package and give you support for that, but this is more heuristics only. It is a common practice to create a placeholder class that does nothing in the root package in case there is no class there. This class can be used to specify `scanBasePackageClasses` as an annotation parameter instead of `scanBasePackages`, that needs `String`. In our example, we have an empty interface, `SpringScanBase`, as a placeholder.

Spring scans all the classes that are on the classpath, recognizes the components and field annotations that it can interpret, and uses this knowledge to create beans without configuration when needed.

Note that the abstract class, `ClassLoader`, included in the JDK does not provide any class scanning method. Since Java environments and frameworks can implement their own `ClassLoaders`, it is possible (but very unlikely) that some implementation does not provide the scanning functionality provided by the `URLClassLoader`. `URLClassLoader` is a non-abstract implementation of the class loading functionality and is part of the *JDK* just as well as `ClassLoader`. We will discuss the intricacies of the class loading mechanism in subsequent chapters.

The `gradle` build file contains the usual things. It specifies the repositories, the plugins for Java, and the IDEs for Spring boot. It also specifies the name of the JAR file that it generates during the build. The most important part is the dependency list:

```
buildscript {
    repositories {
        mavenCentral()
    }
    dependencies {
        classpath("org.springframework.boot:spring-boot-gradle-
plugin:1.4.1.RELEASE")
    }
```

```
}

apply plugin: 'java'
apply plugin: 'eclipse'
apply plugin: 'idea'
apply plugin: 'spring-boot'

jar {
    baseName = 'packt-ch07-microservice'
    version =  '1.0.0'
}

repositories {
    mavenCentral()
}

bootRun {
    systemProperties System.properties
}

sourceCompatibility = 1.10
targetCompatibility = 1.10

dependencies {
    compile("org.springframework.boot:spring-boot-starter-web")
    compile("org.springframework.boot:spring-boot-devtools")
    compile("org.springframework:spring-aop")
    compile("org.springframework:spring-aspects")
    testCompile("org.springframework.boot:spring-boot-starter-test")
}
```

We depend on Spring boot packages, some test packages, AOP support (which we will look at soon), and also on Spring boot devtools.

Spring boot devtools make it possible to restart a web application whenever it is recompiled, without restarting the built-in Tomcat server. Suppose, we start the application by using the following command line:

```
gradle -Dspring.profiles.active=production bootRun
```

Gradle starts up the application. Whenever it sees that the classes it runs are modified, it reloads them, and we can test the modified application within a few seconds.

The `-Dspring.profiles.active=production` argument specifies that the production profile should be active. To be able to use this command-line parameter, we will also need the `bootRun{}` configuration closure in the build file.

Testing the application

The application should have unit tests for each and every class it has, except, perhaps, for the DTO classes that contain no functionality. The setters and getters are created by the IDE and are not typed in by the programmer, so it is unlikely that there will be any errors. If there is some error related to those classes, it is more likely that it is an integration problem that cannot be discovered by using unit tests. Since we discussed unit tests in the previous chapters in detail, we will focus more on integration tests and application tests here.

Integration tests

Integration tests are very similar to unit tests, and in most cases, novice programmers claim that they perform unit testing when they actually perform integration testing.

Integration tests drive the code but do not test the individual classes (units) in isolation, mocking everything that the class may use. Rather, they test the functionality of most of the classes that are needed to perform a test. This way, the integration test does test that the classes are able to work together and not only satisfy their own specifications but also ensure that these specifications work together.

In the integration test, the external world (like external services) and access to the database are mocked. That is because the integration tests are supposed to run on integration servers, in the same environment where the unit tests are executed, and there, these external interfaces may not be available. In most cases, databases are mocked using in-memory SQL, and external services are mocked using some mock classes.

Spring provides a nice environment to execute such integration tests. In our project, we have a sample integration test:

```
package packt.java11.mybusiness.productinformation;

import ...

@RunWith(SpringRunner.class)
@SpringBootTest(classes = Application.class)
@AutoConfigureMockMvc
@ActiveProfiles("local")
public class ProductInformationControllerTest {

    @Autowired
    private MockMvc mockMvc;

    @Test
```

```
    public void noParamGreetingShouldReturnDefaultMessage() throws
Exception {

        this.mockMvc.perform(get("/pi")).andDo(print())
            .andExpect(status().isNotFound());
    }

    @Test
    public void paramGreetingShouldReturnTailoredMessage() throws Exception
{

        this.mockMvc.perform(get("/pi/123"))
            .andDo(print()).andExpect(status().isOk())
            .andExpect(jsonPath("$.title").value("Book Java 9 by
Example"));
    }

}
```

This is far from being a complete and full-fledged integration test. There are many situations that haven't been tested, but here, it is good as an example. To have all the support for the Spring environment, we have to use the `SpringRunner` class. The `@RunWith` annotation is handled by the JUnit framework; all other annotations are for Spring. When the JUnit framework sees that there is a `@RunWith` annotation and a runner class specified, it starts that class instead of the standard runner. `SpringRunner` sets up a Spring context for the test and handles the annotations.

`@SpringBootTest` specifies the applications that we need to test. This helps Spring read that class and the annotation on that class, identifying the packages to be scanned.

`@AutoConfigureMockMvc` tells Spring to configure a mock version of the Model View Controller framework, which can be executed without a servlet container and web protocol. Using that, we can test our REST services without really going to the network.

`@ActiveProfiles` tells Spring that the active profile is local and that Spring has to use the configuration that is denoted by the annotation, `@Profile("local")`. This is a version that uses the `.properties` files instead of external HTTP services; thus, this is appropriate for integration testing.

The test performs `GET` requests inside the mocking framework, executes the code in the controller, and tests the returned value by using the mocking framework and fluent API in a very readable way.

Note that using the properties files and having the service implementation based on properties files is a bit of an overkill. I created this so that it is possible to start up the application interactively without any real backing service. Consider the following command—`gradle -Dspring.profiles.active=local bootRun`. If we issue the preceding command, then the server starts up using this local implementation. If we only aim for integration testing, then the local implementation of the service classes should be under the `test` directory and should be much simpler, mainly only returning constant responses for any expected request and throwing errors if any non-expected request comes.

Application tests

Consider the following command:

```
gradle -Dspring.profiles.active=production bootRun
```

If we start up the application, issuing the preceding command and firing up the browser to the URL `http://localhost:8080/pi/123`, we will get a fat error message on the browser screen. Ouch...

It says `Internal Server Error, status=500` or something similar. That is because our code wants to connect to the backing services, but we do not have any yet. To have some test the application on this level, we should create the backing services or at least something that mocks them. The easiest way to do this is by using the SoapUI program.

SoapUI is a Java program that's available from `https://www.soapui.org/`. There's an open source version and free version of it, and there is a commercial version. For our purposes, the free version is enough. We can install it in the simplest click-forward way as it has a setup wizard. After that, we can start it up and use the graphical user interface.

We will create a new test project, **Catalog and inventory**, and set up two REST mock services in it, **Catalog** and **Inventory**, as shown in the following screenshot:

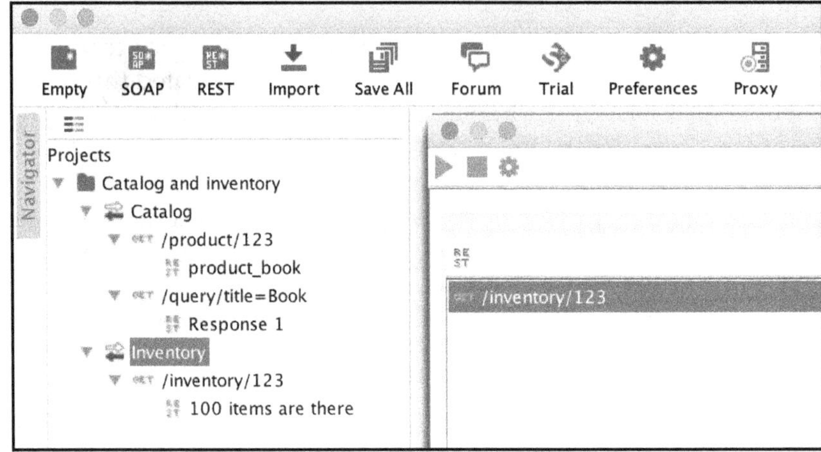

For each of the mock services, we set up requests to be matched, as well as responses. The content of the response is text and can be typed into the text field on the user interface. It is important that we do not forget to set the media type of the response to `application/json` (the default is XML):

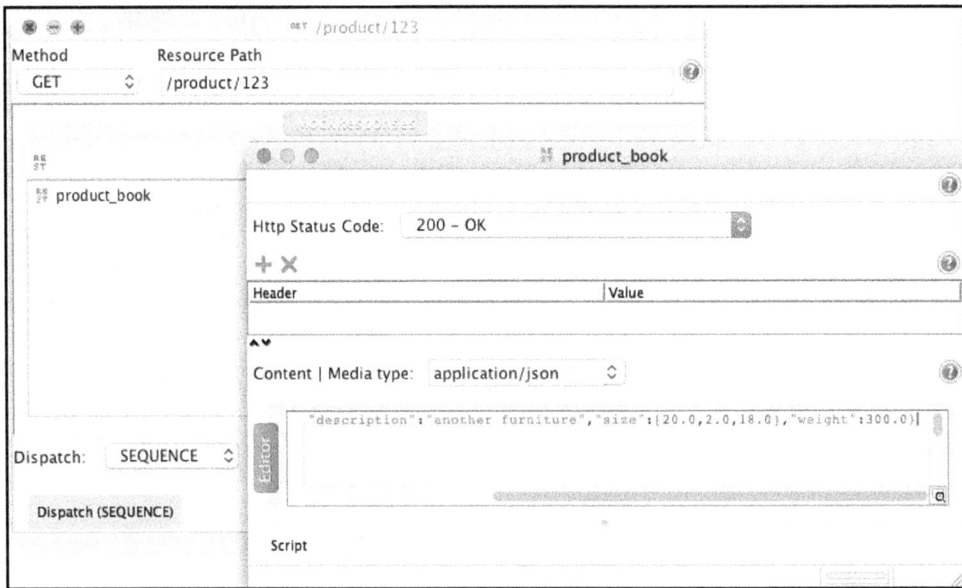

Before starting the services, we have to set the port numbers (by clicking on the cogwheel) to something that is available on the server. Since 8080 is used by the Tomcat server and is executed by Gradle, and 8082 is used by SoapUI to list the mock services that are currently running, I will set the catalog to listen on port 8081 and the inventory to listen on port 8083. You can also see these port numbers in the listing of the `ProductInformationServiceUrlBuilder` class.

The soapUI saves the project in an XML file, and it is available for you on GitHub in the `project` directory.

After starting the mock services, the error message disappears from the browser screen when we press refresh:

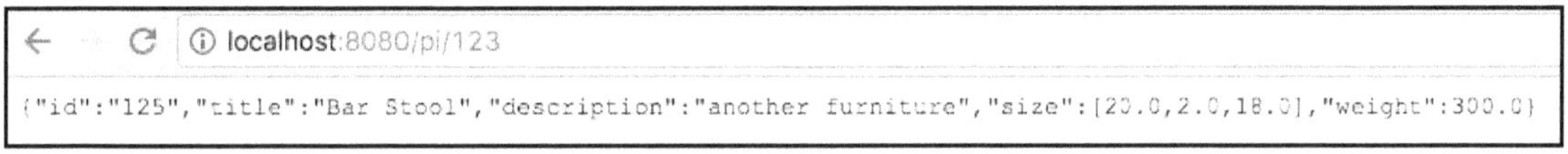

```
localhost:8080/pi/123
{"id":"125","title":"Bar Stool","description":"another furniture","size":[20.0,2.0,18.0],"weight":300.0}
```

What we see is exactly what we typed into SoapUI.

Now, if I change the inventory mock service to return 0 instead of 100, as in the original version, what I get is the following empty record:

```
{"id":"","title":"","description":"","size":[0.0,0.0,0.0],"weight":0.0}
```

The testing, even on this level, can be automated. Now, we were playing around, using the browser, and this is something nice. Somehow, I feel like I am producing something when there is a program that is really doing something, and I can see that there is some response in the browser window. However, after a while, this becomes boring, and testing manually that the application is still working is cumbersome. It is especially boring for those functions that were not changed. The fact is that they do change miraculously multiple times, even when we do not touch the code that influences them. We do actually touch the code that influences the function, but we are not aware of it. Poor design, poor coding, or maybe we just forgot, but it happens. The regression test is inevitable.

Although browser testing user interfaces can also be automated, this time, we are using a REST service that we can test—this is what SoapUI is for. We have already installed the tool, we have already started it, and we have some mock services running in it. The next thing is to add a **New REST service from URI** to the project and specify the URL `http://localhost:8080/pi/{id}`, exactly the same way as we did for Spring:

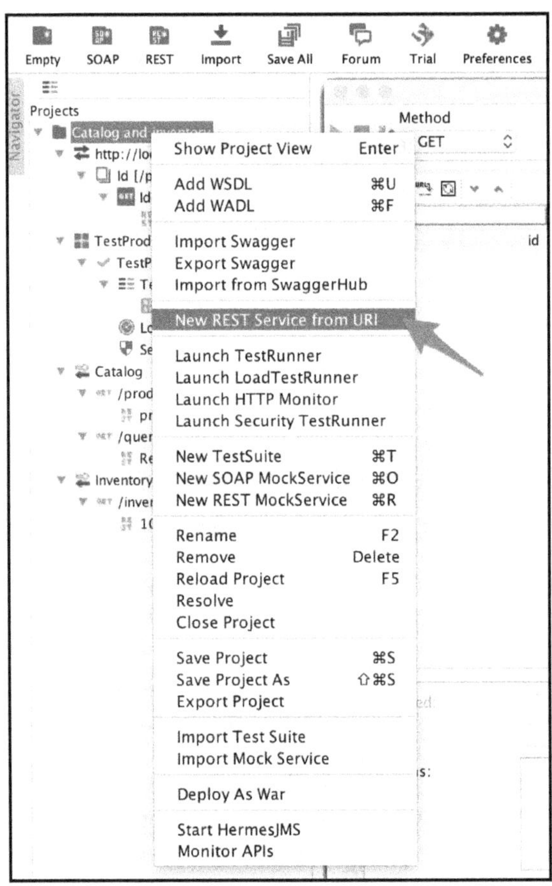

When we have a REST service defined in the project, we can create a new Test Suite and a Test Case inside the suite. We can then add a step to the Test Case that will call the REST service using the parameter `123` if we modify the default value, which is the same as the name of the parameter, in this case, `id`. We can run the test step using the green triangle on the upper-left corner of the window, and since we have the tested application and the SoapUI mock services running, we should get an answer in JSON. We have to select JSON on the response side; otherwise, SoapUI tries to interpret the response as XML, and since we have a JSON response, it is not too fruitful. What we see is the following window:

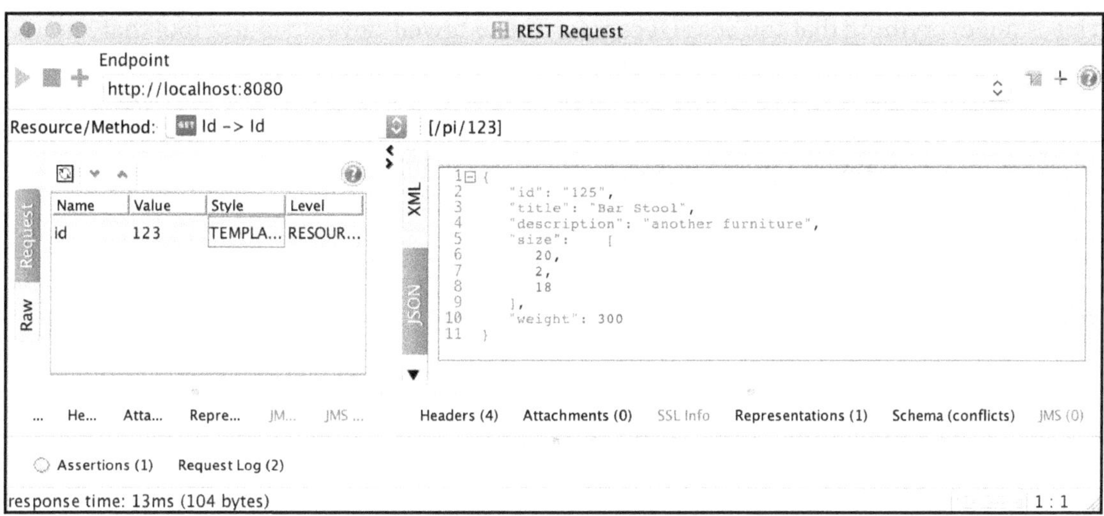

It is the same response that we saw in the browser. There are no miracles when we program computers. Sometimes, we do not understand what happens, and some things are so complex that they seem to be a miracle, but they are actually not. There is an explanation for everything—it may just not be known to us. In this case, we certainly know what is happening, but why is it any better to see the JSON on the screen of SoapUI than it is on the browser? The reason is that SoapUI can execute assertions and, in some cases, further test steps based on the result of the REST invocation, and the final result is a simple YES or NO. The test is OK, or it FAILS.

To add an assertion, click on the **Assertions** text on the lower-left corner of the window. As you can see in the preceding screenshot, I have already added one that compares the `"title"` field of the returned JSON with the text `"Bar Stool"`. When we add the assertion, the default value it suggests is the one that was actually returned, which is just a very handy feature.

After this, running the whole test suite again will run all the test cases (we only have one), and all the test steps, one after the other (again, we only have one), and finally it will display a green **FINISHED** bar on the UI, as shown in the following screenshot:

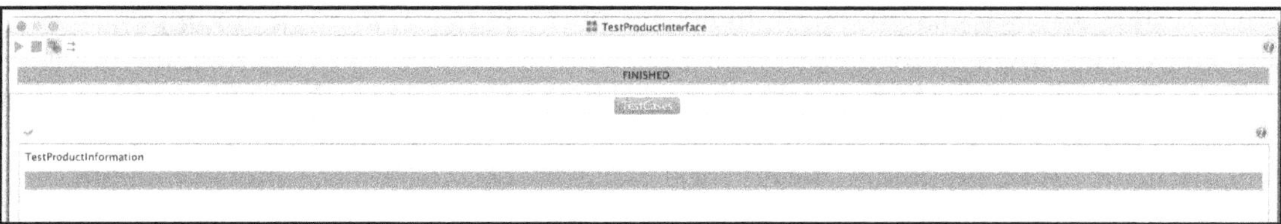

This is not everything that the SoapUI can do. This is a well-developed test tool that has been in the market for many years. SoapUI can test SOAP services and REST services, and it can handle JMS messages. You can create tests of many steps with these calls, loops, and assertions in calls or in separate tests, and in case all else fails, you can do just about anything by creating programmed steps in the Groovy language or by creating extensions in Java.

Servlet filters

By now, the services should work fine and anyone can query the details of our products. This may be a problem. The details of the products are not necessarily public information. We have to ensure that we only serve the data to partners who are eligible to see it.

To ensure that, we need something in the request that proves that the request comes from a partner. This information is typically a password or some other secret. It could be placed into the `GET` request parameters or into the HTTP request header. It is better to put it into the header because the information is secret and not to be seen by anybody.

The GET parameters are a part of the URL, and the browser history remembers that. It is also very easy to enter this information into the browser location window, copy/paste it, and send it over a chat channel or over email. This way, a user of the application who is not so educated and concerned about security may disclose secret information. Although it is not impossible to do the same with the information that is sent in an HTTP header, it is not likely to happen. If the information is in the header and somebody sends this information in an email, they probably know what they are doing; they cross a security border willingly and not by simple negligence.

To send authentication information along the HTTP request, Spring provides a security module that can be easily configured with annotations and configuration XMLs and/or classes. This time, we will do it a bit differently to introduce servlet filters.

We will require that the vendors insert the `X-PartnerSecret` header into the request. This is a non-standard header, and thus it must have the `X-` prefix. Following this approach is also an extra security feature. This way, we can prevent the user from reaching the service using a simple browser. There is, at least, a need for an extra plugin that can insert a custom header or some other program such as SoapUI. This way, it will ensure that our partners will use the interface programmatically, or if ever they need to test the interface ad hoc, only users with a certain level of technology can do so. This is important to keep the support costs controlled.

Since this secret has to be checked in the case of each and every service, we'd better not insert the checking code into each and every service controller. Even if we create the code properly and factor the check for the secret into a separate class, the invocation of the method asserting that the secret is there and is correct will have to be inserted into each and every controller. The controller does the service; checking the client's authenticity is an infrastructure issue. They are different concerns, and thus, they have to be separated.

The best way that the servlet standard provides this for us is via a servlet filter. A servlet filter is a class invoked by the servlet container before the servlet itself if the filter is configured. The filter can be configured in the `web.xml` configuration file of the servlet container or by using an annotation when we use Spring boot. The filter does not only get the request and response as parameters, but also a third argument of the `FilterChain` type that it should use to call the servlet or the next filter in the chain.

There can be more than one filter defined, and they get chained up. The filter may, at its discretion, decide to call or not to call the next one in the chain:

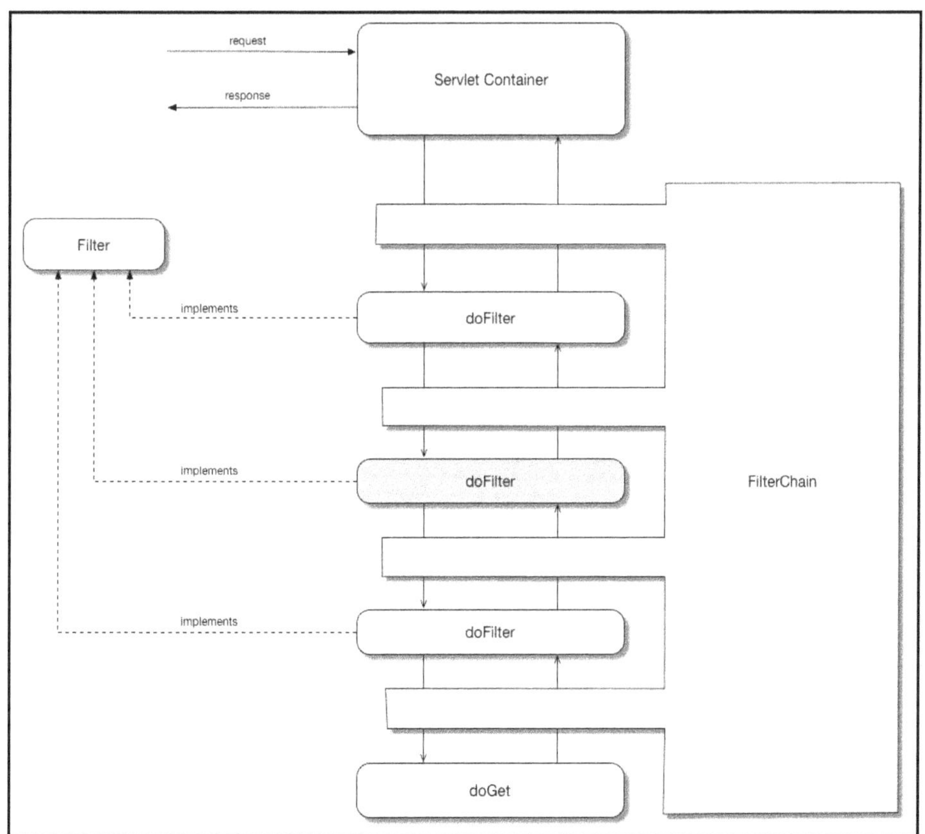

We put our servlet filter into the `auth` subpackage of our application:

```
package packt.java11.mybusiness.productinformation.auth;

import ...

@Component
public class AuthFilter implements Filter {
    public static final int NOT_AUTHORIZED = 401;
    private static Logger log = LoggerFactory.getLogger(AuthFilter.class);

    @Override
    public void init(FilterConfig filterConfig)
        throws ServletException {
    }

    @Override
    public void doFilter(ServletRequest request,
                         ServletResponse response,
                         FilterChain chain)
        throws IOException, ServletException {

        HttpServletRequest httpRequest = (HttpServletRequest) request;
        final String secret = httpRequest.getHeader("X-PartnerSecret");
        log.info("Partner secret is {}", secret);
        if (true || "packt".equals(secret)) {
            chain.doFilter(request, response);
        } else {
            HttpServletResponse httpResponse = (HttpServletResponse)
response;
            httpResponse.sendError(NOT_AUTHORIZED);
        }
    }

    @Override
    public void destroy() {
    }
}
```

The filter implements the `Filter` interface, which defines three methods. In our case, we do not have any parameters to consider in the filter, and we do not allocate any resources to release; thus, both the `init` and `destroy` methods are empty. The main work of the filter is the `doFilter` method. It has three parameters; two of them are the same as the parameters of a servlet, and the third is `FilterChain`.

The request is converted to `HttpServletRequest` so that we can get access to the `X-PartnerSecret` header through the `getHeader` method. If the value sent in this header field is good, we call the next one in the chain. In our application, there are no more filters being configured; therefore, the next in the chain is the servlet. If the secret is not acceptable, then we do not call the next in the chain. Instead, we return the *401 Not Authorized* HTTP error to the client.

In this application, the secret is very simple. This is the constant string `packt`. This is not really a big secret, especially now that it is published in this book. A real-life application would require something more cryptic and less known. It is very probable that each partner would use different secrets and that the secret has to change from time to time.

When there is an error condition in a servlet that our program handles, it is a good practice to use the HTTP error handling mechanism. Instead of sending back a message with the status code *200 OK* and explaining, for example, in a JSON format that the authentication was not successful, we have to send back the *401 code*. This is defined by the standard and does not need any further explanation or documentation.

There is one thing left in our program, and that is audit logging.

Audit logging and AOP

We have logged in our sample code and for that, we used slf4j, which we covered in the previous chapter. Logging is more or less the decision of the developer and supports technical levels of operation. There, we also touched on a few sentence audit loggings. This type of logging is usually explicitly required in a functional requirement.

Generally, AOP is separating the different aspects of code functionality into separate code fragments, and is implementing them independently of each other. This is very much the single responsibility principle. This time, it is implemented in a way where not only are the different functionalities implemented separately, but where we can connect them together. This is defined separately. What is executed before and after the other parts are encoded separately and gets to the Spring configuration? We have seen something similar already. The dependencies that a class needs to properly operate are defined in a separate segment (XML or Java code). It is not a surprise that in the case of AOP, the same is done using Spring. Aspects are configured in the configuration file or class.

A typical aspect is audit logging, and we will use this as an example. There are many topics that can be implemented using aspects, and some of them are even worth implementing that way.

We do not want to implement the audit logging code in each business method or class that needs it. Instead, we implement a general aspect and configure the wiring so that whenever a bean method that needs audit logging is invoked, Spring invokes the audit logging.

There are other important terminologies that we should understand for AOP and especially how AOP can be configured in Spring.

The first and most important is the aspect. This is the functionality that we want to implement, which in our example is the audit logging.

Joinpoint is the point in execution when an aspect is invoked. When using a full-scale aspect solution in Java that modifies the bytecode of the generated class, a join point can be almost anything. It can be access to a field, read or write; it can be the invocation of a method or exception throwing. In the case of Spring, the class bytecode is not modified; thus, Spring is not able to identify the access of a field or an exception being thrown. Using Spring, a join point is always used when a method is invoked.

A piece of advice is how the aspect is invoked at the join point. It can be before advice, after advice, or around advice. When the advice is before, the aspect is invoked before the method is called. When the advice is after, the aspect is invoked after the method is invoked. Around means that the aspect is invoked before the method call, and the aspect also has an argument to call the method and still perform some actions after the method is called. This way, the around advice is very similar to servlet filters.

The before advice is called before the method call, and after it returns, the framework will invoke the method. There is no way for the aspect to prevent the invocation of the original method. The only exception is when the aspect, well, throws an exception.

The after advice is also affected by exceptions. There can be an after returning advice that is invoked when the method is returning. The after throwing is only invoked if the method was throwing an exception. Finally, after is invoked in the case of an exception or return.

The pointcut is a special string expression that identifies join points. A pointcut expression may match zero, one, or more join points. When the aspect is associated with a pointcut expression, the framework will know the join points and when and where to invoke the aspect. In other words, the pointcut is the string that tells you when and for which method to invoke the aspect.

Even though Spring implementation of AOP does not use AspectJ and does not modify the bytecode that was created for the classes, it supports the pointcut expression language. Although this expression language provides more features than what Spring implements, it is a well-established and widely used and accepted expression language to describe pointcuts, and it just would not make sense to invent something new.

Introduction is adding methods or fields to a type that already exists, and does so during runtime. Spring allows this AOP functionality to add an interface to an existing type and add an implementation of the interface in the form of an advice class. In our example, we do not use this functionality.

Target object is the object that is being advised by the aspect. This is the bean that contains the method around the aspect, that is, before or after the aspect is invoked.

That was just a condensed set of definitions, almost like in a math book. If you did not get the point just reading this, don't worry. I did not understand it either when I first read it. That is why we have the following example, after which all we just covered will make more sense:

```
package packt.java11.mybusiness.productinformation;

import ...
@Configuration
@Aspect
public class SpringConfigurationAspect {
    private static Logger log = LoggerFactory.getLogger("AUDIT_LOG");

    @Around("execution(* byId(..))")
    public ProductInformation byIdQueryLogging(ProceedingJoinPoint jp)
throws Throwable {
        log.info("byId query is about to run");
        ProductInformation pi = (ProductInformation)
jp.proceed(jp.getArgs());
        log.info("byId query was executed");
        return pi;
    }

    @Around("execution(* url(..))")
    public String urlCreationLogging(ProceedingJoinPoint jp) throws
Throwable {
        log.info("url is to be created");
        var url = (String) jp.proceed(jp.getArgs());
        log.info("url created was " + url);
        return url;
    }
}
```

The class is annotated with the `@Configuration` annotation so that Spring knows that this class contains the configuration. The `@Aspect` annotation denotes that this configuration may also contain aspect definitions. The `@Around` annotation on the methods gives the type of advice, and the argument string for the annotation is the pointcut expression. If the type of advice is different, one of the annotations, `@Before`, `@After`, `@AfterReturning`, or `@AfterThrowing`, should be used.

In our example, we use the `@Around` aspect to demonstrate the most complex scenario. We logged the execution of the target method before and after the execution of the method, and we also called the original method through the `ProceedingJoinPoint` object. Because the two objects returned different types and we want to log differently, we defined two aspect methods.

The argument of the advice annotation is the pointcut string. In this case, it is a simple one. The first one, `execution(* byId(..))`, says that the aspect should be invoked for any execution of any method that has the name byId and has any arguments. The second is very similar, except the name of the method is different. These are simple pointcut expressions, but in a large application that heavily uses AOP, they can be very complex.

The pointcut expression syntax in Spring mainly follows the syntax used by AspectJ. The expression uses the notion of **point cut designator** (**PCD**), which is usually execution. It is followed by the pattern that defines which method to intercept. The general format is as follows:

```
execution(modifiers-pattern? ret-type-pattern declaring-type-pattern?name-
pattern(param-pattern) throws-pattern?)
```

Except for the return type part, all other parts are optional. For example, we can write the following:

```
execution(public * *(..))
```

This will intercept all `public` methods. The following expression intercepts all methods that have a name starting with `set` characters:

```
execution(* set*(..))
```

We can use the `*` character as a joker in the same way as we can use it on the command line in Windows or on a Unix shell. The argument matching definition is a bit more complex. `(..)` means any arguments, `()` means no arguments, and `(*)` means exactly one argument of any type. The last one can also be used when there are more arguments; for example, `(*,Integer)` means that there are two arguments, the second being an `Integer`, and we just do not care what the type of the first one is.

Pointcut expressions can be more complex, joining together match expressions with the `&&` (and) and `||` (or) logical operators, or using the `!` (negation) unary operator.

Using the `@Pointcut()` annotation, the configuration can define pointcuts, putting the annotations on methods. For example, consider the following:

```
@Pointcut("execution(* packt.java.9.by.example.service.*.*(..))")
public void businessService() {}
```

It will define a join point for any method that is implemented in any class in the `packt.java.9.by.example.service` package. This merely defines the pointcut expression and assigns it to the name `businessService`, which is given by the name of the method. Later, we can refer to this expression in aspect annotations, for example:

```
@After("businessService()")
```

Note that the use of this method is purely for its name. This method is not invoked by Spring. It is only used to borrow its name from the expression that is defined on it by using the `@Pointcut` annotation. There is a need for something, such as a method, to put this annotation on, and since methods have names, why not use it? Spring does it. When it scans the configuration classes and sees the annotation, it assigns it in its internal structures to the name of the method, and when that name (along with the parenthesis, to confuse the novice programmer mimicking a method call) is used, it looks up the expression for that name.

AspectJ defines other designators. Spring AOP recognizes some of them, but it throws `IllegalArgumentException` because Spring only implements method execution pointcuts. AspectJ, on the other hand, can also intercept object creation for which the PCD is initialization, as an example. Some other PCDs, in addition to execution, can limit an execution PCD. For example, the PCD, `within`, can be used to limit the aspect to join points belonging to classes within certain packages, or the `@target` PCD can be used to limit the matching to methods in objects that have the annotation given between `(` and `)` after the keyword `@target` in the pointcut expression.

There is a PCD that Spring uses that does not exist in AspectJ. This is a bean. You can define a pointcut expression that contains `bean(name pattern)` to limit the join point to method executions that are in the named bean. The pattern can be the entire name or it can be, as almost any PCD expression that's matching, `*`, as a joker character.

Dynamic proxy-based AOP

Spring AOP, when first presented to Java programmers, seemed like magic. How do we have a variable of `classX` and we call a method on that object? Instead, it executes some aspect before or after the method execution, or even around it, intercepting the call.

The technique that Spring uses is called a dynamic proxy. When we have an object which implements an interface, we can create another object – the proxy object – that also implements that interface, but each and every method implementation invokes a different object called handler, implementing the JDK interface, `InvocationHandler`. When a method of the interface is invoked on the proxy object, it will call the following method on the handler object:

```
public Object invoke(Object target, Method m, Object[] args)
```

This method is free to do anything, even calling the original method on the target object with the original or modified argument:

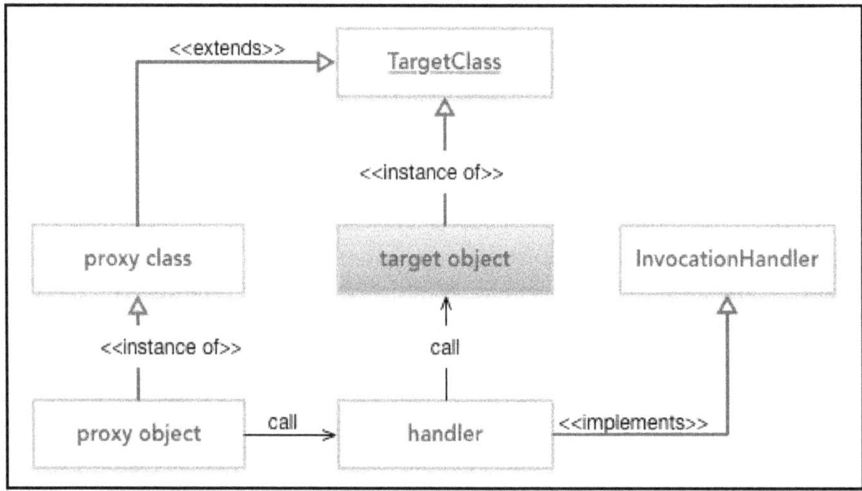

When we do not have an interface at hand that the class to be proxied implements, we cannot use JDK methods. Luckily, there are widely used libraries, such as `cglib`, which are also used by Spring that can do something similar. `Cglib` can create a proxy object that extends the original class and implements its methods, invoking the handler object's invoke method in a way similar to how the JDK version does for the interface methods.

These technologies create and load classes into the Java memory during runtime, and they are very deep technical tools. They are advanced topics. I do not say not to play with them while being a novice Java programmer. After all, what can happen? Java is not a loaded gun. It is, however, important that you do not lose interest when you do not understand some of the details or something does not work at first. Or second. Or third... Keep swimming.

AOP implementation in Spring works by generating proxy objects for the target objects, and the handlers invoke the aspects that we define in the Spring configuration. This is the reason you cannot put aspects on `final` classes or on `final` methods. Also, you cannot configure aspects on `private` or `protected` methods. The `protected` methods could be proxied in principle, but this is not a good practice, and thus Spring AOP does not support it. Similarly, you cannot put aspects on classes that are not Spring beans. They are created by the code directly, not through Spring, and have no chance to return a proxy instead of the original object when the object is created. Simply put, if Spring is not asked to create the object, it cannot create a custom one. The last thing we want to do is execute the program and see how the aspects perform. The implementation of our audit logging is extremely simple. We use the standard logging, which is not really sufficient for a real-life application of audit logging. The only special thing we do is that we use a logger identified by the name `AUDIT_LOG` and not by the name of a class. This is a legitimate use of the loggers in most of the logging frameworks. In spite of the fact that we usually use the class to identify the logger, it is absolutely possible to use a string to identify a logger. In the case of our logging, this string will also be printed on the console in the log lines, and it will visually stand out.

Consider the following command:

```
gradle -Dspring.profiles.active=production bootRun
```

If we start the application with the preceding command, start SoapUI for the project, start the mock services, and execute the test, we will see the following log lines that the aspects print on the console:

```
2023-10-07 23:42:07.559  INFO 74643 --- [nio-8080-exec-1]
o.a.c.c.C.[Tomcat].[localhost].[/]       : Initializing Spring
FrameworkServlet 'dispatcherServlet'
2023-10-07 23:42:07.567  INFO 74643 --- [nio-8080-exec-1]
o.s.web.servlet.DispatcherServlet        : FrameworkServlet
'dispatcherServlet': initialization started
2023-10-07 23:42:07.626  INFO 74643 --- [nio-8080-exec-1]
o.s.web.servlet.DispatcherServlet        : FrameworkServlet
'dispatcherServlet': initialization completed in 59 ms
2023-10-07 23:42:07.629  INFO 74643 --- [nio-8080-exec-1]
```

```
p.j.b.e.m.p.auth.AuthFilter              : Partner secret is packt
2023-10-07 23:42:07.655  INFO 74643 --- [nio-8080-exec-1] AUDIT_LOG
: byId query is about to run
2023-10-07 23:42:07.666  INFO 74643 --- [nio-8080-exec-1] AUDIT_LOG
: url is to be created
2023-10-07 23:42:07.691  INFO 74643 --- [nio-8080-exec-1] AUDIT_LOG
: url created was http://localhost:8083/inventory/{id}
2023-10-07 23:42:07.715  INFO 74643 --- [nio-8080-exec-1]
p.j.b.e.m.p.l.RestClientProductLookup    : amount {id: 123, amount: 100}.
2023-10-07 23:42:07.716  INFO 74643 --- [nio-8080-exec-1]
p.j.b.e.m.p.l.RestClientProductLookup    : There items from 123. We are
offering
2023-10-07 23:42:07.716  INFO 74643 --- [nio-8080-exec-1] AUDIT_LOG
: url is to be created
2023-10-07 23:42:07.716  INFO 74643 --- [nio-8080-exec-1] AUDIT_LOG
: url created was http://localhost:8081/product/{id}
2023-10-07 23:42:07.725  INFO 74643 --- [nio-8080-exec-1] AUDIT_LOG
: byId query was executed
```

Summary

In this chapter, we built a simple business application that supports business-to-business transactions. We implemented a REST service in a microservices (almost) architecture using the features that are provided by the de facto standard enterprise framework—Spring. Looking back at this chapter, it is amazing how few lines of code we wrote to achieve all the functionality, and that is good. The less code we need to develop what we want, the better. This proves the power of the framework.

We discussed microservices, HTTP, REST, JSON, and how to use them using the MVC design pattern. We learned how Spring is built up, what modules are there, how dependency injection works in Spring, and we even touched on AOP a bit. This was very important because, along with AOP, we discovered how Spring works using dynamic proxy objects, and this is something that is very valuable when you need to debug Spring or some other framework that uses a similar solution (and there are a few that are frequently used).

We started to test our code using a simple browser, but after that, we realized that REST services are better tested using a professional testing tool, and for that, we used SoapUI and built up a simple REST test suite with REST test steps and mock services.

Having learned all that, nothing will stop us from extending this application using very modern and advanced Java technologies, such as reflection (which we already touched on a bit when we discussed the JDK dynamic proxy), Java streams, lambda expressions, and scripting on the server side.

8

Extending Our E-Commerce Application

In the last chapter, we started developing an e-commerce application and we created the functionality to look up products based on their ID and, also, on the basis of several parameters. In this chapter, we will extend this functionality so that we can also order the products we selected. While doing so, we will learn new technologies, focusing on functional programming in Java and on some other language features, such as reflection and annotation handling during runtime, and a scripting interface.

As we did in the previous chapters, we will develop the application step by step. As we discover the newly learned technologies, we will refactor the code to enroll the new tools and methods to produce more readable and effective code. We will also mimic the development of real-life projects in the sense that, at the start, we will have simple requirements, and later, new requirements will be set as our imagined business develops and sells more and more products. We will become imagined millionaires.

We will use the code base of the previous chapter, and we will develop it further, though, for a new project. We will use Spring, Gradle, Tomcat, and SoapUI, which are not new, as we became acquainted with these in the previous chapter. In this chapter, you will learn about the following topics:

- Annotation processing
- Using reflection
- Functional programming in Java using:
- Lambda expressions
- Streams
- Invoking scripts from Java

The MyBusiness ordering

The ordering process is a little bit more complicated than just looking up products. The order form itself lists products and amounts, and identifies who the customer for that order is. All that we have to do is check that the products are available in our store, and that we can deliver them to the given customer. This is the simplest approach; however, with some products, there are more restrictions. For example, when somebody orders a desk-side lamp, we deliver the power cord separately. The reason for this is that the power cord is specific to the country. We deliver different power cords to the United Kingdom and to Germany. One possible approach could be to identify the country of the customer. But this approach does not take into account the fact that our customers are resellers. All customers could be located in the United Kingdom and, at the same time, they may want to deliver the lamp with the power cable to Germany. To avoid such situations and ambiguity, it would be apt that our customers order the desk-side lamp and the power cord as separate items in the same order. In some cases, we deliver the desk-side lamp without the power cord, but this is a special case. We need a degree of logic to identify these special cases. Therefore, we have to implement logic to see whether there is a power cord for a desk-side lamp and, if there is no automatic handling of the order, it is refused. It does not mean that we will not deliver the product. We will merely put the order in a queue and an operator will have to look at it.

The problem with this approach is that the desk-side lamp is only one product that needs configuration support. The more products we have, the more specialties they may have, and the piece of code that checks the consistency of an order becomes more and more complex until it reaches a level of complexity that is not manageable. When a class or method becomes too complex, the programmers refactor it, splitting up the method or class into smaller pieces. We have to do the same with product checking. We shouldn't try to create one huge class that checks for the product and all the possible order constellations, but rather we should have many smaller checks so that each checks only one small set.

Checking for consistency is simpler in some cases. Checking whether the lamp has a power cord has a complexity any novice programmer can program. We use this example in our code because we want to focus on the actual structure of the code, and not on the complex nature of the check itself. In real life, however, the checks can be fairly complex. Imagine a shop that sells computers. It puts a configuration together: power supply, graphics cards, and motherboard, the appropriate CPU, and the memory. There are many choices, and some of them may not work together. In a real-life situation, we need to check that the motherboard is compatible with the memory selected, that it has as many banks as are in the order, that they are appropriately paired (some memories can only be installed in pairs), that there is a compatible slot for the graphics card, and that the power has enough watts to reliably run the whole configuration. This is very complex and is best not confused with the code that checks whether there is a power cord for a lamp.

Setting up the project

Since we are still using Spring Boot, the build file does not need any modification; we will use the same file as in the last chapter. The package structure, however, is a bit different. This time, we do something more complicated than getting a request and responding to whatever the backend services deliver to us. Now, we have to implement complex business logic that, as we will see, needs many classes. When we have more than 10 classes, give or take, in a certain package, it is time to think about putting them into separate packages. The classes that are related to each other and have a similar functionality should be put into one package. This way, we will have a package for the following:

- The controllers (though we have only one in this example, but usually there are more)
- Data storing beans that have no functionality other than storing data, hence, fields, setters, and getters
- Checkers that will help us check power cords when a desk-side lamp is ordered
- Services that perform different services for the controller
- The main package for our program that contains the `Application` class, `SpringConfiguration`, and several interfaces

Order controller and DTOs

When a request comes to the server to order a bunch of products, it comes in an HTTPS `POST` request. The body of the request is encoded in JSON. Till now, we had controllers that were handling `GET` parameters. Handling `POST` requests are not much more difficult when we can rely on the data marshaling of Spring. The controller code itself is simple:

```
package packt.java11.bulkorder.controllers;

import ...

@RestController
public class OrderController {
    private static final Logger log =
LoggerFactory.getLogger((OrderController.class));
    private final Checker checker;

    public OrderController(@Autowired Checker checker) {
        this.checker = checker;
    }
```

```
        @RequestMapping("/order")
        public Confirmation getProductInformation(@RequestBody Order order) {
            if (checker.isConsistent(order)) {
                return Confirmation.accepted(order);
            } else {
                return Confirmation.refused(order);
            }
        }
    }
```

There is only one request that we handle in this controller`order`. This is mapped to the URL, `/order`. The order is automatically converted from JSON to an order object from the request body. This is what the `@RequestBody` annotation asks Spring to do for us. The functionality of the controller simply checks the consistency of the order. If the order is consistent, then we accept the order; otherwise, we refuse it. The real-life example will also check that the order is not only consistent but also comes from a customer who is eligible for buying those products and that the products are available in the warehouse or, at least, can be delivered, based on the promises and lead time from the producers.

To check the consistency of the order, we need something that does this job for us. As we know that we have to modularize the code and not implement too many things in a single class, we need a checker object. This is provided automatically based on the annotation on the class and also on the constructor of the controller by `@Autowired`.

The `Order` class is a simple bean, simply listing the items:

```
package packt.java11.bulkorder.dtos;

import ...

public class Order {
    private String orderId;
    private List<OrderItem> items;
    private String customerId;


    // ... setters and getters ...
}
```

The name of the package is `dtos`, which stands for the plural of **Data Transfer Object** (**DTO**). DTOs are objects that are used to transfer data between different components, usually over the network. Since the other side can be implemented in any language, the marshaling can be JSON, XML, or some other format that is capable of delivering nothing but data. These classes do not have real methods. DTOs usually have only fields, setters, and getters.

The following is the class that contains one item in an order:

```
package packt.java11.bulkorder.dtos;

public class OrderItem {
    private double amount;
    private String unit;
    private String productId;

    // ... setters and getters ...
}
```

The order confirmation is also in this package, and though this is also a true DTO, it has a few simple auxiliary methods:

```
package packt.java11.bulkorder.dtos;

public class Confirmation {
    private final Order order;
    private final boolean accepted;

    private Confirmation(Order order, boolean accepted) {
        this.order = order;
        this.accepted = accepted;
    }

    public static Confirmation accepted(Order order) {
        return new Confirmation(order, true);
    }

    public static Confirmation refused(Order order) {
        return new Confirmation(order, false);
    }

    public Order getOrder() {
        return order;
    }

    public boolean isAccepted() {
```

```
            return accepted;
        }
    }
```

We provide two factory methods for the class. This is a little violation of the single responsibility principle that purists hate. Most of the time, when the code becomes more complex, such shortcuts bite back, and the code has to be refactored to be cleaner. The purist solution would be to create a separate factory class. Utilization of the factory methods, either from this class or from a separated class, makes the code of the controller more readable.

The major task we have is the consistency check. The code, up to this point, is almost insignificant.

Consistency checker

We have a consistency checker class, and an instance of it is injected into the controller. This class is used to check the consistency, but it does not actually perform the check itself. It only controls the different checkers that we provide and invokes them one by one to do the real work.

We require that a consistency checker, such as the one that checks whether the order contains a power cord when a desk-side lamp is ordered, implements the `ConsistencyChecker` interface:

```
package packt.java11.bulkorder;

import packt.java11.bulkorder.dtos.Order;

public interface ConsistencyChecker {

    boolean isInconsistent(Order order);
}
```

The method `isInconsistent` should return `true` if the order is inconsistent. It returns `false` if it does not know whether the order is inconsistent or not, but, from the aspect that the actual checker examines the order, there is no inconsistency. Having several `ConsistencyChecker` classes, we have to invoke one after the other until one returns `true` or we are out of them. If none of them returns `true`, then we can safely assume, at least from the automated checkers' point of view, that the order is consistent.

We know at the start of the development that we will really have a lot of consistency checkers and not all are relevant for all of the orders. We want to avoid the invocation of each checker for each order. To do so, we implement some filtering. We let products specify what type of checks they need. This is a piece of product information, such as the size or the description. To accommodate this, we need to extend the `ProductInformation` class.

We will create each `ConsistencyChecker` interface, implementing the class to be a Spring bean (annotated with the `@Component` annotation), and, at the same time, we will annotate them with an annotation that specifies what type of checks they implement. At the same time, `ProductInformation` is extended, containing a set of `Annotation` class objects that specify which checkers to invoke. We could simply list the checker classes instead of the annotations, but this gives us some extra freedom in configuring the mapping between the products and the annotations. The annotation specifies the nature of the products, and the checker classes are annotated. The desk-side lamp is the `PoweredDevice` type, and the checker class, `NeedPowercord`, is annotated with the `@PoweredDevice` annotation. If there is any other type of product that also needs a power cord, then the annotation of that type should be added to the `NeedPowercord` class, and our code will work. Since we are starting to diving deep into annotations and annotation handling, we have to first learn what annotations really are. We have already used annotations since, `Chapter 3`, *Optimizing the Sort - Making Code Professional*, but all we knew was how to use them, and that is usually dangerous without understanding what we did.

Annotations

Annotations are used with the `@` character in front of them and can be attached to packages, classes, interfaces, fields, methods, method parameters, generic type declaration and use, and, finally, to annotations. Annotations can be used almost everywhere and they are used to describe some program meta information. For example, the `@RestController` annotation does not directly alter the behavior of the `OrderController` class. The behavior of the class is described by the Java code that is inside it. The annotation helps Spring to understand what the class is and how it can and should be used. When Spring scans all the packages and classes to discover the different Spring beans, it sees the annotation on the class and takes it into account. There can be other annotations on the class that Spring does not understand. They may be used by some other framework or program code. Spring ignores them as any well-behaving framework. For example, as we will see later, in our code base, we have the `NeedPowercord` class, which is a Spring bean and, as such, annotated with the `@Component` annotation. At the same time, it is also annotated with the `@PoweredDevice` annotation. Spring has no idea about what a powered device is. This is something that we define and use. Spring ignores this.

Packages, classes, interfaces, fields, and so on, can have many annotations attached to them. These annotations should simply be written in front of the declaration of the syntactical unit they are attached to.

In the case of packages, the annotation has to be written in front of the package name in the `package-info.java` file. This file can be placed in the directory of the package and can be used to edit the *JavaDoc* for the package and also to add an annotation to the package. This file cannot contain any Java class since the name, `package-info`, is not a valid identifier.

We cannot just write anything in front of anything as an annotation. Annotations should be declared. They are in the runtime of Java special interfaces. The Java file that declares the `@PoweredDevice` annotation, for example, looks like this:

```
package packt.java11.bulkorder.checkers;

import java.lang.annotation.Retention;
import java.lang.annotation.RetentionPolicy;

@Retention(RetentionPolicy.RUNTIME)
public @interface PoweredDevice {
}
```

The `@` character in front of the `interface` keyword shows us that this is a special one—an annotation type. There are some special rules; for example, an annotation interface should not extend any other interface, not even an annotation one. On the other hand, the compiler automatically makes the annotation interface so that it extends the JDK interface, `java.lang.annotation.Annotation`.

Annotations are in the source code and, thus, they are available during the compilation process. They can also be retained by the compiler and put into the generated class files, and when the class loader loads the class file, they may also be available during runtime. The default behavior is that the compiler stores the annotation along with the annotated element in the class file, but the class loader does not keep it available for runtime.

To handle annotations during the compilation process, the Java compiler has to be extended using annotation processors. This is a fairly advanced topic and there are only a few examples you can meet while working with Java. An annotation processor is a Java class that implements a special interface and is invoked by the compiler when it processes an annotation in the source file that the processor is declared to have an interest in.

Annotation retention

Spring and other frameworks usually handle annotations during runtime. The compiler and the class loader have to be instructed that the annotation is to be kept available during runtime. To do so, the annotation interface itself has to be annotated using the `@Retention` annotation. This annotation has one parameter of the `RetentionPolicy` type, which is an `enum`. We will soon discuss how annotation parameters should be defined.

It is interesting to note that the `@Retention` annotation on the annotation interface has to be available in the class file; otherwise, the class loaders would not know how to treat an annotation. How do we signal that an annotation is to be kept by the compiler after the compilation process? We annotate the annotation interface declaration. Thus, the declaration of `@Retention` is annotated by itself and declared to be available at runtime.

The annotation declaration can be annotated using `@Retention(RetentionPolicy.SOURCE)`, `@Retention(RetentionPolicy.CLASS)`, or `@Retention(RetentionPolicy.RUNTIME)`.

Annotation target

The final retention type will be the one that's most frequently used. There are also other annotations that can be used on annotation declarations. The `@Target` annotation can be used to restrict the use of the annotation to certain locations. The argument to this annotation is either a single `java.lang.annotation.ElementType` value or an array of these values. There is good reason to restrict the use of annotations. It is much better to get a compilation time error when we place an annotation in the wrong place than hunting during runtime as to why the framework is ignoring our annotation.

Annotation parameters

Annotations, as we saw previously, can have parameters. To declare these parameters in the `@interface` declaration of the annotation, we use methods. These methods have a name and a return value, but they should not have an argument. You may try to declare some parameters, but the Java compiler will be strict and will not compile your code.

The values can be defined at the place where the annotation is used, using the name of the method and with the = character, assigning to them a value that is compatible with the method type. For example, let's suppose that we modify the declaration of the `PoweredDevice` annotation to the following:

```
public @interface ParameteredPoweredDevice {
    String myParameter();
}
```

In such a case, at the use of the annotation, we should specify a value for the parameter, such as the following:

```
@Component
@ParameteredPoweredDevice(myParameter = "1966")
public class NeedPowercord implements ConsistencyChecker {
...
```

If the name of the parameter is a value and, at the place of use of the annotation, there is no other parameter defined, then the name *value* may be skipped. For example, modifying the code as follows is a handy shorthand when we have only one parameter:

```
public @interface ParameteredPoweredDevice{
    String value();
}
...
@Component
@ParameteredPoweredDevice("1966")
public class NeedPowercord implements ConsistencyChecker {
...
```

We can define optional parameters also using the `default` keyword following the method declaration. In this case, we have to define a default value for the parameter. Modifying the sample annotation we have further, we still can, but need not, specify the value. In the latter case, it will be an empty string:

```
public @interface ParameteredPoweredDevice {
    String value() default "";
}
```

Since the value we specify should be constant and calculable during compile time, there is not much use of complex types. Annotation parameters are usually strings, integers, and, on occasion, doubles, or other primitive types. The exact list of the types given by the language specification is as follows:

- Primitive (`double`, `int`, and so on)
- String
- Class
- An enum
- Another annotation
- An array of any of the aforementioned types

We have seen examples of `String` and also that `enum:Retention` and `Target` both have `enum` parameters. The interesting part we want to focus on is the last two items in the preceding list.

When the value of the parameter is an array, the value can be specified as comma-separated values between the `{` and `}` characters. For example:

```
String[] value();
```

This can then be added to the `@interface` annotation and we can write the following:

```
@ParameteredPoweredDevice({"1966","1967","1991"})
```

However, in case there is only one value we want to pass as the parameter value, we can still use the format:

```
@ParameteredPoweredDevice("1966")
```

In this case, the value of the attribute will be an array of length `1`. When the value of an annotation is an array of annotation types, things get a bit more complex. We create an `@interface` annotation (note the plural in the name):

```
@Retention(RetentionPolicy.RUNTIME)
public @interface PoweredDevices {
ParameteredPoweredDevice[] value() default {};
}
```

The use of this annotation could be as follows:

```
@PoweredDevices(
        {@ParameteredPoweredDevice("1956"),
@ParameteredPoweredDevice({"1968", "2018"})}
)
```

Note that this is not the same as having the `ParameteredPoweredDevice` annotation with three parameters. This is an annotation that has two parameters. Each parameter is an annotation. The first has one string parameter and the second has two.

As you can see, annotations can be fairly complex, and some of the frameworks (or rather the programmers who created them) ran amok using them. Before you start writing a framework, conduct research to see whether there is already a framework that you can use. Also, check whether there is another way to solve your problem. 99% of annotation handling code could be avoided and made simpler. The less code we write for the same functionality, the happier we are. Us programmers are lazy, and this is the way it has to be.

The last example, where the parameter of the annotation is an array of annotations, is important to understand regarding how we can create repeatable annotations.

Repeatable annotations

Annotate the declaration of the annotation with `@Repeatable` to denote that the annotation can be applied multiple times at one place. The parameter to this annotation is an annotation type that should have a parameter of type, which is an array of this annotation. Don't try to understand! I'll give an example instead. I already have, in fact—we have `@PoweredDevices`. It has an argument that is an array of `@ParameteredPoweredDevice`. Consider that we now annotate this `@interface` as the following:

```
...
@Repeatable(PoweredDevices.class)
public @interface ParameteredPoweredDevice {
...
```

Then, we can simplify the use of `@ParameteredPoweredDevice`. We can repeat the annotation multiple times, and the Java runtime will automatically enclose it in the wrapping class, which, in this case, is `@PoweredDevices`. In this case, the following two will be equivalent:

```
...
@ParameteredPoweredDevice("1956")
@ParameteredPoweredDevice({"1968", "2018"})
public class NeedPowercord implements ConsistencyChecker {
...

@PoweredDevices(
```

```
        {@ParameteredPoweredDevice("1956"),
@ParameteredPoweredDevice({"1968", "2018"})}
)
public class NeedPowercord implements ConsistencyChecker {
...
```

The reason for this complex approach is again an example of backward compatibility that Java strictly follows. Annotations were introduced in Java 1.5 and repeatable annotations have been available only since version 1.8. We will soon talk about the reflection API that we use to handle the annotations during runtime. This API in the `java.lang.reflect.AnnotatedElement` interface has a `getAnnotation(annotationClass)` method, which returns an annotation. If a single annotation can appear more than once on a class, method, and so on, then there is no way of calling this method to get all the different instances with all the different parameters. Backward compatibility was ensured by introducing the containing type that wraps the multiple annotations.

Annotation inheritance

Annotations, just like methods or fields, can be inherited between class hierarchies. If an annotation declaration is marked with `@Inherited`, then a class that extends another class with this annotation can inherit it. The annotation can be overridden in case the child class has the annotation. Because there is no multiple inheritance in Java, annotations on interfaces cannot be inherited. Even when the annotation is inherited, the application code that retrieves the annotation of a certain element can distinguish between the annotations that are inherited and those that are declared on the entity itself. There are methods to get the annotations and separate methods to get the declared annotations that are declared on the actual element, and not inherited.

@Documented annotation

The `@Documented` annotation expresses the intent that the annotation is part of the contract of the entity and, this way, it has to get into the documentation. This is an annotation that the *JavaDoc* generator looks at when creating the documentation for an element that references the `@Documented` annotation.

JDK annotations

There are other annotations defined in the JDK in addition to those that are to be used to define annotations. We have already seen some of these. The most frequently used is the `@Override` annotation. When the compiler sees this annotation, it checks that the method really does override an inherited method. Failing to do so will result in an error, saving us from a miserable runtime debugging.

The `@Deprecated` annotation signals in the documentation of a method, class, or some other element that the element is not to be used. It is still there in the code, because some users may still use it, but in the case of a new development that depends on the library containing the element, the newly developed code should not use it. The annotation has two parameters. One parameter is `since`, which can have a string value and may deliver version information about how long or since which version of the method, or class is deprecated. The other parameter is `forRemoval`, which should be `true` if the element will not appear in the future versions of the library. Some methods may be deprecated because there are better alternatives but the developers do not intend to remove the method from the library. In such a case, `forRemoval` can be set to `false`.

The `@SuppressWarning` annotation is also a frequently used one, though its use is questionable. It can be used to suppress some of the warnings of the compiler. It is recommended to write code, if possible, which can be compiled without any warning.

The `@FunctionalInterface` annotation declares that an interface intends to have only one method. Such interfaces can be implemented as lambda expressions. You will learn about lambda expressions later in this chapter. When this annotation is applied on an interface and there is more than one method declared in the interface, the compiler will signal a compilation error. This will prevent any developer early on from adding another method to an interface intended to be used together with functional programming and lambda expressions.

Using reflection

Now that you have learned how to declare annotations and how to attach them to classes and methods, we can return to our `ProductInformation` class. You may recall that we wanted to specify the type of products in this class and that each product type is represented by an `@interface` annotation. We have already listed it in the previous few pages, the one we will implement in our `@PoweredDevice` example. We will develop the code assuming that later, there will be many such annotations, product types, and consistency checkers that are annotated with `@Component` and with one or more of our annotations.

Getting annotations

We will extend the `ProductInformation` class with the following field:

```
private List<Class<? extends Annotation>> check;
```

Since this is a DTO, and Spring needs the setters and getters, we will also add a new getter and setter to it. This field will contain the list of classes that each class implements for one of our annotations and also the built-in JDK interface, `Annotation`, because that is the way the Java compiler generates them. At this point, this may be a bit murky, but I promise that the dawn will break and that there will be light at the end of the tunnel.

To get the product information, we have to look it up according to ID. This is the interface and service that we developed in the last chapter, except that this time, we have another new field. This is, in fact, a significant difference, although the `ProductLookup` interface did not change at all. In the last chapter, we developed two versions. One of the versions was reading the data from a properties file, while the other one was connecting to a REST service.

Properties files are ugly and an old technology, but a must if ever you intend to pass a Java interview or work on enterprise applications developed at the start of the 21st century. I had to include it in the last chapter. It was included in this book at my insistence. At the same time, while coding for this chapter, I did not have the stomach to keep using it. I also wanted to show you that the same content could be managed in a JSON format.

Now, we will extend the implementation of `ResourceBasedProductLookup` to read the product information from JSON formatted resource files. Most of the code remains the same in the class; therefore, we only list the difference here:

```
package packt.java11.bulkorder.services;
import ...

@Service
public class ResourceBasedProductLookup implements ProductLookup {
    private static final Logger log =
        LoggerFactory.getLogger(ResourceBasedProductLookup.class);

    private ProductInformation fromJSON(InputStream jsonStream) throws
IOException {
        final var mapper = new ObjectMapper();
        return mapper.readValue(jsonStream, ProductInformation.class);
    }

// ...
    private void loadProducts() {
        if (productsAreNotLoaded) {
            try {
                final var resources = new
PathMatchingResourcePatternResolver().
                        getResources("classpath:products/*.json");
                for (final var resource : resources) {
                    loadResource(resource);
                }
                productsAreNotLoaded = false;
            } catch (IOException ex) {
                log.error("Test resources can not be read", ex);
            }
        }
    }

    private void loadResource(Resource resource) throws IOException {
        final var dotPos = resource.getFilename().lastIndexOf('.');
        final var id = resource.getFilename().substring(0, dotPos);
        final var pi = fromJSON(resource.getInputStream());
        pi.setId(id);
        products.put(id, pi);
        if( pi.getCheck() != null )
        log.info("Product {} check is {}",id,pi.getCheck().get(0));
    }
// ...
```

In the `project resources/products` directory, we have a few JSON files. One of them contains the desk lamp product information:

```
{
  "id" : "124",
  "title": "Desk Lamp",
  "check": [
    "packt.java11.bulkorder.checkers.PoweredDevice"
  ],
  "description": "this is a lamp that stands on my desk",
  "weight": "600",
  "size": [ "300", "20", "2" ]
}
```

The type of product is specified in a JSON array. In this example, this array has only one element, and that element is the fully qualified name of the annotation interface that represents the type of product. When the JSON marshaller converts the JSON to a Java object, it recognizes that the field that needs this information is a `List`, so it converts the array to a list and, also, the elements from `String` to `Class` objects representing the annotation interface.

Now that we have the resources loaded from JSON formatted resources and we have seen how easy it is to read JSON data when using Spring, we can get back to the order consistency check. The `Checker` class implements the logic to collect the pluggable checkers and to invoke them. It also implements the annotation-based screening so as not to invoke the checkers we don't really need for the actual products in the actual order:

```
package packt.java11.bulkorder.services;


import ...

@Component()
@RequestScope
public class Checker {
    private static final Logger log =
LoggerFactory.getLogger(Checker.class);

    private final Collection<ConsistencyChecker> checkers;
    private final ProductInformationCollector piCollector;
    private final ProductsCheckerCollector pcCollector;


    public Checker(@Autowired Collection<ConsistencyChecker> checkers,
                   @Autowired ProductInformationCollector piCollector,
                   @Autowired ProductsCheckerCollector pcCollector
```

```
    ) {
        this.checkers = checkers;
        this.piCollector = piCollector;
        this.pcCollector = pcCollector;
    }

    public boolean isConsistent(Order order) {
        final var map = piCollector.collectProductInformation(order);
        if (map == null) {
            return false;
        }
        final var annotations = pcCollector.getProductAnnotations(order);
        for (final var checker : checkers) {
            for (final var annotation :
checker.getClass().getAnnotations()) {
                if (annotations.contains(annotation.annotationType())) {
                    if (checker.isInconsistent(order)) {
                        return false;
                    }
                    break;
                }
            }
        }
        return true;
    }
}
```

One of the interesting things to mention is that the Spring autowiring is very clever. We have a field with the `Collection<ConsistencyChecker>` type. Usually, autowiring works if there is exactly one class that has the same type as the resources to wire. In our case, we do not have any such candidate since this is a collection, but we have many `ConsistencyChecker` classes. All our checkers implement this interface and Spring recognizes it, instantiates them all, magically creates a collection of them, and injects the collection into this field.

Usually, a good framework works logically. I was not aware of this feature of Spring, but I thought that this would be logical and, magically, it worked. If things are logical and just work, you do not need to read and remember the documentation. A bit of caution does not do any harm, however. After I realized that this functionality works this way, I looked it up in the documentation to see that this is really a guaranteed feature of Spring and not something that just happens to work, but may change in future versions without notice. Using only guaranteed features is extremely important, but is frequently neglected in our industry.

When the `isConsistent()` method is invoked, it first collects the product information into `HashMap`, assigning a `ProductInformation` instance to each `OrderItem`. This is done in a separate class. After this, `ProductsCheckerCollector` collects the `ConsistencyChecker` instances needed by one or more product items. When we have this set, we need to invoke only those checkers that are annotated with one of the annotations that are in this set. We do that in a loop.

In this code, we use reflection. We loop over the annotations that each checker has. To get the collection of annotations, we invoke `checker.getClass().getAnnotations()`. This invocation returns a collection of objects. Each object is an instance of some JDK runtime generated class that implements the interface we declared as an annotation in its own source file. There is no guarantee, though, that the dynamically created class implements only our `@interface` and not some other interfaces. Therefore, to get the actual annotation class, we have to invoke the `annotationType()` method.

The `ProductCheckerCollector` and `ProductInformationCollector` classes are very simple, and we will discuss them later when we learn about streams. They will serve as a good example at that point, when we implement them using loops and, right after that, using streams.

Having them all, we can finally create our actual checker classes. The one that helps us see that there is a power cord ordered for our lamp is the following:

```
package packt.java11.bulkorder.checkers;

//SNIPPET SKIL TILL "import ..."

import org.slf4j.Logger;
import org.slf4j.LoggerFactory;
import org.springframework.stereotype.Component;
import packt.java11.bulkorder.ConsistencyChecker;
import packt.java11.bulkorder.dtos.Order;

import ...
@Component
@PoweredDevice
public class NeedPowercord implements ConsistencyChecker {
    private static final Logger log =
LoggerFactory.getLogger(NeedPowercord.class);

    @Override
    public boolean isInconsistent(Order order) {
        log.info("checking order {}", order);
        var helper = new CheckHelper(order);
        return !helper.containsOneOf("126", "127", "128");
```

```
        }
    }
```

The helper class contains simple methods that will be needed by many of the checkers, for example:

```
    public boolean containsOneOf(String... ids) {
        for (final var item : order.getItems()) {
            for (final var id : ids) {
                if (item.getProductId().equals(id)) {
                    return true;
                }
            }
        }
        return false;
    }
```

Invoking methods

In this example, we used only a single reflection call to get the annotations attached to a class. Reflection can do many more things. Handling annotations is the most important use of these calls since annotations do not have their own functionality and cannot be handled in any other way during runtime. Reflection, however, does not stop telling us what annotations a class or any other annotation holding element has. Reflection can be used to get a list of the methods of a class, the name of the methods as strings, the implemented interfaces of a class, the parent class it extends, the fields, the types of fields, and so on. Reflection generally provides methods and classes to walk through the actual code structure down to the method level, programmatically.

This walkthrough does not only allow reading types and code structure, but also makes it possible to set field values and call methods without knowing the method's name at compile time. We can even set fields that are `private` and are not generally accessible by the outside world. It should also be noted that accessing the methods and fields through reflection is usually slower than through compiled code because it always involves lookup according to the name of the element in the code.

The rule of thumb is that if you see that you have to create code using reflection, then realize that you are probably creating a framework (or writing a book about Java that details reflection). Does this sound familiar?

Spring also uses reflection to discover the classes, methods, and fields, and also to inject an object. It uses the URL class loader to list all the JAR files and directories that are on the classpath, loads them, and examines the classes.

For a contrived example, for the sake of demonstration, let's assume that the `ConsistencyChecker` implementations were written by many external software vendors, and the architect who originally designed the program structure just forgot to include the `isConsistent()` method in the interface. (At the same time, to preserve our mental health, we can also imagine that this person is no longer working in the company for doing so.) As a consequence, the different vendors delivered Java classes that "implement" this interface, but we cannot invoke the method, not only because we do not have a common parent interface that has this method, but also because the vendors just happened to use different names for their methods.

What can we do in this situation? Business-wise, asking all the vendors to rewrite their checkers is ruled out because them knowing we are in trouble attaches a hefty price tag to the task. Our managers want to avoid that cost and us developers also want to show that we can rectify the situation and perform miracles (I will comment on that later).

We could just have a class that knows every checker and how to invoke each of them in many different ways. This would require us to maintain said class whenever a new checker is introduced to the system, and we want to avoid that. The whole plugin architecture we are using was invented for this very purpose in the first place.

How can we invoke a method on an object that we know has only one declared method, which accepts an order as a parameter? That is where reflection comes into the picture. Instead of calling `checker.isInconsistent(order)`, we implement a small `private` method, `isInconsistent()`, which calls the method, whatever its name is, via reflection:

```
private boolean isInconsistent(ConsistencyChecker checker, Order order) {
    final var methods = checker.getClass().getDeclaredMethods();
    if (methods.length != 1) {
        log.error("The checker {} has zero or more than one methods",
            checker.getClass());
        return false;
    }
    final var method = methods[0];
    final boolean inconsistent;
    try {
        inconsistent = (boolean) method.invoke(checker, order);
    } catch (InvocationTargetException |
        IllegalAccessException |
        ClassCastException e) {
        log.error("Calling the method {} on class {} threw exception",
            method, checker.getClass());
```

```
            log.error("The exception is ", e);
            return false;
        }
        return inconsistent;
    }
```

We can get the class of the object by calling the `getClass()` method and, on the object that represents the class itself, we can call `getDeclaredMethods`. Fortunately, the checker classes are not littered by many methods, so we check that there is only one method declared in the checker class. Note that there is also a `getMethods()` method in the reflection library, but it will always return more than one method. It returns the declared and the inherited methods. Because each and every class inherits from `java.lang.Object`, at least the methods of the `Object` class will be there.

After this, we try to invoke the class using the `Method` object that represents the method in the reflection class. Note that this `Method` object is not directly attached to an instance. We retrieved the method from the class and, hence, when we invoke it, we should pass the object it should work on as a first parameter. This way, `x.y(z)` becomes `method.invoke(x,z)`. The last parameter of `invoke()` is a variable number of arguments that are passed as an `Object` array. In most cases, when we invoke a method, we know the arguments in our code, even if we do not know the name of the method and have to use reflection. When even the arguments are not known, but are available as a matter of calculation, then we have to pass them as an `Object` array.

Invoking a method via reflection is a risky call. If we try to call a method the normal way, which is `private`, then the compiler will signal an error. If the number of arguments or types are not appropriate, the compiler will again give us an error. If the returned value is not `boolean`, or there is no return value at all, then we again get a compiler error. In the case of reflection, the compiler is clueless. It does not know what method we will invoke when the code is executing. The `invoke()` method, on the other hand, can, and will, notice all these failures when it is invoked. If any of the aforementioned problems occur, then we will get exceptions. If the `invoke()` method itself sees that it cannot perform what we ask of it, then it will throw `InvocationTargetException` or `IllegalAccessException`. If the conversion from the actual return value to `boolean` is not possible, then we will get `ClassCastException`.

Regarding performing magic, it is a natural urge that we feel like making something extraordinary, something outstanding. This is okay when we are experimenting with something, doing something for fun, but it is definitely not okay when we are working on a professional job. Average programmers, who do not understand your brilliant solution, will maintain the code in an enterprise environment. They will turn your nicely combed code into haystack while fixing some bugs or implementing some minor new features. Even if you are the Mozart of programming, they will be, at best, no-name singers. A brilliant code in an enterprise environment can be a requiem, with all the implications that metaphor entails.

Last but not least, the sad reality is that we are usually not the Mozarts of programming.

Note that in case the return value of the original value is primitive, then it will be converted to an object by reflection, and then we will convert it back to the primitive value. If the method does not have a return value, in other words, if it is `void`, then the reflection will return a `java.lang.Void` object. The `Void` object is only a placeholder. We cannot convert it to any primitive value or any other type of object. It is needed because Java is strict and `invoke` has to return an `Object`, so the runtime needs something that it can return. All we can do is check that the returned value class is really `Void`.

Let's continue with our story and our solution. We submitted the code, and it works in production for a while until a new update from a software vendor breaks it. We debug the code in the test environment and see that the class now contains more than one method. Our documentation clearly states that they should only have one `public` method, and they provided a code that has...hmm...we realize that the other methods are `private`. They are right; they can have `private` methods according to the contract, so we have to amend the code. We replace the lines that look up the one and only method:

```
final var methods = checker.getClass().getDeclaredMethods();
if (methods.length != 1) {
...
}
final var method = methods[0];
```

The new code will be as follows:

```
final var method = getSingleDeclaredPublicMethod(checker);
if (method == null) {
    log.error(
            "The checker {} has zero or more than one methods",
            checker.getClass());
    return false;

}
```

The new method that we write to look up the one and only `public` method is as follows:

```
private Method getSingleDeclaredPublicMethod(
    ConsistencyChecker checker) {
    final var methods = checker.getClass().getDeclaredMethods();
    Method singleMethod = null;
    for (final var method : methods) {
        if (Modifier.isPublic(method.getModifiers())) {
            if (singleMethod != null) {
                return null;
            }
            singleMethod = method;
        }
    }
    return singleMethod;
}
```

To check whether the method is `public` or not, we use a `static` method from the `Modifier` class. There are methods to check all possible modifiers. The value that the `getModifiers()` method returns is an `int` bit field. Different bits have different modifiers, and there are constants that define these. Bits that can only be used for other types of reflection objects will never be set.

There is one exception, which is `volatile`. This bit is reused to signal bridge methods. Bridge methods are created by the compiler automatically and can have deep and complex issues that we do not discuss in this book. The reuse of the same bit does not cause confusion because a field can be `volatile`, but, as a field, it cannot be a bridge method. Obviously, a field is a field and not a method. In the same way, a method cannot be a `volatile` field. The general rule is as follows: do not use methods on reflection objects where they do not have a meaning; or else, know what you are doing.

Making the storyline even more intricate, a new version of a checker accidentally implements the checking method as a `private` package. The programmer simply forgot to use the `public` keyword. For the sake of simplicity, let's assume that the classes declare only one method again, but it is not public. How do we solve this problem using reflection?

Obviously, the simplest solution is to ask the vendors to fix the problem—it is their fault. In some cases, however, we must create a workaround over some problems. There is another solution—creating a class with a `public` method in the same package, invoking the `private` package methods from the other class, thus relaying the other class. As a matter of fact, this solution, as a workaround for such a bug, seems to be more logical and cleaner, but this time, we want to use reflection.

To avoid `java.lang.IllegalAccessException`, we have to set the `method` object as accessible. To do so, we have to insert the following line in front of the invocation:

```
method.setAccessible(true);
```

Note that this will not change the method to `public`. It will only make the method accessible for invocation through the very instance of the `method` object that we set as accessible.

I have seen code that checks whether a method is accessible by calling the `isAccessible()` method and saves this information; it sets the method as accessible if it was not accessible and restores the original accessibility after the invocation. This is totally useless. As soon as the `method` variable goes out of scope, and there is no reference to the object we set the accessibility flag to, the effect of the setting wears off. Also, there is no penalty for setting the accessibility of a `public` or an otherwise callable method.

Setting fields

We can also call `setAccessible` on `Field` objects, and then we can even set the value of private fields using reflection. Without further fake stories, just for the sake of this example, let's make a `ConsistencyChecker` named `SettableChecker`:

```
@Component
@PoweredDevice
public class SettableChecker implements ConsistencyChecker {
    private static final Logger log =
LoggerFactory.getLogger(SettableChecker.class);

    private boolean setValue = false;

    public boolean isInconsistent(Order order) {
        return setValue;
    }
}
```

This checker will return `false`, unless we set the field to `true` using reflection. We do set it as such. We create a method in the `Checker` class and invoke it from the checking process for each checker:

```
private void setValueInChecker(ConsistencyChecker checker) {
    Field[] fields = checker.getClass().getDeclaredFields();
    for( final Field field : fields ){
        if( field.getName().equals("setValue") &&
            field.getType().equals(boolean.class)){
```

```
                field.setAccessible(true);
                try {
                    log.info("Setting field to true");
                    field.set(checker,true);
                } catch (IllegalAccessException e) {
                    log.error("SNAFU",e);
                }
            }
        }
    }
```

The method goes through all the declared fields and, if the name is `setValue` and the type is `boolean`, then it sets it to `true`. This will essentially render all orders that contain a powered device as rejected.

Note that although `boolean` is a built-in language primitive, which is not a class by any means, it still has a class so that reflection can compare the type of the field against the class that `boolean` artificially has. Now, `boolean.class` is a class literal in the language and, for each primitive, a similar constant can be used. The compiler identifies these as class literals and creates the appropriate pseudo class references in the bytecode so that primitives can also be checked in this way, as demonstrated in the sample code of the `setValueInChecker()` method.

We checked that the field has the appropriate type, and we also called the `setAccessible()` method on the field. Even though the compiler does not know that we really did everything to avoid `IllegalAccessException`, it still believes that calling `set` on `field` can throw such an exception, as it is declared. However, we know that it should not happen (famous last words of a programmer?). To handle this situation, we surround the method call with a `try` block and, in the `catch` branch, we log the exception.

Functional programming in Java

Since we have created a lot of code in our example for this chapter, we will look at the functional programming features of Java, which will help us to delete many lines from our code. The less code we have, the easier it is to maintain the application; thus, programmers love functional programming. But this is not the only reason why functional programming is so popular. It is also an excellent way to describe certain algorithms in a more readable and less error-prone manner than conventional loops.

Functional programming is not a new thing. The mathematical background behind it was developed in the 1930s. One of the first (if not the first) functional programming languages was LISP. It was developed in the 1950s and is still in use, so much so that there is a version of the language implemented on the JVM (Clojure).

Functional programming, in short, means that we express the program structure in terms of functions. In this meaning, we should think of functions as in mathematics and not as the term is used in programming languages, such as C. In Java, we have methods, and when we are following the functional programming paradigm, we create and use methods that behave like mathematical functions. A method is functional if it gives the same result no matter how many times we invoke it, just as *sin(0)* is always zero. Functional programming avoids changing the state of objects, and because the state is not changing, the results are always the same. This also eases debugging.

If a function has once returned a certain value for the given arguments, it will always return the same value. We can also read the code as a declaration of the calculation more than as commands that are executed one after the other. If the execution order is not important, then the readability of the code may also increase.

Java helps functional programming style with lambda expressions and streams. Note that these streams are not I/O streams and do not really have any relation to those.

We will first take a short look at lambda expressions and what streams are, and then, we will convert some parts of our program to use these programming constructs. We will also see how much more readable these codes become.

Readability is a debatable topic. A code may be readable to one developer and may be less readable to another. It very much depends on what they got used to. From my experience, I know that developers frequently get distracted by streams. When developers first meet streams, the way to think about them and how they look is just strange. But this is the same as starting to learn to ride a bicycle. While you are still learning how to ride, and you fall off more than you actually move forward, it is definitely slower than walking. On the other hand, once you have learned how to ride...

Lambda

We have already used lambda expressions in `Chapter 3`, *Optimizing the Sort - Making Code Professional,* when we wrote the exception-throwing test. In that code, we set the comparator to a special value that was throwing `RuntimeException` at each invocation:

```
sort.setComparator((String a, String b) -> {
        throw new RuntimeException();
    });
```

The argument type is `Comparator`; therefore, what we have to set there should be an instance of a class that implements the `java.util.Comparator` interface. That interface defines only one method that implementations have to define—`compare`. Thus, we can define it as a lambda expression. Without lambda, if we need an instance, we have to type a lot. We have to create a class, name it, declare the `compare()` method in it, and write the body of the method, as shown in the following code segment:

```
public class ExceptionThrowingComparator implements Comparator {
  public int compare(T o1, T o2){
    throw new RuntimeException();
  }
}
```

Where it is used, we should instantiate the class and pass it as an argument:

```
sort.setComparator(new ExceptionThrowingComparator());
```

We may save a few characters if we define the class as an anonymous class, but the overhead is still there. What we really need is the body of the one and single method that we have to define. This is where lambda comes into the picture.

We can use a lambda expression in any place where we would otherwise need an instance of a class that only has one method. The methods that are defined and inherited from `Object` do not count, and we also do not care about the methods that are defined as `default` methods in the interface. They are there. Lambda defines the one that is not yet defined. In other words, lambda clearly depicts, with much less overhead as an anonymous class, that the value is a functionality, and we pass that as a parameter.

The simple form of a lambda expression is as follows:

```
parameters -> body
```

The parameters can be enclosed between parentheses or, if there is only one, then it can stand without. The body similarly can be enclosed between the `{` and `}` characters, or it can be a simple expression. This way, a lambda expression can reduce the overhead to a minimum, using the parentheses only where they are really needed.

It is also an extremely useful feature of lambda expressions that we do not need to specify the types of the parameters in case it is obvious from the context where we use the expression. Thus, the preceding code segment can even be shorter, as follows:

```
sort.setComparator((a, b) -> {
    throw new RuntimeException();
});
```

Or, we can write the following:

```
sort.setComparator((var a, var b) -> {
    throw new RuntimeException();
});
```

The parameters, `a` and `b`, will have the type as needed. To make it even simpler, we can also omit the `(` and `)` characters around the parameters in case there is only one.

The parentheses are not optional if there is more than one parameter. This is to avoid ambiguity in some situations. For example, the method call `f(x,y->x+y)` could have been a method with two arguments—`x`, and a lambda expression that has one parameter, `y`. At the same time, it could also be a method call with a lambda expression that has two parameters, `x` and `y`. When there are multiple arguments and the type of the argument can be calculated by the compiler, the `var` keyword can be used since the Java 11 release.

Lambda expressions are very handy when we want to pass functionality as an argument. The declaration of the type of argument at the place of the method declaration should be a functional interface type. These interfaces can optionally be annotated using `@FunctionalInterface`. The Java runtime has many such interfaces defined in the `java.util.function` package. We will discuss some of them in the next section, along with their use in streams. For the rest, the standard Java documentation is available from Oracle.

Streams

Streams were also new in Java 8, just like lambda expressions. They work together very strongly, so their appearance at the same time is not a surprise. Lambda expressions, as well as streams, support the functional programming style.

The very first thing to clarify is that streams do not have anything to do with input and output streams, except the name. They are totally different things. Streams are more like collections with some significant differences. (If there were no differences, they would just have been collections.) Streams are essentially pipelines of operations that can run sequentially or in parallel. They obtain their data from collections or other sources, including data that is manufactured on-the-fly.

Streams support the execution of the same calculation on multiple data. This structure is referred to as **Single Instruction Multiple Data** (**SIMD**). Don't be afraid of the expression. This is a very simple thing. We have already done that many times in this book. Loops are also a kind of SIMD structure. When we loop through the checker classes to see whether any of those oppose the order, we perform the same instruction for each and every checker. Multiple checkers mean multiple data.

One problem with loops is that we define the order of execution when it is not needed. In the case of checkers, we do not really care what order the checkers are executed in. All we care about is that all are okay with the order. We still specify some order when we program the loop. This comes from the nature of loops, and there is no way we could change that. That is how they work. However, it would be nice if we could just, somehow, say *"do this and that for each and every checker"*. This is where streams come into play.

Another point is that code that uses loops is more imperative rather than descriptive. When we read the program of a loop construct, we focus on the individual steps. We first see what the commands in the loop do. These commands work on the individual elements of the data and not on the whole collection or array.

When we then put the individual steps together in our brain, we realize what the big picture is, what the loop is for. In the case of streams, the description of operations is a level higher. Once we learn the stream methods, it is easier to read them. Stream methods work on the whole stream and not on the individual elements, and thus are more descriptive.

`java.lang.Stream` is an interface. An object with a type implementing this interface represents many objects and provides methods that can be used to perform instructions on these objects. The objects may or may not be available when we start the operation on one of them, or may just be created when needed. This is up to the actual implementation of the `Stream` interface. For example, suppose we generate a stream that contains `int` values using the following code:

```
IntStream.iterate( 0, (s) -> s+1 )
```

In the preceding code snippet, all the elements cannot be generated because the stream contains an infinite number of elements. This example will return the numbers 0, 1, 2, and so on until further stream operations, which are not listed here, terminate the calculation.

When we program `Stream`, we usually create a stream from a `Collection`—not always, but frequently. The `Collection` interface was extended in Java 8 to provide the `stream` and `parallelStream()` methods. Both of them return stream objects that represent the elements of the collection. While `stream` returns the elements in the same order as they are in the collection in case there is a natural order, the `parallelStream` creates a stream that may be worked on in a parallel manner. In this case, if some of the methods that we use on the stream are implemented in that way, the code can use the multiple processors available in the computer.

As soon as we have a stream, we can use the methods that the `Stream` interface defines. The one to start with is `forEach()`. This method has one argument, which is usually provided as a lambda expression, and will execute the lambda expression for each element of the stream.

In the `Checker` class, we have the `isConsistent()` method. In this method, there is a loop that goes through the annotations of the checker class. If we wanted to log the interfaces that the annotation in the loop implements, we could add the following:

```
for (ConsistencyChecker checker :checkers) {
  for (Annotation annotation : checker.getClass().getAnnotations()) {
    Arrays.stream(annotation.getClass().getInterfaces()).forEach(
      t ->log.info("annotation implemented interfaces {}",t));
...
```

In this example, we create a stream from an array using the factory method from the `Arrays` class. The array contains the interfaces returned by the reflection method, `getInterfaces()`. The lambda expression has only one parameter; thus, we do not need to use parentheses around it. The body of the expression is a method call that returns no value; thus, we also omit the `{` and `}` characters.

Why all this hassle? What is the gain? Why couldn't we just write a simple loop that logs the elements of the array? The gains are readability and maintainability. When we create a program, we have to focus on *what* the program should do and not on *how* it should do it. In an ideal world, a specification would just be executable. We may actually get there in the future when programming work will be replaced by artificial intelligence. (Not the programmers, though.) We are not there, yet. We have to tell the computers how to do what we want to achieve. We used to have to enter binary codes on the console of PDP-11 to get machine code deployed into the memory to have it executed. Later, we had assemblers; later still, we had FORTRAN and other high-level programming languages that have replaced much of the programming work as it was 40 years ago. All these developments in programming shift the direction from *how* toward *what*. Today, we program in Java 11, and the road still has miles to go. The more we can express what to do, instead of how to do it, the shorter and more understandable our programs will be. It will contain the essence and not some artificial litter that is needed by the machines to just do what we want. When I see a loop in a code I have to maintain, I assume that there is some importance of the order in which the loop is executed. There may be no importance at all. It may be obvious after a few seconds. It may need minutes or more to realize that the ordering is not important. This time is wasted and can be saved with programming constructs that better express the *what to do* part, instead of the *how to do part*.

Functional interfaces

The argument to the method should be `java.util.function.Consumer`. This is an interface that requires the `accept()` method to be defined, and this method is `void`. The lambda expression or a class that implements this interface will *consume* the argument of the `accept()` method and does not produce anything.

There are several other interfaces defined in that package, each serving as a functional interface used to describe some method arguments that can be given as lambda expressions in the actual parameters.

For example, the opposite of `Consumer` is `Supplier`. This interface has a method named `get()` that does not need any argument, but that gives some `Object` as a return value.

If there is an argument and also a returned value, the interface is called `Function`. If the returned value has to be the same type as the argument, then the `UnaryOperator` interface is our friend. Similarly, there is a `BinaryOperator` interface, which returns an object of the same type as the arguments. Just as we got from `Function` to `UnaryOperator`, we can see that in the other direction, there is also `BiFunction` in case the arguments and the return values do not share the type.

These interfaces are not defined independently of each other. If a method requires `Function` and we have `UnaryOperator` to pass, it should not be a problem. `UnaryOperator` is essentially the same as `Function`, with the same type of arguments. A method that can work with `Function`, which accepts an object and returns an object, should not have a problem if they have the same type. Those can be, but need not be, different. To let that happen, the `UnaryOperator` interface extends `Function` and thus can be used in place of `Function`.

The interfaces in this class that we have met so far are defined using generics. Because generic types cannot be primitives, the interfaces that operate on primitive values should be defined separately. `Predicate`, for example, is an interface that defines `booleantest(T t)`. It is a function that returns a `boolean` value and is often used in stream methods.

There are also interfaces, such as `BooleanSupplier`, `DoubleConsumer`, `DoubleToIntFunction`, and more, that work with primitive `boolean`, `double`, and `int`. The number of possible combinations of the different argument types and return values is infinite... almost.

Fun fact: To be very precise, it is not infinite. A method can have at most 254 arguments. This limit is specified in the JVM and not in the Java language specification. Of course, one is useless without the other. There are 8 primitive types (plus `Object`, plus the possibility that there are less than 254 arguments), which means that the total number of possible functional interfaces is 10^{254}, give or take a few magnitudes. Almost infinite!

We should not expect to have all the possible interfaces defined in the JDK in this package. These are only those interfaces that are the most useful. There is no interface, for example, that uses `short` or `char`. If we need anything like that, then we can define the `interface` in our code. Or just think hard and find out how to use an already defined one. (I have never used the `short` type during my professional carrier. It was never needed.)

How are these functional interfaces used in streams? The `Stream` interface defines the methods that have some functional interface types as arguments. For example, the `allMatch()` method has a `Predicate` argument and returns a `Boolean` value, which is `true` if all the elements in the stream match `Predicate`. In other words, this method returns `true` if, and only if, `Predicate`, supplied as an argument, returns `true` for each and every element of the stream.

In the following code, we will rewrite some of the methods that we implemented in our sample code using loops to use streams, and, through these examples, we will discuss the most important methods that streams provide. We saved up two classes, `ProductsCheckerCollector` and `ProductInformationCollector`, to demonstrate the stream usage. We can start with these. `ProductsCheckerCollector` goes through all the products that are contained in the `Order` and collects the annotations that are listed in the products. Each product may contain zero, one, or many annotations. These are available in a list. The same annotation may be referenced multiple times. To avoid duplicates, we use `HashSet`, which will contain only one instance of the elements, even if there are multiple instances in the products:

```
public class ProductsCheckerCollector {
    private static final Logger log =
            LoggerFactory.getLogger(ProductsCheckerCollector.class);

    private final ProductInformationCollector pic;

    public ProductsCheckerCollector
            (@Autowired ProductInformationCollector pic) {
        this.pic = pic;
    }

    public Set<Class<? extends Annotation>> getProductAnnotations(Order
order) {
        var piMap = pic.collectProductInformation(order);
        final var annotations = new HashSet<Class<? extends Annotation>>();
        for (var item : order.getItems()) {
            final var pi = piMap.get(item);
            if (pi != null && pi.getCheck() != null) {
                for (final var check : pi.getCheck()) {
                    annotations.addAll(pi.getCheck());
                }
            }
        }
        return annotations;
    }
```

Now, let's see how this method looks when we recode it using streams:

```
public Set<Class<? extends Annotation>> getProductAnnotations(Order order)
{
    var piMap = pic.collectProductInformation(order);
    return order.getItems().stream()
            .map(piMap::get)
            .filter(Objects::nonNull)
            .peek(pi -> {
                if (pi.getCheck() == null) {
                    log.info("Product {} has no annotation", pi.getId());
                }
            })
            .filter(ProductInformation::hasCheck)
            .peek(pi -> log.info("Product {} is annotated with class {}",
pi.getId(), pi.getCheck()))
            .flatMap(pi -> pi.getCheck().stream())
            .collect(Collectors.toSet());
}
```

The major work of the method goes into a single, though huge, stream expression. We will cover the elements of the expression in the coming pages.

`List` returned by `order.getItems` is converted calling the `stream()` method:

```
return order.getItems().stream()
```

As we have already mentioned it briefly, the `stream()` method is part of the `Collection` interface. Any class that implements the `Collection` interface will have this method, even those that were implemented before streams were introduced in Java 8. This is because the `stream()` method is implemented in the interface as a `default` method. This way, if we happen to implement a class implementing this interface, even if we do not need streams, we get it for free as an extra.

The `default` methods in Java 8 were introduced to support backward compatibility of interfaces. Some of the interfaces of the JDK were to be modified to support lambda and functional programming. One example is the `stream()` method. With the pre-Java 8 feature set, the classes implementing some of the modified interfaces should have been modified. They would have been required to implement the new method. Such a change is not backward compatible, and Java as a language and JDK was paying keen attention to be backward compatible. Thus, `default` methods were introduced. These let a developer extend an interface and still keep it backward compatible, providing a default implementation for the methods, which are new. Contrary to this philosophy, brand new functional interfaces of Java 8 JDK also have `default` methods, though, having no prior version in the JDK, they have nothing to be compatible with. In Java 9, interfaces were also extended and now they can contain not only `default` and `static` methods, but also `private` methods. This way, interfaces became kind of equivalent to abstract classes, though there are no fields in an interface except constant `static` fields. This interface functionality extension is a much-criticized feature, which just poses the programming style and structural issues that other languages allowing multiple class inheritance face. Java was avoiding this until the appearance of Java 8 and Java 9.
What is the takeaway from this? Be careful with `default` methods and also with `private` methods in interfaces. Use them wisely, if at all.

The elements of this stream are `OrderItem` objects. We need `ProductInformation` for each `OrderItem`.

Method references

It is lucky that we have `Map`, which pairs order items with product information, so we can invoke `get()` on `Map`:

```
.map(piMap::get)
```

The map() method is again something that has the same name as something else in Java, and should not be confused. While the Map class is a data structure, the map() method in the Stream interface performs mapping of the stream elements. The argument of the method is a Function (recall that this is a functional interface that we recently discussed). This function converts a value, T, which is available as the element of the original stream (Stream<T>), to a value, R, and the return value of the map() method is Stream<R>. The map() method converts Stream<T> to Stream<R> using the given Function<T,R>, calling it for each element of the original stream and creating a new stream from the converted elements.

We can say that the Map interface maps keys to values in a data structure in a static way, and the stream method, map(), maps one type of value to another (or the same) type of values dynamically.

We have already seen that we can provide an instance of a functional interface in the form of a lambda expression. This argument is not a lambda expression. This is a method reference. It says that the map() method should invoke the get() method on Map piMap using the actual stream element as an argument. We are lucky that get() also needs one argument, aren't we? We could also write it as follows:

```
.map( orderItem ->piMap.get(orderItem))
```

However, this would have been exactly the same as piMap::get.

This way, we can reference an instance method that works on a certain instance. In our example, the instance is the one referenced by the piMap variable. It is also possible to reference static methods. In this case, the name of the class should be written in front of the :: characters. We will soon see an example of this when we use the static method, nonNull, from the Objects class (note that the class name is in plural form, and it is in the java.util package and not java.lang).

It is also possible to reference an instance method without giving the reference on which it should be invoked. This can be used in places where the functional interface method has an extra first parameter, which will be used as the instance. We have already used this in Chapter 3, *Optimizing the Sort - Making Code Professional*, when we passed String::compareTo, when the expected argument was a Comparator. The compareTo() method expects one argument, but the compare() method in the Comparator interface needs two. In such a situation, the first argument will be used as the instance on which compare() has to be invoked, and the second argument is passed to compare(). In this case, String::compareTo is the same as writing the lambda expression (String a, String b) -> a.compareTo(b).

Last but not least, we can use method references to constructors. When we need a `Supplier` of (let's keep it simple) `Object`, we can write `Object::new`.

The next step is to filter out the `null` elements from the stream. Note that, at this point, the stream has `ProductInformation` elements:

```
.filter(Objects::nonNull)
```

The `filter()` method uses `Predicate` and creates a stream that contains only the elements that match the predicate. In this case, we used the reference to a `static` method. The `filter()` method does not change the type of stream. It only filters out the elements.

The next method we apply is a bit anti-functional. Pure functional stream methods do not alter the state of an object. They create new objects that they return but, other than that, there is no side effect. `peek()` itself is no different because it only returns a stream of the same elements as the one it is applied on. However, this *no-operation* feature lures the novice programmer to do something non-functional and write code with side effects. After all, why use it if there is no (side) effect in calling it?

```
.peek(pi -> {
    if (pi.getCheck() == null) {
        log.info("Product {} has no annotation", pi.getId());
    }
})
```

While the `peek()` method itself does not have any side effects, the execution of the lambda expression may have. However, this is also true for any of the other methods. It is just the fact that, in this case, it is more tempting to do something inadequate. Don't. We are disciplined adults. As the name of the method suggests, we may peek into the stream but we are not supposed to do anything else. With programming being a particular activity, in this case, peeking is adequate. And that is what we actually do in our code: we log something.

After this, we get rid of the elements that have no `ProductInformation`; we want to get rid of the elements that have it as well, but there is no checker defined:

```
.filter(pi -> pi.getCheck() != null)
```

In this case, we cannot use method references. Instead, we use a lambda expression. As an alternative solution, we may create a `boolean hasCheck()` method in `ProductInformation`, which returns `true` if the `private` field check is not `null`. This would then read as follows:

```
.filter(ProductInformation::hasCheck)
```

This is totally valid and works, although the class does not implement any functional interface and has many methods, not only this one. However, the method reference is explicit and specifies which method to invoke.

After this second filter, we log the elements again:

```
.peek(pi -> log.info(
     "Product {} is annotated with class {}", pi.getId(),
                                              pi.getCheck()))
```

The next method is `flatMap`, and this is something special and not easy to comprehend. At least for me, it was a bit more difficult than understanding `map()` and `filter()` when I learned functional programming:

```
.flatMap(pi ->pi.getCheck().stream())
```

This method expects that the lambda, method reference, or whatever is passed to it as an argument, to create a whole new stream of objects for each element of the original stream the method is invoked on. The result is, however, not a stream of streams, which also could be possible, but rather the returned streams are concatenated into one huge stream.

If the stream we apply it to is a stream of integer numbers, such as 1, 2, 3, ..., and the function for each number *n* returns a stream of three elements, *n*, *n+1*, and *n+2*, then the resulting stream, `flatMap()`, produces a stream containing 1, 2, 3, 2, 3, 4, 3, 4, 5, 4, 5, 6, and so on.

Finally, the stream we have should be collected to a `Set`. This is done by calling the `collector()` method:

```
.collect(Collectors.toSet());
```

The argument to the `collector()` method is (again, an overused expression) `Collector`. It can be used to collect the elements of the stream into a collection. Note that `Collector` is *not* a functional interface. You cannot just collect something using a lambda or a simple method. To collect the elements, we definitely need some place where the elements are collected as the ever-newer elements come from the stream. The `Collector` interface is not simple. Fortunately, the `java.util.streams.Collectors` class (again, note the plural) has a lot of `static` methods that create and return `Object` fields, which, in turn, create and return `Collector` objects.

One of these is `toSet()`, which returns a `Collector` that helps collect the elements of the stream into a `Set`. The `collect()` method will return the `Set` when all the elements are there. There are other methods that help collect the stream elements by summing up the elements, calculating the average, or to a `List`, `Collection`, or to a `Map`. Collecting elements to a `Map` is a special thing, since each element of a `Map` is actually a key-value pair. We will see the example of that when we look at `ProductInformationCollector`.

The `ProductInformationCollector` class code contains the `collectProductInformation()` method, which we will use from the `Checker` class as well as from the `ProductsCheckerCollector` class:

```
private Map<OrderItem, ProductInformation> map = null;

public Map<OrderItem, ProductInformation> collectProductInformation(Order
order) {
    if (map == null) {
        log.info("Collecting product information");
        map = new HashMap<>();
        for (OrderItem item : order.getItems()) {
            final ProductInformation pi = lookup.byId(item.getProductId());
            if (!pi.isValid()) {
                map = null;
                return null;
            }
            map.put(item, pi);
        }
    }
    return map;
}
```

The simple trick is to store the collected value in `Map`, and if that is not `null`, then just return the already calculated value, which may save a lot of service calls in case this method is called more than once handling the same HTTP request.

There are two ways of coding such a structure. One is by checking the non-nullity of the `Map` and returning if the `Map` is already there. This pattern is widely used and has a name. This is called guarding *if*. In this case, there is more than one return statement in the method, which may be seen as a weakness or anti-pattern. On the other hand, the tabulation of the method is one tab shallower. It is a matter of taste and, in case you find yourself in the middle of a debate about one or the other solution, just do yourself a favor and let your peer win on this topic and save your stamina for more important issues, for example, whether you should use streams or just plain old loops.

Now, let's see how we can convert this solution into a functional style:

```
public Map<OrderItem, ProductInformation> collectProductInformation(Order
order) {
    if (map == null) {
        log.info("Collecting product information");
        map =
        order.getItems()
                .stream()
                .map(item -> tuple(item, item.getProductId()))
                .map(t -> tuple(t.r, lookup.byId((String) t.s)))
                .filter(t -> ((ProductInformation)t.s).isValid())
                .collect(Collectors.toMap(t -> (OrderItem)t.r, t ->
(ProductInformation)t.s));
        if (map.keySet().size() != order.getItems().size()) {
            log.error("Some of the products in the order do " +
                    "not have product information, {} != {} ",
                map.keySet().size(),order.getItems().size());
            map = null;
        }
    }
    return map;
}
```

We use a helper class, `Tuple`, which is nothing but two `Object` instances named `r` and `s`. We will list the code for this class later. It is very simple.

In the streams expression, we first create the stream from the collection, and then we map the `OrderItem` elements to a stream of `OrderItem` and `productId` tuples. Then, we map these tuples to tuples that now contain `OrderItem` and `ProductInformation`. These two mappings could be done in a single mapping call, which would perform the two steps in one. I decided to create the two to have simpler steps in each line in the vain hope that the resulting code will be easier to comprehend.

The filter step is also nothing new. It just filters out invalid product information elements. There should actually be none. It happens if the order contains an order ID to a non-existent product. This is checked in the next statement when we look at the number of collected product information elements to see that all the items have proper information.

The interesting code is how we collect the elements of the stream into a `Map`. To do so, we again use the `collect()` method and also the `Collectors` class. This time, the `toMap()` method creates the `Collector`. This needs two `Function` resulting expressions. The first one should convert the elements of the stream to the key and the second should result in the value to be used in the `Map`. Because the actual type of the key and the value is calculated from the result of the passed lambda expressions, we explicitly have to cast the fields of the tuple to the types required.

Finally, the simple `Tuple` class is as follows:

```
public class Tuple<R, S> {
    final public R r;
    final public S s;

    private Tuple(R r, S s) {
        this.r = r;
        this.s = s;
    }

    public static <R, S> Tuple tuple(R r, S s) {
        return new Tuple<>(r, s);
    }
}
```

There are still some classes in our code that deserve to be converted to functional style. These are the `Checker` and `CheckerHelper` classes.

In the `Checker` class, we can rewrite the `isConsistent()` method:

```
public boolean isConsistent(Order order) {
    var map = piCollector.collectProductInformation(order);
    if (map == null) {
        return false;
    }
    final var as = pcCollector.getProductAnnotations(order);
    return !checkers.stream().anyMatch(
            c -> Arrays.stream(c.getClass().getAnnotations()
            ).filter(a -> as.contains(a.annotationType())
            ).anyMatch(x -> c.isInconsistent(order)
            ));
}
```

Since you have already learned most of the important stream methods, there is hardly any new issues here. We can mention the `anyMatch()` method, which will return `true` if there is at least one element so that the `Predicate` parameter passed to `anyMatch()` is `true`. It may also need some accommodation so that we could use a stream inside another stream. It very well may be an example when a stream expression is overly complicated and needs to split up into smaller pieces using local variables.

Finally, before we leave the functional style, we rewrite the `containsOneOf()` method in the `CheckHelper` class. This contains no new elements and will help you check what you have learned about `map()`, `filter()`, `flatMap()`, and `Collector`. Note that this method, as we discussed, returns `true` if `order` contains at least one of the order IDs given as strings:

```
public boolean containsOneOf(String... ids) {
    return order.getItems().parallelStream()
        .map(OrderItem::getProductId)
        .flatMap(itemId -> Arrays.stream(ids)
            .map(id -> tuple(itemId, id)))
        .filter(t -> Objects.equals(t.s, t.r))
        .collect(Collectors.counting()) > 0;
}
```

We create the stream of the `OrderItem` objects, and then we map it to a stream of the IDs of the products contained in the stream. Then, we create another stream for each of the IDs with the elements of the ID and one of the string IDs given as the argument. Then, we flatten these substreams into one stream. This stream will contain `order.getItems().size()` times `ids.length` elements: all possible pairs. We will filter out those pairs that contain the same ID twice, and finally, we will count the number of elements in the stream.

Scripting in Java

We are almost ready with our sample program for this chapter. There is one issue, though it is not professional. When we have a new product that needs a new checker, we have to create a new release of the code.

Programs in professional environments have releases. When the code is modified, bugs are fixed, or a new function is implemented, there are numerous steps that the organization requires before the application can go into production. These steps comprise the release process. Some environments have lightweight release processes; others require rigorous and expensive checks. This is not down to the preferences of the people in the organization, however. When the cost of a non-working production code is low and it does not matter whether there is an outage or incorrect functioning in the program, then the release process can be simple. This way, releases get out faster and cheaper. An example may be a chat program that is used for fun by the users. In such a situation, it may be more important to release new fancy features instead of ensuring bug-free working. At the other end of the spectrum, if you create code that controls an atomic power plant, the cost of failure can be pretty high. Serious testing and careful checking of all the features, even after the smallest change, can pay off.

In our example, simple checkers may be an area that is not likely to induce serious bugs. It is not impossible, but the code is so simple...Yes, I know that such an argument is a bit fishy, but let's assume that these small routines could be changed with less testing and in an easier way than the other parts of the code. How can the code for these little scripts be separated, then, so that they do not require a technical release, a new version of the application, and not even a restarting of the application? We have a new product that needs a new check and we want to have some way of injecting this check into the application environment without any service disruption.

The solution we choose is scripting. Java programs can execute scripts written in *JavaScript*, *Groovy*, *Jython* (which is the *JVM* version of the language *Python*), and many other languages. Except for *JavaScript*, the language interpreters of these languages are not a part of the JDK, but they all provide a standard interface, which is defined in the JDK. The consequence is that we can implement script execution in our code and the developers, who provide the scripts, are free to choose any of the available languages; we do not need to care about executing a *JavaScript* code. We will use the same API as to execute *Groovy* or *Jython*. The only thing we should know is what language the script is in. This is usually simple—we can guess that from the file extension, and, if guessing is not enough, we can demand that the script developers put *JavaScript* into files with the `.js` extension, *Jython* into files with `.jy` or `.py`, *Groovy* into files with `.groovy`, and so on. It is also important to note that if we want our program to execute one of these languages, we should make sure that the interpreter is on the classpath. In the case of *JavaScript*, this is a given; therefore, by way of a demonstration in this chapter, we will write our scripts in *JavaScript*. There will not be a lot; this is, after all, a Java book and not a *JavaScript* book.

Scripting is usually a good choice when we want to pass the ability of programmatically configuring or extending our application. This is our case now.

The first thing we have to do is extend the production information. In case there is a script that checks the consistency of an order that a product is in, we need a field where we can specify the name of the script:

```
private String checkScript;

public String getCheckScript() {
    return checkScript;
}

public void setCheckScript(String checkScript) {
    this.checkScript = checkScript;
}
```

We do not want to specify more than one script per product; therefore, we do not need a list of script names. We have only one script specified by the name.

To be honest, the data structure for the checker classes and the annotations, allowing multiple annotations per product and also per checker class, was too complicated. However, we could not avoid having a sufficiently complex structure that could demonstrate the power and capability of stream expressions. Now that we are over that subject, we can go on using simpler data structures, focusing on script execution.

We also have to modify the `Checker` class to not only use the checker classes, but also the scripts. We cannot throw away the checker classes because, by the time we realize that we need better scripts for the purpose, we already have a lot of checker classes and we have no financing to rewrite them to be scripts. Well yes, we are in a book and not in real life, but in an enterprise, that would be the case. That is why you should be very careful while designing solutions for a business. The structures and the solutions will be there for a long time and it is not easy to throw a piece of code out just because it is technically not the best. If it works and is already there, the business will be extremely reluctant to spend money on code maintenance and refactoring.

In summary—we modify the `Checker` class. We need a new class that can execute our scripts; thus, we have to insert a new `final` field, as follows:

```
private final CheckerScriptExecutor executor;
```

We also have to modify the constructor by adding a new argument to initialize the `final` field.

We also have to use this `executor` in the `isConsistent()` method:

```
public boolean isConsistent(Order order) {
    final var map = piCollector.collectProductInformation(order);
    if (map == null) {
        return false;
    }
    final var annotations = pcCollector.getProductAnnotations(order);
    var needAnntn = (Predicate<Annotation>) an ->
            annotations.contains(an.annotationType());
    var consistent = (Predicate<ConsistencyChecker>) c ->
            Arrays.stream(c.getClass().getAnnotations())
                    .parallel()
                    .unordered()
                    .filter(needAnntn)
                    .anyMatch(x -> c.isInconsistent(order));
    final var checkersOK = !checkers.stream().anyMatch(consistent);
    final var scriptsOK = !map.values().parallelStream().
            map(ProductInformation::getCheckScript).
            filter(Objects::nonNull).
            anyMatch(s -> executor.notConsistent(s, order));
    return checkersOK && scriptsOK;
}
```

Note that in this code, we use parallel streams because, why not? Whenever it is possible, we can use parallel streams, even unordered, to tell the underlying system, and also the programmer fellows maintaining the code, that the order is not important.

We also modify one of our product JSON files to reference a script instead of a checker class through some annotation:

```
{
  "id" : "124",
  "title": "Desk Lamp",
  "checkScript" : "powered_device",
  "description": "this is a lamp that stands on my desk",
  "weight": "600",
  "size": [ "300", "20", "2" ]
}
```

Even JSON is simpler. Note that, as we decided to use JavaScript, we do not need to specify the filename extension when we name the script.

We may later consider further development where we will allow the product checker script maintainers to use different scripting languages. In such a case, we may still require that they specify the extension and, in case there is no extension, it will be added by our program as `.js`. In our current solution, we do not check that, but we may devote a few seconds to thinking about it in order to be sure that the solution can be developed further. It is important that we do not develop extra code for the sake of further development. Developers are not fortune tellers and cannot tell reliably what the future needs will be. That is the task of business people.

We put the script into the `resource` directory of our project under the `scripts` directory. The name of the file has to be `powered_device.js` because this is the name we specified in the JSON file:

```
function isInconsistent(order){
    isConsistent = false
    items = order.getItems()
    for( i in items ){
    item = items[i]
    print( item )
        if( item.getProductId() == "126" ||
            item.getProductId() == "127" ||
            item.getProductId() == "128"  ){
            isConsistent = true
            }
    }
    return ! isConsistent
}
```

This is an extremely simple JavaScript program. As a side note, when you iterate over a list or an array in JavaScript, the loop variable will iterate over the indexes of the collection or the array. Since I rarely program in JavaScript, I fell into this trap and it took me more than half an hour to debug the error I made.

We have prepared everything we need to call the script. We still have to invoke it. To do so, we use the JDK scripting API. First, we need a `ScriptEngineManager`. This manager is used to get access to the JavaScript engine. Although the JavaScript interpreter has been a part of the JDK since Java 7, it is still managed in an abstract way. It is one of the many possible interpreters that a Java program can use to execute a script. It just happens to be there in the JDK, so we do not need to add the interpreter JAR to the classpath. `ScriptEngineManager` discovers all the interpreters that are on the classpath and registers them.

It does so using the service provider specification, which has been a part of the JDK for a long time, and, by Java 9, it also got extra support in module handling. This requires the script interpreters to implement the `ScriptEngineFactory` interface and also to list the class that does it in the `META-INF/services/javax.script.ScriptEngineFactory` file. These files, from all the JAR files that are part of the classpath, are read as resources by `ScriptEngineManager`, and, through this, it knows which classes implement script interpreters. The `ScriptEngineFactory` interface requires that the interpreters provide methods such as `getNames()`, `getExtensions()`, and `getMimeTypes()`. The manager calls these methods to collect the information about the interpreters. When we ask a JavaScript interpreter, the manager will return the one created by the factory that said that one of its names is `JavaScript`.

To get access to the interpreters through the name, the filename extension or mime-type is just one of the functions of `ScriptEngineManager`. The other one is to manage `Bindings`.

When we execute a script from within the Java code, we don't do it because we want to increase our dopamine levels. In the case of scripts, it does not happen. We want some results. We want to pass parameters and, following the execution of the script, we want values back from the script that we can use in the Java code. This can happen in two ways. One is by passing parameters to a method or function implemented in the script and getting the return value from the script. This usually works, but it may even happen that some scripting language does not even have the notion of the function or method. In such a case, it is not a possibility. What is possible is to pass an environment to the script and read values from the environment after the script is executed. This environment is represented by `Bindings`.

`Bindings` is a map that has `String` keys and `Object` values.

In the case of most scripting languages, for example, in JavaScript, `Bindings` is connected to global variables in the script we execute. In other words, if we execute the following command in our Java program before invoking the script, then the JavaScript global variable, `globalVariable`, will reference the `myObject` object:

```
myBindings.put("globalVariable",myObject)
```

We can create `Bindings` and pass it to `ScriptEngineManager`, but it is just as well that we can use the one that it creates automatically, and can call the `put()` method on the engine object directly.

There are two `Bindings` when we execute scripts. One is set on the `ScriptEngineManager` level. This is named global binding. There is also one managed by `ScriptEngine` itself. This is the local `Bindings`. From the script point of view, there is no difference. From the point of view of embedding, there is a degree of difference. In case we use the same `ScriptEngineManager` to create multiple `ScriptEngine` instances, then the global bindings are shared by them. If one gets a value, all of them see the same value; if one sets a value, all the others will later see that changed value. The local binding is specific to the engine it is managed by. Since we only introduce Java scripting API in this book, we do not go into more detail and will not use `Bindings`. We are good with invoking a JavaScript function and obtaining a result from it.

The class that implements the script invocation is `CheckerScriptExecutor`. It starts with the following lines:

```
package packt.java11.bulkorder.services;
import ...

@Component
public class CheckerScriptExecutor {
    private static final Logger log =
            LoggerFactory.getLogger(CheckerScriptExecutor.class);

    private final ScriptEngineManager manager = new ScriptEngineManager();

    public boolean notConsistent(String script, Order order) {

        try {
            final var scriptReader = getScriptReader(script);
            final var result = evalScript(script, order, scriptReader);
            assertResultIsBoolean(script, result);
            log.info("Script {} was executed and returned {}", script,
result);
            return (boolean) result;

        } catch (Exception wasAlreadyHandled) {
            return true;
        }
    }
```

The only `public` method, `notConsistent()`, gets the name of the script to execute and also `order`. The latter has to be passed to the script. First, it gets `Reader`, which can read the script text, evaluate it, and finally return the result in case it is `boolean` or can at least be converted to `boolean`. If any of the methods invoked from here that we implemented in this class are erroneous, it will throw an exception, but only after appropriately logging it. In such cases, the safe way is to refuse an order.

Actually, this is something that the business should decide. If there is a check script that cannot be executed, it is clearly an erroneous situation. In this case, accepting an order and later handling the problems manually has certain costs. Refusing an order or confirmation because of some internal bug is also not a happy path for the order process. We have to check which approach causes the least damage to the company. It is certainly not the duty of the programmer. Our situation is an easy situation.

We assume that the business representatives said that the order in such a situation should be refused. In real life, similar decisions are refused by the business representatives, saying that it just should not happen and that the IT department has to ensure that the program and the whole operation is totally bug-free. There is a psychological reason for such a response, but this really takes us extremely far away from Java programming.

Engines can execute a script passed through `Reader` or as `String`. Because now we have the script code in a resource file, it seems to be a better idea to let the engine read the resource instead of reading it to a `String`:

```
private Reader getScriptReader(String script) throws IOException {
    final Reader scriptReader;
    try (final var scriptIS = new ClassPathResource(
            "scripts/" + script + ".js").getInputStream()) {
        scriptReader = new InputStreamReader(scriptIS);
    } catch (IOException ioe) {
        log.error("The script {} is not readable", script);
        log.error("Script opening exception", ioe);
        throw ioe;
    }
    return scriptReader;
}
```

To read the script from a resource file, we use the Spring `ClassPathResource` class. The name of the script is prepended with the `scripts` directory and appended by the `.js` extension. The rest is fairly standard and nothing we have not seen in this book. The next method that evaluates the script is more interesting:

```
private Object evalScript(String script, Order order, Reader scriptReader)
        throws ScriptException, NoSuchMethodException {
    final Object result;
    final var engine = manager.getEngineByName("JavaScript");
    try {
        engine.eval(scriptReader);
        final var inv = (Invocable) engine;
        result = inv.invokeFunction("isInconsistent", order);
    } catch (ScriptException | NoSuchMethodException se) {
        log.error("The script {} thruw up", script);
        log.error("Script executing exception", se);
```

```
            throw se;
        }
        return result;
    }
```

To execute the method in the script, first of all, we need a script engine that is capable of handling JavaScript. We get the engine from the manager by its name. If it is not JavaScript, we should check that the returned `engine` is not `null`. In the case of JavaScript, the interpreter is part of the JDK, and checking that the JDK conforms to the standard would be paranoid.

If ever we want to extend this class to handle not only JavaScript, but also other types of scripts, this check has to be done, and also the script engine should probably be requested from the manager according to the filename extension, which we do not have access to in this `private` method. But that is a development for the future and is not part of this book.

When we have the engine, we have to evaluate the script. This will define the function in the script so that we can invoke it afterwards. To invoke it, we need some `Invocable` object. In the case of JavaScript, the engine also implements an `Invocable` interface. Not all script engines implement this interface. Some scripts do not have functions or methods, and there is nothing to invoke in them. Again, this is something to do later, when we want to allow not only JavaScript scripting but also other types of scripting.

To invoke the function, we pass its name to the `invokeFunction()` method and also the arguments that we want to pass on. In this case, this is the `order`. In the case of JavaScript, the integration between the two languages is fairly developed. As in our example, we can access the field and the methods of the Java objects that are passed as arguments and the returned JavaScript `true` or `false` value is also magically converted to `Boolean`. There are some situations when access is not that simple though:

```
    private void assertResultIsBoolean(String script, Object result) {
        if (!(result instanceof Boolean)) {
            log.error("The script {} returned non boolean", script);
            if (result == null) {
                log.error("returned value is null");
            } else {
                log.error("returned type is {}", result.getClass());
            }
            throw new IllegalArgumentException();
        }
    }
```

The final method of the class checks that the returned value, which can be anything since this is a script engine, can be converted into a `boolean`.

It is important to note that the fact that some of the functionality is implemented in a script does not guarantee that the application works seamlessly. There may be several issues, and scripts may affect the inner workings of the entire application. Some scripting engines provide special ways of protecting the application from bad scripts, while others do not. The fact that we do not pass, but give orders to, the script does not guarantee that a script cannot access other objects. Using reflection, `static` methods, and other techniques, there are ways of accessing just about anything inside our Java program. We may be a bit easier with the testing cycle when only a script changes in our code base, but it does not mean that we should blindly trust any script.

In our example, it would probably be a very bad idea to let the producers of the products upload scripts to our system. They may provide their check scripts, but these scripts have to be reviewed from the security point of view before being deployed into the system. If this is done properly, then scripting is an extremely powerful extension to the Java ecosystem, giving great flexibility to our programs.

Summary

In this chapter, we have developed the ordering system of our enterprise application. Along with the development of the code, we encountered many new things. You learned about annotations and how they can be handled by reflections. Although not strongly related, you learned how to use lambda expressions and streams to express several programming constructs simpler than conventional loops. In the last part of this chapter, we extended the application using scripting by invoking JavaScript functions from Java, and also by invoking Java methods from JavaScript.

In fact, with all of this knowledge, we matured to a Java level that is needed for enterprise programming. The rest of the topics this book covers are for the aces. But you want to be one, don't you? This is why I wrote the remaining chapters. Read on!

9

Building an Accounting Application Using Reactive Programming

In this chapter, we will develop a sample program that does the inventory management part of the company we created the order handling code for. Do not expect a fully developed, ready-to-use, professional application. Also, do not expect that we will get into the details of accounting and bookkeeping. That is not our aim. We will focus more on the programming technique in question—**reactive programming**. Sorry, pals; I know that bookkeeping and accounting are fun, but this is not the book for those topics.

Reactive programming is an old (well, what is old in computer science?) approach that has come recently to Java. Java 9 was the first release that supports some of the aspects of reactive programming in the standard JDK. To sum it up in one sentence, reactive programming is about focusing more on how the data flows and less on how the implementation handles the data flow. As you may recall, this is also a step toward describing *what we want to do* from the description of *how to do it*.

After going through this chapter, you will understand what reactive programming is and what tools there are in Java that you can utilize. You will also understand what reactive programming is good for and when and how you can utilize this principle in the future, as there will be more and more frameworks supporting reactive programming in Java. In this chapter, you will learn about the following topics:

- Reactive programming in general
- Reactive streams in Java
- How to implement our sample code in a reactive way

Reactive... what?

There is reactive programming, reactive systems, and reactive streams. These are three different things that are related to one another. It is not without reason that all three are called *reactive*.

Reactive programming is a programming paradigm similar to object-oriented programming and functional programming. A **reactive system** is a system design that sets certain aims and technological constraints on how certain types of information systems should be designed to be reactive. There are a lot of resemblances to reactive programming principles in this. A **reactive stream** is a set of interface definitions that help to achieve a similar coding advantage to reactive systems, which can be used to create reactive systems. Reactive stream interfaces are part of JDK 9. They are available in Java and in other languages.

We will look at these in separate sections; at the end of these sections, you should have a better understanding of why each of them is called *reactive*.

Reactive programming in a nutshell

Reactive programming is a paradigm that focuses more on where the data flows during computation than on how to compute the result. The problem is best described as several computations that depend on the output of one another, but if several may be executed independently of the other, reactive programming may come into the picture. As a simple example, we can have the following computation that calculates the value of `h` from some given `b`, `c`, `e`, and `f` values, using `f1`, `f2`, `f3`, `f4`, and `f5` as simple computational steps:

```
a = f1(b,c)
d = f2(e,f)
k = f3(e,c)
g = f4(b,f,k)
h = f5(d,a,g)
```

If we write these in Java in a conventional way, the methods `f1` to `f5` will be invoked one after the other. If we have multiple processors and we are able to make the execution parallel, we may also perform some of the methods parallel. This, of course, assumes that these methods are purely computational methods and do not change the state of the environment, and, in this way, they can be executed independently of one another. For example, `f1`, `f2`, and `f3` can be executed independently of one another. The execution of the `f4` function depends on the output of `f3`, and the execution of `f5` depends on the output of `f1`, `f2`, and `f4`.

If we have two processors, we can execute `f1` and `f2` together, followed by the execution of `f3`, then `f4`, and, finally, `f5`. These are the four steps. If we look at the preceding calculation not as commands but rather as expressions and how the calculations depend on one another, then we do not dictate the actual execution order, and the environment may decide to calculate `f1` and `f3` together, then `f2` and `f4`, and, finally `f5`, saving one step. This way, we can concentrate on the data flow and let the reactive environment act upon it without putting in extra constraints:

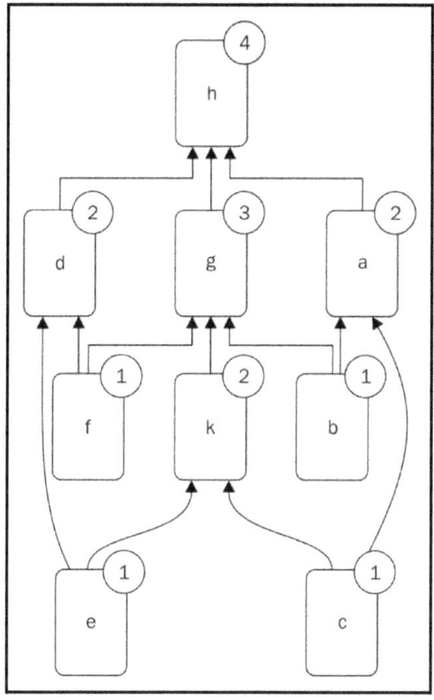

This is a very simple approach of reactive programming. The description of the calculation in the form of expressions gives the data flow, but in the explanation, we still assumed that the calculation is executed synchronously. If the calculations are executed on different processors located on different machines connected to a network, then the calculation may not and does not need to be synchronous. Reactive programs can be asynchronously executed if the environment is asynchronous. It may happen that the different calculations, `f1` to `f4`, are implemented and deployed on different machines. In such a case, the values calculated are sent from one to the other over the network, and the nodes execute the calculation every time there is a change in the inputs. This is very similar to good old analog computers that were created using simple building blocks, and the calculations were done using analog signals.

The program was implemented as an electronic circuit, and when the input voltage or current (usually voltage) changed in the inputs, the analog circuits followed it at light speed, and the result appeared in the output. In such a case, the signal propagation was limited by the speed of light on the wires and analog circuitry speed in the wired modules, which was extremely fast and may beat digital computers.

When we talk about digital computers, the propagation of the *signal* is digital, and this way, it needs to be sent from one calculation node to the other one, be it some object in JVM or some program on the network. A node has to execute its calculation if either of the following apply:

- Some of the values in the input have changed
- The output of the calculation is needed

If the input has not changed, then the result should eventually be the same as the last time; thus, the calculation does not need to be executed again—it would be a waste of resources. If the result of the calculation is not needed, then there is no need to perform the calculation, even if the result would not be the same as the last one. No one cares.

To accommodate this, reactive environments implement two approaches to propagate the values. The nodes may pull the values from the output of other modules. This will ensure that no calculation that is not needed will be executed. The modules may push their output to the next module that depends on them. This approach will ensure that only changed values ignite calculation. Some of the environments may implement a hybrid solution.

When values change in the system, the change is propagated toward the other nodes that again propagate the changes to another node, and so on. If we imagine the calculation dependencies as a directed graph, then the changes travel towards the transitive closure of the changed values along the nodes connected. The data may travel with all the values from one node output to the other node input, or only the change may travel. The second approach is more complex because it needs the changed data and also meta information that describes what has changed. On the other hand, the gain may be significant when the output and input set of data is huge, and only a small portion of it is changed. It may also be important to calculate and propagate only the actual delta of the change when there is a high probability that some of the nodes do not change the output for many of the different inputs. In such a case, the change propagation may stop at the node where there is no real change in spite of the changed input values. This can save up a lot of calculation in some of the networks.

In the configuration of the data propagation, the directed acyclic graph can be expressed in the code of the program; it can be configured, or it can even be set up and changed during the execution of the code dynamically. When the program code contains the structure of the graph, the routes and the dependencies are fairly static. To change the data propagation, the code of the program has to be changed, recompiled, and deployed. If there are multiple network node programs, this may even need multiple deployments that should be carefully furnished to avoid different incompatible versions running on different nodes. There should be similar considerations when the graph is described in some configuration. In such a case, the compilation of the program(s) may not be needed when only the wiring of the graph is changed, but the burden to have compatible configuration on different nodes in the case of a network execution is still there.

Letting the graph change dynamically also does not solve this problem. The setup and the structure are more flexible and, at the same time, more complex. The data propagated along the edges of the graph may contain not only computational data but also data that drives changes in the graph. Many times, this leads to a very flexible model called **higher-order reactive programming**.

Reactive programming has a lot of benefits, but, at the same time, it may be very complex, sometimes too complex, for simple problems. It is to be considered when the problem to be solved can easily be described using data graph and simple data propagations. We can separate the description of the problem and the order of the execution of the different blocks. This is the same consideration that we discussed in the previous chapter. We describe more about the *what to do* part and less about the *how to do* part.

On the other hand, when the reactive system decides the order of execution, what is changed, and how that should be reflected on the output of other blocks, it should do so without knowing the core of the problem that it is solving. In some situations, coding the execution order manually based on the original problem could perform better.

> This is similar to the memory management issue. In modern runtime environments, such as the JVM, Python runtime, Swift programming, or even Golang, there is some automated memory management. When programming in C, the programmer has full control over memory allocation and memory release. In the case of real-time applications, where the performance and response time is of the utmost importance, there is no way to let an automated garbage collector take time and delay the execution from time to time. In such a case, the C code can be optimized to allocate memory when needed; there is a resource for the allocation and release of memory when possible, and there is time to manage memory. These programs are better performing than the ones created for the same purpose using a garbage collector. Still, we do not use C in most of the applications because we can afford the extra resources needed for automated memory collection. Even though it would be possible to write a faster code by managing the memory manually, automated code is faster than what an average programmer would have created using C, and also the frequency of programming errors is much lower.

Just as there are some issues that we have to pay attention to when using automated memory management, we have to pay attention to some issues in a reactive environment, which would not exist in the case of manual coding. Still, we use the reactive approach for its benefits.

The most important issue is to avoid loops in the dependency graph. Although it is absolutely perfect to write the definition of calculations, a reactive system would probably not be able to cope with these definitions. Some reactive systems may resolve in some simple-case cyclic redundancy, but that is an extra feature, and we generally just have to avoid that. Consider the following computations:

```
a = b + 3
b = 4 / a
```

Here, `a` depends on `b`, so when `b` changes, `a` is calculated. However, `b` also depends on `a`, which is recalculated, and, in this way, the system gets into an infinite loop. The preceding example seems to be simple, but that is the feature of a good example. Real-life problems are not simple, and in a distributed environment, it is extremely hard sometimes to find cyclic redundancy.

Another problem is called a **glitch**. Consider the following definition:

```
a = b + 3
q = b + a
```

When the parameter `b` is changed, for example, from `3` to `6`, the value of `a` will change from `6` to `9`, and, thus, `q` will change from `9` to `15`. This is very simple. However, the execution order based on the recognition of the changes may first alter the value of `q` from `9` to `12` before modifying it to `15` in the second step. This can happen if the calculating node responsible for the calculation of `q` recognizes the change in `b` before the value of `a` as a consequence of the change in the value of `b`. For a short period of time, the value of `q` will be `12`, which does not match the previous one and also does not match the changed state. This value is only a glitch in the system that happens after an input changes and also disappears without any further change in the input in the system:

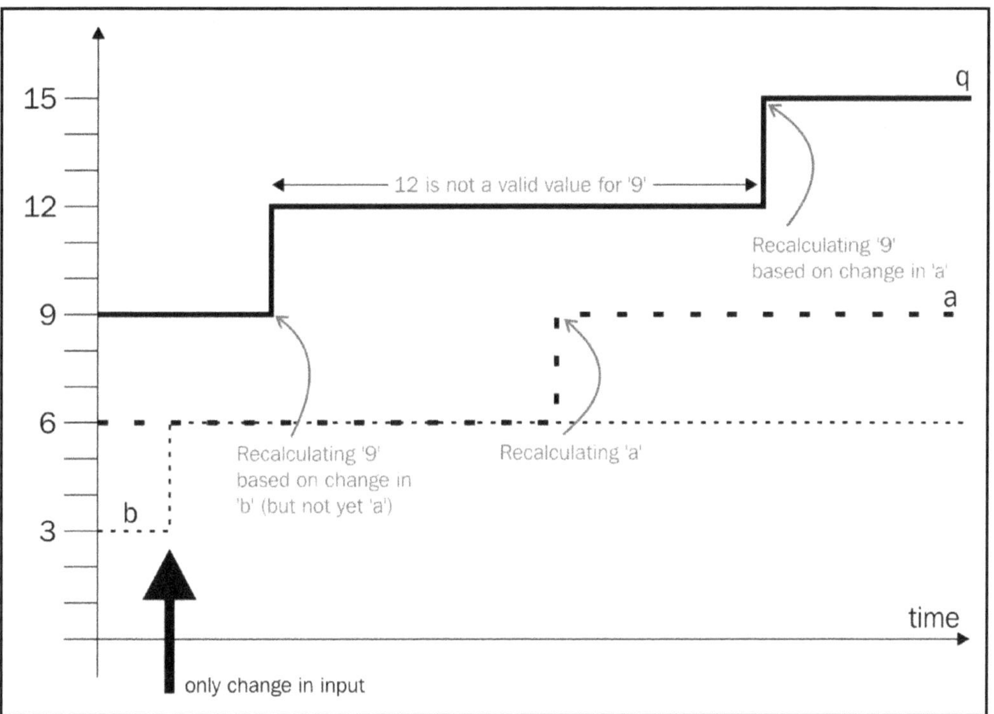

If you have ever learned the design of logical circuits, then **static hazards** may ring a bell. They are exactly the same phenomenon.

Reactive programming also assumes that the calculations are stateless. The individual nodes that perform the calculation may have a state in practice and, in most cases, they do. It is not inherently evil to have a state in some calculation. However, debugging something that has a state is significantly more complex than debugging something that is stateless, and functional.

It is also an important aid to the reactive environment, letting it perform different optimizations based on the fact that the calculations are functional. If the nodes have a state, then the calculations may not be rearranged freely because the outcome may depend on the actual evaluation order. These systems may not really be *reactive*, or, at least, this may be debated.

Reactive systems

A **reactive system** is defined in the reactive manifesto at `http://www.reactivemanifesto.org/`. The creators of the manifesto realized that, with the change of technology, new system patterns will need to be developed in enterprise computing to leverage the new technology and yield better outcomes. The manifesto envisions systems are as follows:

- Responsive
- Resilient
- Elastic
- Message-driven

The first three features are user values; the last one is more of a technological approach to get the values.

Responsive

A system is *responsive* if it gives results in a reliable manner. If you talk to me, I will answer your question or, at least, tell you that I do not know the answer or that I was not able to understand the question. Yes, it would be better to get the answer, but if a system cannot give that to you, it is still expected to give something back. If you have past experience with client-operating systems from just ten years ago, and some old computers, you can understand this. Getting a rotating hourglass is frustrating. You just do not know whether the system is working to get you the answer or whether it is totally frozen.

A reactive system has to be responsive. The response should come in a timely manner. The actual timing depends on the actual system. It may be milliseconds, seconds, or even hours if the system is running on a spaceship traveling toward the other side of Jupiter. The important thing is that the system should guarantee some *soft* upper limit for the response time. This does not necessarily mean that the system should be a real-time solution, which is a much stricter requirement.

The advantage of responsiveness is not only that the user does not become nervous in front of the computer. After all, most of these services are used by other services that mainly communicate with one another. The real advantage is that error discovery is more reliable. If a reactive system element becomes non-responsive, it is certainly an error condition, and something should be done about it, outside the scope of normal operations (replace a faulty communication card, restart a system, and so on). The sooner we can identify an error state, the cheaper it is to fix it. The more we can identify where the problem is, the less time and money we could spend localizing the error. Responsiveness is not about speed; it is about better operation and better quality.

Resilient

Resilient systems keep working, even when there is an error. Well, not any error. That would be a miracle, or simply nonsense! An error generally is an error. If armageddon comes and it is the end of the world as we know it, even resilient systems will not be responsive. For smaller disruptions, however, there may be some cure to make the systems resilient.

There are techniques that may help if only a disk fails, there is a power outage, or there is a programming error. Systems may be replicated, so when one of the instances stops responding, some other instance may take up the task of the failing one and can go on working. Systems prone to errors may be isolated from one another in terms of space or time. When there is an earthquake or flood at one location, the other location may still go on working. If different components do not need to communicate in real-time and messages are stored and forwarded in a reliable manner, then this is not a problem, even if the two systems are never available at the same time. They can still cooperate by taking up the messages, performing the task they are supposed to, and sending out the resulting message afterward.

Errors in the system have to be addressed, even if the system remains responsive. Errors do not affect the responsiveness of a resilient system, but the level of resilience decreases and should be restored.

Elastic

Elasticity means that the system is adapting to the load. We can have a huge system, with lots of processors capable of serving the largest anticipated demand, but this is not elasticity because the demand is not constant and, most of the time, is smaller than the maximum, so the resources of such a system are idle. This wastes time, CPU cycle, and energy, and thus creates an ecological footprint:

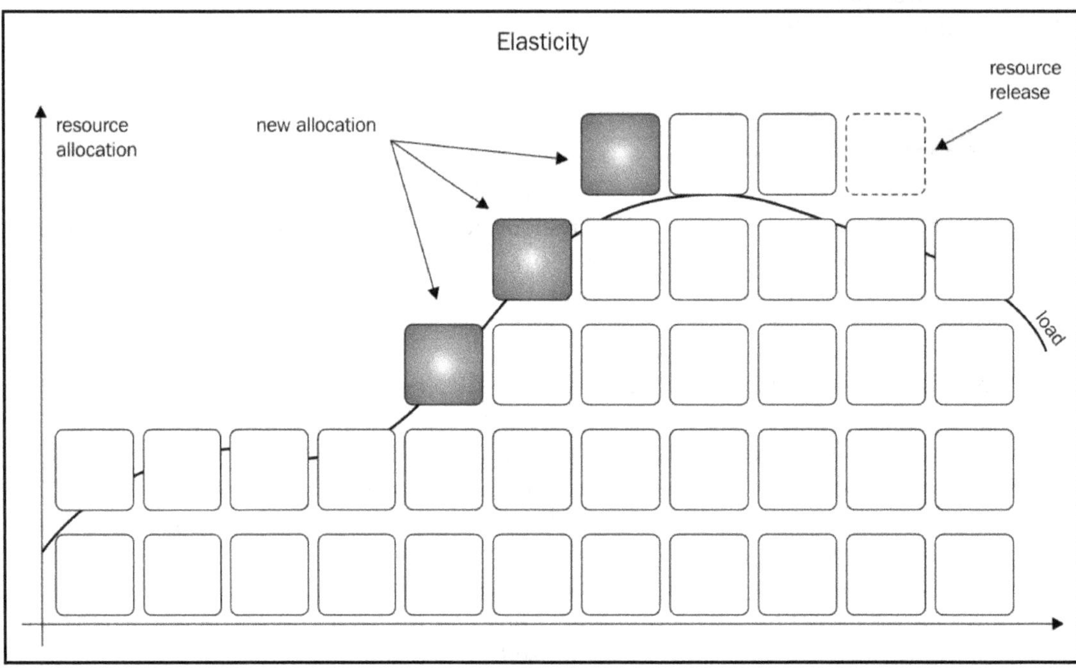

Having systems run on the cloud can avoid such losses. The cloud is nothing more than many computers that somebody operates for multiple applications, even for multiple corporations, and each rents only the CPU cycles that it really needs, and only when it needs them. At other times, when the load is smaller, the CPU and the electric power can be used by someone else. Since different applications and different corporations have different peak times, the loss of resources is less with this model. There are many issues that have to be solved, such as data isolation and protection of information from eavesdropping, but these are mainly solved. Secret-service corporations will not rent resources from a cloud service to run their computations (perhaps, they'd do for some other purpose), and some other paranoid companies may also refrain from doing that, but most of the companies will do. It is more effective and is thus cheaper, even after considering all the possible side effects.

Elasticity means that the allocated resources follow, or rather anticipate, needs. When the system anticipates higher-capacity needs, it allocates more resources, and at the off-peak time, it releases the resources so that other cloud customers can use it.

Elasticity also assumes that the system is scalable. These two things, elasticity, and scalability, are closely related, but are not the same. *Scalability* means that the application can accommodate a higher load, allocating more resources. Scalability does not care whether this allocation is the static buying and powering of huge computer boxes in a computing center dedicated to the application or dynamic allocation of resources from the cloud on demand. Scalability simply means that if the demand doubles, then the resources can also be multiplied to meet the demand. If the multiplication factor in the resources needed is the same or is not more than the factor in demand, then the application is scalable. If we need more resources to meet the demand, or if we cannot meet the demand, even if the demand increases only moderately, then the application is not scalable. Elastic applications are always scalable; otherwise, they cannot be elastic.

Message-driven

Reactive systems are **message-driven**, not because we need message-driven systems, but rather because message-driven systems are those that can deliver responsiveness, resilience, and elasticity at the same time.

Message-driven architecture means that the information travels between the components that are disconnected. One component sends a message and then *forgets* it. It does not wait for the other component to act upon the message. When the message is sent, all the tasks on behalf of the sending component are performed, and all the resources needed to handle the tasks are released, resulting in the message being released and ready to be used for the next task.

Message-driven does not necessarily mean *networking*. Messages can travel between objects, threads, and processes inside the same machine. On the other hand, if the interfaces to the messaging architecture are well-designed, then the components do not need to be modified if the infrastructure changes, and the messages that were previously passing between threads will now have to travel through the ocean in IP packets.

Sending messages makes it possible to isolate the sender and the receiver in space and time, just as we described, as a means for elasticity. The receiver may pick up the message some time after it arrived when it has the resources to do so. Responsiveness, though, requires that this time is not in the unreachable distant future but in some limited distance. If the message cannot be processed successfully, another message may signal the error. An error message is not the result we expect, but it is still a response, and the system remains responsive to all the benefits it gives.

Back-pressure

Message handling, with the appropriate messaging interfaces and implementation, supports **back-pressure**. Back-pressure is a means to lessen the burden on a component when it cannot or can barely handle more messages. Messages may be queued for processing, but no real-life queue has unlimited capacity, and reactive systems should not lose a message that's uncontrolled. Back-pressure signals the load of the component to the message producers, asking them to lessen the production. It is like a water pipe. If you start closing the outlet of the pipe, the pressure starts to increase in the pipe backwards, the water source forcing it to deliver less and less water.

Back-pressure is an effective way of handling load because it moves load handling to the component that can really do it. In old-fashioned queuing systems, there is a queue that stores the items till the component receiving them can consume them, doing its job. A queue design can be good if there is a well-defined limit for the size of the load and for the maximum size of the queue. If the queue is ever full, the items cannot be delivered, and the system stalls.

Applying back-pressure is a bit different. A queue may still be used in front of the components for performance optimization and to ensure responsiveness. The producer of the item can still put the produced item in the queue and return to attending to its own duties and does not need to wait until the consumer can attend to the item. This is decoupling, as we mentioned earlier. Seeing that the queue is full or almost full can also act as a very simple back-pressure. It is not true if someone says that queues are totally missing this feature. At times, it may simply be totally sufficient just to look at the capacity of a queue, and also the items in it, to see whether there is some need to lessen the load on the receiver the queue belongs to. But the producer does this, not the receiver, and that is an essential problem.

The producer sees that the receiver is not keeping pace with the supply, but the producer does not have any information about the cause, and not knowing the cause cannot predict the future behavior. Having a back-pressure information channel from the receiver to the producer makes the story more fine-grained.

The producer may see that there are, say, 10 slots in the queue, and it thinks that there is no problem; the producer decides to deliver eight more items in the next 150ms. One item usually takes 10ms to process, give or take; thus, the items are expected to be processed in less than 100ms, which is just better than the required 200ms maximum. The producer only knows that an item *usually* takes 10ms to process. The receiver, on the other hand, sees that the last item it got into the queue requires so much processing that, by itself, it will require 200ms. To signal this, it can tell the producer over the back-pressure not to deliver new items till further notice. The receiver knows that the items would have fitted into the queue well but would not have been processed in a timely manner. Using this information, the producer will issue some commands to the cloud control, to allocate another processing, and sends the next eight items to the new receiver, letting the old one do its cumbersome job it has to with that far above average item.

Back-pressure lets you aid the data load control, with information created by the receivers that have the most information about processing the items.

Reactive streams

Reactive streams started as an initiative to provide a standard of handling data streams in an asynchronous mode by regulating the push of the data using back-pressure. The original site of the project is `http://www.reactive-streams.org/`.

Reactive streams are now implemented in JDK 9 in the `java.util.concurrent` package.

The aim of the definition of reactive streams is to define the interface that can handle the propagation of the generated data in a totally asynchronous way without the need on the receiving side to buffer the unlimited created data. When data is created in a stream and is made available to be worked on, the worker that gets the data has to be fast enough to handle all the data that is generated. The capacity should be high enough to handle the highest production. Some intermediate buffers may handle peaks, but if there is no control that stops or delays production when the consumer is at the top of its capacity, the system will fail. Reactive system interfaces are designed to provide a way to support back-pressure. Back-pressure is a process to signal the producer of the data to slow down or even to stop the production to the level that fits the consumer. Every call the interfaces define is asynchronous so that the performance of one part is not affected by the delays in the execution of other parts.

The initiative did not aim to define the way in which data is transferred between production and consumption. It focuses on the interfaces, to give a clear structure for the programs and also to give an API that will work with all the implementations.

Reactive programming in Java

Java is not a reactive language. However, this does not mean that we cannot create reactive programs in Java. There are libraries that support different reactive programming approaches. I should mention that the Akka framework and ReactiveX also exist for other languages as well. With Java 9, the JDK starts to support reactive programming, providing a few classes and interfaces for this purpose. We will focus on these features now.

The JDK contains the `java.util.concurrent.Flow` class, which contains related interfaces and some static methods to support flow controlled programs. The model that this class supports is based on `Publisher`, `Subscriber`, and `Subscription`.

As a very simple explanation, a `Publisher` accepts a subscription from a `Subscriber`. A `Subscriber` gets the data it subscribed to when the data is available. The interfaces focus on the very core of the data-flow control of the communication, and they are a bit abstract, so they are interfaces. However, it may not be simple to understand how they work, at first.

The `Publisher` interface defines the `subscribe()` method. This is the only method this interface defines and that is because this is the only thing that a *real* publisher can be asked. You can subscribe to the publications. The argument of the method is a `Subscriber` that subscribes to the publications:

```
void subscribe(Flow.Subscriber<? super T> subscriber)
```

There is a readily available `Publisher` class in the JDK that we will look at later. When the `subscribe()` method of the `Publisher` is called, it has to decide whether the subscriber can get the subscription. Usually, the subscription is accepted, but the implementation has the freedom to refuse a subscription attempt. `Publisher` may refuse a subscription if, for example, the subscription for the actual subscriber was already performed and the `Publisher` implementation does not allow multiple subscriptions from the same subscriber.

The implementation of the method is required to call the `onError()` method of `subscriber`, with `Throwable` as the argument. In the case of multiple subscriptions, `IllegalStateException` seems to be suitable, as the JDK documentation defines at the moment.

If the subscription is successful, `Publisher` is expected to call the `onSubscribe()` method of `subscriber`. The argument to this method is a `Subscription` object (an instance of a class that implements the interface `Subscription`). This way, the `Publisher` notifies the `Subscriber` that the subscription request was accepted, and also passes an object to manage the subscription.

Managing the subscription as an abstraction could be imagined as a complex task, but in the case of reactive streams, it is very simple. All the subscriber can and should do is set the number of items it can receive at the moment, and the subscription can be canceled.

Why should the `Publisher` call back the `onSubscribe` method of `Subscriber`? Why doesn't it simply return the subscription or throw some error? The reason for this complex behavior is that it may not be the `Subscriber` that invokes the `subscribe()` method. Just as in real life, I can subscribe and pay for a year for a magazine subscription as a Christmas gift. (This is the season when I am writing this part of the book.) In our code, some wiring component responsible for who is notified about certain data-change calls `subscribe` and not necessarily the subscriber. The `Subscriber` is only responsible for the minimal things that a subscriber should be responsible for. The other reason is that the whole approach is asynchronous. When we subscribe to something, the subscription may not be available and ready immediately. There could be some long-running processes that need to finish until the subscription will be available, and the caller that is calling `subscribe` does not need to wait for the completion of the process. When the subscription is ready, it is passed to the subscriber, to the very entity that really needs it.

The `Subscriber` interface defines the `onSubscribe()`, `onError()` (we have already talked about these), `onComplete()`, and `onNext()` methods.

It is important in the definition of these interfaces that the subscriber gets the items from `Publisher` or from some other object to which the `Publisher` delegates this task via some push. The subscriber does not need to go to the *newsstand* to get the next issue; someone calling the `onNext` method delivers the issue to it directly.

This also bears the consequence that, unless there are some controls in the hands of the `Subscriber`, it could happen that the `Publisher` floods the `Subscriber` with items. Not every `Subscriber` is capable of handling unlimited items. The `Subscriber` gets a `Subscription` object upon performing the subscription, and this object can be used to control the flow of the item objects.

The Publisher creates the Subscription object, and the interface defines two methods—cancel and request. The cancel() method should be called by the Subscriber to notify the Publisher that it should not deliver more items. The subscription is cancelled. The request(long n) method specifies that the subscriber is prepared to get at most n items via subsequent calls to the onNext() method:

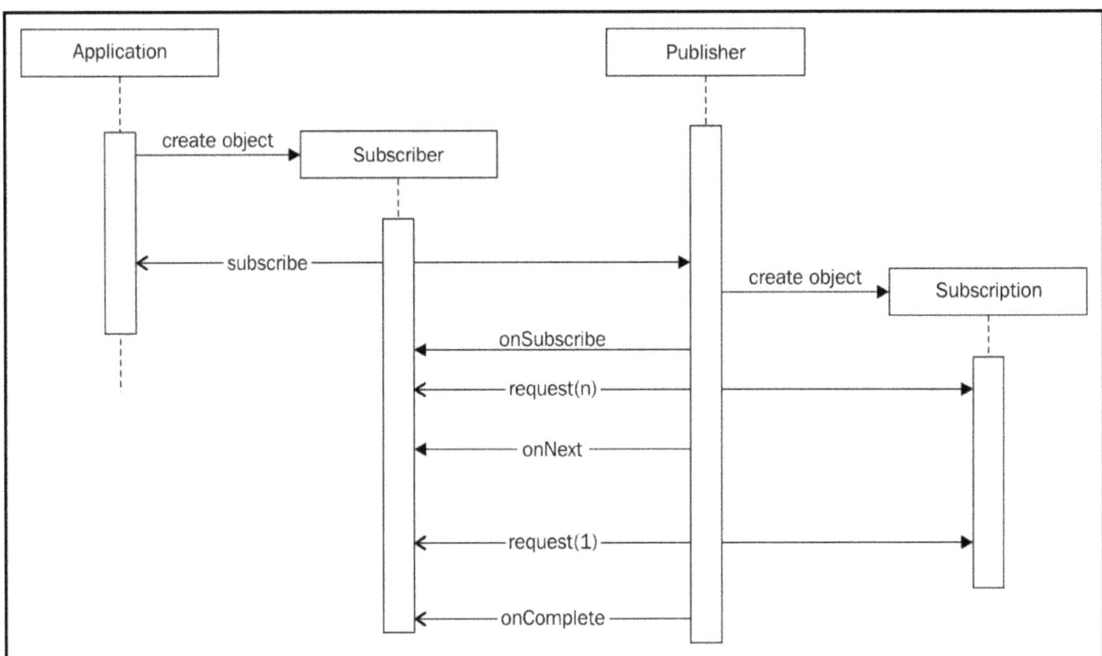

If the subscriber has already invoked the request() method, the specified number is added to the subscription counter. In other words, the specified long value does not reflect the actual state of the subscriber. It is a *delta*, increasing some counters maintained by the Publisher that counts the number of items that can be delivered, adding the value of the long argument and decrementing by *one* on each item delivered to the Subscriber. The most usual approach is to call request(1) each time the Subscriber has finished processing a request.

If the request() method is invoked with the Long.MAX_VALUE argument, the Publisher may just send any item that it can without counting and without limit. This is essentially switching off the back-pressure mechanism.

The specification also mentions that the call to `cancel` does not necessarily mean that there will be no more issues delivered at all. Cancellation is done on best effort. Just as in real life, when you send your mail to the daily paper with your intent to cancel the subscription, the publisher will not send an agent to stop the postman before they drop the issue to your mailbox. If something was already on its way when the cancellation arrived to the publisher, it continues to go on its way. If the `Publisher` has already started some asynchronous process that cannot reasonably be stopped, then the `onNext()` method will be invoked with some of the elements.

The `Publisher` and `Subscriber` interfaces have a generic parameter, `T`. This is the type of item that the `Publisher` interface publishes and the `Subscriber` interface gets in the `onNext()` method. To be a bit more precise, the `Subscriber` interface can have an `R` type, which is a superclass of `T`; thus, it is compatible with the `Publisher` interface. For example, if `Publisher` publishes `Long` values, then the `Subscriber` interface can accept `Long`, `Number`, or `Object` in the argument of the `onNext()` method, depending on the declaration of the class that implements `Subscriber`.

The `Flow` class also contains a `Processor` interface that extends both `Publisher` and `Subscriber`. This interface is there to be implemented by classes that also accept data and send data to other components in the reactive flow. Such elements are very common in reactive stream programs because many elements that perform some tasks get the items to work on from other reactive stream elements; thus, they are `Subscriber`s and, at the same time, they send it after they have finished their tasks; thus, they are `Publisher`s.

Implementing the inventory

Now that we have discussed a lot of technologies and programming approaches, it is time to implement some sample code. We will implement inventory, keeping in our application using reactive streams. For the example, the inventory will be very simple. It is a `Map<Product,InventoryItem>` that holds the number of items for each product. The actual map is `ConcurrentHashMap` and the `InventoryItem` class is a bit more complex than a `Long` number to properly handle concurrency issues. When we design a program that is built on responsive streams, we do not need to deal with much concurrency locking, but we still should be aware that the code runs in a multithread environment and may exhibit strange behavior if we do not follow some rules.

The code for the `Inventory` class is fairly simple, since it handles only a map:

```
package packt.java11.mybusiness.inventory;

import ...
```

```
@Component
public class Inventory {
    private final Map<Product, InventoryItem> inventory =
            new ConcurrentHashMap<>();

    private InventoryItem getItem(Product product) {
        inventory.putIfAbsent(product, new InventoryItem());
        return inventory.get(product);
    }

    public void store(Product product, long amount) {
        getItem(product).store(amount);
    }

    public void remove(Product product, long amount)
            throws ProductIsOutOfStock {
        if (getItem(product).remove(amount) != amount)
            throw new ProductIsOutOfStock(product);
    }
}
```

The inventory item maintaining the class is a bit more complex, since this is the level where we handle a bit of concurrency or, at least, this is the class where we have to pay some attention:

```
package packt.java11.mybusiness.inventory;

import java.util.concurrent.atomic.AtomicLong;

public class InventoryItem {
    private final AtomicLong amountOnStock =
            new AtomicLong(0);

    void store(long n) {
        amountOnStock.accumulateAndGet(n,
                (stock, delta) -> stock + delta);
    }

    long remove(long delta) {
        class ClosureData {
            long actNr;
        }
        var d = new ClosureData();
        amountOnStock.accumulateAndGet(delta,
                (stock, n) ->
                        stock >= n ?
                                stock - (d.actNr = n) :
                                stock - (d.actNr = 0));
```

```
            return d.actNr;
        }
    }
```

When we add products to the inventory, we have no limit. The storage shelves are extremely huge, and we do not model that they may get full and the inventory may not be able to accommodate more items. When we want to remove items from the repository, however, we have to deal with the fact that there may not be enough items from the product. In such a case, we do not remove any items from the repository. We serve the customer to the full satisfaction or we do not serve at all.

To maintain the number of the items in the inventory, we use `AtomicLong`. This class has the `accumulateAndGet()` method. This method gets a `Long` parameter and a `LongBinaryOperator` that we provide in our code as a lambda. This code is invoked by the `accumulateAndGet()` method to calculate the new value of the stock. If there are enough items, then we remove the requested number of items. If there are not enough items on stock, then we remove zero. The method returns the number of items that we actually return. Since that number is calculated inside the lambda, it has to escape from there. To do so, we use `ClosureData`, which is defined inside the method.

Note that, for example, in Groovy, we could simply use a `Long d` variable and alter the variable inside the closure. Groovy calls lambda to closures, so to speak. In Java, we cannot do so because the variables that we can access from inside the method should be effectively final. However, this is nothing more than a bit more explicit notation that belongs to the closure environment. The `ClosureData d` object is final, as opposed to the field the class has, which can be modified inside the lambda.

The most interesting class that we are really interested in this chapter is `InventoryKeeper`. This class implements the `Subscriber` interface and is capable of consuming orders to maintain the inventory:

```
package packt.java11.mybusiness.inventory;

import ...

public class InventoryKeeper implements Flow.Subscriber<Order> {
    private static final Logger log =
LoggerFactory.getLogger(InventoryKeeper.class);
    private static final long WORKERS = 3;
    private final Inventory inventory;
    private Flow.Subscription subscription = null;
    private ExecutorService service = Executors.newFixedThreadPool((int)
WORKERS);
```

```
    public InventoryKeeper(@Autowired Inventory inventory) {
        this.inventory = inventory;
    }

    @Override
    public void onSubscribe(Flow.Subscription subscription) {
        log.info("onSubscribe was called");
        subscription.request(3);
        this.subscription = subscription;
    }

    @Override
    public void onNext(Order order) {
        service.submit(() -> {
                    log.info("Thread {}",
Thread.currentThread().getName());
                    for (final var item : order.getItems()) {
                        try {
                            inventory.remove(item.getProduct(),
item.getAmount());
                            log.info("{} items removed from stock",
item.getAmount());
                        } catch (ProductIsOutOfStock exception) {
                            log.error("Product out of stock");
                        }
                    }
                    subscription.request(1);
                }
        );
    }

    @Override
    public void onError(Throwable throwable) {
        log.info("onError was called for {}", throwable);
    }

    @Override
    public void onComplete() {
        log.info("onComplete was called");
    }
}
```

The `onSubscribe()` method is invoked after the object is subscribed. The subscription is passed to the object and is also stored in a field. Since the subscriber needs this subscription in subsequent calls, when an item passed in `onNext` is processed and a new item is acceptable, a field is a good place to store this object in. In this method, we also set the initial request to three items. The actual value is simply demonstrative. Enterprise environments should be able to configure such parameters:

```
private ExecutorService service =
                    Executors.newFixedThreadPool((int) WORKERS);
```

The most important part of the code is the `onNext()` method. What it does is actually go through all the items of the order and then removes the number of items from the inventory. If some of the items are out of stock, then it logs an error. This is the boring part. The interesting part is that it does this through an executor service. This is because the call to `onNext` should be asynchronous. The publisher calls `onNext` to deliver the item, but we should not make it wait for the actual processing. When the postman brings your favorite magazine, you don't start reading it immediately and make the postman wait for your signature approving acceptance. All you have to do in `onNext()` is fetch the next order and make sure that this will be processed in due time.

The actual implementation in this code uses `ThreadPool` with three threads in it. Also, the number of required items is three. This is a logical coincidence—each thread works on a single item. It does not need to be like that, even if in most cases it is. Nothing can stop us from making more threads working on the same item, if that makes sense. The opposite is also true. One single thread may be created to work on multiple items. These codes will probably be more complex, and the whole idea of these complex execution models is to make the coding and the logic simpler, move the multithreading, coding, and implementation issues into the framework, and focus on the business logic in the application code. But I cannot tell that there may not be an example for a subscriber working multiple threads on multiple items, intermingled.

The last code we have to look at in this chapter is the unit test that drives the code with some examples:

```
@Test
public void testInventoryRemoval() throws InterruptedException {
    Inventory inventory = new Inventory();
    try (SubmissionPublisher<Order> p = new SubmissionPublisher<>();) {
```

We create `Publisher` using the JDK class, `SubmissionPublisher`, which neatly implements this interface by delivering multithread functionality for us without much hassle:

```
p.subscribe(new InventoryKeeper(inventory));
```

We create an inventory keeper and we subscribe to the publisher. This does not start delivering anything because there are no publications yet, but it creates a bond between the subscriber and the publisher, telling them that whenever there is a product submitted, the subscriber wants it.

After that, we create the products and store them in the inventory, 20 pieces altogether, and we also create an order that wants 10 products to be delivered. We will execute this order many times. This is a bit of simplification, but for the test, there is no reason to create separate order objects that have the same products and the same amounts in the list of items:

```
Product product = new Product();
inventory.store(product, 20);
OrderItem item = new OrderItem();
item.setProduct(product);
item.setAmount(10);
Order order = new Order();
List<OrderItem> items = new LinkedList<>();
items.add(item);
order.setItems(items);
```

After all, this has been done; we submit the order to the `Publisher` 10 times. This means that there are 10 orders for the same product, each asking for 10 pieces, which is 100 pieces altogether. Those are 100 pieces against the warehouse where we have only 20 of them. What we should expect is that only the first two orders will be fulfilled and the rest will be rejected, and that is what will actually happen when we execute this code:

```
for (int i = 0; i < 10; i++)
    p.submit(order);
log.info("All orders were submitted");
```

After all the orders are published, we wait for half a second so that the other threads have time to execute, and then we finish:

```
    for (int j = 0; j < 10; j++) {
        log.info("Sleeping a bit...");
        Thread.sleep(50);
    }
}//try( p )
```

Note that this is not a regular unit-test file. It is some test code to play around with, which I also recommend for you to execute, debug, and look at the different log outputs.

Summary

In this short chapter, we had a look at reactive programming, reactive systems, and reactive streams. We discussed the similarities and the differences between these that may lead to confusion. We paid special attention to Java reactive streams (introduced in Java 9) that have practically nothing to do with `Stream` classes and methods.

In the second half of this chapter, we discussed a very simple example that uses reactive streams.

After reading this chapter, you have learned a lot about the Java language and programming. We did not detail all the small bits of Java, as that is not possible in a book. I dare say that there is no human on Earth, or around it on an orbital route, wherever humans are, who knows everything about Java. We do, however, know enough by now to start coding in an enterprise environment and to learn more and more on the go till we retire, or even after that. What is still left is a little bit of programming. In the previous sentence, I used the word *coding* to make a distinction. Coding is not the same as programming. Coding is a technique used in the profession of programming. During the last chapter, we will see the aspects of programming and how it can, and should, be done in a professional manner. This is rarely covered in an introductory book, but I am happy that we could agree on this topic with the publisher. This way, you can finish the book, not only with the knowledge that you learn from this book but also with a vision, looking ahead on the road, you will walk up the hillside to the top. You will know the topics, areas, and subjects that you can go on learning.

10
Finalizing Java Knowledge to a Professional Level

By now, you have learned the most important areas and topics needed for a professional Java developer. What we still have ahead of us is to discuss some topics that will lead you from being a junior developer to a senior developer. Reading this chapter will not make anyone a senior developer, though. The previous chapters were the roads that we walked down. This chapter is only the map. If each of the previous chapters covered a short walk of a few miles in the journey of coding to reach the harbor, then this chapter is the nautical map to discover a new continent.

We will briefly bite into some very deep and high-level professional areas, such as creating a Java agent, compile-time annotation processing, polyglot programming, a bit of architecture design, tools, and techniques to work in teams. We'll provide a taster of these areas. Now, you have enough knowledge to understand the importance of these topics, and getting a taste will create an appetite for the coming years of self-development, or, at least, it is my intention to make you, the reader, addicted.

Java deep technologies

In this section, we will cover three technologies:

- Java agent
- Polyglot programming
- Annotation processing

Knowing them is not a must for a Java professional. Knowing about them is. Java agents are used mainly in development environments and in operations. They are complex runtime technologies that interact with the already-running *JVM*. Annotation processing is another area. Annotation processors are plugged into the Java compiler. Polyglot programming is in the middle. It is JVM programming, just like programming in Java, but using a different language or, perhaps, a different language and Java together. Or even many languages, such as Jython, Groovy, or Clojure, and Java together.

We will discuss these technologies so that you get an idea about what they are and where to look for more information in case you want to learn more about them.

Java agent

A Java agent is a Java program that is loaded by the Java runtime in a special way and can be used to interfere with the bytecode of the loaded classes, to alter them. They can be used to do the following:

- List or log, and report the loaded classes during runtime as they are loaded
- Modify the classes so that the methods will contain extra code to report runtime behavior
- Support debuggers to alter the content of a class as the developer modifies the source code

This technology is used in, for example, the **JRebel** and **XRebel** products from `https://zeroturnaround.com/`.

Although Java agents work in the deep details of Java, they are not magic. They are a bit complex and you need a deep understanding of Java, but anyone who can program in Java can write a Java agent. All that is required is that the class, which is the agent, has some predefined methods packaged into a JAR file along with the other classes of the agent and has a `META-INF/MANIFEST.MF` file that defines the names of the classes implementing the `premain()` and/or `agentmain()` methods, and some other fields.

The detailed and precise reference documentation is part of the *JDK JavaDoc* available at: `https://docs.oracle.com/javase/8/docs/technotes/guides/instrumentation/index.html` in the documentation of the `java.lang.instrument` package.

When a Java application is started with a Java agent, the command line has to contain the following option:

```
-javaagent:jarpath[=options]
```

Here, `jarpath` points to the JAR file that contains the agent class and the manifest file. The class must have a method named `premain` or `agentmain`. It may have one or two arguments. The JVM tries to call the two-argument version first after the JVM is initialized:

```
public static void premain(String agentArgs, Instrumentation inst);
```

If a two-argument version does not exist, then the one-argument version is used, which is essentially the same as the two-argument version but misses the instrumentation argument, which, in my opinion, does not make too much sense since a Java agent cannot do much without the `Instrumentation` object:

```
public static void premain(String agentArgs);
```

The `agentArgs` parameter is the string passed as an option on the command line. The second argument, `Instrumentation`, provides methods to register class transformers that can modify class bytecodes and methods that can ask the JVM to perform the redefinition or retransformation of classes during runtime.

Java applications can also load an agent after the program has already started. In such a case, the agent cannot be invoked before the main method of the Java application, since it has already started by that time. To separate the two cases, JVM calls `agentmain` in such a scenario. Note that either `premain` or `agentmain` is invoked for an agent and never both. A single agent can implement both so that it is capable of performing its task loaded at the startup, specified on the command line or after the JVM starts.

If `agentmain` is used, it has the same arguments as `premain`.

There is one major and important difference between the invocation of `premain()` and `agentmain()`. If an agent cannot be loaded during startup, for example, if it cannot be found, if the JAR file does not exist, if the class does not have the `premain()` method, or if it throws an exception, the JVM will abort. If the agent is loaded after the JVM is started (in this case, `agentmain` is to be used), the JVM will not abort if there is some error in the agent.

This approach is fairly reasonable. Imagine that there is a server application that runs on the Tomcat servlet container. When a new version is started, the system enters a down for maintenance period. If the new version cannot be started because the agent is not behaving well, it is better not started. The damage to debug the situation and fix it, or roll back the application to the old version and call for a longer fixing session, may be less than starting up the application and not having the proper agent functionality. If the application starts up only without the agent, then the suboptimal operation may not immediately be recognized. On the other hand, when an agent is attached later, the application is already running. An agent is attached to an already-running application to get information from an already-running instance. To stop the already-running instance and fail it, especially in an operational environment, is more damaging than not attaching the agent. It may not go unnoticed anyway because the agent that is most probably attached is used by operational personnel.

A `premain` or `agentmain` agent gets an `Instrumentation` object as the second argument. This object implements several methods. One of them is:

```
void addTransformer(ClassFileTransformer transformer)
```

The agent implements the transformer, and it has the `transform()` method signature:

```
byte[] transform(Module module, ClassLoader loader,
                 String className,
                 Class<?> classBeingRedefined,
                 ProtectionDomain protectionDomain,
                 byte[] classfileBuffer)
throws IllegalClassFormatException
```

This method is called by the JVM when a class is loaded or when it is to be transformed. The method gets the class object itself, but, more importantly, it gets the byte array that contains the bytecode of the class. The method is expected to return the bytecode of the transformed class. Modifying the bytecode requires some knowledge of how the bytecode is built and the structure of the class file. There are libraries that help to do that, such as Javassist (`http://www.javassist.org/`) or ASM (`http://asm.ow2.org/`). Nevertheless, I will not start coding before getting acquainted with the structure of the bytecode.

Agents, running in a separate thread and presumably interacting with the user or the filesystem and based upon some external observation at any time, may call the following method to perform the retransformation of the classes using the registered transformers:

```
void retransformClasses(Class<?>... classes)
```

The agent can also call the following method, which will redefine the classes given as arguments:

```
void redefineClasses(ClassDefinition... definitions)
```

The `ClassDefinition` class is simply a `Class` and `byte[]` pair. This will redefine the classes through the class-maintaining mechanism of the JVM.

Note that these methods and Java agents interact with the deep, low-level part of the JVM. This also bears the consequence that it is very easy to destroy the whole JVM. The bytecode is not checked, unlike during the loading of the class, and thus, if there is some error in it, the consequence may not only be an exception but also the crashing of the JVM. Also, the redefinition and the transformations should not alter the structure of the classes. They should not change their inheritance footprint, add, rename, or remove methods, or change the signature of the methods, and this is also true for fields.

Also, note that the already-created objects will not be affected by the changes; they will still use the old definition of the class and only new instances will be affected.

Polyglot programming

Polyglot programming is the technique where there are different programming languages used in the same application. Such an approach is not only appropriate when a different part of the application runs on a different environment. For example, the client executes in the browser using JavaScript, CSS, and HTML while the server is programmed to run in a Tomcat environment in Java. This is a different story, and, usually, this is not the typical use case when someone is speaking about polyglot programming.

When the application that runs on the server partially runs in Java and also in some other language, then we can refer to it as polyglot programming. For example, we create the order-handling application in Java and some of the code that checks the correctness of the order based on the product-specific codes that the order contains is written in JavaScript. Does it ring a bell? We have already done that in this book to demonstrate the scripting API of the JDK. That was real polyglot programming even if we did not mention it that way.

The JVM that runs the compiled Java code is a very good target for different language compilers, and thus, there are many languages that compile for it. When the JVM runs the bytecode of a class, it does not know what the source language was, and it does not really care; the compiler is created by the bytecode and it just executes that.

We can use different languages, such as Jython, Groovy, and Scala, to name a few popular ones, that compile for the JVM. We can write one class using one language and the other one using another. When they are put together into a JAR, WAR, or EAR file, the runtime system will just run them.

When do we use polyglot programming?

Polyglot configuration

Usually, we turn toward polyglot programming when we want to create an application that is more flexible and configurable. Applications that get installed in many instances, usually, at different customer sites, have some configurations. These configurations can be XML files, properties files, and INI files (those come from Windows). As the programs develop, these static-configuration possibilities reach their limits. Application developers soon see that they need to configure a functionality that is cumbersome to describe using these technologies. Configuration files start getting larger and the code that reads and interprets the configuration files grows to be too large. Good developers have to realize that this is the situation, and before the configuration files and the code that handles them become unmanageable, some scripting configuration, polyglot programming, has to be implemented:

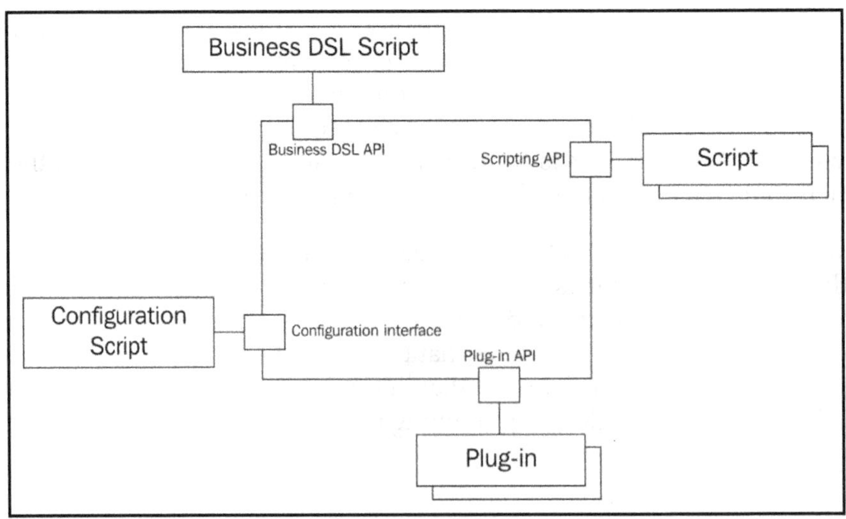

Decent developer teams may reach a point when they develop their configuration language and the interpreter of that language. It can be based on XML, or it can just be any other language. After all, writing a language is fun; I have done it a few times myself. Most of these were, however, hobbies and not professional projects. Usually, there is no customer value in crafting another language. It is better to use an existing one.

In the case of configuration, Groovy is a very handy language that supports complex closure and meta-class syntax and implementation. This way, the language is extremely suitable for creating a domain-specific language. Since Groovy is compiled to JVM, Groovy classes can be invoked directly from Java, and reading the configuration is essentially invoking the class compiled from the configuration file. The compilation can be during application build-time, but in the case of configuration, it makes more sense to do it during application startup. We have already seen that the Groovy implementation of the scripting API or the special API that Groovy provides is absolutely capable of doing that.

Have we seen examples of this in the book? It may be a surprise to you, but we have in fact used Groovy to describe configurations many times. *Gradle* build files are nothing more than Groovy DSL developed mainly in Groovy to support the project's build configuration.

Polyglot scripting

Configuration is not the only application of polyglot programming. Configuration is executed at the program's startup and the configuration data is used as static data afterward. We can execute scripts during the application's execution any time and not only during its startup. This can be used to provide extra functionality to the program's user with installations that use the same application but are furnished with different scripts.

One of the first applications that provided this scripting capability was the emacs editor. The core of the application was written in the C language and it contained a Lisp interpreter that let the user write scripts, which were executed in the editor environment. AutoCAD, an engineering program, also used a Lisp interpreter for similar purposes. Why was Lisp used for this purpose? Lisp has very simple syntax, and therefore, it is easy to parse Lisp code. At the same time, the language is powerful, and there were open source Lisp interpreters (at least one) available at that time.

To get this kind of flexibility, applications often provide plugin APIs that a developer can use to extend the application. This requires that the developer set up coding tools, including the IDE, build tool, and continuous integration, that is, a professional programming environment. When the task to be solved by the plugin is simple, the overhead is simply too large. In such a case, a scripting solution is handier.

Scripting is not a solution for everything. When the scripts extending the application become too complex, it means that the scripting possibility is just too much. It is difficult, however, to take back a toy from a child. If users get used to the scripting possibility, then they will not take it well if the next version of the application we release does not provide that possibility. Thus, it is extremely important to assess the possible use of the scripting capability in our application. Scripting and, more generally, any feature of our program, will not be used in the way we intended. They will be used for whatever it is possible to use them for. Users can go beyond all imagination when it comes to abusing a feature. It may be a good idea to think about limiting the scripting possibility beforehand or limiting the running time of the scripts or the size of the script our program agrees to work with. If these limitations are set reasonably, and the users understand and accept these, a plugin structure in addition to the scripting capability has to be considered.

The security of an application, including a plugin or scripting extension, is also very important. The scripts or plugins run on the same JVM as the core application. Some scripting languages provide a fence around the scripts that limits the access to the core application's objects and classes, but this is an exception. Usually, scripts run with the same privilege as the core application and that way they can do just about anything. Thus, scripts should be trusted in the same way as the core application. Script installation or modification should never be possible for an unprivileged user of the application. Such an action is almost always reserved for the system administrator.

If an unprivileged user can upload a script to the server and then have it executed, we just opened a security hole in our application. Since access restrictions are enforced by the application, it is easy to override these limitations using an uncontrolled script. The hacker can just access other users' data easily, which they are not entitled to, and read and modify our database.

Business DSL

Polyglot programming may also come into the picture when the application's code can be separated into business code and technology code. The business code contains the top-level business logic that we actually write the application for, and this is the code that contains the logic that the customer pays for. The technology code is to support the algorithms coded in the business DSL.

Most enterprise applications contain these two types of code but many do not separate them. This leads to a monolithic application that contains repetitive code. When you feel that you are writing the same type of code when you need persistence or networking, and the same type of code again while coding some business rules, then this code smell suggests that the two code types are not separated. DSL and scripting are not a magic wand and do not solve all the problems that stem from an incorrect application structure. In such a situation, the code has to be refactored first to separate the business logic and the infrastructure code, and it is only the second step to implement a DSL and a business API supporting it and to rewrite the business code into the DSL. Every step of such a project delivers value for the application and even if it never gets to DSL and scripting, the effort invested is not wasted.

The business DSL scripting is very similar to pluggable scripts, except that this time it is not the application that calls the scripts to execute some special extension functionality. Instead, the DSL code calls the application through the business API that it provides. The advantage of providing the API and using a DSL is that the code that implements the business logic gets rid of the technical details, can be very abstract, and, in this way, can be much closer to a business-level description of the problem rather than just program code. Even a businessperson can understand business DSL, and though it is not a goal in real-life examples, they could even write code.

At TU Vienna, we also used a similar approach to make semiconductor simulation more usable for the semiconductor design engineer. The core calculating code was written in Fortran, a C language framework that handled the massive simulation data input and output and that embedded the XLISP interpreter that executed these programs. The Lisp code contained the simulation configuration data and could also contain simple loops when the simulation was to be executed for many configuration points. It was polyglot programming, except it wasn't called that at the time.

Problems with polyglot

Polyglot programming is not only all about advantages. Before jumping into this direction, developers have to consider a lot of things.

Using another language for the application needs knowledge. Finding people who can code in the languages that are used is eventually more difficult than finding developers who only know Java. (This is also true if the kernel application language is not Java.) Different languages require different mindsets and, often, different people. The team should also have some members who are proficient in both languages, and it is also an advantage if most of the people know at least a bit about the other language.

The toolset that supports Java is outstanding. The build tools, integrated development environment, libraries, debugging possibilities, and logging frameworks, to name a few, are all extremely good compared with other languages. Polyglot development needs support for the other language as well, which may not be as advanced as the support for Java. Often, it is really an issue to debug DSL solutions and IDE support may also be lagging.

When we program in Java, we often take for granted that the IDE reads the meta-data of the libraries and whenever we need to call a method, or reference a class, the IDE suggests the best possibility. XML and properties files may also be supported and the IDE may know some of the most-used frameworks, such as *Spring*, and understand the XML configuration handling the names of the classes as hyperlinks, even when the class names are inside some attribute strings.

It is far from being this easy in the case of other languages. For the languages that have a wide user base, the tooling support may be good, but if you pick an exotic language, you are on your own. The more exotic the language, the less support you may have.

You can create a tool to support your DSL. It is not hard to do so using tools such as `http://www.eclipse.org/Xtext/`. In such a case, you are tied to *Eclipse*, which may or may not be a problem. You can pick a special language, for example, *Kotlin*, which is extensively supported by *IntelliJ*, because the same company supports the language and the IDE, but again, you buy into a special technology that can be expensive to replace if you have to. It is generally true not only for languages but also for any technology you include into your development. When you select one, you should consider the support and the cost of getting off the horse if or when it starts dying.

Annotation processing

We have already discussed annotations in great detail. You may recall that we defined our annotation interfaces using the following annotation:

```
@Retention(RetentionPolicy.RUNTIME)
```

This tells the Java compiler to keep the annotation and put it into the JVM code so that the code can access it during runtime using reflection. The default value is `RetentionPolicy.CLASS`, which means that the annotation gets into the bytecode, but the JVM does not make it available for the runtime system. If we use `RetentionPolicy.SOURCE`, the annotation does not even get into the class file. In this case, there is only one possibility to do anything with the annotation—compile time.

How can we write code that runs during compile-time? Java supports the notion of annotation processors. If there is a class on the classpath of the compiler that implements the `javax.annotation.processing.Processor` interface, the compiler will invoke the implemented methods one or more times, passing information about the source file that the compiler is actually processing. The methods will be able to access the compiled methods, classes, or whatever is annotated, and also the annotation that triggered the processor invocation. It is important, however, that this access is not the same as in runtime. What the annotation processor accesses is neither a compiled nor a loaded class, that is, it is available when the code uses reflection. The source file at this time is under compilation; thus, the data structures that describe the code are actually structures of the compiler, as we will see in our next example.

The annotation processor is called one or more times. The reason it is invoked many times is that the compiler makes it possible for the annotation processors to generate source code based on what it sees in the partially-compiled source code. If the annotation processor generates a Java source file, the compiler has to compile the new source code and perhaps compile some of the already-compiled files again. This new compilation phase needs annotation-processor support until there are no more rounds to execute.

Annotation processors are executed one after the other, and they work on the same set of source files. There is no way to specify the order of the annotation-processor executions; thus, two processors working together should perform their tasks, no matter in what order they are invoked. Also, note that these codes run inside the compiler. If an annotation processor throws an exception, the compilation process will probably fail. Thus, throwing an exception out of the annotation processor should only be done if there is an error that cannot be recovered and the annotation processor decides that the compilation after that error cannot be completed.

When the compiler gets to the phase to execute the annotation processors, it looks at the classes that implement the `javax.annotation.processing.Processor` interface and creates instances of these classes. These classes have to have a public no-argument constructor. To streamline the execution of the processors and to invoke a processor only for the annotations that it can handle, the interface contains two methods:

- `getSupportedSourceVersion()`: Returns the latest version the annotation processor can support
- `getSupportedAnnotationTypes()`: Returns a set of `String` objects that contain the fully-qualified class name of the annotations that this processor can handle

If an annotation processor was created for Java 1.8, it may work with Java 9, but it may also not work. If it declares that the latest supported version is 1.8, then the compiler in a Java 9 environment will not invoke it. It is better not to invoke an annotation processor than calling it and messing up the compilation process, which may even create compiled but erroneous code.

The values returned by these methods are fairly constant for an annotation processor. An annotation processor will return the same source version it can handle and will return the same set of annotations. Therefore, it would be clever to have some way to define these values in the source code in a declarative manner.

It can be done when we extend the `javax.annotation.processing.AbstractProcessor` class instead of directly implementing the `Processor` interface. This abstract class implements these methods. Both of them get the information from the annotation so that we can decorate the class that extends the abstract class. For example, the `getSupportedAnnotationTypes()` method looks at the `SupportedAnnotationTypes` annotation and returns an array of annotation type strings that are listed in the annotation.

Now, this is a bit brain-twisting and can also be confusing at first. We are executing our annotation processor during compile-time. But the compiler itself is a Java application, and in this way, the time is runtime for the code that runs inside the compiler. The code of `AbstractProcessor` accesses the `SupportedAnnotationTypes` annotation as a runtime annotation using reflection methods. There is no magic in it. The method in the JDK 9 is as follows:

```
public Set<String> getSupportedAnnotationTypes() {
    SupportedAnnotationTypes sat = this.getClass()
                        .getAnnotation(SupportedAnnotationTypes.class);
    if  (sat == null) {
        ... error message is sent to compiler output ...
```

```
            return Collections.emptySet();
        }
        else
            return arrayToSet(sat.value());
    }
```

(The code has been edited for brevity. In Java 11, the code is a bit more complex as it handles modules introduced in Java 9, but the structure is essentially the same.)

To see an example, we will look at the code of a polyglot annotation processor. Our very simple annotation processor will process one simple annotation, `com.javax0.scriapt.CompileScript`, that can specify a script file. The annotation processor will load the script file and execute it using the scripting interface of Java 9.

I developed this code as a demonstration code a few years ago; it is available with the Apache license from GitHub. Thus, the package of the classes is retained.

The annotation processor contains two code files. One is the annotation itself that the processor will work on:

```
@Retention(RetentionPolicy.SOURCE)
@Target(ElementType.TYPE)
public @interface CompileScript {
    String value();
    String engine() default "";
}
```

As you can see, this annotation will not get into the class file after compilation; thus, there will be no trace during runtime so that any class source may occasionally use this annotation. The `Target` of the annotation is `ElementType.TYPE` means that this annotation can only be applied to those Java 9 language constructs that are some kind of types—`class`, `interface`, and `enum`.

The annotation has two parameters. The value should specify the name of the script file, and the engine may define the type of the script that is in that file. The implementation we'll create will try to identify the type of the script from the filename extension, but if somebody would like to bury some Groovy code into a file that has the `.jy` extension (which is usually for Jython), so be it.

The processor extends `AbstractProcessor` and, in this way, some of the methods are inherited at the expense of some annotations used in the class:

```
package com.javax0.scriapt;
import ...
@SupportedAnnotationTypes("com.javax0.scriapt.CompileScript")
@SupportedSourceVersion(SourceVersion.RELEASE_11)
public class Processor extends AbstractProcessor {
```

There is no need to implement the `getSupportedAnnotationTypes()` and `getSupportedSourceVersion()` methods. These are replaced by the use of the annotations on the class. We support only one annotation in this processor, the one that we defined in the previously-listed source file, and we are prepared to manage the source code up to Java version 11. The only method we have to override is `process()`:

```
@Override
public boolean process(final Set<? extends TypeElement> annotations,
                       final RoundEnvironment roundEnv) {
    for (final var element : roundEnv.getRootElements()) {
        processClass(element);
    }
    return false;
}
```

This method gets two arguments. The first is the set of annotations it was invoked for. The second is the round environment. Because the processor can be invoked many times, the different invocations may have different environments. Each invocation is in around and the `RoundEnvironment` argument is an object that can be used to get information about the given round. It can be used to get the root elements of the round for which this annotation is invoked. In our case, this will be a set of class elements that have the `CompileScript` annotation. We iterate over this set, and for each class, we invoke the `processClass()` method. See the next code snippet:

```
private static void processClass(final AnnotatedConstruct element) {
    for (final var ann : element.getAnnotationMirrors()) {
        processAnnotation(ann);
    }
}
```

The actual annotation is not available during compile-time, as we already mentioned. Hence, what we have available is only a compile-time mirror image of the annotation. It has the `AnnotationMirror` type, which can be used to get the actual type of the annotation and, also, the values of the annotation. The type of the annotation is available during compile time. The compiler needs it; otherwise, it could not compile the annotation. The values are available from the annotation itself. Our `processAnnotation()` method handles each annotation it gets as an argument:

```
private static void processAnnotation(final AnnotationMirror mirror) {
    final var script = FromThe.annotation(mirror).getStringValue();
    final var engine = FromThe.annotation(mirror).getStringValue("engine");
    execute(script, engine);
}
```

Our `@CompileScript` annotation defines two parameters. The first value is the script filename and the second one is the scripting engine name. If the second one is not specified, an empty string is set as the default value. The `execute()` method is called for each and every occasion of the annotation:

```
private static void execute(final String scriptFileName, final String
engineName) {
    final var manager = new ScriptEngineManager();
    final ScriptEngine engine;
    if (engineName != null && !engineName.isEmpty()) {
        engine = manager.getEngineByName(engineName);
    } else {
        final var ext = getExtensionFrom(scriptFileName);
        engine = manager.getEngineByExtension(ext);
    }
    try (final var reader = new FileReader(new File(scriptFileName),
StandardCharsets.UTF_8)) {
        engine.eval(reader);
    } catch (final IOException | ScriptException e) {
        throw new RuntimeException(e);
    }
}
```

The method tries to load the script, based on the filename, and tries to instantiate the script engine, based on the given name. If there is no name given, the filename extension is used to identify the scripting engine. By default, the JavaScript engine is on the classpath as it is part of the JDK. If any other JVM-based scripting engine is in use, it has to be made available on the classpath or on the module path.

The last method of the class is a simple script-manipulation method, nothing special. It just chops off the filename extension so that the engine can be identified based on the extension string:

```
private static String getExtensionFrom(final String scriptFileName) {
    final int extPos = scriptFileName.lastIndexOf('.');
    return extPos == -1 ? "" : scriptFileName.substring(extPos + 1);
}
```

And just for the sake of completeness, we have the closing bracket of the class:

```
}
```

Programming in the enterprise

When a professional works for an enterprise, they do not work alone. There are a lot of people—developers as well as other coworkers—we have to cooperate with. The older the IT department of the enterprise the larger the enterprise is, and the more specialized roles people are in. You will meet business analysts, project managers, test engineers, build engineers, subject-matter experts, testers, architects, scrum masters, and automation engineers, to name a few roles. Some of these roles may overlap; each person may have a specific responsibility, while in other cases, some roles could even be more specialized. Some of the roles are very technical and require less business-related knowledge; others are more business-oriented.

Working as a team with so many people and with so many different roles is not simple. The complexity of the task may be overwhelming for a novice developer and cannot be done without definite policies that all members of the operation follow, more or less. Perhaps your experience will show that it is more often less than more, but that is a different story.

For the way developers work together, there are well-established industry practices. These support the **Software Development Lifecycle** (**SDLC**) using waterfall, agile, or a mix of the two models in some way. In the following sections, we will look at tools and techniques that are, or at least should be used in every software-development organization. These are:

- Static code-analysis tools that control the quality of the code examining the source code
- Source code version-control that stores all the versions of the source code and helps get the source code for any old version of the development process
- Software versioning to keep some order to how we identify the different versions and do not get lost among them

- Code-review and tools that help to pinpoint bugs that are not revealed by tests, and to aid knowledge-sharing
- Knowledge-based tools to record and document the findings
- Issue-tracking tools that record bugs, customer issues, and other tasks that somebody has to attend to
- A selection process and considerations for external products and libraries
- The continuous integration that keeps the software in a consistent state and reports errors immediately before the error propagates to other versions or other code, depending on how the erroneous code gets developed
- Release management, which keeps track of the different release versions of the software
- A code repository, which stores the compiled and packed artifacts

The following diagram shows the most widely used tools for these tasks:

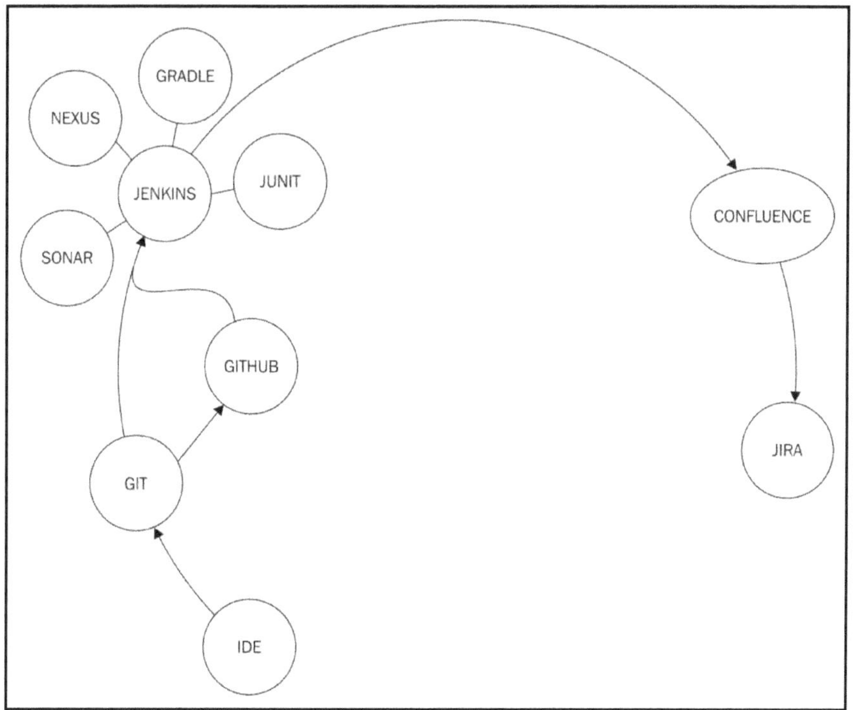

Static code analysis

Static code-analysis tools read the code just like the compiler and analyze it, but instead of compilation, they try to find errors or mistakes in it. Not the syntax errors. For that, we already have the Java compiler. Mistakes, such as using a loop variable outside of a loop, which may be absolutely valid but is usually bad style and, often, such usage comes from a simple mistake. They also check that the code follows the styling rules we set.

Static code analyzers help identify many small and obvious errors in the code. Sometimes, they are annoying, warning about something that may not really be a problem. In such a case, it is better to code the program a bit differently, and not because we want the static code analysis to run without warning. We should never modify the code because of a tool. If we code something in such a way that it passes a quality-check tool and not because it is better that way, then we are serving the tools instead of the tools serving us.

The reason to change the code to pass the code analysis is that it is very probable that the code is more readable to an average programmer if it does not violate the coding style. You, or the other team members, can be excellent programmers who understand the code very well even if it uses a special construct. However, you cannot say that about all the programmers who will maintain your code in the future. The code lives a long life. I work with some programs that were written 50 years ago. They are still running and are maintained by young professionals; they were not even born when the code was developed. It can easily happen that the person who will maintain your code has not yet been born when you are writing the code. You cannot know anything about their competence and coding practices. The best you can do is prepare for the average and that is exactly what static code-analysis tools are for.

The checks that these tools perform are not hardwired into the tools. Some special language inside the tools describes the rules and they can be deleted, other rules can be added, and rules can be modified. This way, you can accommodate the coding standards of the enterprise you work for. The different rules can be categorized as cosmetic, minor, major, and critical. Cosmetic things are mainly warnings and we do not really care about them, even though it is nice to fix even these issues. Sometimes, these small things may signal a really big issue. We can set limits for the number of minor and major bugs before the check is declared as failing and also for the critical errors. In the last case, this limit is usually zero. If a coding error seems to be critical, then it's better to not have any in the code.

The most frequently-used tools are **Checkstyle**, **FindBugs**, and **PMD**. The execution of these tools is usually automated, and though they can be executed from the IDE or from the developer's command line, their main use is on the **continuous integration** (**CI**) server. During the build, these tools are configured on the CI server to run, and it can be configured such that the build should be broken if the static code analysis fails with some limit. Executing the static code analysis is usually the next step after compilation and unit-test execution, and before the actual packaging.

SonarQube (`https://www.sonarqube.org/`) is a special tool in addition to being a static code analysis tool. SonarQube maintains the history of the previous checks, supports unit-test code coverage, and can report the change of the quality over time. This way, you can see how the quality, coverage percentage, and number of different qualifications of code style errors have changed. Often, when approaching the release date, the code quality decreases as people are in a rush. This is very bad because this is the time when most of the bugs should be eliminated. Having a statistic about the quality may help change the practice by seeing the trends before the quality, and thus the maintainability of the code gets out of hand.

Source code version-control

Source code version-control systems store different versions of the source code. These days, we cannot imagine professional software development without it. This was not always the case, but the availability of free online repositories encouraged hobby developers to use some version-control, and when these developers worked for enterprises later, it was evident that the use of these systems is kind of a must.

There are many different version-control systems. The most widely-used one is Git. The version-control that was previously widely used was **SVN** and, even before that, **CVS**. These are less and less used these days. We can see **SVN** as a successor of **CVS** and Git as a successor of **SVN**. In addition to these, there are other version-control systems, such as **Mercurial**, **Bazaar**, or **Visual Studio Team Services**. For a comprehensive list of the available tools, visit the Wikipedia page at `https://en.wikipedia.org/wiki/List_of_version_control_software`.

My bet is that you will meet Git first and there is a high probability of you coming across SVN when programming for an enterprise. Mercury may appear in your practice but any of the others that currently exist are very rare, are used for a specific area, or are simply extinct.

Version-control systems allow the development team to store the different versions of the software in an organized manner on storage that is maintained (backed up regularly in a reliable manner). This is important for different purposes.

Different versions of the software may be deployed to different instances. If we develop software for clients and we have many clients with whom we hope to make a terrific business, then different clients may have different versions. This is not only because some clients are reluctant to pay for the upgrade, and we just do not want to give the new version for free. Often, the costs that arise on the side of the customer prevent the upgrade for a long time. Software products do not work on their own in an isolated environment. Different clients have different integrated environments; the software communicates with different applications. When a new version is to be introduced in an enterprise environment, it has to be tested for whether it works with all the systems it has to cooperate with. This testing takes a lot of effort and money. If the new features or other values that the new version delivers over the old one do not justify the cost, it would be a waste of money to deploy the new version. The fact that there is a new version of our software does not mean that the old versions are not usable.

If there is some bug at the customer's end, it is vital we fix the bug in that version. To do so, the bug has to be reproduced in the development environment, which eventually means that the source code for that version has to be available for the developers.

This does require the customer database to contain references to the different versions of our software products that are installed at the customer site. To make it more complicated, a customer may have more than one version at a time in different systems and may also have different licenses, so the issue is more complex than it first seems. If we do not know which version the client has, we are in trouble. Since the database registering the versions for the customers and real life may get unsynchronized, software products log their version at startup. We have a separate section about versioning in this chapter.

If the bug is fixed in the version that the client has, the incident at the customer's end may be solved after deployment. The problem, though, still remains if the version is not the previous version of the software. The bug fix introduced to an old version of the software may still be lurking around in the later or, for that matter, earlier versions. The development team has to identify which versions are relevant to clients. For example, an old version that is not installed anymore at any of the clients' sites does not deserve the investigation. After that, the relevant versions have to be investigated to check whether they exhibit the bug. This can only be done if we have the source version. Some old versions may not have the bug if the code causing the bug is introduced in later versions. Some new versions may also be immune to the bug because the bug was already fixed in the previous version, or simply because the piece of code that caused the bug was refactored even before the bug manifested. Some bugs may even affect a specific version instead of a range of products. Bug-fixing may be applied to different versions and they may need slightly different fixes. All this needs a maintained source-version repository.

Even when we do not have different customers with different versions, it is more than likely that we have more than one version of our software in development. The development of a major release is coming to an end, and therefore, one part of the team responsible for testing and bug-fixing focuses on those activities. At the same time, the development of features for the next version still goes on. The code implementing the functionalities for the next version should not get into the version that is about to be released. The new code may be very fresh, untested, and may introduce new bugs. It is common to introduce freeze times during the release process. For example, it may be forbidden to implement any new feature of the upcoming release. This is called a feature freeze.

Revision-control systems deal with these freeze periods, maintaining different branches of the code. The release will be maintained in one branch and the version for later releases in a different one. When the release goes out, the bug fixes that were applied to it should also be propagated to the newer version; otherwise, it might happen that the next version will contain bugs that were already fixed in the previous version. To do so, the release branch is merged with the ongoing one. Thus, version-control systems maintain a graph of the versions, where each version of the code is a node in the graph and the changes are vertices.

Git goes very far in this direction. It supports branch-creation and merging so well that developers create separate branches for each change that they create and then they merge it back with the master branch when the feature development is done. This also makes for a good opportunity for code review. The developer making the feature development or bug fix creates a pull request in the GitHub application, and another developer is requested to review the change and perform the pull. This is a kind of four-eyed principle applied to code development.

Some of the revision-control systems keep the repository on a server and any change gets to the server. The advantage of this is that any change committed gets to a server disk that is regularly backed up and is thus safe. Since the server-side access is controlled, any code sent to the server cannot be rolled back without trace. All versions, even the wrong versions, are stored on the server. This may be required legally. On the other hand, if the commit requires network access and server interaction, it may be slow and this will, in the long run, motivate developers not to commit their changes frequently. The longer a change remains on the local machine, the more risk we have of losing some of the code, and merging becomes more and more difficult with time. To heal this situation, Git distributes the repository and the commit happens to the local repository, which is exactly the same as the remote one on a server. The repositories are synchronized when one repository pushes the changes to another one. This encourages the developers to make frequent commits to the repository, providing short commit messages, which helps to track the change made to the code.

Some older version-control systems support file locking. This way, when a developer checks out a code file, others cannot work on the same piece of code. This essentially avoids collisions during code merging. Over the years, this approach did not seem to fit the development methodologies. Merge issues are less of a problem than files that are checked out and forgotten. SVN supports file locking but this is not really serious and does not prevent one developer from committing changes to a file that somebody else locked. It is more of a suggestion than real locking.

Source code repositories are very important but should not be confused with release repositories, which store the compiled released version of the code in binary. Source and release repositories work together.

Software versioning

Software versioning is magic. Think about the different versions of Windows or *Star Wars* movies. Well, the latter is not really software versioning but it shows that the issue is very general. In the case of Java, versioning is not that complex. First of all, the version of Java we use now is 9. The previous version was 1.8, before that 1.7, and so on, down to 1.0. Earlier versions of Java were called Oak, but that is history. After all, who can tell what Java 2 was?

Fortunately, when we create a Java application, the situation is simpler. There has been a suggestion from Oracle, from the time of Java 1.3, about how to version JARs: `http://docs.oracle.com/javase/7/docs/technotes/guides/extensions/versioning.html`.

This document distinguishes between specification versions and implementation versions. If the specification of the JAR content changes, the code has to behave differently from how it was behaving till then; the specification version should change. If the specification is not changed but the implementation is – for example, when we fix a bug – then the implementation version changes.

In practice, nobody uses this scheme, although it is a brilliant idea to separate the implementation and specification versions, at least, in theory. I even bet that most of your colleagues have never heard of this versioning. What we use in practice is semantic versioning.

Semantic versioning (`http://semver.org/`) mixes the specification and implementation versions into one single version number triplet. This triplet has the format of **mmp,** that is:

- **m**: Major version number
- **m**: Minor version number
- **p**: Patch number

The specification says that these numbers start with zero and increase by one. If the major number is zero, it means that the software is still in development. In this state, the API is not stable and may change without a new major version number. The major version number gets to one when the software is released. Later, it has to be increased when the API of the application (library) has changed from the previous version and the application is not backward-compatible with the previous version. The minor version number is increased when the change affects only the implementation but the change is significant; perhaps even the API is also changing but in a backward-compatible manner. The patch version is increased when some bug is fixed, but the change is not major and the API does not change. The minor and the patch levels have to be reset to zero if any version number in the triplet in front of any of them is increased: a major-version-number increase resets both the minor and patch version; a minor-version-number increase resets the patch number.

This way, semantic versioning keeps the first element of the triplet for the specification version. The minor is a mix of the specification and implementation versions. A patch version change is clearly an implementation version change.

In addition to these, semantic versioning allows us to append a pre-release string, such as `-RC1` and `-RC2`. It also allows the appending of metadata, such as a date after a plus sign, for example, `+20160120` as a date.

The use of semantic versioning helps those that use the software to easily spot compatible versions and to see which version is older and which is newer.

Code review

When we create programs in a professional way, it is done in teams. There is no one-man show in programming other than as a hobby or going along with tutorials. This is not only because it is more effective to work in teams, but also because one person is vulnerable. If you work alone and get hit by a bus or you win the lottery and lose your ability or motivation to work on the project, your customer is in trouble. That is not professional. Professional projects should be resilient to any member falling off.

Teamwork needs cooperation and one form of cooperation is code review. This is the process where a developer or a group of developers reads a part of the code that other team members have written. There are direct gains from this activity:

- The developers reading the code get more knowledge about the code; they learn the code. This way, if the developer creating the code leaves the process for any reason, the others can continue the work with minimal issues.

- Coding styles can be aligned. Developers, even seniors, need to pay careful attention to coding mistakes. There may be bugs or a coding style violation. Coding style is important because the more readable the code is, the less likely it is to have unnoticed bugs. It is also important that the coding style is the same for the team. All team members should use the same style. Looking at a code that has a different style from the one I wrote is a bit harder to follow and understand. The differences may distract the reader, and the team members have to be able to read the code. The code belongs to the team and not a single developer. Any team member should know the code and be able to modify it.
- During code review, a lot of bugs can be discovered. The parties looking at the code and trying to understand the workings of it may occasionally discover bugs in the structure of the code, which are otherwise hard to discover using tests. If you like, code review is the whitest white-box test. People think differently and different mindsets catch different bugs.

Code review can be done online and offline. It can be done in teams or peer-to-peer.

Most teams follow the code review process that GitHub supports, which is the simplest. Changes to the code are committed to a branch and are not merged with the code directly but, rather, a pull request is created on the web interface. The local policy may require that a different developer perform the pull. The web interface will highlight the changes and we can add comments to the changed code. If the comments are significant, the original developer requesting the pull should modify the code to answer the comments and request the pull again. This ensures that at least two developers see any changes; the knowledge is shared.

Feedback is peer-to-peer. It is not a senior teaching a junior. That requires a different channel. Comments in GitHub are not good for this purpose; at least, there are better channels, such as talking face-to-face. Comments may come from a senior to a junior or from a junior to a senior. In this work, and in giving feedback on the quality of the code, seniors and juniors are equal.

The simplest and perhaps the most frequent comment is the following—*I can see that* `Xyz.java` *was changed in the modification but I see no change made to* `XyzTest.java`. This is almost an instant refusal for the merge. If a new feature is developed, unit tests have to be created to test that feature. If a bug is fixed, unit tests have to be created to prevent the bug from coming back. I personally get this comment many times, even from juniors. One of them told me, "We know that you are only testing us if we dare to give feedback." God knows, I was not. They did not believe. There is one case when a change in `Xyz.java` does not need to be followed by a change in `XyzTest.java`—when the change does not alter the functionality of the class, it only alters a non-functional feature, such as the performance.

While change review and GitHub are good tools during development, it may not be appropriate when a larger chunk of code has to be reviewed. In such a case, other tools, such as **FishEye**, have to be used. In this tool, we can select the source files for review even if they were not recently changed. We can also select reviewers and deadlines. Commenting is similar to GitHub. Finally, this type of code review finishes with a code review session, where the developers gather and discuss the code in person.

When organizing such a session, it is important that a person who has experience managing other people mediates these sessions. Code and discussion on styles can get very personal. At the same time, when attending such a meeting, you should pay attention so as not to get personal. There will be enough participants who may not know this or are less disciplined.

Never attend a review session without reviewing the code first using the online tools. When you make comments, the language should be very polite for the reason I have already mentioned. Finally, the mediator should be able to separate important and not-so-important issues and to stop any debate on bagatelle things. Somehow, the less important issues are more sensitive. I personally do not care about formatting the tab size if it is two or four spaces and whether the file should contain only spaces or whether tab characters are allowed, but people tend to like to waste time on such issues.

The most important issue during code-review sessions is that we are professionals. It may happen that I review and comment your code today, but tomorrow, it will be just the opposite, and we have to work together as a team.

Knowledge base

Knowledge base was a buzzword a few years ago. A few companies were evangelizing the idea of wiki technology and nobody was using it. Today, the landscape of the knowledge base is totally different. All enterprises use some kind of wiki implementation that is there to share knowledge. They mostly use Confluence, but there are also other wiki solutions available, commercial and free as well.

Knowledge bases store information that you, as a developer, would write down in a paper notebook for your later reference, for example, the IP address of the development server, directories for where to install the JAR files, what commands to use, what libraries you have collected, and why you use them. The major difference is that you write it in a formatted way into a wiki and it is available immediately for other developers. It is a bit of a burden on the developer to write these pages, and it requires some self-discipline at first. Sticking to the example of the IP address of the development server and the install directories, you have to write not only the IP address of the server but also some text explaining what the information is, because the others may not understand it otherwise. It is also a bit of work to place the page with the information in the wiki system with a good name, link it to other pages, or find the appropriate position of the page in the tree of pages. If you were using a paper notebook, you could just write down the IP address and the directories on the first free page of the book and you would remember all others.

The wiki approach will pay dividends when coworkers do not need to find the information themselves; you can find the information in an easier way because other coworkers have also recorded their findings in the knowledge base and, a few months later, you can find the information you recorded yourself. In the case of a paper notebook, you would turn the pages to find the IP address and you may or may not remember which one is the primary and which is the secondary server. You may even forget by then that there are two servers (or was it a double cluster?).

To view a long list of available wiki software, visit `https://en.wikipedia.org/wiki/Comparison_of_wiki_software`.

Issue tracking

Issue-tracking systems keep track of issues, bugs, and other tasks. The first issue-tracking systems were created to maintain the list of bugs and also the state of the bug-fixing process to ensure that a bug, identified and recorded, would not get forgotten. Later, these software solutions developed and became full-fledged issue trackers and are unavoidable project-management tools in every enterprise.

The most widely-used issue-tracking application is Jira, but on the `https://en.wikipedia.org/wiki/Comparison_of_issue-tracking_systems` page, you can find many other applications.

The most important feature of an issue-tracking application is that it has to record an issue in detail in an editable manner. It has to record the person who recorded the issue in case more information is needed during issue handling. The source of the issue is important. Similarly, issues have to be assigned to a responsible person, who is accountable for the progress of issue handling.

Modern issue tracking systems provide complex access control, workflow management, relation management, and integration with other systems.

Access control will only allow the person who has something to do with an issue access to it, so others cannot alter the state of an issue or even read the information attached to it.

An issue may go through different workflow steps depending on the type of issue—a bug may be reported or reproduced, a root cause analyzed, a fix developed or tested, a patch created, a fix merged with the next release version or published in the release. This is a simple workflow with a few states.

Relation management allows us to set different relations between issues and allows the user to navigate from issue to issue along these relations. For example, a client reports a bug, and the bug is identified as being the same as another that was already fixed. In such a case, it would be insane to go through the original workflow and create a new patch for the same bug. Instead, the issue gets a relation pointing to the original issue and sets the state to closed.

Integration with other systems is also useful to keep a consistent development state. Version control may require that, for every commit, the commit message contains a reference to the issue that describes the requirement, bug, or changes that the code modification supports. Issues may be linked to knowledge base articles or agile project management software tools using web links.

Testing

We already discussed testing when we talked about unit testing. Unit testing is extremely important in agile development and it helps keep the code clean and reduce the number of errors. But this is not the only type of testing that you will see in enterprise development.

Types of tests

Testing is performed for many reasons but there are at least two reasons we have to mention. One is to hunt for bugs and create error-free code as much as possible. The other is to prove that the application is usable and can be utilized for the purpose it was meant for. It is important from the enterprise point of view and considers a lot of aspects that the unit test does not. While the unit test focuses on one unit and, thus, is an extremely good tool to point out where the error is, it is totally unusable when it comes to discovering bugs that come from erroneous interfaces between modules. The unit tests mock external modules and, thus, tests that the unit works as expected. However, if there is an error in this expectation and the other modules do not behave in the same way as the unit test mock, the error will not be discovered.

To discover the errors on this level, which is the next level above unit test, we have to use integration tests. During integration tests, we test how individual units can work together. When we program in Java, the units are usually classes; thus, the integration test will test how the different classes work together. While there is a consensus (more or less) about what a unit test is in Java programming, this is less so in the case of integration tests.

In this regard, the external dependencies, such as other modules reachable via the network or database layers, may be mocked, or may be set up using some test instance during integration testing. The argument is not about whether these parts should be mocked or not, only the terminology. Mocking some components, such as the database, has advantages as well as drawbacks. As in the case of any mock, the drawback is the cost of setting up the mock as well as the fact that the mock behaves differently from the real system. Such a difference may result in some bugs still remaining in the system and lurking there until a later case of testing or, God forbid, production is used.

Integration tests are usually automated in a way similar to unit tests. However, they usually require more time to execute. This is why these tests are not executed at each source code change. Usually, a separate maven or Gradle project is created, which has a dependency on the application JAR and contains only integration test code. This project is usually compiled and executed daily.

It may happen that daily execution is not frequent enough to discover the integration issues in a timely manner, but a more frequent execution of the integration tests is still not feasible. In such a case, a subset of the integration test cases is executed more frequently, for example, every hour. This type of testing is called smoke-testing. The following diagram shows the position of the different testing types:

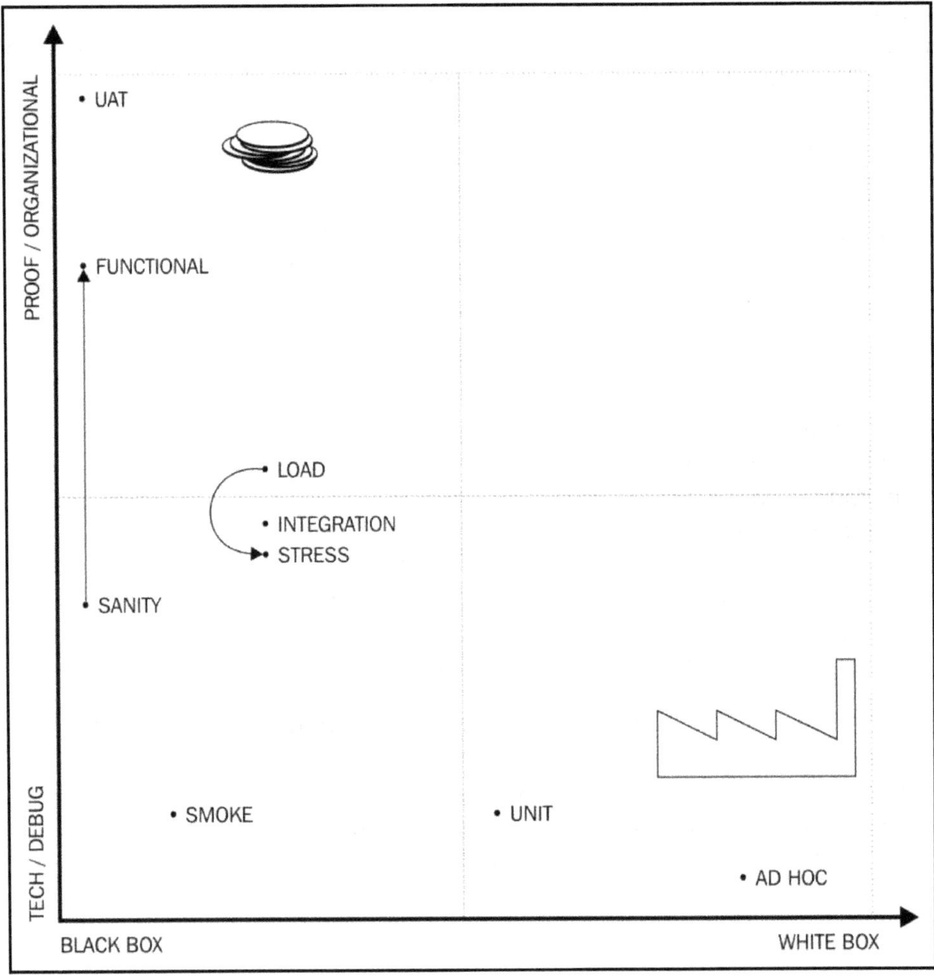

When the application is tested in a fully set up environment, the testing is called system testing. Such testing should discover all the integration bugs that may have been lurking and covered during the previous testing phases. The different type of system tests can also discover non-functional issues. Both functional testing and performance testing are done on this level.

Functional testing checks the functions of the application. It ensures that the application functions as expected or at least has functions that are worth installing in the production environment and can lead to cost savings or profit increase. In real life, programs almost never deliver all the functions that were envisioned in any requirement documentation, but if the program is usable in a sane manner, it is worth installing, assuming there are no security issues or other issues.

If there are a lot of functions in the application, functional testing may cost a lot. In such a case, some companies perform a sanity test. This test does not check the full functionality of the application, only a subset to ensure that the application reaches a minimal quality requirement and it is worth spending the money on the functional testing.

There may be some test cases that are not envisioned when the application was designed and thus there is no test case in the functional test plan. It may be some weird user action, such as a user pressing a button on the screen when nobody thought it was possible. Users, even if benevolent, may happen to press or touch anything and enter all possible unrealistic input into a system. Ad-hoc testing tries to amend this shortage. During ad-hoc testing, a tester tries all the possible ways to use the application that they can imagine at the moment the test is executed.

This is also related to security testing, also called penetration testing, when the vulnerabilities of the system are discovered. These are special types of tests that are performed by professionals who have their core area of expertise in security. Developers usually do not have that expertise, but at least, the developers should be able to discuss issues that are discovered during such a test and amend the program to fix the security holes. This is extremely important in the case of internet applications.

Performance testing checks that the application, in a reasonable environment, can handle the expected load that the user puts on the system. A load test emulates the users who attack the system and measures the response time. If the response time is appropriate, that is, lower than the required maximum under the maximum load, the test passes; otherwise, it fails. If a load test fails, it is not necessarily a software error. It may be that the application needs more or faster hardware. Load tests usually test the functionality of the application in only a limited way and only test usecase scenarios that pose read load on the application.

Many years ago, we were testing a web application that had to have a response time of two seconds. The load test was very simple—issue `GET` requests so that there were a maximum of 10,000 requests active at the same time. We started with 10 clients, and then a script increased the concurrent users to 100, then 1,000, and then stepping up by 1,000 every minute. This way, the load test was 12 minutes long. The script printed the average response time, and we were ready to execute the load test at 4:40 p.m. on a Friday. The average response time started from a few milliseconds and went up to 1.9 seconds as the load was increased to 5,000 concurrent users, and from there, it descended down to 1 second as the load was increased to 10,000 users. You can understand the attitude of the people on a Friday afternoon, being happy that we met the requirements. My colleagues left for the weekend happily. I stayed to test a bit more because I was bothered by the phenomenon that the response time decreases as we increase the load above 5,000. First, I reproduced the measurement and then started looking at the log files. At 7 pm, I already knew the reason. When the load went above 5,000, the connections the Apache server was managing started to exhaust and the web server started to send back 500 internal error codes. That is something that Apache can do very effectively. It is very fast in telling you that you cannot be served. When the load was around 10,000 concurrent users, 70% of the responses already had 500 errors. The average went down, but the users were actually not served. I reconfigured the Apache server so that it could serve all the requests and forward each to our application just to learn that the response time of our application was around 10 seconds at the maximum load. Around 10 p.m., when my wife was calling my mobile for the third time, I also knew how large a memory I should set in the Tomcat startup file in the options for the JVM to get the desired 2-second response time in case of 10,000 concurrent users.

A stress test is a type of performance test that you may also face. This type of test increases the load on the system until it cannot handle the load. That test should ensure that the system can recover from the extreme load automatically or manually but, in no case, will do something that it shouldn't. For example, a baking system should never commit an unconfirmed transaction, no matter how big the load is. If the load is too high, it should leave the dough raw but should not bake extra bread.

The most important test at the top of the hierarchy is the user-acceptance test. This is usually an official test that the customer, who buys the software, executes and in the case of successful execution, pays the price for the software. Thus, this is extremely important in professional development.

Test automation

Tests can be automated. It is not a question of whether it is possible to automate a test, only whether it is worth doing so. Unit tests and integration tests are automated, and as time advances, more and more tests get automated as we move along to higher steps toward the **user acceptance test** (**UAT**). UAT is not likely to be automated. After all, this test checks the integration between the application and the user. While the user, as an external module, can be mocked using automation in lower levels, we should reach the level where the integration test happens without mocks.

There are many tools that help the automation of tests. The blocker for test automation, these days, is the cost of the tools to do so, the cost of learning and developing the tests, and the fear that the automated tests are not discovering some of the errors.

It is true that it is easier to do something wrong with a program than without. This is true for almost anything, not just testing. And we still do use programs; why else would you read this book? Some of the errors may not be discovered during automated functional testing, which would otherwise have been discovered using manual tests. At the same time, when the same test is executed the hundredth time by the same developer, it is extremely easy to miss an error. An automated test will never do that. And most importantly, the cost of the automated test is not 100 times the cost of running it once.

We have used test-automation tools in this book. **SoapUI** is a tool that helps you create tests that can be executed automatically. Other testing tools that are worth looking at are **Cucumber**, **Concordion**, **Fintnesse**, and **JBehave**. There is a good comparison of tools at `https://www.qatestingtools.com/`.

Black box versus white box

You may have heard many times that a test is a black-box test. This simply means that the test does not know anything about how the **system under test** (**SUT**) is implemented. The test relies only on the interface of the SUT that is exported for the outside world. A white box test, on the other end of the scale, tests the internal working of the SUT and very much relies on the implementation:

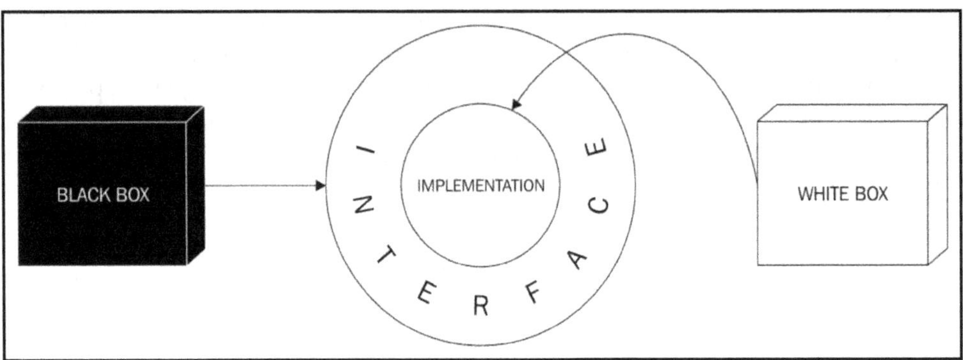

Both approaches have advantages and disadvantages. We should use one, or a mixture of the two approaches, when it fits the purpose of the testing needs the most. A black-box test that doesn't rely on the implementation does not need to change if the implementation changes. If the interface of the tested system changes, the test should also be changed. A white-box test may need changes if the implementation changes, even if the interface remains the same. The advantage of the white-box test is that, often, it is easier to create such a test and the testing can be more effective.

To get the best of both worlds, systems are designed to be testable. Be careful, though. It often means that the functionality internal to the tested system is propagated to the interface. That way, the test will use only the interface and, thus, can be declared to be a black box, but it does not help. If something changes in the internal workings of the tested system, the test has to follow it. The only difference is that you may call it a black-box test if the interface also changes. That does not save any work. Rather, it increases it—we have to check all the modules that rely on the interface if they also need any changes.

I do not say that we should not pay attention to creating testable systems. Often, making a system testable results in cleaner and simpler code. If the code, however, gets messier and much longer because we want to make it testable, we are probably not going in the right way.

Selecting libraries

Programming for the enterprise or even programming a moderately sized project cannot be done without the use of external libraries. In the Java world, most of the libraries we use are open source and, more or less, free. When we buy a library, there is usually a standard process enforced by the purchasing department. In such a case, there is a written policy about how to select the vendor and the library. In the case of "free" software, they do not usually care, though they should. In such a case, the selection process mainly lies with the IT department and it is therefore important to know the major points to be considered before selecting a library even if it's free.

In the previous paragraph, I put the word free between quotes. That is because no software is really free. There is no such thing as a free lunch, as they say. You have heard this many times, but it may not be obvious in the case of an open source code library or framework you are going to select. The major selection factor for any purchase or implementation is the cost, the price. If the software is free, it means that you do not need to pay an upfront fee for the software. However, there is a cost of integrating and using it. Support costs money. Somebody may say that the support is community support and also available free of charge. The thing is that the time you spend hunting for a workaround that helps you to get over a bug is still money. It is your time, or if you are a manager, it is the time of the professional in your department whose time you pay for, or, it can be an external contractor who will hand you a huge bill if you do not have the in-house expertise to solve the issue.

Since free software does not have a price tag attached, we have to look at the other factors that are important in the selection process. At the end of the day, they will all affect the cost in some way. Sometimes, the way a criterion alters the cost is not obvious or easily calculable. However, for each one, we can set no-go levels that are based on technology decisions, and we can compare libraries for being better or worse along with each of the criteria.

Fit for the purpose

This is perhaps the most important factor. Other factors may be argued about in terms of the scale of importance, but if a library is not appropriate for our purpose, this is certainly not something to select, no matter what. It may be obvious in many cases, but you may be surprised how many times I have seen a product selected because it was the favorite of a person in some other project and the library was forced to be used in the new project even though the requirements were totally different.

License

The license is an important question as not all free software is free for all uses. Some of the licenses allow free use for hobby projects and education but require you to purchase the software for professional, profit-oriented use.

The most widely used licenses and their explanations (and the whole text of the license) are available on the web page of the **Open Source Initiative** (`https://opensource.org/licenses`). It lists nine different licenses, and to make the situation a bit more complex, these licenses have versions.

One of the oldest licenses is the **General Public License** (**GPL**) standing for GNU. This license contains the following sentences:

> *"For example, if you distribute copies of such a program, whether gratis or for a fee, you must pass on to the recipients the same freedoms that you received. You must make sure that they, too, receive or can get the source code."*

If you create software for a for-profit enterprise and the company intends to sell software, you probably cannot use any line of code that is from a GPL-licensed software. It would imply that you are required to pass on your own source code, which may not be the best sales strategy. An Apache license, on the other hand, may be OK for your company. This is something that your lawyers should decide.

Even though this is lawyer's work, there is one important point that we developers must be aware of and pay close attention to. Sometimes, the libraries contain code from other projects and their license, as advertised, may not be the real one. A library may be distributed under the Apache license but contains code that is GPL-licensed. This is obviously a violation of the GPL license, which was committed by some open source developers. Why would you care? Here comes the explanation via an imagined situation.

You develop software for an enterprise. Let's say that this company is one of the largest car manufacturers in the world, or one of the largest banks, pharma, whatever. The owner of the GPL software seeks remedies for the misuse of their software. Will they sue the software developer, John Doe, who has a total wealth of $200,000, or your company, claiming that you did not duly check the license of the code? They certainly will not dig for gold where there is none. Suing the company you work for may not be successful, but certainly not a good process you or anyone at the company wants.

What can we, as software professionals, do?

We have to use libraries that are well known and used widely. We can check the source code of the library to see whether there is any copied code. Some package names may present clues. You can Google part of the source code to find matches. Last but not least, the company can subscribe to services that provide similar research for the libraries.

Documentation

Documentation is an important aspect. If the documentation is not appropriate, it will be hard to learn how to use the library. Some of the team members may already know the library, but, again, this may not be the case for newer team members. We should consider our colleagues, who are expected to be average programmers, as they will have to learn to use the library. Thus, documentation is important.

When we speak about documentation, we should not only think about the *JavaDoc* reference documentation but also tutorials and books if they are available.

An alive project

It is important not to select a library for use that is not alive. Have a look at the roadmap of the library, the last time a release was shipped, and the frequency of the commits. If the library is not alive, we should consider not using it. Libraries work in an environment and the environment changes. The library may connect to a database. The new version of the database may provide new features that give us better performance only if the library is modified to accommodate these new features. The library communicates over HTTP; will it support the new 2.0 version of the protocol? If nothing else, the version of the Java environment will change over the years and the library we use should sooner or later follow it to leverage the new features.

There is no guarantee that an alive library will always stay alive. However, a library that is already dead will certainly not resurrect.

Even if the project is alive at the moment, there are some points that may give some hints about the future of the library. If the company developing it is well-established and financially stable, and the library is developed with a reasonable business model, then there is a low risk that the project dies. If there are a lot of companies who use the library, then it is likely that the project will stay alive even if the original team stops working on it or the original financing structure changes. However, these are only small factors and not well-established facts. There is no guarantee, and telling the future is more an art than a science.

Maturity

Maturity is similar to the previous criterion. A project may very well be alive when just starting up, but if it is in its infancy, we better not use the library for a large project. When a project is in its early phase, a lot of bugs can be in the code, the API may change radically, and presumably, there may only be a small number of companies that rely on the code. This also means that the community support is lower.

Of course, if all the projects select only mature, open source code, then no open source project would ever get to the mature state. We should assess the importance of the project. Is the project business-critical? Will the project become business-critical?

If the project is not business-critical, the company can afford to invent a fresh library that is not that mature. It may be reasonable if there are no mature libraries for the purpose because the technology you are going to use is relatively new. In such a case, the project in the company is probably also new and not business-critical yet. It will be business-critical, we hope, after some time, but by that time, the library will be mature, or may just die and we can select a competing solution before the project becomes too expensive to switch.

Judging the maturity of a library is always difficult and has to be aligned with the maturity and importance of the project that we want to use the library for.

Number of users

If the library is alive and mature but there are not many users, something is wrong. Why don't people use the library if it is good? If the number of users for a library or framework is low and there are no large corporations among its users, it is probably not a good one. If nobody is using it, this may signal that our assessment of the other criteria may not be appropriate.

Also note that if there are only a few users of the library, the knowledge in the community is also scarce and we may not be able to get community support.

The "I like it" factor

Last but not least, the "I like it" factor is extremely important. The question is not whether you like the library but how much the developers like it. Developers will like a library that is easy to use and fun to work with, and this will result in low cost. If the library is hard to use and developers do not like it, they will not learn to use it to the level that is required for good quality, only to the level that is needed. The end result will be suboptimal software.

Continuous integration and deployment

Continuous integration means that whenever a new version is pushed to the source code repository, the continuous integration server kicks in, pulls the code to its disk, and starts the build. It compiles the code first, runs the unit tests, fires the static code-analysis tools, and if all goes right, packages a snapshot release and deploys it on a development server.

CI servers have web interfaces that can be used to create a release. In such a case, the deployment can even go to the test servers or to production depending on local business needs and on the policy that was created accordingly.

Automating the build and deployment process has the same advantages as any other automation—repeated tasks can be performed without manual intervention, which is tedious, boring, and, thus, error-prone if done by a human. The outstanding advantage is that if there is an error in the source code that can be discovered by the automated build process, it will be discovered. Novice developers say that it is cheaper and easier to build the code locally, which the developers do anyway, and then push the code to the server if the build process is already checked. This is partly true. Developers have to check that the code is of a good quality and builds well before sending it to the central repo. However, this cannot always be achieved. Some errors may not manifest on local environments.

It may so happen that one developer accidentally uses a newer version of Java than the one supported and uses a new feature of the new version. Enterprises do not generally use the latest technology. They tend to use versions that are proven, have many users, and are mature. This year, in 2018, when Java 11 is going to be released in September, huge enterprises still use Java 1.6 and 1.7. Since Java 9, 10 and 11 have many new features that are not trivial to implement, I expect that the adoption of the technology may take even longer than the adoption of Java 1.8, which gave us functional programming and Lambda.

It may also happen that a new library is added to the dependencies of the build and the developer who added it to the build file (`pom.xml` or `build.gradle`) could use it without any problem on their local machine. It does not mean that the library is officially added to the project, and it may not be available in the central code repository (Artifactory, Nexus, or other implementations of the code repository). The library may have only been on the local repository of the developer, and they may have assumed that since the code compiles, the build is OK.

Some large organizations use different code repositories for different projects. The libraries get into these repositories following meticulous examination and decisions. Some libraries may get there, while others may not. The reason to have different repositories could be numerous. A project is developed for a customer who has a different policy about an open source project than another. If the enterprise develops code for itself, it may happen that a library is phased out or not supported anymore, and can only be used for projects that are old. A maintenance release may not need to replace a library, but new projects may not be allowed to use a dying software library.

The CI server can run on a single machine or it can run on several machines. If it serves many projects, it may be set up as a central server with many agents running on different machines. When a build process has to be started, the central server delegates this task to one of the agents. The agents may have different loads, running several different build processes, and may have different hardware configurations. The build process may have requirements regarding the speed of the processor or about the available memory. Some agents may run simpler builds for smaller projects but would fail to execute the build of a large project or of some small project that still has a huge memory requirement to execute some tests.

When a build fails, the build server sends out emails to the developers, and the person who sent the last update to the code repository is obligated to fix the bug without delay. This encourages the developers to commit frequently. The smaller the change, the fewer chances there are of a build problem. The build-server web interface can be used to see the actual state of the projects, which project is failing to build, and which is just fine. If a build fails, there is a red sign in the line of the build, and if the build is OK, the sign is green.

Often, these reports are continually displayed on an old machine using a huge display so that every developer or anybody who enters the room can see the actual state of the builds. There is even special hardware that you can buy that has red, yellow, and green lamps to follow the state of the build and rings a bell when the build fails.

Release management

Developing software means a continuously changing code base. Not every version of the software is supposed to be installed in production. Most of the versions are pushed to the repository on a branch that is half complete. Some versions are meant only for testing and a few are meant to be installed in production even if only some of those will finally get to production.

Almost all the time, the releases follow the semantic versioning that we discussed in an earlier section. The versions that are meant only to be tested usually have the `-SNAPSHOT` modifier at the end of the version number. For example, the `1.3.12-SNAPSHOT` version is the version that was once debugged, and is going to become the `1.3.12` version. The snapshot versions are not definite versions. They are the code as it is by then. Because a snapshot release never gets installed in production, it is not needed to reproduce a snapshot version for maintenance. Thus, the snapshot versions are not increased continually. Sometimes, they may be changed, but that is a rare exception.

It may happen that we work on a bug fix, `1.3.12-SNAPSHOT`, and during development, we change so much code that we decide that it has to be `1.4.0` when it is released, so we rename the snapshot to `1.4.0-SNAPSHOT`. This is a rare case. Often, the release creation creates a `1.4.0` version from `1.3.12-SNAPSHOT` as the decision about the new release number is made by the time the release is created.

When the release process is started, usually from the web interface of the CI server, the developer creating the release has to specify the release version. This is usually the same as the snapshot version without the `-SNAPSHOT` postfix. The build process not only creates the build but also tags the source code repository version it was using and loads the packaged program (artifact) to the code repository. The tag can be used later to access the exact version of the source code that was used to create the release. If there is a bug in a specific version, then this version has to be checked out on a developer machine to reproduce the bug and find the root cause.

If the build of a release fails, it can be rolled back, or you can skip that release number and note it as a failed release build. An existing release can never have two versions. The source code is the only one that is for that release and the generated code has to be exactly the one in any storage. Subsequent compilation of the same source may result in slightly different code, for example, if a different version of Java is used to create the latter one. Even in such a case, the one that was created by the build server in the first place is the version that belongs to the release. When a bug is reproduced and the code is recompiled from the exact same source, it is already a snapshot version. Multiple releases may be possible from the same source version, for example, compiled with Java versions from 1.5 to 1.8 and version 9 but a single release always belongs to the exact same source code.

If a release that was supposed to be a release version fails during QA checks, then a new release has to be created and the failed release has to be noted as such. The version that marketing uses to name the different versions should not be related to the technical version numbers we work with. Often it is, and it causes a lot of headaches. If you realize that the two are totally different things and one does not have to do anything with the other, life gets simpler. Look at the different versioning of the Windows operating system or Java. As marketing, Java used 1.0 then 1.1, but Java 1.2 was advertised as Java 2 and still the code contained 1.2 (which now, seven major releases later, also becomes 9 instead of 1.9)

The last part of release management is that deployments should register the version numbers. The company has to know which release is installed on which server, and of which client.

The code repository

The code repository stores the libraries and helps manage the dependencies of the different libraries. Ages ago, when Java projects used ANT as a build tool and without the later-added Ivy dependency management, the libraries that were needed by a project were downloaded to the source code, usually to the `lib` library. If a library needed another library, those were also downloaded and stored manually, and this continued until all the libraries that one of the already downloaded libraries needed were copied to the source code tree.

This was a lot of manual work and, also, the library code was stored in the source code repository as many copies. A compiled library is not a source code and has nothing to do in the source code repository. Manual work that can be automated has to be automated. This is not because developers are lazy (yes, we are and we have to be), but because manual work is error-prone and, thus, expensive.

This was when Apache Ivy was invented and Maven, following ANT, already supported repository management. Libraries were structured in directories and supported metadata that described the dependencies to other libraries. Luckily, Gradle did not invent its own code repository. Instead, it supports both the Maven and Ivy repositories.

Using the repository, the build tools automatically download the libraries that are needed. If a library has a new version, the developer only has to update the version of the needed library in the build configuration and then all the tasks, including downloading all the new versions of the other libraries that are needed by that version, are done automatically.

Walking up the ladder

At this point, you have a lot of information that will rocket your start as an enterprise Java developer. You have a base of knowledge that you can build on. There is a long way to go to become a professional Java developer. There is a lot of documentation to read, a lot of code to scan and understand, and also a lot of code to write till you can claim to be a professional Java developer. You may probably face many years of continuous education. The good thing is that even after that, you can continue your journey and you can educate yourself, as being a professional Java developer is rarely a job people retire from. No, no! Not because they die while at it! Rather, professional software developers with experience start to code less and less and support the development process in different ways, which leverages more of their experience. They can become business analysts, project managers, test engineers, subject-matter experts, architects, scrum masters, automation engineers, and so on. Is it a familiar list? Yes, these are the people you will work with as a developer. Many of them may have started as a developer themselves. The following diagram shows the relative positions of these roles:

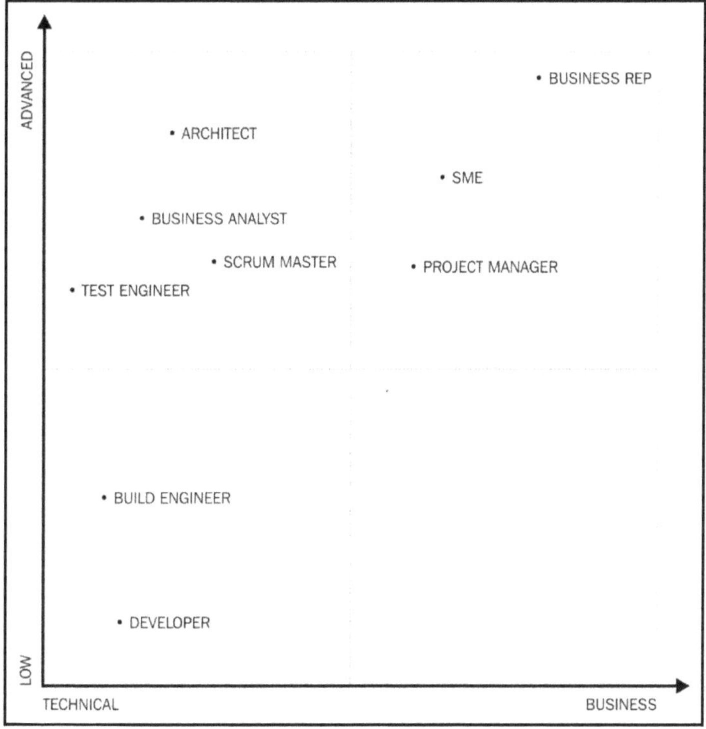

Let's take a more detailed look into what these roles do in enterprise development:

- Business analysts work with the client and create the documents, specifications, use cases, and user stories needed by the developers to develop the code.
- Project managers administer the projects and help the team to get things done in cooperation with other teams, caring for all the project matters that developers cannot attend to or would unnecessarily burn time on that they should devote to coding.
- Subject-matter experts are more advanced in knowing the business needs, so it is a bit rare for a developer to become one, but if the industry you work in is technology oriented, it may not be impossible to become one.
- Test engineers control the QA process; they understand not only the test methodologies and requirements of testing but also the development process, so that they can support bug fixes and not only identify them, which would be poor.
- Architects work with BAs and design a high-level structure for the applications and code, and document it in a way that helps the developers to focus on the actual tasks they have to perform. Architects are also responsible for the solution to use technologies, solutions, and structures that fit the purpose, are future-proof, and are affordable.
- Scrum mates help the development team to follow the agile methodology and guide the team in controlling the administration and resolving problems.

There are many different future paths you could take as a software developer and I only listed some of the positions that you can find in an enterprise today. As technology develops, I can imagine that in 20 years from now, software developers will teach and curate artificial intelligence systems and that will be what we refer to as programming. Who can tell?

Summary

Going in this direction is a good choice. Being a Java developer and becoming a senior is a profession that will pay well in the coming 10 to 20 years and perhaps even longer. At the same time, I personally find this technology fascinating and interesting, and after more than 10 years of Java programming and more than 35 years of programming, I still learn something new every day.

In this book, you learned the basics of Java programming. I also mentioned issues, suggested directions, and warned you about pitfalls that are not Java specific. However, we also did the homework of learning about the Java language, the infrastructure, the libraries, development tools, and networking in Java. You also learned about the most modern approaches that come only with Java 8 and 9, such as functional programming in Java, streams, and reactive programming. Now you can start working as a Java developer. What's next? Go and find the joy in programming and in Java!

Other Books You May Enjoy

If you enjoyed this book, you may be interested in these other books by Packt:

Java: High-Performance Apps with Java 9
Mayur Ramgir, Nick Samoylov

ISBN: 9781789130515

- Familiarize with modular development and its impact on performance
- Learn various string-related performance improvements, including compact string and modify string concatenation
- Explore various underlying compiler improvements, such as tiered attribution and Ahead-of-Time (AOT) compilation
- Learn security manager improvements
- Understand enhancements in graphics rasterizers
- Use of command-line tools to speed up application development
- Learn how to implement multithreading and reactive programming
- Build microservices in Java 9
- Implement APIs to improve application code

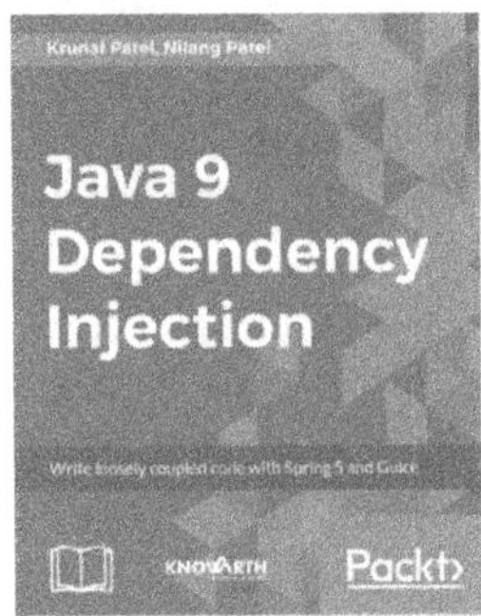

Java 9 Dependency Injection
Krunal Patel, Nilang Patel

ISBN: 9781788296250

- Understand the benefits of DI and fo from a tightly coupled design to a cleaner design organized around dependencies
- See Java 9's new features and modular framework
- Set up Guice and Spring in an application so that it can be used for DI
- Write integration tests for DI applications
- Use scopes to handle complex application scenarios
- Integrate any third-party library in your DI-enabled application
- Implement Aspect-Oriented Programming to handle common cross-cutting concerns such as logging, authentication, and transactions
- Understand IoC patterns and anti-patterns in DI

Leave a review - let other readers know what you think

Please share your thoughts on this book with others by leaving a review on the site that you bought it from. If you purchased the book from Amazon, please leave us an honest review on this book's Amazon page. This is vital so that other potential readers can see and use your unbiased opinion to make purchasing decisions, we can understand what our customers think about our products, and our authors can see your feedback on the title that they have worked with Packt to create. It will only take a few minutes of your time, but is valuable to other potential customers, our authors, and Packt. Thank you!

Index

J

L

M

N

O

P

Q

R

S

T

U

V

W

X

Y

www.ingramcontent.com/pod-product-compliance
Lightning Source LLC
Chambersburg PA
CBHW060639060326
40690CB00020B/4456
9781789131895